PRIVATE LAW

A CASEBOOK FOR MASTER'S DEGREE STUDENTS

■ ■ ■

Russell Korobkin
Richard C. Maxwell Distinguished Professor,
UCLA School of Law

AMERICAN CASEBOOK SERIES®

WEST ACADEMIC

860 Blue Gentian Road, Suite 350
Eagan, MN 55121
1-877-888-1330

Published in the United States of America

ISBN: 978-1-68561-111-8

For Deirdre

PREFACE

The American law school curriculum is designed for the benefit of Juris Doctor (or "J.D.") students, who devote three years of full-time, post-graduate study to earning their degree. For decades, the standard approach has been one year of required introductory courses that provide students with a broad, foundational knowledge of law followed by two years of more specialized, elective courses that enable students to build deeper knowledge in their areas of interest. Roughly half of that first year of required, foundational study includes courses in contract, tort, and property law—subjects rooted in the common law that regulate the legal relationships between private actors (hence, "private law").

In the 21st century, however, the law school population has changed, and students enroll in law school master's degree programs in increasing numbers. Lawyers trained in other countries began to come to the United States in the latter part of the 20th century for one year of American legal study to earn a Master of Laws (or "LL.M.") degree. Today, most American law schools offer at least one LL.M. program. Approximately 7500 students per year apply to one or more of these, 90 percent of whom earned their first law degree at a law school outside of the country. In the past 15 years, many schools launched a new type of master's degree program, known generally as "Legal Master's" programs, for non-lawyer professionals, who seek to both broaden and deepen their understanding of how the law operates but do not wish to qualify for the bar examination or become a licensed attorney. There are no reliable national figures, but applications for these programs, which go by a variety of names including Master of Legal Studies, Master of Studies in Law, and Juris Master, probably now number in the low thousands and are likely to eclipse those of LL.M. programs in coming years.

Most students enrolled in either type of master's program earn their degrees in one year of full-time study or its part-time equivalent, meaning that they complete approximately 1/3 of the number of courses that J.D. students complete. For these students to have sufficient time to study law in the specialized fields that brought them to law school, the number of foundational courses must be reduced. But how?

Many schools require one course (often an abbreviated course that lasts only one or two weeks) that provides a brief overview of American law and then allow master's students devote the rest of their time to specialized elective courses. Other schools require master's students to select one or more courses from the list of required, first-year JD courses, meaning that students might obtain deep knowledge of one or two foundational subjects but little or none of the other subjects.

When we began to design our Master of Legal Studies program at the UCLA School of Law, we thought that the first of these approaches provides too thin of a foundation for a serious student of American law and that the second approach provides too spotty of a foundation. Our approach was to design a new foundational curriculum as broad as the first year J.D. curriculum in its scope but more abbreviated in its depth.

I took on the responsibility of designing and teaching a course in "Private Law," which would cover core substantive topics of property, torts, and contracts, teach common law reasoning and analysis, and introduce carefully selected theoretical concepts useful to understanding any area of law. This casebook is a result of that initial work and several iterations of teaching the course. It is my hope that its availability will motivate instructors with a background in property, tort, *or* contract law to now offer a private law course that provides their master's students with a firm foundation in all three. The casebook is appropriate for sophisticated students with little or no knowledge of American law, whether they be master's students with a law degree from a non-U.S. law school, master's degree students studying law for the first time, or even highly motivated undergraduate students interested in learning through the traditional law school case method.

Many thanks are due for what has been, of course, a group effort. Our then-Dean Jennifer Mnookin chose to create our Master of Legal Studies program and gave me, as Vice Dean, the task of designing it. Associate Dean Tracey Parr was an outstanding partner in that process. Professors Iman Anabtawi, Doug Lichtman, Tim Malloy, Cynthia Merrill, Peter Reich and Clyde Spillinger worked with me to design the program's "core" curriculum, of which the Private Law course is part. Assistant Dean Jason Fiske brought tremendous expertise and energy to launching the program and building it into a success. UCLA law students Parker Johnson, Antonia Spatafore, and Guy Schnitkes provided critical research assistance for the book. Professors Peter Reich, Rick Sander, Rebecca Stone and Ken Vandevelde, along with the fabulous students in the first and second classes of the UCLA Master of Legal Studies program, provided valuable feedback on some or all of the text itself. Amanda Avella at West Publishing added the final editing touches.

Much of the material in the chapters on contract law draws heavily on materials created previously for my contract law casebook, *K: A Common Law Approach to Contracts*, now in its fourth edition, co-authored with Professor Tracey George and published by Aspen Publishing. My deepest thanks are due to both Professor George and Aspen for their generous permission to draw on their intellectual property in a significant way in creating this book.

RUSSELL KOROBKIN
LOS ANGELES, CALIFORNIA

February 2025

SUMMARY OF CONTENTS

TABLE OF CONTENTS

TABLE OF CASES

The principal cases are in bold type.

PRIVATE LAW

A CASEBOOK FOR MASTER'S DEGREE STUDENTS

INTRODUCTION

■ ■ ■

"Private Law" is a term used to describe the bodies of law that govern the relationships between private individuals or entities. "Public Law," in contrast, describes the range of legal subjects that govern the rights and responsibilities of private actors in relation to government entities and the relationship of different government entities to one another.

Public law disputes garner more media headlines: May states prohibit abortions or outlaw private ownership of guns? Can the police require motorists to share their mobile phone passwords? What power do administrative agencies have to interpret statutes? But private law disputes are the bread and butter of the legal system. Which driver is liable for damages resulting from an automobile accident? Is a seller who provides goods two weeks later than promised liable to the buyer for damages? May one landowner build a structure that blocks the view of her neighbor? The vast majority of lawsuits filed in state courts, where 90 percent of all litigation occurs, are matters of private law. A basic understanding of how law works in our society requires a sophisticated understanding of the private law system. The goal of this course, is to provide you with this understanding.

Most courses taught in law school on topics of substantive law, as opposed to courses dealing with the practice of law (such as Trial Advocacy) or the rules governing the practice of law (such as Civil Procedure), can be classified as private law or public law, but the line between the two categories is not perfectly clear, for two reasons:

First, some subjects, by virtue of the way they have been conceived traditionally, include some topics from both categories. Property law is *mostly* private law, as its primary focus is the rights of private parties to control resources vis-à-vis other private parties, but Property courses usually include coverage of the topic of "takings," which concerns the extent to which the government may requisition land from private citizens under the Fifth and Fourteenth Amendments to the U.S. Constitution. Administrative law is mostly public law, as its focus is on how government agencies exercise regulatory power for the protection of society generally, but some statutes and regulations provide private parties with the ability to recover compensation from other private parties. For example, workers compensation regimes, creatures of administrative law, provide detailed rules that allow workers who suffer injuries on the job to recover damages from employers.

Second, the purposes or effects of some areas of law are simultaneously both private and public in nature in ways that cannot be disentangled. Successful plaintiffs in a tort lawsuit recover damages for themselves (serving a private function) but the precedent serves as a deterrent of future wrongful conduct for the protection of society (arguably a public function). At some level, the conceptual distinction between the two categories can even be questioned. Private law always has a public element, as private law is enforced by private parties through the mechanisms of public courts. Even if the parties choose to resolve their dispute through a private arbitration rather than a court, public enforcement of an arbitral judgment looms in the background and ensures that the losing party will abide by the decision.

These complications notwithstanding, dividing the vast universe of substantive legal subjects into the binary categories of private law and public law provides one sensible way to organize and frame the subject matter of the law. In private law, an individual's or a private organization's rights and responsibilities are defined in relation to other private parties. And when conflict cannot be avoided or resolved, a private party may seek to vindicate its rights through a legal action brought against another private party. If the plaintiff prevails, the court will order the defendant to pay financial compensation to the plaintiff or issue an injunction requiring the defendant to take some action toward or refrain from taking some action concerning the plaintiff in the future.

There are many substantive areas of private law, but the most fundamental of these are property law, tort law, and contract law. These bodies of law are considered so fundamental to a proper legal education that nearly every law school in the United States requires students studying for a J.D. (Juris Doctor) degree to take a course in each of these subjects in their first year of a three-year program of study. Until the late 20th Century, most law schools required J.D. students to study each of these subjects for a full year. Today, most J.D. programs require only a one-semester course in each of these topics, but each carry at least four semester-units of credit at most schools. This means that Property, Torts, and Contracts make up nearly a full one-half year of study for J.D. students.

In a perfect world, every law student would receive at least four-units of instruction in each of these important subjects. But master's degree students—whether earning a Master of Laws (LL.M.) degree or a Master of Legal Studies (sometimes also called a Master of Studies in Law or Juris Master degree)—usually earn their degrees in only one year (if studying full time) or the equivalent of one year (if studying part time). It makes sense for J.D. students, enrolled in a three-year program, to allocate a semester's worth of coursework to these three foundational subjects. For master's degree students, most of whom have other areas of particular interest that draw them to law school, twelve units (or more) of instruction in property, torts, and contract law is neither advisable nor feasible.

This book, and your Private Law course, take seriously both the importance of these subjects and the limitations on the time required for master's degree students (or, in some cases, advanced undergraduate students) by providing you with core concepts of each of these three subjects, along with critical skills in legal reasoning, in a single course. You will not—obviously!—study as many different topics that fall within these three subject areas as you would if you enrolled in a J.D. program, but you will learn the most fundamental concepts of the private law system. After mastering the materials in this book, you will be able to hold your own with J.D. students in a discussion or debate about private law issues or problems, and you will be prepared to enroll in any advanced law school courses that fall under the general umbrella of private law.

This book follows a three-part narrative arc. It begins by addressing the question of how the American legal system assigns and determines the extent of rights to control valuable resources as between competing claimants, the core subject matter of property law. Most property law textbooks focus their attention on "real property" (land and fixed structures) and "personal property" (movable "things"). As intellectual property becomes increasingly important in the modern economy, many property law texts include some coverage of this area of law as well, even though it remains a subject covered separately in upper-level law school classes. The first portion of this book—Chapters 1–5—explores how property rights are allocated and defined.

Our bodies are the most valuable possession that most of us have. Unless you are blessed with very rich and generous relatives, you will obtain real, personal, and intellectual property primarily by selling your labor in the employment market and using your earnings to purchase other valuable resources. Since the eradication of chattel slavery by the 13th Amendment to the U.S. Constitution in 1865 and the emancipation of women from the legal control of men in subsequent decades, there has been little serious debate concerning who possesses legal rights in one's body—the individual does—at least vis-à-vis other private actors. (Property rights in one's body vis-à-vis the state is arguably a more complicated question, as anyone who has served time in prison, been drafted into the military, paid taxes, or tried to obtain an abortion in a state that prohibits the procedure might attest.) So, when you consider questions of who has what property rights and why, consider the scope of the subject to include the human body and its capacity for labor, in addition to real, personal, and intellectual property.

The second portion of the book considers the question of how the American legal system protects the property rights of private individuals or entities from encroachment by others. This is the basic subject matter of the law of torts. The word "tort," meaning "wrong" in French, was imported by English lawyers. Through criminal law, an area of public law, the government, acting as a party, meets out punishments for a variety of wrongs, which can be incarceration or monetary fines payable to the public treasury. But it is tort law that provides private parties with the ability to file a civil lawsuit and obtain personal compensation or other relief from those who cause harm to their person or possessions.

Torts textbooks often divide torts into three categories: "intentional torts" are a variety of different injuries caused by a party that intends to commit the act that results in the injury; the general tort of "negligence" (along with several subsidiary "negligence torts") results from accidents caused by careless behavior that is deemed wrongful even though the injury is not intentional; and "strict liability" torts are injuries for which the party who caused the injury is responsible even in the absence of wrongful behavior of any kind. Chapter 6's exploration of the tort of battery not only teaches you the legal doctrine concerning one specific intentional tort but also serves as an introduction to the subject of intentional torts more generally by exploring the nature of the "intent" that the law requires. Chapter 7 explores the difference between torts that require negligence and those that assess strict liability. Chapters 8–10 delve into elements that constitute of the tort of negligence, the most common of the sources of harm to persons and belongings that give rise to private legal actions for compensation.

Much social interaction, and nearly all business, involves private parties exchanging their property rights. The third section of the book, making up approximately half of the total material, explores the substantive law that facilities and enforces these exchanges.

Chapter 11 surveys the law concerning gifts, abandonment, and found property. These three doctrines, usually covered in a Property course, concern the transfer of property rights from one private party to another. Chapters 12–24 concern the law governing contracts, by far the most prevalent method by which property rights are reallocated. These topics, unsurprisingly, are typically taught in law schools in a Contracts course.

In contrast to transfers by gift (primarily, but also abandonment or finding), contracts are defined by a mutual exchange between two (or more) parties. As part of a transaction, both parties give up valuable rights or forego some action that they otherwise have the legal right to take, either now or at some time in the future. The mechanism of contract facilitates my willingness to sell you my land, my car, my ideas, my services, or my forbearance, or to loan you money. Contract law's pledge of state power to enforce private agreements substitutes for trust in the integrity of one's counterpart to fulfill its promises. This enables buyers to be confident that a seller will deliver the goods or perform the services promised and sellers to be confident that a buyer will pay, even in the absence of familial ties or personal connections that might have facilitate exchanges in simpler times.

Chapter 12 explores the basic requirements for making a private agreement enforceable as a contract, and Chapters 13–15 explore the grounds that enable a party to avoid enforcement because of the behavior of the contracting counterpart or the nature of the contract itself. Chapters 16–18 consider how courts interpret the obligations embodied in contracts when the parties disagree as to the precise nature of their rights and responsibilities, and Chapters 19–20 probe how courts interpret the parties' rights and responsibilities when unexpected events occur after a contract is signed. Chapters 16–20 collectively relate to contract interpretation, the subject of most litigated disputes on contract law. The final four chapters, Chapters 21–24 explore the remedies available to parties who are the victim of a breach of contract (that is, nonperformance) by their counterparts.

Although the arc of this book runs generally from property law to tort law to contract law, the distinctions between these subject areas are not always so clear. It bears noting that property law effectively merges with tort law in some instances and contract law in others.

When one party believes that another has interfered with their property rights, their legal claim often sounds in tort law. But, in addition to being the procedural mechanism for protecting most property rights (that is, a party whose property rights are infringed files a tort lawsuit), the parameters of tort law often define the nature and extent of the underlying property rights. Chapters 3 and 4 concern the extent of landowners' rights to use and to exclude other from their parcels, topics traditionally covered in Property courses. But the law of nuisance and trespass, the legal doctrines that define the extent of the landowners' rights in these chapters, are torts. Unlike the torts of nuisance and trespass, the tort of battery (Chapter 6) is never considered a topic that falls within the subject of property law, but one might understand battery law as determining the extent, on one dimension, of individuals' property rights in their bodies. If someone punches you in the nose or gropes you, that is a battery; if someone pushes you to squeeze onto a crowded city bus, that almost certainly is not. This tells you a lot about the extent to which you have the right to exclude others from touching your person.

When parties' property rights are determined entirely or in part by their agreements with one another, property law becomes difficult to distinguish from contract law. For example, easements and servitudes provide rights to use or benefit from real property that is primarily owned by another party. Although sometimes established by operation of law, these types of property rights are often established by agreement between two parties. Easements and servitudes are topics almost always covered in the law school Property course (but are not covered in this book). But the question of whether these property rights were created and, if so, the extent of the rights, is often essentially a matter of contract law.

There is also overlap between tort law and contract law. In certain instances, a legal claim might sound in both tort and contract. If a seller lies to a buyer about the fundamental nature of its goods or services, the buyer might bring a lawsuit seeking money damages under tort law (the tort is called "fraud" in some states, "deceit" in others) or seek to avoid enforcement of the contract under the doctrine of misrepresentation. If a party breaches a contract, the counterpart is entitled under contract law to recover compensatory damages (the amount of money necessary to compensate for the breach) but not punitive damages (an amount meant to punish). But if the breaching party never intended to perform its obligations, the non-breaching party has a claim for the tort of fraud (more specifically, the subcategory of "promissory fraud"), under which it can recover punitive damages.

Law is complicated. Recognizing how different bodies of law are related to one another is important to being a skilled legal analyst and problem solver. If you were to take separate courses in Property, Torts, and Contracts, you might never think about the relationship between these private law subjects. The opportunity to better understand these relationships is one advantage to studying private law in a single course.

* * *

The foundations of American private law can be traced back to the English courts of the Middle Ages. Most private law is "common law," meaning that it was developed by courts incrementally over time, and it continues to evolve to this day as judicial opinions serve as precedent for the resolution of future disputes. The "law" is comprised of judicial decisions built upon the edifice of prior judicial decisions, built upon prior judicial decisions.

Common law in the United States is state law. Most cases involving state law are litigated in state courts, so most judicial opinions in common law subjects (and most decisions excerpted in this book) are published by state courts. In the limited set of cases in which federal courts have jurisdiction to rule on state law disputes—most importantly, when the parties reside in different states—the federal courts must judge according to the rules of state law. (Which state's law is relevant to decide a case is a subject of its own, called Conflict of Laws, which you will not have the time to broach in this course.)

The most important implication of all of this for purposes of your study of private law is that, for most of the topics covered in this book, the precise contours of the law vary somewhat from state to state. What you will learn in this course, then, is not exactly *the* law.

Following an introductory narrative, most chapters of this book include relevant sections of various "restatements" of the law. Restatements are scholarly efforts, sponsored by the non-profit American Law Institute, to describe the legal rules of particular subjects as they generally exist. They include statements of rules known as "black letter law," because these are traditionally published in bold-face type, and comments that provide additional description and examples. Restatements are not law—that is, they have no precedential force—although they are sometimes relied on by judges as guidance. For the purposes of this course, unless your professor tells you otherwise, you should assume that the black letter law as provided by the relevant restatement approximates what the relevant law is. Always remember, however, that a restatement's description might not be exactly the law in your state, and, on some occasions, the law might be quite different in different states. In some chapters of this book, you will read decisions of courts from different states that contradict one another, demonstrating that in the United States common law is not unitary.

The statement that *most* private law is common law is subject to two very different qualifications. The first is that during the 20th century, many states codified some or much of their common law. This means that, depending on your state, there might be statutes, enacted by the legislature, that cover much of the same ground as the sections of the various restatements that you encounter in this book. Because the substance of these statutes originated in common law judicial opinions, and because statutes often do not provide enough detail to cover the variety of factual situations that arise, it continues to be the case that private law develops largely from judicial decisions that rest on earlier judicial opinions. If you live in a state that has largely codified its common law, when a private law problem arises in your professional life, you will want to be sure to consult the text of the relevant state law. Unlike a restatement section, codified provisions of the common law are *the* law. Most of the time you will find that the state legislation is generally consistent with guidance provided by the authors of the restatements, just like most of the time an opinion excerpted in this book from a court of one state will be generally consistent with the law of other states. But this is not always the case.

The second qualification is that not all modern private law is common law. Both state legislatures and the U.S. Congress regularly enact statutes that amend or change preexisting common law rules or that create entirely new bodies of law to deal with modern problems. Statutes take precent over common law, so when a legislature enacts a new statute, the law in the relevant field evolves through judicial interpretation of the statute, rather than through judicial interpretation of the common law.

The most important example of this in this course is intellectual property law. The U.S. Constitution provides Congress with the authority "[t]o promote the progress of science and useful arts, by securing for limited times to authors and inventors the exclusive right to their respective writings and discoveries." As a result, copyright, patent, and trademark law are governed by federal statutes that apply in every state (although, to point out one additional wrinkle, sometimes the federal circuit courts in different parts of the country will interpret the federal law differently, which makes the law effectively different in different circuits unless the U.S. Supreme Court settles the question at issue). A party whose copyrights, patents, or trademarks are infringed invokes the rules and remedies provided by relevant federal statute, not by the common law of torts.

The root source of contract law is even more confusing. The common law of contracts descends, of course, from the common law. The Uniform Commercial Code (U.C.C.) is a model statute that has been adopted in large part (but not entirely) by every state legislature except for Louisiana. The U.C.C. essentially carves out areas of commercial law from the common law for the purpose of establishing a body of law that is consistent across the United States in order to better facilitate commerce. Most relevant to this course is Article 2 of the U.C.C., which governs contracts for the sale of goods. As a practical matter, the almost universal ratification of Article 2 means that contracts for services and for real and intellectual property are governed by the common law of contracts, but contracts for movable goods are governed by the U.C.C. The good news, from the student's perspective, is that Article 2 of the U.C.C. is mostly consistent with principles of the common law of contracts. If a problem arises in your professional life concerning a contract for the sale of goods, you need to research the U.C.C. and judicial decisions interpreting it. But for purposes of this course, unless your professor tells you that a certain rule is different under Article 2, you should assume that the common law of contracts is generally applicable even to contracts for goods.

* * *

Learning the foundations of American private law in just one semester will be a challenging but rewarding endeavor. Each of the following 24 chapters that will guide you in this endeavor includes an introduction, a set of judicial opinions ("cases," for short), and a set of discussion problems.

The introduction includes a narrative description of the chapter's topic that provides context, describes the main issues or questions that will be discussed, and explains how the cases that follow fit into this landscape. In nearly every chapter, the narrative description is followed by selected provisions of the relevant restatement, which will provide you with clear statements of the basic legal rules relevant to the topic. Chapters 2 and 5, which focus entirely or partially on intellectual property law, contain relevant statutory provisions.

The cases, which make up the most significant portion of each chapter, serve a variety of purposes that differ somewhat across topics: they provide further description of the legal rules, reasoning behind the rules, examples of how courts apply the rules in specific factual situations, and/or extensions of the rules to situations not addressed by the "black letter law." In some chapters, the cases will address different issues, providing you with a greater range of knowledge about the topic; in other chapters, cases might address the same or very similar issues and produce different outcomes, forcing you to determine whether the cases can be distinguished on their facts or whether the courts have different interpretations of the law.

Having studied the introductory materials and the cases, you should have a foundational knowledge of the law in the relevant topic area. The discussion problems provide you with an opportunity to apply your knowledge to an unfamiliar factual situation, which is the fundamental competency of legal analysis. Each discussion problem is an abbreviated description of an actual, decided case. When considering the discussion problems, you should assume the chapter's introductory materials and the cases make up the relevant body of law. Approach each problem by first identifying the best legal arguments for each party and then by determining what you believe to be the best resolution of the case under the law.

None of the discussion problems are truly easy cases—they have been selected, in part, because there are colorable arguments that can be made on both sides. But you will find that for some of the problems, the weight of the argument seems to be heavily on one side, while for others, the outcome might seem indeterminate given the law that you have learned. Importantly, exactly the same thing can be said about legal problems that you will confront in the real world! Whether or not you have time in your class to actively debate these problems, your professor will tell you how the court ruled in the case and why.

You are now set to begin your study of Private Law. Enjoy the journey!

CHAPTER 1

INITIAL ACQUISITION OF PROPERTY

■ ■ ■

INTRODUCTION

Dating back to the early days of the United States, the initial assignment of rights in physical property was largely governed by the rules of "discovery" and of "capture." In the early U.S. Supreme Court case of *Johnson v. M'Intosh*, Chief Justice John Marshall describes the principles by which land previously undiscovered (by Europeans) was allocated first as between sovereigns, and then between individuals through the sovereign. In *Pierson v. Post*, a New York court considers the allocation of previously unowned, wild foxes as between competing claimants. The rules described by both courts might be both be considered to apply the principle of *first possession* to disputes concerning property rights, but in subtly different ways.

The foundational rules of property law illustrated by *Johnson* and *Pierson* have little practical significance in the 21st century, as most physical property is already subject to clear title. Today, we acquire almost all of our physical property through transfer, often by contract (e.g., selling our labor to an employer) or by gift (including bequests), rather than by first possession. But the basic doctrines concerning unowned land and movable physical property ("chattels") are still useful in understanding fundamental principles of private property, and, as the discussion problems indicate, the issues in these cases do arise occasionally in the modern world.

As you read this pair of cases, consider the broader question of why private ownership of property is central to how we organize our society. Philosopher John Locke argued that natural law provides individuals with property rights in "the fruits of the earth" that they gather and in land that they enclose and improve, thus privatizing resources that were originally held in common by mixing them with labor. John Locke, *Second Treatise on Civil Government* (1690). Three-hundred years later, scholars writing in the "Law and Economics" tradition contend that private ownership is necessary for the efficient use of resources because it provides incentives to develop property that would otherwise be underutilized and prevents the overuse of common resources. See, e.g., Richard A. Posner, *Economic Analysis of Law* (7th ed., 2007). How do the reasons for *why* private ownership of property is important suggest *how* unowned physical property should be allocated as between competing claimants? Should a tract of land be treated differently than a wild animal, or is one rule or the other better in both situations? More broadly, does the principle of first possession make sense as a fundamental principle of allocation?

McFall v. Shimp implicitly raises the question of whether it makes sense to conceive of rights to control our own bodies, universally recognized since the abolition of slavery (and God-given, according to John Locke), as property rights. Are the same principles we use to think about rights in land and in chattels applicable? If so, is there an argument that can be made for a different outcome than the one handed down by the court?

CASES

JOHNSON V. M'INTOSH

Supreme Court of the United States
21 U.S. 543 (1823)

MR. CHIEF JUSTICE MARSHALL delivered the opinion of the Court.

The plaintiffs in this cause claim the land, in their declaration mentioned, under two grants, purporting to be made, the first in 1773, and the last in 1775, by the chiefs of certain Indian tribes, constituting the Illinois and the Piankeshaw nations; and the question is, whether this title can be recognised in the Courts of the United States?

. . .

On the discovery of this immense continent, the great nations of Europe were eager to appropriate to themselves so much of it as they could respectively acquire. . . . But, as they were all in pursuit of nearly the same object, it was necessary, in order to avoid conflicting settlements, and consequent war with each other, to establish a principle, which all should acknowledge as the law by which the right of acquisition, which they all asserted, should be regulated as between themselves. This principle was, that discovery gave title to the government by whose subjects, or by whose authority, it was made, against all other European governments, which title might be consummated by possession.

The exclusion of all other Europeans, necessarily gave to the nation making the discovery the sole right of acquiring the soil from the natives, and establishing settlements upon it. It was a right with which no Europeans could interfere. It was a right which all asserted for themselves, and to the assertion of which, by others, all assented.

. . .

While the different nations of Europe respected the right of the natives, as occupants, they asserted the ultimate dominion to be in themselves; and claimed and exercised, as a consequence of this ultimate dominion, a power to grant the soil, while yet in possession of the natives. These grants have been understood by all, to convey a title to the grantees, subject only to the Indian right of occupancy.

The history of America, from its discovery to the present day, proves, we think, the universal recognition of these principles.

. . . .

No one of the powers of Europe gave its full assent to this principle, more unequivocally than England. The documents upon this subject are ample and complete. So early as the year 1496, her monarch granted a commission to the Cabots, to discover countries then unknown to *Christian people*, and to take possession of them in the name of the king of England. Two years afterwards, Cabot proceeded on this voyage, and discovered the continent of North America, along which he sailed as far south as Virginia. To this discovery the English trace their title.

In this first effort made by the English government to acquire territory on this continent, we perceive a complete recognition of the principle which has been mentioned. The right of discovery given by this commission, is confined to countries 'then unknown to all Christian people;' and of these countries Cabot was empowered to take possession in the name of the king of England. Thus asserting a right to take possession, notwithstanding the occupancy of the natives, who were heathens, and, at the same time, admitting the prior title of any Christian people who may have made a previous discovery.

. . . .

Thus has our whole country been granted by the crown while in the occupation of the Indians. These grants purport to convey the soil as well as the right of dominion to the grantees. . . .In some instances, the soil was conveyed by the crown unaccompanied by the powers of government, as in the case of the northern neck of Virginia.

. . . .

The States, having within their chartered limits different portions of territory covered by Indians, ceded that territory, generally, to the United States, on conditions expressed in their deeds of cession, which demonstrate the opinion, that they ceded the soil as well as jurisdiction, and that in doing so, they granted a productive fund to the government of the Union. The lands in controversy lay within the chartered limits of Virginia, and were ceded with the whole country northwest of the river Ohio.

. . . .

The power now possessed by the government of the United States to grant lands, resided, while we were colonies, in the crown, or its grantees. The validity of the titles given by either has never been questioned in our Courts. It has been exercised uniformly over territory in possession of the Indians. The existence of this power must negative the existence of any right which may conflict with, and control it. An absolute title to lands cannot exist, at the same time, in different persons, or in different governments. An absolute, must be an exclusive title, or at least a title which excludes all others not compatible with it. All our institutions recognise the absolute title of the crown, subject only to the Indian right of occupancy, and recognise the absolute title of the crown to extinguish that right.

. . . . The British government, which was then our government, and whose rights have passed to the United States, asserted title to all the lands occupied by Indians, within the chartered limits of the British colonies. It asserted also a limited sovereignty over them, and the exclusive right of extinguishing the title which occupancy gave to them. These claims have been maintained and established as far west as the river Mississippi, by the sword. The title to a vast portion of the lands we now hold, originates in them. It is not for the Courts of this country to question the validity of this title, or to sustain one which is incompatible with it.

. . .

This opinion conforms precisely to the principle which has been supposed to be recognised by all European governments, from the first settlement of America. The absolute ultimate title has been considered as acquired by discovery, subject only to the Indian title of occupancy, which title the discoverers possessed the exclusive right of acquiring. Such a right is no more incompatible with a seisin in fee, than a lease for years, and might as effectually bar an ejectment.

. . . .

. . . .It is supposed to be a principle of universal law, that, if an uninhabited country be discovered by a number of individuals, who acknowledge no connexion with, and owe no allegiance to, any government whatever, the country becomes the property of the discoverers, so far at least as they can use it. They acquire a title in common. The title of the whole land is in the whole society. It is to be divided and parcelled out according to the will of the society, expressed by the whole body, or by that organ which is authorized by the whole to express it.

If the discovery be made, and possession of the country be taken, under the authority of an existing government, which is acknowledged by the emigrants, it is supposed to be equally well settled, that the discovery is made for the whole nation, that the country becomes a part of the nation, and that the vacant soil is to be disposed of by that organ of the government which has the constitutional power to dispose of the national domains, by that organ in which all vacant territory is vested by law.

According to the theory of the British constitution, all vacant lands are vested in the crown, as representing the nation; and the exclusive power to grant them is admitted to reside in the crown, as a branch of the royal prerogative. It has been already shown, that this principle was as fully recognised in America as in the island of Great Britain.

. . . .

After bestowing on this subject a degree of attention which was more required by the magnitude of the interest in litigation, and the able and elaborate arguments of the bar, than by its intrinsic difficulty, the Court is decidedly of opinion, that the plaintiffs do not exhibit a title which can be sustained in the Courts of the United States; and that there is no error in the judgment which was rendered against them in the District Court of Illinois.

Judgment affirmed, with costs.

PIERSON V. POST

Supreme Court of New York
3 Cai. R. 175 (1805)

TOMPKINS, J. delivered the opinion of the court.

. . .

The question submitted by the counsel in this cause for our determination is, whether *Lodowick Post,* by the pursuit with his hounds in the manner alleged in his declaration, acquired such a right to, or property in, the fox, as will sustain an action against *Pierson* for killing and taking him away?

The cause was argued with much ability by the counsel on both sides, and presents for our decision a novel and nice question. It is admitted that a fox is an animal *feræ naturæ,* and that property in such animals is acquired by occupancy only. These admissions narrow the discussion to the simple question of what acts amount to occupancy, applied to acquiring right to wild animals?

If we have recourse to the ancient writers upon general principles of law, the judgment below is obviously erroneous. *Justinian's Institutes,* lib. 2. tit. 1. s. 13. and *Fleta,* lib. 3. c. 2. p. 175. adopt the principle, that pursuit alone vests no property or right in the huntsman; and that even pursuit, accompanied with wounding, is equally ineffectual for that purpose, unless the animal be actually taken. The same principle is recognised by *Bracton,* lib. 2. c. 1. p. 8.

Puffendorf, lib. 4. c. 6. s. 2. and 10. defines occupancy of beasts *feræ naturæ,* to be the actual corporal possession of them, and *Bynkershoek* is cited as coinciding in this definition. It is indeed with hesitation that *Puffendorf* affirms that a wild beast mortally wounded, or greatly maimed, cannot be fairly intercepted by another, whilst the pursuit of the person inflicting the wound continues. The foregoing authorities are decisive to show that mere pursuit gave *Post* no legal right to the fox, but that he became the property of *Pierson,* who intercepted and killed him.

It therefore only remains to inquire whether there are any contrary principles, or authorities, to be found in other books, which ought to induce a different decision. Most of the cases which have occurred in *England,* relating to property in wild animals, have either been discussed and decided upon the principles of their positive statute regulations, or have arisen between the huntsman and the owner of the land upon which beasts *feræ naturæ* have been apprehended; the former claiming them by title of occupancy, and the latter *ratione soli.* Little satisfactory aid can, therefore, be derived from the *English* reporters.

Barbeyrac, in his notes on *Puffendorf,* does not accede to the definition of occupancy by the latter, but, on the contrary, affirms, that actual bodily seizure is not, in all cases, necessary to constitute possession of wild animals. He does not, however, *describe* the acts which, according to his ideas, will amount to an appropriation of such animals to private use, so as to exclude the claims of all other persons, by title of occupancy, to the same animals; and he is far from averring that pursuit alone is sufficient for that purpose. To a certain extent, and as far as *Barbeyrac* appears to me to go, his objections to *Puffendorf's* definition of occupancy are reasonable and correct. That is to say, that actual bodily seizure is not indispensable to acquire right to, or possession of, wild beasts; but that, on the contrary, the mortal wounding of such beasts, by one not abandoning his pursuit, may, with the utmost propriety, be deemed possession of him; since, thereby, the pursuer manifests an unequivocal intention of appropriating the animal to his individual use, has deprived him of his natural liberty, and brought him within his certain control. So also, encompassing and securing such animals with nets and toils, or otherwise intercepting them in such a manner as to deprive them of their natural liberty, and render escape impossible, may justly be deemed to give possession of them to those persons who, by their industry and labour, have used such means of apprehending them. . . .

The case cited from 11 *Mod.* 74–130 I think clearly distinguishable from the present; inasmuch as there the action was for maliciously hindering and disturbing the plaintiff in the exercise and enjoyment of a private franchise; and in the report of the same case, 3 *Salk*. 9. *Holt,* Ch. J. states, that the ducks were in the plaintiff's decoy pond, and *so in his possession,* from which it is obvious the court laid much stress in their opinion upon the plaintiff's possession of the ducks, *ratione soli.*

We are the more readily inclined to confine possession or occupancy of beasts *feræ naturæ,* within the limits prescribed by the learned authors above cited, for the sake of certainty, and preserving peace and order in society. If the first seeing, starting, or pursuing such animals, without having so wounded, circumvented or ensnared them, so as to deprive them of their natural liberty, and subject them to the control of their pursuer, should afford the basis of actions against others for intercepting and killing them, it would prove a fertile source of quarrels and litigation.

However uncourteous or unkind the conduct of *Pierson* towards *Post,* in this instance, may have been, yet his act was productive of no injury or damage for which a legal remedy can be applied. We are of opinion the judgment below was erroneous, and ought to be reversed.

LIVINGSTON, J. My opinion differs from that of the court.

. . .

By the pleadings it is admitted that a fox is a "wild and noxious beast." Both parties have regarded him, as the law of nations does a pirate. . . . His depredations on farmers and on barn yards, have not been forgotten; and to put him to death wherever found, is allowed to be meritorious, and of public benefit. Hence it follows, that our decision should have in view the greatest possible encouragement to the destruction of an animal, so cunning and ruthless in his career. But who would keep a pack of hounds; or what gentleman, at the sound of the horn, and at peep of day, would mount his steed, and for hours together, "*sub jove frigido,*" or a vertical sun, pursue the windings of this wily quadruped, if, just as night came on, and his stratagems and strength were nearly exhausted, a saucy intruder, who had not shared in the honours or labours of the chase, were permitted to come in at the death, and bear away in triumph the object of pursuit?

. . .

. . .I . . . feel great difficulty in determining, whether to acquire dominion over a thing, before in common, it be sufficient that we barely see it, or know where it is, or wish for it, or make a declaration of our will respecting it; or whether, in the case of wild beasts, setting a trap, or lying in wait, or starting, or pursuing, be enough; or if an actual wounding, or killing, or bodily tact and occupation be necessary. . . . After mature deliberation, I embrace that of *Barbeyrac,* as the most rational, and least liable to objection. . . . He ordained, that if a beast be followed with *large dogs and hounds,* he shall belong to the hunter, not to the chance occupant; and in like manner, if he be killed or wounded with a lance or sword; but if chased with *beagles only,* then he passed to the captor, not to the first pursuer. If slain with a dart, a sling, or a bow, he fell to the hunter, if still in chase, and not to him who might afterwards find and seize him.

Now, as we are without any municipal regulations of our own, and the pursuit here, for aught that appears on the case, being with dogs and hounds of *imperial stature,* we are at liberty to adopt one of the provisions just cited, which comports also with the learned conclusion of *Barbeyrac,* that property in animals *feræ naturæ* may be acquired without bodily touch or manucaption, provided the pursuer be within reach, or have a *reasonable* prospect (which certainly existed here) of taking, what he has *thus* discovered an intention of converting to his own use.

When we reflect also that the interest of our husbandmen, the most useful of men in any community, will be advanced by the destruction of a beast so pernicious and incorrigible, we cannot greatly err, in saying, that a pursuit like the present, through waste and unoccupied lands, and which must inevitably and speedily have terminated in corporal possession, or bodily *seisin,* confers such a right to the object of it, as to make any one a wrongdoer, who shall interfere and shoulder the spoil. The *justice's* judgment ought, therefore, in my opinion, to be affirmed.

Judgment of reversal.

MCFALL V. SHIMP

Pennsylvania Court of Common Pleas
10 Pa. D. & C.3d 90 (1978)

FLAHERTY, J.

Plaintiff, Robert McFall, suffers from a rare bone marrow disease and the prognosis for his survival is very dim, unless he receives a bone marrow transplant from a compatible donor. Finding a compatible donor is a very difficult task and limited to a selection among close relatives. After a search and certain tests, it has been determined that only defendant is suitable as a donor. Defendant refuses to submit to the necessary transplant, and before the court is a request for a preliminary injunction which seeks to compel defendant to submit to further tests, and, eventually, the bone marrow transplant.

Although a diligent search has produced no authority, plaintiff cites the ancient statute of King Edward I, 81 Westminster 2, 13 Ed. I, c. 24, pointing out, as is the case, that this court is a successor to the English courts of Chancery and derives power from this statute, almost 700 years old. The question posed by plaintiff is that, in order to save the life of one of its members by the only means available, may society infringe upon ones absolute right to his "bodily security"?

The common law has consistently held to a rule which provides that one human being is under no legal compulsion to give aid or to take action to save another human being or to rescue. A great deal has been written regarding this rule which, on the surface, appears to be revolting in a moral sense. Introspection, however, will demonstrate that the rule is founded upon the very essence of our free society. It is noteworthy that counsel for plaintiff has cited authority which has developed in other societies in support of plaintiff's request in this instance. Our society, contrary to many others, has as its first principle, the respect for the individual, and that society and government exist to protect the individual from being invaded and hurt by another. Many societies adopt a contrary view which has the individual existing to serve the society as a whole. In preserving such a society as we have, it is bound to happen that great moral conflicts will arise and will appear harsh in a given instance. In this case, the chancellor is being asked to force one member of society to undergo a medical procedure which would provide that part of that individual's body would be removed from him and given to another so that the other could live. Morally, this decision rests with defendant, and, in the view of the court, the refusal of defendant is morally indefensible. For our law to *compel* defendant to submit to an intrusion of his body would change every concept and principle upon which our society is founded. To do so would defeat the sanctity of the individual, and would impose a rule which would know no limits, and one could not imagine where the line would be drawn.

. . . .For a society which respects the rights of *one* individual, to sink its teeth into the jugular vein or neck of one of its members and suck from it sustenance for *another* member, is revolting to our hard-wrought concepts of jurisprudence. Forceable extraction of living body tissue causes revulsion to the judicial mind. Such would raise the spectre of the swastika and the Inquisition, reminiscent of the horrors this portends.

This court makes no comment on the law regarding plaintiff's rights in an action at law for damages, but has no alternative but to deny the requested equitable relief. An order will be entered denying the request for a preliminary injunction.

DISCUSSION PROBLEMS

1. The Home Run Ball

In October 2001, San Francisco Giant's slugger Barry Bonds hit a record-breaking 73rd home run into the right field bleachers of PacBell Park. Alex Popov and Patrick Hayashi were waiting with their baseball gloves, hoping for the chance to snag this souvenir, which experts predicted might be worth as much as $1 million if sold at auction.

The ball first landed in the webbing of Popov's glove, which stopped the trajectory of the ball. As the ball hit Popov's glove, he was tackled to the ground by a crowd of fans also attempting to get ahold of it. Buried under the pile, Popov was hit and kicked, but no members of the crowd who assaulted him could be identified, although it was clear that Hayashi was not among them. At some point, the ball was knocked away from Popov and landed on the ground. Video evidence and witness testimony did not definitively establish the extent to which Popov ever had secured the ball. The ball rolled to Hayashi, who had also been knocked to the ground in the melee. He picked it up, stood, and placed it in his pocket. There was no evidence that Hayashi had assaulted Popov.

Popov sued Hayashi for the ball. How should the court rule?

2. The Natural Gas Well

Daniel and Elizabeth Barnard owned 66 acres of land, bordered by James B. Barnard's 156 acres. Pursuant to a lease agreement with James, Monongahela Natural Gas Co. drilled a well on the edge of James's property, only 55 feet away from Daniel's and Elizabeth's property line. That well produced natural gas that was drawn from under both tracts of land. Should Daniel & Elizabeth have a legal claim against Monongahela?

3. Buried Treasure

Jack Schley purchased a house with a half-paved garage and hired a crew to pave the rest. While using a pick to remove the soil from the unpaved portion, a member of the work crew, A.M. Couch, struck a glass jar that contained $1,000 in cash (nearly $10,000 in 2020 dollars). The owner of the money was never identified. Schley and Couch both claimed the found money. Who should the law permit to keep it?

CHAPTER 2

CREATION (PATENT AND COPYRIGHT)

■ ■ ■

INTRODUCTION

Unlike land or chattels, which can be altered or improved but existed in some form before being acquired by any person, "intellectual property" is created (at least in crucial part) by the mind. The types of creative effort that justify treating intellectual creations as property, as well as the nature, scope and duration of those property rights, is highly contested to this day. *Diamond v. Chakrabarty* and *Association for Molecular Pathology v. Myriad Genetics* explores the critical question of what creative work is sufficiently inventive to qualify for patent protection. 35 U.S.C. § 101. *Feist Publications, Inc. v. Rural Telephone Service Co., Inc.* considers an equivalent question in the copyright realm: what type of work is sufficiently creative to qualify as an "original work of authorship" deserving protection. 17 U.S.C. § 102. As you try to understand the lines the courts draw between legally protected and unprotected creative work, also ask yourself whether these lines are stable (can the rules be reliably applied to other cases?) and defensible (is there a moral or consequentialist theory that justifies these lines?).

An important difference between the nature of physical and intellectual property is that the latter is generally non-rivalrous, meaning its use by one person is not inconsistent with a use by another. If you farm your neighbor's land or joyride in his car, he cannot make use of those things (at least not fully), but if you replicate his invention or copy his poem, this does not impede his ability to make full use of either. How, if at all, should this difference matter to the nature of property rights that the law provides? If the law does not recognize his ownership of his farm and thus prevents you from eating his crops, he might lack the incentive to sow the land. Should we fear, in the same way, that he might not write poems if he is unable to prevent you from copying them?

There is also a legal process difference between physical and intellectual property that bears mention. The law of physical property is almost entirely state law and mostly derives from English common law (although much of that has now been codified in many states). Intellectual property has a different pedigree. Article I, Section 8 of the U.S. Constitution delegates to Congress the power to allocate private rights in intellectual property: "To promote the progress of science and useful arts, by securing for limited times to authors and inventors the exclusive right to their respective writings and discoveries." There is some state law governing intellectual property (trade secrets law, for example, is almost entirely a creature of state common law), but as a result of the Constitution's grant of power, the law of intellectual property is largely governed by federal law.

The first congress enacted the Copyright Act of 1790, providing property rights to creators of maps, charts, and books. The Patent Act of 1790 provided a process for securing property rights in inventions. Both federal statutes have been revised dozens of times since, greatly expanding the scope of protection for intellectual property. The first copyright act provided property protection for a narrow category of creative works for 14 years, renewable for another 14. Today, copyright protection is far broader and lasts for the life of the author plus 75 years (or 95 years if the author is a corporation). The first patent act gave a three-person committee made up of the Attorney General, the Secretary of State and the Secretary of War discretion to award patents. Today, a professionalized Patent and Trademark Office issues patents based on a defined set of criteria.

---

35 U.S. Code § 101. Inventions patentable

Whoever invents or discovers any new and useful process, machine, manufacture, or composition of matter, or any new and useful improvement thereof, may obtain a patent therefor, subject to the conditions and requirements of this title.

35 U.S. Code § 102. Conditions for patentability; novelty

(a) NOVELTY; PRIOR ART.—A person shall be entitled to a patent unless—

(1) the claimed invention was patented, described in a printed publication, or in public use, on sale, or otherwise available to the public before the effective filing date of the claimed invention; . . .

35 U.S. Code § 103. Conditions for patentability; non-obvious subject matter

A patent for a claimed invention may not be obtained . . . if the differences between the claimed invention and the prior art are such that the claimed invention as a whole would have been obvious before the effective filing date of the claimed invention to a person having ordinary skill in the art to which the claimed invention pertains. Patentability shall not be negated by the manner in which the invention was made.

35 U.S. Code § 271. Infringement of patent

(a) Except as otherwise provided in this title, whoever without authority makes, uses, offers to sell, or sells any patented invention, within the United States or imports into the United States any patented invention during the term of the patent therefor, infringes the patent.

17 U.S. Code § 102. Subject matter of copyright: In general

(a) Copyright protection subsists, in accordance with this title, in original works of authorship fixed in any tangible medium of expression, now known or later developed, from which they can be perceived, reproduced, or otherwise communicated, either directly or with the aid of a machine or device. Works of authorship include the following categories:

(1) literary works;

(2) musical works, including any accompanying words;

(3) dramatic works, including any accompanying music;

(4) pantomimes and choreographic works;

(5) pictorial, graphic, and sculptural works;

(6) motion pictures and other audiovisual works;

(7) sound recordings; and

(8) architectural works.

(b) In no case does copyright protection for an original work of authorship extend to any idea, procedure, process, system, method of operation, concept, principle, or discovery, regardless of the form in which it is described, explained, illustrated, or embodied in such work.

17 U.S. Code § 302. Duration of copyright: Works created on or after January 1, 1978

(a) IN GENERAL.—Copyright in a work created on or after January 1, 1978, subsists from its creation and, except as provided by the following subsections, endures for a term consisting of the life of the author and 70 years after the author's death.

. . .

(c) ANONYMOUS WORKS, PSEUDONYMOUS WORKS, AND WORKS MADE FOR HIRE.—In the case of an anonymous work, a pseudonymous work, or a work made for hire, the copyright endures for a term of 95 years from the year of its first publication, or a term of 120 years from the year of its creation, whichever expires first.

CASES

DIAMOND V. CHAKRABARTY

Supreme Court of the United States
447 U.S. 303 (1980)

MR. CHIEF JUSTICE BURGER delivered the opinion of the Court.

We granted certiorari to determine whether a live, human-made micro-organism is patentable subject matter under 35 U.S.C. § 101.

I

In 1972, respondent Chakrabarty, a microbiologist, filed a patent application, assigned to the General Electric Co63+

. The application asserted 36 claims related to Chakrabarty's invention of "a bacterium from the genus *Pseudomonas* containing therein at least two stable energy-generating plasmids, each of said plasmids providing a separate hydrocarbon degradative pathway. This human-made, genetically engineered bacterium is capable of breaking down multiple components of crude oil. Because of this property, which is possessed by no naturally occurring bacteria, Chakrabarty's invention is believed to have significant value for the treatment of oil spills.

Chakrabarty's patent claims were of three types: first, process claims for the method of producing the bacteria; second, claims for an inoculum comprised of a carrier material floating on water, such as straw, and the new bacteria; and third, claims to the bacteria themselves. The patent examiner allowed the claims falling into the first two categories, but rejected claims for the bacteria. His decision rested on two grounds: (1) that micro-organisms are "products of nature," and (2) that as living things they are not patentable subject matter under 35 U.S.C. § 101.

Chakrabarty appealed the rejection of these claims to the Patent Office Board of Appeals, and the Board affirmed the Examiner on the second ground. Relying on the legislative history of the 1930 Plant Patent Act, in which Congress extended patent protection to certain asexually reproduced plants, the Board concluded that § 101 was not intended to cover living things such as these laboratory created micro-organisms.

The Court of Customs and Patent Appeals, by a divided vote, reversed. . . .

II

The Constitution grants Congress broad power to legislate to "promote the Progress of Science and useful Arts, by securing for limited Times to Authors and Inventors the exclusive Right to their respective Writings and Discoveries." Art. I, § 8, cl. 8. The patent laws promote this progress by offering inventors exclusive rights for a limited period as an incentive for their inventiveness and research efforts. The authority of Congress is exercised in the hope that "[t]he productive effort thereby fostered will have a positive effect on society through the introduction of new products and processes of manufacture into the economy, and the emanations by way of increased employment and better lives for our citizens." *Kewanee, supra*, 416 U.S., at 480, 94 S.Ct., at 1885–86.

The question before us in this case is a narrow one of statutory interpretation requiring us to construe 35 U.S.C. § 101, which provides:

> "Whoever invents or discovers any new and useful process, machine, manufacture, or composition of matter, or any new and useful improvement thereof, may obtain a patent therefor, subject to the conditions and requirements of this title."

Specifically, we must determine whether respondent's micro-organism constitutes a "manufacture" or "composition of matter" within the meaning of the statute.

III

In cases of statutory construction we begin, of course, with the language of the statute. And "unless otherwise defined, words will be interpreted as taking their ordinary, contemporary common meaning. We have also cautioned that courts "should not read into the patent laws limitations and conditions which the legislature has not expressed."

Guided by these canons of construction, this Court has read the term "manufacture" in § 101 in accordance with its dictionary definition to mean "the production of articles for use from raw or prepared materials by giving to these materials new forms, qualities, properties, or combinations, whether by hand-labor or by machine." Similarly, "composition of matter" has been construed consistent with its common usage to include "all compositions of two or more substances and . . . all composite articles, whether they be the results of chemical union, or of mechanical mixture, or whether they be gases, fluids, powders or solids." In choosing such expansive terms as "manufacture" and "composition of matter," modified by the comprehensive "any," Congress plainly contemplated that the patent laws would be given wide scope.

The relevant legislative history also supports a broad construction. The Patent Act of 1793, authored by Thomas Jefferson, defined statutory subject matter as "any new and useful art, machine, manufacture, or composition of matter, or any new or useful improvement [thereof]." Act of Feb. 21, 1793, § 1, 1 Stat. 319. The Act embodied Jefferson's philosophy that "ingenuity should receive a liberal encouragement. Subsequent patent statutes in 1836, 1870, and 1874 employed this same broad language. In 1952, when the patent laws were recodified, Congress replaced the word "art" with "process," but otherwise left Jefferson's language intact. The

Committee Reports accompanying the 1952 Act inform us that Congress intended statutory subject matter to "include anything under the sun that is made by man."

This is not to suggest that § 101 has no limits or that it embraces every discovery. The laws of nature, physical phenomena, and abstract ideas have been held not patentable. Thus, a new mineral discovered in the earth or a new plant found in the wild is not patentable subject matter. Likewise, Einstein could not patent his celebrated law that $E=mc^2$; nor could Newton have patented the law of gravity. Such discoveries are "manifestations of . . . nature, free to all men and reserved exclusively to none."

Judged in this light, respondent's micro-organism plainly qualifies as patentable subject matter. His claim is not to a hitherto unknown natural phenomenon, but to a nonnaturally occurring manufacture or composition of matter—a product of human ingenuity "having a distinctive name, character [and] use." The point is underscored dramatically by comparison of the invention here with that in *Funk*. There, the patentee had discovered that there existed in nature certain species of root-nodule bacteria which did not exert a mutually inhibitive effect on each other. He used that discovery to produce a mixed culture capable of inoculating the seeds of leguminous plants. Concluding that the patentee had discovered "only some of the handiwork of nature," the Court ruled the product nonpatentable:

> "Each of the species of root-nodule bacteria contained in the package infects the same group of leguminous plants which it always infected. No species acquires a different use. The combination of species produces no new bacteria, no change in the six species of bacteria, and no enlargement of the range of their utility. Each species has the same effect it always had. The bacteria perform in their natural way. Their use in combination does not improve in any way their natural functioning. They serve the ends nature originally provided and act quite independently of any effort of the patentee." 333 U.S., at 131, 68 S.Ct., at 442.

Here, by contrast, the patentee has produced a new bacterium with markedly different characteristics from any found in nature and one having the potential for significant utility. His discovery is not nature's handiwork, but his own; accordingly it is patentable subject matter under § 101.

IV

. . . .

To buttress his argument, the petitioner, with the support of *amicus*, points to grave risks that may be generated by research endeavors such as respondent's. The briefs present a gruesome parade of horribles. Scientists, among them Nobel laureates, are quoted suggesting that genetic research may pose a serious threat to the human race, or, at the very least, that the dangers are far too substantial to permit such research to proceed apace at this time. We are told that genetic research and related technological developments may spread pollution and disease, that it may result in a loss of genetic diversity, and that its practice may tend to depreciate the value of human life. These arguments are forcefully, even passionately, presented; they remind us that, at times, human ingenuity seems unable to control fully the forces it creates—that with Hamlet, it is sometimes better "to bear those ills we have than fly to others that we know not of."

It is argued that this Court should weigh these potential hazards in considering whether respondent's invention is patentable subject matter under § 101. We disagree.

. . . .

Our task, rather, is the narrow one of determining what Congress meant by the words it used in the statute; once that is done our powers are exhausted. Congress is free to amend § 101 so as to exclude from patent protection organisms produced by genetic engineering. Cf. 42 U.S.C. § 2181(a), exempting from patent protection inventions "useful solely in the utilization of special nuclear material or atomic energy in an atomic weapon." Or it may chose to craft a statute specifically designed for such living things. But, until Congress takes such action, this Court must construe the language of § 101 as it is. The language of that section fairly embraces respondent's invention.

Accordingly, the judgment of the Court of Customs and Patent Appeals is *Affirmed.*

ASSOCIATION FOR MOLECULAR PATHOLOGY v. MYRIAD GENETICS, INC.

Supreme Court of the United States
569 U.S. 576 (2013)

JUSTICE THOMAS delivered the opinion of the Court.

Respondent Myriad Genetics, Inc. (Myriad), discovered the precise location and sequence of two human genes, mutations of which can substantially increase the risks of breast and ovarian cancer. Myriad obtained a number of patents based upon its discovery. This case involves claims from three of them and requires us to resolve whether a naturally occurring segment of deoxyribonucleic acid (DNA) is patent eligible under 35 U.S.C. § 101 by virtue of its isolation from the rest of the human genome. We also address the patent eligibility of synthetically created DNA known as complementary DNA (cDNA), which contains the same protein-coding information found in a segment of natural DNA but omits portions within the DNA segment that do not code for proteins. For the reasons that follow, we hold that a naturally occurring DNA segment is a product of nature and not patent eligible merely because it has been isolated, but that cDNA is patent eligible because it is not naturally occurring. We, therefore, affirm in part and reverse in part the decision of the United States Court of Appeals for the Federal Circuit.

I

A

Genes form the basis for hereditary traits in living organisms. See generally *Association for Molecular Pathology v. United States Patent and Trademark Office,* 702 F.Supp.2d 181, 192–211 (S.D.N.Y.2010). The human genome consists of approximately 22,000 genes packed into 23 pairs of chromosomes. Each gene is encoded as DNA, which takes the shape of the familiar "double helix" that Doctors James Watson and Francis Crick first described in 1953. Each "cross-bar" in the DNA helix consists of two chemically joined nucleotides. The possible nucleotides are adenine (A), thymine (T), cytosine (C), and guanine (G), each of which binds naturally with another nucleotide: A pairs with T; C pairs with G. The nucleotide cross-bars are chemically connected to a sugar-phosphate backbone that forms the outside framework of the DNA helix. Sequences of DNA nucleotides contain the information necessary to create strings of amino acids, which in turn are used in the body to build proteins. Only some DNA nucleotides, however, code for amino acids; these nucleotides are known as "exons." Nucleotides that do not code for amino acids, in contrast, are known as "introns."

Creation of proteins from DNA involves two principal steps, known as transcription and translation. In transcription, the bonds between DNA nucleotides separate, and the DNA helix unwinds into two single strands. A single strand is used as a template to create a complementary ribonucleic acid (RNA) strand. The nucleotides on the DNA strand pair naturally with their counterparts, with the exception that RNA uses the nucleotide base uracil (U) instead of thymine (T). Transcription results in a single strand RNA molecule, known as pre-RNA, whose nucleotides form an inverse image of the DNA strand from which it was created. Pre-RNA still contains nucleotides corresponding to both the exons and introns in the DNA molecule. The pre-RNA is then naturally "spliced" by the physical removal of the introns. The resulting product is a strand of RNA that contains nucleotides corresponding only to the exons from the original DNA strand. The exons-only strand is known as messenger RNA (mRNA), which creates amino acids through translation. In translation, cellular structures known as ribosomes read each set of three nucleotides, known as codons, in the mRNA. Each codon either tells the ribosomes which of the 20 possible amino acids to synthesize or provides a stop signal that ends amino acid production.

DNA's informational sequences and the processes that create mRNA, amino acids, and proteins occur naturally within cells. Scientists can, however, extract DNA from cells using well known laboratory methods. These methods allow scientists to isolate specific segments of DNA—for instance, a particular gene or part of a gene—which can then be further studied, manipulated, or used. It is also possible to create DNA synthetically through processes similarly well known in the field of genetics. One such method begins with an mRNA molecule and uses the natural bonding properties of nucleotides to create a new, synthetic DNA molecule. The result is the inverse of the mRNA's inverse image of the original DNA, with one important distinction: Because the natural creation of mRNA involves splicing that removes introns, the synthetic DNA created from mRNA also contains only the exon sequences. This synthetic DNA created in the laboratory from mRNA is known as complementary DNA (cDNA).

Changes in the genetic sequence are called mutations. Mutations can be as small as the alteration of a single nucleotide—a change affecting only one letter in the genetic code. Such small-scale changes can produce an entirely different amino acid or can end protein production altogether. Large changes, involving the deletion, rearrangement, or duplication of hundreds or even millions of nucleotides, can result in the elimination, misplacement, or duplication of entire genes. Some mutations are harmless, but others can cause disease or increase the risk of disease. As a result, the study of genetics can lead to valuable medical breakthroughs.

B

This case involves patents filed by Myriad after it made one such medical breakthrough. Myriad discovered the precise location and sequence of what are now known as the BRCA1 and BRCA2 genes. Mutations in these genes can dramatically increase an individual's risk of developing breast and ovarian cancer. The average American woman has a 12- to 13-percent risk of developing breast cancer, but for women with certain genetic mutations, the risk can range between 50 and 80 percent for breast cancer and between 20 and 50 percent for ovarian cancer. Before Myriad's discovery of the BRCA1 and BRCA2 genes, scientists knew that heredity played a role in establishing a woman's risk of developing breast and ovarian cancer, but they did not know which genes were associated with those cancers.

Myriad identified the exact location of the BRCA1 and BRCA2 genes on chromosomes 17 and 13. Chromosome 17 has approximately 80 million nucleotides, and chromosome 13 has approximately 114 million. Within those chromosomes, the BRCA1 and BRCA2 genes are each about 80,000 nucleotides long. If just exons are counted, the BRCA1 gene is only about 5,500 nucleotides long; for the BRCA2 gene, that number is about 10,200. *Ibid.* Knowledge of the location of the BRCA1 and BRCA2 genes allowed Myriad to determine their typical nucleotide sequence. That information, in turn, enabled Myriad to develop medical tests that are useful for detecting mutations in a patient's BRCA1 and BRCA2 genes and thereby assessing whether the patient has an increased risk of cancer.

Once it found the location and sequence of the BRCA1 and BRCA2 genes, Myriad sought and obtained a number of patents. [C]laim 1 asserts a patent claim on the DNA code that tells a cell to produce the string of BRCA1 amino acids listed in SEQ ID NO:2.

Claim 2 of the '282 patent operates similarly. It claims "[t]he isolated DNA of claim 1, wherein said DNA has the nucleotide sequence set forth in SEQ ID NO:1." *Id.*, at 822. [T]he Federal Circuit recognized that claim 2 asserts a patent on the cDNA nucleotide sequence listed in SEQ ID NO:1, which codes for the typical BRCA1 gene.

Claim 5 of the '282 patent claims a subset of the data in claim 1. In particular, it claims "[a]n isolated DNA having at least 15 nucleotides of the DNA of claim 1." App. 822. The practical effect of claim 5 is to assert a patent on any series of 15 nucleotides that exist in the typical BRCA1 gene. Because the BRCA1 gene is thousands of nucleotides long, even BRCA1 genes with substantial mutations are likely to contain at least one segment of 15 nucleotides that correspond to the typical BRCA1 gene. Similarly, claim 6 of the '282 patent claims "[a]n isolated DNA having at least 15 nucleotides of the DNA of claim 2." *Ibid.* This claim operates similarly to claim 5, except that it references the cDNA-based claim 2. The remaining claims at issue are similar, though several list common mutations rather than typical BRCA1 and BRCA2 sequences.

C

Myriad's patents would, if valid, give it the exclusive right to isolate an individual's BRCA1 and BRCA2 genes (or any strand of 15 or more nucleotides within the genes) by breaking the covalent bonds that connect the DNA to the rest of the individual's genome. The patents would also give Myriad the exclusive right to synthetically create BRCA cDNA. In Myriad's view, manipulating BRCA DNA in either of these fashions triggers its "right to exclude others from making" its patented composition of matter under the Patent Act. 35 U.S.C. § 154(a)(1); see also § 271(a) ("[W]hoever without authority makes . . . any patented invention . . . infringes the patent").

But isolation is necessary to conduct genetic testing, and Myriad was not the only entity to offer BRCA testing after it discovered the genes. The University of Pennsylvania's Genetic Diagnostic Laboratory (GDL) and others provided genetic testing services to women. Petitioner Dr. Harry

Ostrer, then a researcher at New York University School of Medicine, routinely sent his patients' DNA samples to GDL for testing. After learning of GDL's testing and Ostrer's activities, Myriad sent letters to them asserting that the genetic testing infringed Myriad's patents. App. 94–95 (Ostrer letter). In response, GDL agreed to stop testing and informed Ostrer that it would no longer accept patient samples. Myriad also filed patent infringement suits against other entities that performed BRCA testing, resulting in settlements in which the defendants agreed to cease all allegedly infringing activity. 689 F.3d, at 1315. Myriad, thus, solidified its position as the only entity providing BRCA testing.

Some years later, petitioner Ostrer, along with medical patients, advocacy groups, and other doctors, filed this lawsuit seeking a declaration that Myriad's patents are invalid under 35 U.S.C. § 101. The District Court then granted summary judgment to petitioners on the composition claims at issue in this case based on its conclusion that Myriad's claims, including claims related to cDNA, were invalid because they covered products of nature. The Federal Circuit reversed. . . .

With respect to the merits, the court held that both isolated DNA and cDNA were patent eligible under § 101. The central dispute among the panel members was whether the act of *isolating* DNA—separating a specific gene or sequence of nucleotides from the rest of the chromosome—is an inventive act that entitles the individual who first isolates it to a patent. Each of the judges on the panel had a different view on that question. Judges Lourie and Moore agreed that Myriad's claims were patent eligible under § 101. . . . Judge Lourie relied on the fact that the entire DNA molecule is held together by chemical bonds and that the covalent bonds at both ends of the segment must be severed in order to isolate segments of DNA. This process technically creates new molecules with unique chemical compositions. Judge Lourie found this chemical alteration to be dispositive, because isolating a particular strand of DNA creates a nonnaturally occurring molecule, even though the chemical alteration does not change the information-transmitting quality of the DNA.

. . . .

Finally, Judge Bryson concurred in part and dissented in part, concluding that isolated DNA is not patent eligible. As an initial matter, he emphasized that the breaking of chemical bonds was not dispositive: "[T]here is no magic to a chemical bond that requires us to recognize a new product when a chemical bond is created or broken." *Id.,* at 1351. Instead, he relied on the fact that "[t]he nucleotide sequences of the claimed molecules are the same as the nucleotide sequences found in naturally occurring human genes." *Id.,* at 1355. Judge Bryson then concluded that genetic "structural similarity dwarfs the significance of the structural differences between isolated DNA and naturally occurring DNA, especially where the structural differences are merely ancillary to the breaking of covalent bonds, a process that is itself not inventive." *Ibid.* . . .

Although the judges expressed different views concerning the patentability of isolated DNA, all three agreed that patent claims relating to cDNA met the patent eligibility requirements of § 101. *Id.,* at 1326, and n. 9 (recognizing that some patent claims are limited to cDNA and that such claims are patent eligible under § 101); *id.,* at 1337 (Moore, J., concurring in part); *id.,* at 1356 (Bryson, J., concurring in part and dissenting in part) ("cDNA cannot be isolated from nature, but instead must be created in the laboratory . . . because the introns that are found in the native gene are removed from the cDNA segment"). We granted certiorari. 568 U.S. ___, 133 S.Ct. 694, 184 L.Ed.2d 496 (2012).

II

A

Section 101 of the Patent Act provides:

> "Whoever invents or discovers any new and useful . . . composition of matter, or any new and useful improvement thereof, may obtain a patent therefor, subject to the conditions and requirements of this title." 35 U.S.C. § 101.

We have "long held that this provision contains an important implicit exception[:] Laws of nature, natural phenomena, and abstract ideas are not patentable." *Mayo,* 566 U.S., at ___, 132 S.Ct., at 1293 (internal quotation marks and brackets omitted). Rather, " 'they are the basic tools of scientific and technological work' " that lie beyond the domain of patent protection. *Id.,* at ___, 132 S.Ct., at 1293. As the Court has explained, without this exception, there would be considerable danger that the grant of patents would "tie up" the use of such tools and thereby "inhibit future innovation premised upon them." *Id.,* at ___, 132 S.Ct., at 1301. This would be at odds with the very point of patents, which exist to promote creation.

The rule against patents on naturally occurring things is not without limits, however, for "all inventions at some level embody, use, reflect, rest upon, or apply laws of nature, natural phenomena, or abstract ideas," and "too broad an interpretation of this exclusionary principle could eviscerate patent law." 566 U.S., at ___, 132 S.Ct., at 1293. As we have recognized before, patent protection strikes a delicate balance between creating "incentives that lead to creation, invention, and discovery" and "imped[ing] the flow of information that might permit, indeed spur, invention." *Id.,* at ___, 132 S.Ct., at 1305. We must apply this well-established standard to determine whether Myriad's patents claim any "new and useful . . . composition of matter," § 101, or instead claim naturally occurring phenomena.

B

It is undisputed that Myriad did not create or alter any of the genetic information encoded in the BRCA1 and BRCA2 genes. The location and order of the nucleotides existed in nature before Myriad found them. Nor did Myriad create or alter the genetic structure of DNA. Instead, Myriad's principal contribution was uncovering the precise location and genetic sequence of the BRCA1 and BRCA2 genes within chromosomes 17 and 13. The question is whether this renders the genes patentable.

Myriad recognizes that our decision in *Chakrabarty* is central to this inquiry. Brief for Respondents 14, 23–27. In *Chakrabarty,* scientists added four plasmids to a bacterium, which enabled it to break down various components of crude oil. 447 U.S., at 305, and n. 1, 100 S.Ct. 2204. The Court held that the modified bacterium was patentable. It explained that the patent claim was "not to a hitherto unknown natural phenomenon, but to a nonnaturally occurring manufacture or composition of matter—a product of human ingenuity 'having a distinctive name, character [and] use.' " *Id.,* at 309–310, 100 S.Ct. 2204 (quoting *Hartranft v. Wiegmann,* 121 U.S. 609, 615, 7 S.Ct. 1240, 30 L.Ed. 1012 (1887); alteration in original). The *Chakrabarty* bacterium was new "with markedly different characteristics from any found in nature," 447 U.S., at 310, 100 S.Ct. 2204, due to the additional plasmids and resultant "capacity for degrading oil." *Id.,* at 305, n. 1, 100 S.Ct. 2204. In this case, by contrast, Myriad did not create anything. To be sure, it found an important and useful gene, but separating that gene from its surrounding genetic material is not an act of invention.

Groundbreaking, innovative, or even brilliant discovery does not by itself satisfy the § 101 inquiry. In *Funk Brothers Seed Co. v. Kalo Inoculant Co.,* 333 U.S. 127, 68 S.Ct. 440, 92 L.Ed. 588 (1948), this Court considered a composition patent that claimed a mixture of naturally occurring strains of bacteria that helped leguminous plants take nitrogen from the air and fix it in the soil. *Id.,* at 128–129, 68 S.Ct. 440. The ability of the bacteria to fix nitrogen was well known, and farmers commonly "inoculated" their crops with them to improve soil nitrogen levels. But farmers could not use the same inoculant for all crops, both because plants use different bacteria and because certain bacteria inhibit each other. *Id.,* at 129–130, 68 S.Ct. 440. Upon learning that several nitrogen-fixing bacteria did not inhibit each other, however, the patent applicant combined them into a single inoculant and obtained a patent. *Id.,* at 130, 68 S.Ct. 440. The Court held that the composition was not patent eligible because the patent holder did not alter the bacteria in any way. *Id.,* at 132, 68 S.Ct. 440 ("There is no way in which we could call [the bacteria mixture a product of invention] unless we borrowed invention from the discovery of the natural principle itself"). His patent claim thus fell squarely within the law of nature exception. So do Myriad's. Myriad found the location of the BRCA1 and BRCA2 genes, but that discovery, by itself, does not render the BRCA genes "new . . . composition[s] of matter," § 101, that are patent eligible.

Indeed, Myriad's patent descriptions highlight the problem with its claims. For example, a section of the '282 patent's Detailed Description of the Invention indicates that Myriad found the location of a gene associated with increased risk of breast cancer and identified mutations of that gene that increase the risk. See App. 748–749. In subsequent language Myriad explains that the location of the gene was unknown until Myriad found it among the approximately eight million nucleotide pairs contained in a subpart of chromosome 17. See *Ibid.* The '473 and '492 patents contain similar language as well. Many of Myriad's patent descriptions simply detail the "iterative process" of discovery by which Myriad narrowed the possible locations for the gene sequences that it sought. Myriad seeks to import these extensive research efforts into the § 101 patent-eligibility inquiry. Brief for Respondents 8–10, 34. But extensive effort alone is insufficient to satisfy the demands of § 101.

Nor are Myriad's claims saved by the fact that isolating DNA from the human genome severs chemical bonds and thereby creates a nonnaturally occurring molecule. Myriad's claims are simply not expressed in terms of chemical composition, nor do they rely in any way on the chemical changes that result from the isolation of a particular section of DNA. Instead, the claims understandably focus on the genetic information encoded in the BRCA1 and BRCA2 genes. If the patents depended upon the creation of a unique molecule, then a would-be infringer could arguably avoid at least Myriad's patent claims on entire genes (such as claims 1 and 2 of the '282 patent) by isolating a DNA sequence that included both the BRCA1 or BRCA2 gene and one additional nucleotide pair. Such a molecule would not be chemically identical to the molecule "invented" by Myriad. But Myriad obviously would resist that outcome because its claim is concerned primarily with the information contained in the genetic *sequence,* not with the specific chemical composition of a particular molecule.

. . . .

C

cDNA does not present the same obstacles to patentability as naturally occurring, isolated DNA segments. As already explained, creation of a cDNA sequence from mRNA results in an exons-only molecule that is not naturally occurring. Petitioners concede that cDNA differs from natural DNA in that "the non-coding regions have been removed." Brief for Petitioners 49. They nevertheless argue that cDNA is not patent eligible because "[t]he nucleotide sequence of cDNA is dictated by nature, not by the lab technician." *Id.,* at 51. That may be so, but the lab technician unquestionably creates something ne3w when cDNA is made. cDNA retains the naturally occurring exons of DNA, but it is distinct from the

DNA from which it was derived. As a result, cDNA is not a "product of nature" and is patent eligible under § 101, except insofar as very short series of DNA may have no intervening introns to remove when creating cDNA. In that situation, a short strand of cDNA may be indistinguishable from natural DNA.

III

It is important to note what is *not* implicated by this decision. First, there are no method claims before this Court. Had Myriad created an innovative method of manipulating genes while searching for the BRCA1 and BRCA2 genes, it could possibly have sought a method patent. But the processes used by Myriad to isolate DNA were well understood by geneticists at the time of Myriad's patents "were well understood, widely used, and fairly uniform insofar as any scientist engaged in the search for a gene would likely have utilized a similar approach," 702 F.Supp.2d, at 202–203, and are not at issue in this case.

Similarly, this case does not involve patents on new *applications* of knowledge about the BRCA1 and BRCA2 genes. Judge Bryson aptly noted that, "[a]s the first party with knowledge of the [BRCA1 and BRCA2] sequences, Myriad was in an excellent position to claim applications of that knowledge. Many of its unchallenged claims are limited to such applications." 689 F.3d, at 1349.

FEIST PUBLICATIONS, INC. V. RURAL TELEPHONE SERVICE COMPANY, INC.

Supreme Court of the United States
499 U.S. 340 (1991)

JUSTICE O'CONNOR delivered the opinion of the Court.

This case requires us to clarify the extent of copyright protection available to telephone directory white pages.

I

Rural Telephone Service Company, Inc., is a certified public utility that provides telephone service to several communities in northwest Kansas. It is subject to a state regulation that requires all telephone companies operating in Kansas to issue annually an updated telephone directory. Accordingly, as a condition of its monopoly franchise, Rural publishes a typical telephone directory, consisting of white pages and yellow pages. The white pages list in alphabetical order the names of Rural's subscribers, together with their towns and telephone numbers. The yellow pages list Rural's business subscribers alphabetically by category and feature classified advertisements of various sizes. Rural distributes its directory free of charge to its subscribers, but earns revenue by selling yellow pages advertisements.

Feist Publications, Inc., is a publishing company that specializes in area-wide telephone directories. Unlike a typical directory, which covers only a particular calling area, Feist's area-wide directories cover a much larger geographical range, reducing the need to call directory assistance or consult multiple directories. The Feist directory that is the subject of this litigation covers 11 different telephone service areas in 15 counties and contains 46,878 white pages listings—compared to Rural's approximately 7,700 listings. Like Rural's directory, Feist's is distributed free of charge and includes both white pages and yellow pages. Feist and Rural compete vigorously for yellow pages advertising.

As the sole provider of telephone service in its service area, Rural obtains subscriber information quite easily. Persons desiring telephone service must apply to Rural and provide their names and addresses; Rural then assigns them a telephone number. Feist is not a telephone company, let alone one with monopoly status, and therefore lacks independent access to any subscriber information. To obtain white pages listings for its area-wide directory, Feist approached each of the 11 telephone companies operating in northwest Kansas and offered to pay for the right to use its white pages listings.

Of the 11 telephone companies, only Rural refused to license its listings to Feist. Rural's refusal created a problem for Feist, as omitting these listings would have left a gaping hole in its area-wide directory, rendering it less attractive to potential yellow pages advertisers. . . .

Unable to license Rural's white pages listings, Feist used them without Rural's consent. Feist began by removing several thousand listings that fell outside the geographic range of its area-wide directory, then hired personnel to investigate the 4,935 that remained. These employees verified the data reported by Rural and sought to obtain additional information. As a result, a typical Feist listing includes the individual's street address; most of Rural's listings do not. Notwithstanding these additions, however, 1,309 of the 46,878 listings in Feist's 1983 directory were identical to listings in Rural's 1982–1983 white pages. Four of these were fictitious listings that Rural had inserted into its directory to detect copying.

Rural sued for copyright infringement in the District Court for the District of Kansas taking the position that Feist, in compiling its own directory, could not use the information contained in Rural's white pages. Rural asserted that Feist's employees were obliged to travel door-to-door or conduct a telephone survey to discover the same information for themselves. Feist responded that such efforts were economically impractical and, in any event, unnecessary because the information copied was beyond the scope of copyright protection. . . .

II

A

This case concerns the interaction of two well-established propositions. The first is that facts are not copyrightable; the other, that compilations of facts generally are. Each of these propositions possesses an impeccable pedigree. That there can be no valid copyright in facts is universally understood. The most fundamental axiom of copyright law is that "[n]o author may copyright his ideas or the facts he narrates." Rural wisely concedes this point, noting in its brief that "[f]acts and discoveries, of course, are not themselves subject to copyright protection." Brief for Respondent 24. At the same time, however, it is beyond dispute that compilations of facts are within the subject matter of copyright. Compilations were expressly mentioned in the Copyright Act of 1909, and again in the Copyright Act of 1976.

There is an undeniable tension between these two propositions. Many compilations consist of nothing but raw data—*i.e.,* wholly factual information not accompanied by any original written expression. On what basis may one claim a copyright in such a work? Common sense tells us that 100 uncopyrightable facts do not magically change their status when gathered together in one place. Yet copyright law seems to contemplate that compilations that consist exclusively of facts are potentially within its scope.

The key to resolving the tension lies in understanding why facts are not copyrightable. The *sine qua non* of copyright is originality. To qualify for copyright protection, a work must be original to the author. See *Harper & Row, supra,* at 547–549, 105 S.Ct., at 2223–2224. Original, as the term is used in copyright, means only that the work was independently created by the author (as opposed to copied from other works), and that it possesses at least some minimal degree of creativity. 1 M. Nimmer & D. Nimmer, Copyright §§ 2.01[A], [B] (1990) (hereinafter Nimmer). To be sure, the requisite level of creativity is extremely low; even a slight amount will suffice. The vast majority of works make the grade quite easily, as they possess some creative spark, "no matter how crude, humble or obvious" it might be. *Id.,* § 1.08 [C] [1]. Originality does not signify novelty; a work may be original even though it closely resembles other works so long as the similarity is fortuitous, not the result of copying. To illustrate, assume that two poets, each ignorant of the other, compose identical poems. Neither work is novel, yet both are original and, hence, copyrightable.

Originality is a constitutional requirement. The source of Congress' power to enact copyright laws is Article I, § 8, cl. 8, of the Constitution, which authorizes Congress to "secur[e] for limited Times to Authors . . . the exclusive Right to their respective Writings." . . .

In *The Trade-Mark Cases,* the Court addressed the constitutional scope of "writings." For a particular work to be classified "under the head of writings of authors," the Court determined, "originality is required." The Court explained that originality requires independent creation plus a modicum of creativity: "[W]hile the word *writings* may be liberally construed, as it has been, to include original designs for engraving, prints, &c., it is only such as are *original,* and are founded in the creative powers of the mind. The writings which are to be protected are *the fruits of intellectual labor,* embodied in the form of books, prints, engravings, and the like." *Ibid.* (emphasis in original).

It is this bedrock principle of copyright that mandates the law's seemingly disparate treatment of facts and factual compilations. "No one may claim originality as to facts." *Id.,* § 2.11[A], p. 2–157. This is because facts do not owe their origin to an act of authorship. The distinction is one between creation and discovery: The first person to find and report a particular fact has not created the fact; he or she has merely discovered its existence. . . .

Factual compilations, on the other hand, may possess the requisite originality. The compilation author typically chooses which facts to include, in what order to place them, and how to arrange the collected data so that they may be used effectively by readers. These choices as to selection and arrangement, so long as they are made independently by the compiler and entail a minimal degree of creativity, are sufficiently original that Congress may protect such compilations through the copyright laws. Nimmer §§ 2.11[D], 3.03; Denicola 523, n. 38. Thus, even a directory that contains absolutely no protectible written expression, only facts, meets the constitutional minimum for copyright protection if it features an original selection or arrangement.

. . . .

This inevitably means that the copyright in a factual compilation is thin. Notwithstanding a valid copyright, a subsequent compiler remains free to use the facts contained in another's publication to aid in preparing a competing work, so long as the competing work does not feature the same selection and arrangement. As one commentator explains it: "[N]o matter how much original authorship the work displays, the facts and ideas it exposes are free for the taking. . . . [T]he very same facts and ideas may be divorced from the context imposed by the author, and restated or reshuffled by second comers, even if the author was the first to discover the facts or to propose the ideas." Ginsburg 1868.

It may seem unfair that much of the fruit of the compiler's labor may be used by others without compensation. As Justice Brennan has correctly observed, however, this is not "some unforeseen byproduct of a statutory scheme." *Harper & Row,* 471 U.S., at 589, 105 S.Ct., at 2245 (dissenting opinion). It is, rather, "the essence of copyright," *ibid.*, and a constitutional requirement. The primary objective of copyright is not to reward the labor of authors, but "[t]o promote the Progress of Science and useful Arts." Art. I, § 8, cl. 8. Accord, *Twentieth Century Music Corp. v. Aiken,* 422 U.S. 151, 156, 95 S.Ct. 2040, 2044, 45 L.Ed.2d 84 (1975). To this end, copyright assures authors the right to their original expression, but encourages others to build freely upon the ideas and information conveyed by a work. *Harper & Row, supra,* 471 U.S., at 556–557, 105 S.Ct., at 2228–2229. This principle, known as the idea/expression or fact/expression dichotomy, applies to all works of authorship. As applied to a factual compilation, assuming the absence of original written expression, only the compiler's selection and arrangement may be protected; the raw facts may be copied at will. This result is neither unfair nor unfortunate. It is the means by which copyright advances the progress of science and art.

B

As we have explained, originality is a constitutionally mandated prerequisite for copyright protection. The Court's decisions announcing this rule predate the Copyright Act of 1909, but ambiguous language in the 1909 Act caused some lower courts temporarily to lose sight of this requirement. . . .

Making matters worse, these courts developed a new theory to justify the protection of factual compilations. Known alternatively as "sweat of the brow" or "industrious collection," the underlying notion was that copyright was a reward for the hard work that went into compiling facts. The classic formulation of the doctrine appeared in *Jeweler's Circular Publishing Co.,* 281 F., at 88:

"The right to copyright a book upon which one has expended labor in its preparation does not depend upon whether the materials which he has collected consist or not of matters which are publici juris, or whether such materials show literary skill *or originality,* either in thought or in language, or anything more than industrious collection. The man who goes through the streets of a town and puts down the names of each of the inhabitants, with their occupations and their street number, acquires material of which he is the author" (emphasis added).

The "sweat of the brow" doctrine had numerous flaws, the most glaring being that it extended copyright protection in a compilation beyond selection and arrangement—the compiler's original contributions—to the facts themselves. Under the doctrine, the only defense to infringement was independent creation. . . .

Decisions of this Court applying the 1909 Act make clear that the statute did not permit the "sweat of the brow" approach. The best example is *International News Service v. Associated Press,* 248 U.S. 215, 39 S.Ct. 68, 63 L.Ed. 211 (1918). In that decision, the Court stated unambiguously that the 1909 Act conferred copyright protection only on those elements of a work that were original to the author. International News Service had conceded taking news reported by Associated Press and publishing it in its own newspapers. Recognizing that § 5 of the Act specifically mentioned " 'periodicals, including newspapers,' " § 5(b), the Court acknowledged that news articles were copyrightable. *Id.,* at 234, 39 S.Ct., at 70. It flatly rejected, however, the notion that the copyright in an article extended to the factual information it contained: "[T]he news element—the information respecting current events contained in the literary production—is not the creation of the writer, but is a report of matters that ordinarily are *publici juris;* it is the history of the day." *Ibid.*

Without a doubt, the "sweat of the brow" doctrine flouted basic copyright principles. Throughout history, copyright law has "recognize[d] a greater need to disseminate factual works than works of fiction or fantasy." *Harper & Row,* 471 U.S., at 563, 105 S.Ct., at 2232. Accord, Gorman, Fact or Fancy: The Implications for Copyright, 29 J. Copyright Soc. 560, 563 (1982). But "sweat of the brow" courts took a contrary view; they handed out proprietary interests in facts and declared that authors are absolutely precluded from saving time and effort by relying upon the facts contained in prior works. In truth, "[i]t is just such wasted effort that the proscription against the copyright of ideas and facts . . . [is] designed to prevent." *Rosemont Enterprises, Inc. v. Random House, Inc.,* 366 F.2d 303, 310 (CA2 1966), cert. denied 385 U.S. 1009, 87 S.Ct. 714, 17 L.Ed.2d 546 (1967). "Protection for the fruits of such research . . . may in certain circumstances be available under a theory of unfair competition. But to accord copyright protection on this basis alone distorts basic copyright principles in that it creates a monopoly in public domain materials without the necessary justification of protecting and encouraging the creation of 'writings' by 'authors.' " Nimmer § 3.04, p. 3–23 (footnote omitted).

III

There is no doubt that Feist took from the white pages of Rural's directory a substantial amount of factual information. At a minimum, Feist copied the names, towns, and telephone numbers of 1,309 of Rural's subscribers. Not all copying, however, is copyright infringement. To establish infringement, two elements must be proven: (1) ownership of a valid copyright, and (2) copying of constituent elements of the work that are original. See *Harper & Row,* 471 U.S., at 548, 105 S.Ct., at 2224. The first element is not at issue here; Feist appears to concede that Rural's directory, considered as a whole, is subject to a valid copyright because it contains some foreword text, as well as original material in its yellow pages advertisements. See Brief for Petitioner 18; Pet. for Cert. 9.

The question is whether Rural has proved the second element. In other words, did Feist, by taking 1,309 names, towns, and telephone numbers from Rural's white pages, copy anything that was "original" to Rural? Certainly, the raw data does not satisfy the originality requirement. Rural may have been the first to discover and report the names, towns, and telephone numbers of its subscribers, but this data does not " 'ow[e] its origin' " to Rural. *Burrow-Giles,* 111 U.S., at 58, 4 S.Ct., at 281. Rather, these bits of information are uncopyrightable facts; they existed before Rural reported them and would have continued to exist if Rural had never published a telephone directory. The originality requirement "rule[s] out protecting . . . names, addresses, and telephone numbers of which the plaintiff by no stretch of the imagination could be called the author." Patterson & Joyce 776.

Rural essentially concedes the point by referring to the names, towns, and telephone numbers as "preexisting material." Brief for Respondent 17. Section 103(b) states explicitly that the copyright in a compilation does not extend to "the preexisting material employed in the work."

The question that remains is whether Rural selected, coordinated, or arranged these uncopyrightable facts in an original way. As mentioned, originality is not a stringent standard; it does not require that facts be presented in an innovative or surprising way. It is equally true, however, that the selection and arrangement of facts cannot be so mechanical or routine as to require no creativity whatsoever. The standard of originality is low, but it does exist. As this Court has explained, the Constitution mandates some minimal degree of creativity, see *The Trade-Mark Cases, 100 U.S., at 94;* and an author who claims infringement must prove "the existence of . . . intellectual production, of thought, and conception."

The selection, coordination, and arrangement of Rural's white pages do not satisfy the minimum constitutional standards for copyright protection. As mentioned at the outset, Rural's white pages are entirely typical. Persons desiring telephone service in Rural's service area fill out an application and Rural issues them a telephone number. In preparing its white pages, Rural simply takes the data provided by its subscribers and lists it alphabetically by surname. The end product is a garden-variety white pages directory, devoid of even the slightest trace of creativity.

Rural's selection of listings could not be more obvious: It publishes the most basic information—name, town, and telephone number—about each person who applies to it for telephone service. This is "selection" of a sort, but it lacks the modicum of creativity necessary to transform mere selection into copyrightable expression. Rural expended sufficient effort to make the white pages directory useful, but insufficient creativity to make it original.

. . . .

Nor can Rural claim originality in its coordination and arrangement of facts. The white pages do nothing more than list Rural's subscribers in alphabetical order. This arrangement may, technically speaking, owe its origin to Rural; no one disputes that Rural undertook the task of alphabetizing the names itself. But there is nothing remotely creative about arranging names alphabetically in a white pages directory. It is an age-old practice, firmly rooted in tradition and so commonplace that it has come to be expected as a matter of course. See Brief for Information Industry Association et al. as *Amici Curiae* 10 (alphabetical arrangement "is universally observed in directories published by local exchange telephone companies"). It is not only unoriginal, it is practically inevitable. This time-honored tradition does not possess the minimal creative spark required by the Copyright Act and the Constitution.

We conclude that the names, towns, and telephone numbers copied by Feist were not original to Rural and therefore were not protected by the copyright in Rural's combined white and yellow pages directory. As a constitutional matter, copyright protects only those constituent elements of a work that possess more than a *de minimis* quantum of creativity. Rural's white pages, limited to basic subscriber information and arranged alphabetically, fall short of the mark. As a statutory matter, 17 U.S.C. § 101 does not afford protection from copying to a collection of facts that are selected, coordinated, and arranged in a way that utterly lacks originality. Given that some works must fail, we cannot imagine a more likely candidate. Indeed, were we to hold that Rural's white pages pass muster, it is hard to believe that any collection of facts could fail.

Because Rural's white pages lack the requisite originality, Feist's use of the listings cannot constitute infringement. This decision should not be construed as demeaning Rural's efforts in compiling its directory, but rather as making clear that copyright rewards originality, not effort. As this Court noted more than a century ago, " 'great praise may be due to the plaintiffs for their industry and enterprise in publishing this paper, yet the law does not contemplate their being rewarded in this way.' " *Baker v. Selden,* 101 U.S., at 105.

The judgment of the Court of Appeals is *Reversed.*

DISCUSSION PROBLEMS

1. Drug Dosage

Thiopurine drugs are used to treat gastrointestinal disorders such as ulcerative colitis and Crohn's disease. These drugs affect people differently, making it difficult for doctors to determine the appropriate dosage. The scientific community knew how to measure the amount of a metabolite (6-thioguanine) in a patient's blood, and it knew that the measurement correlated with whether the dosage of the prescribed drug was too high, too low, or effective, but the field did not know the precise levels that indicated whether the dose was too high (likely toxic) or too low (likely ineffective) and should be adjusted.

Prometheus Laboratories, Inc. determined, with greater accuracy than anyone before, the actual levels of 6-thioguanine that signaled whether administered drugs were generally helpful or potentially harmful. It then developed a straightforward test to measure blood levels of 6-thioguanine. It obtained a patent not just for the test itself, but also for the general process of measuring 6-thioguanine blood levels and determining from the results whether the patient's drug dosage should be increased or decreased.

Prometheus produced and sold diagnostic tests based on this process. Mayo Collaborative Services ("Mayo") produced a different diagnostic test that also measured 6-thioguanine levels in the blood and Prometheus sued for infringement. Has Mayo illegally infringed on Prometheus's patent?

2. Maple Flooring

Mannington Mills and Home Legend both sell laminate flooring, which is composed of a balancing layer (made of water-resistant resin), a core board of wood fiber mixed with resin, and a transparent wear-resistant overlay. Often companies will add a decorative layer, called décor paper, beneath the transparent overlay to improve the aesthetics of the laminate. The décor paper is a two-dimensional artwork that could be any type of design but is usually made to look like typical flooring material.

Mannington Mills created a design known as "Glazed Maple," which is a photo depicting fifteen stained and "time-worn" maple planks. This design was created by staining, sanding, gouging, denting, darkening and adding other imperfections to new maple planks to create a worn look. Electronic scans of the planks were then compiled into a single image that was rearranged and retouched. Mannington Mills registered a copyright of the resulting two-dimensional image, which was then incorporated into its laminate flooring product.

Home Legend sold laminate flooring with a similar design, which it called "Distressed Maple Mendocino. Mannington alleged that Home Legend's design was "virtually identical in every respect," and it sued Home Legend for copyright infringement.

Distressed Maple Mendocino

Glazed Maple

Is Mannington entitled to copyright protection for its Glazed Maple design and therefore able to prevent Home Legend from copying it?

3. Asteroids

In 1979, Atari created an arcade video game called "Asteroids" that became the best-selling video game ever at that time. It was played on a coin-operated gaming cabinet with a display screen, a joystick, and buttons. Amusement World created a game called "Meteors." which was similar.

In both games, the player operates a spaceship that is able to rotate, use thrust, and shoot missiles. Both games feature three sizes of rocks that can be shot into smaller pieces and other spaceships that could shoot the player's craft. Meteors awarded the player points similarly to Asteroids and awarded the player additional spacecraft for scoring an identical number of points ($10,000). In Meteors, the display is in color (Asteroids is black and white), the background is different, the rocks are designed with three-dimensional shading (Asteroids' rocks are two-dimensional), the starting point of the player's spaceship is different, the spaceship rotates and fires faster, and the game moves at a faster rate of speed.

Did Amusement World infringe Atari's copyright?

CHAPTER 3

INCOMPATIBLE USES (NUISANCE)

■ ■ ■

INTRODUCTION

Although lay people usually think of property as *things*, lawyers and legal scholars think of property as a set of rights vis-à-vis other people in relation to things. For example, if you hold a painting in your hands, you have possession of it, but what makes it your property is that you have the right to hang it on your wall or sell it to a collector. In a crowded world, people who possess things will often wish to use them in a way that is inconsistent with other people's ability to use and enjoy their things. In the case of such incompatible uses, property law must necessarily favor one claimant over another. In this Chapter, we consider the problem of incompatible uses of land, although the problem is not limited to this particular context.

One way that law can address the problem of incompatible uses is by establishing a clear, broadly applicable "rule" in favor of one type of use over another, which can be known by parties before disputes arise. Rules can be established by judges through adjudication or by legislative bodies through statutes. As an example of the first, consider the judicial doctrine of ancient lights, which was imported from England and recognized in the early days of the United States but fell out of favor in the mid-19th century. Under this rule, landowners were prohibited from erecting buildings that would block a neighbor's windows from sunlight. In the modern era, nearly all urban areas have zoning ordinances that establish, via rule, what uses may and may not be made of land in different geographical areas. For example, in a specified residential area, landowners might be permitted to build structures up to three stories tall but no taller, and they might be prohibited from using their land for industrial purposes.

Alternatively, the law can address incompatible use conflicts by providing a "standard" that requires legal decisionmakers to examine and balance a broader range of factors that differ across the factual circumstances of particular disputes. One variety of standard describes a set of factors that a judge or jury is instructed to consider, leaving to the decisionmaker how to weigh the facts in a particular case. Another variety of standard establishes that a certain behavior is permissible if "reasonable" under the circumstances. Compared to rules, standards give courts the flexibility to take into account a greater number of relevant factors when applying the law, but this flexibility also makes it more difficult for parties to predict in advance exactly how the law applies to their particular circumstances, and it risks inconsistent application of the law across similar cases.

The law of nuisance (technically, the law of "private nuisance") provides an excellent example of a legal standard. A "nuisance" is a non-trespassory interference with another party's use and enjoyment of her land that is "intentional and unreasonable." Rest. (2d) Torts § 822. Prior to the rise of rule-based zoning ordinances in the early 20th century, the law of nuisance was the primary method that property law adjudicated land use disputes between landowners. Although zoning has supplanted nuisance as the primary law of land use, nuisance law continues to govern disputes over competing uses in a broad range of circumstances.

In *Campbell v. Seaman* and *Henricks v. Stalnaker*, courts struggle to articulate a principled basis for resolving incompatible use disputes under the standard of nuisance law. Is there a way for the courts in these cases to root their results in generally applicable rules that can be applied in future cases? If not, would it be appropriate for the "reasonableness" determination to be left to juries rather than judges? *Spurr Industries v. Del E. Webb Developers* is an important case, not for its holding (it has not been widely followed), but because of how the court grapples both with the question of whether the timing of a use—that is, who was "there first"—should matter and how the costs of incompatible uses should be allocated.

A final question to consider is whether the legal status of a particular land use actually matters to the question of which landowner will end up instituting his preferred use and which will yield to the preferences of the other. The "Coase Theorem," as described in Ronald Coase's famous article, "The Problem of Social Cost," suggests, counterintuitively, that under certain assumptions, the law of nuisance is irrelevant to how land is actually used.

To borrow one of Coase's examples, assume that a cattle ranch abuts a farm, and in the absence of a fence the cattle will damage the farmer's crops. One possible legal rule is that the rancher is liable to the farmer for the value of any crops destroyed by the cattle. An alternative rule is that the rancher is not liable. In the first case, if the value of the meat from the cattle exceeds the value of the crops, the rancher will herd the cattle and pay the farmer for the damage, keeping what remains from the sale of the meat as profit. If the crops are more valuable than the meat, the rancher will stop herding cattle, as the liability will not justify the investment. In the second case, if the value of the cattle exceeds that of the crops, the rancher will continue to herd, of course. But if the crops are more valuable, the farmer will pay the rancher not to keep cattle. Under either legal rule, cattle will roam if they are more valuable than the crops, and they will be prevented from roaming if the crops are more valuable. If both the cattle and the crops are worth more than the cost of a fence, a fence will be built under either rule, with the only difference being which landowner will pay for it. R.H. Coase, "The Problem of Social Cost," 3 *Journal of Law & Economics* 1 (1960). If Coase's analysis is correct, how does this effect whether you think the courts should rule for Campbell or Seaman, Henricks or Stalnaker, or Spurr Industries or Del Webb?

The Coase Theorem can be generalized beyond land use issues as follows: parties will resolve incompatible use disputes, concerning not only property but all legal rights, by allocating the rights to the party that places the highest value on them, as long as the costs of using private contracts to reallocate rights are low. This insight can be useful in analyzing the consequences of many different legal rules.

Restatement (Second) of Torts
§ 821D. Private Nuisance

A private nuisance is a non-trespassory invasion of another's interest in the private use and enjoyment of land.

Comment:

b. Interest in use and enjoyment of land. . . .The phrase "interest in the use and enjoyment of land" is used in this Restatement in a broad sense. It comprehends not only the interests that a person may have in the actual present use of land for residential, agricultural, commercial, industrial and other purposes, but also his interests in having the present use value of the land unimpaired by changes in its physical condition. Thus the destruction of trees on vacant land is as much an invasion of the owner's interest in its use and enjoyment as is the destruction of crops or flowers that he is growing on the land for his present use. "Interest in use and enjoyment" also comprehends the pleasure, comfort and enjoyment that a person normally derives from the occupancy of land. Freedom from discomfort and annoyance while using land is often as important to a person as freedom from physical interruption with his use or freedom from detrimental change in the physical condition of the land itself.

d. Trespass distinguished. A trespass is an invasion of the interest in the exclusive possession of land, as by entry upon it. A nuisance is an interference with the interest in the private use and enjoyment of the land, and does not require interference with the possession.

Restatement (Second) of Torts § 822. General Rule

One is subject to liability for a private nuisance if, but only if, his conduct is a legal cause of an invasion of another's interest in the private use and enjoyment of land, and the invasion is either

(a) Intentional and unreasonable, or

(b) Unintentional and otherwise actionable under the rules controlling liability for negligent or reckless conduct, or for abnormally dangerous conditions or activities.

Comment:

d. ... An injunction may be obtained in a proper case against a threatened private nuisance, but an action cannot be maintained at law [i.e., a claim for monetary damages—*ed.*] unless harm already has been suffered. Even when there is present harm, it is one thing to say that a defendant should pay damages for the harm his factory is causing but it is a different thing to say that he must close his factory if the harm cannot be stopped. For the purpose of determining liability for damages for private nuisance, an invasion may be regarded as unreasonable even though the utility of the conduct is great and the amount of harm Is relatively small. But for the purpose of determining whether the conduct producing the invasion should be enjoined, additional factors must be considered. It may be reasonable to continue an important activity if payment is made for the harm it is causing but unreasonable to initiate or continue it without paying.

Thus denial of relief by way of injunction is not always a precedent for denial of relief by way of damages.

g. ...Not every intentional and significant invasion of a person's interest in the use and enjoyment of land is actionable, even when he is the owner of the land in fee simple absolute and the conduct of the defendant is the sole and direct cause of the invasion. Life in organized society and especially in populous communities involves an unavoidable clash of individual interests. Practically all human activities unless carried on in a wilderness interfere to some extent with others or involve some risk of interference, and these interferences range from mere trifling annoyances to serious harms. It Is an obvious truth that each individual in a community must put up with a certain amount of annoyance, inconvenience and Interference and must take a certain amount of risk in order that all may get on together. The very existence of-organized society depends upon the principle of "give and take, live and let live," and therefore the law of torts does not attempt to impose liability or shift the loss in every case in which one person's conduct has some detrimental effect on another. Liability for damages is imposed in those cases in which the harm or risk to one is greater than he ought to be required to bear under the circumstances, at least without compensation. . . .This rule is expressed in terms of unreasonableness and, as stated in this Section, requires that an intentional invasion be unreasonable before one is liable for causing it.

CASES

CAMPBELL V. SEAMAN

Court of Appeals of New York
63 N.Y. 568 (1876)

EARL, J.

The plaintiffs owned about forty acres of land, situate in the village of Castleton, on the east bank of the Hudson river, and had owned it since about 1849. During the years 1857, 1858 and 1859 they built upon it an expensive dwelling-house, and during those years, and before and since, they improved the land by grading and terracing, building roads and walks through the same, and planting trees and shrubs, both ornamental and useful.

The defendant had for some years owned adjoining lands, which he had used as a brick-yard. The brick-yard is southerly of plaintiffs' dwelling-house about 1,320 feet, and southerly of their woods about 567 feet. In burning bricks defendant had made use of anthracite coal. During the burning of a kiln sulphuric acid gas is generated, which is destructive to some kinds of trees and vines. The evidence shows, and the referee found, that gas coming from defendant's kilns had, during the years 1869 and 1870, killed the foliage on plaintiff's white and yellow, pines and Norway spruce, and had, after repeated attacks, killed and destroyed from 100 to 150 valuable pine and spruce trees, and had injured their grape vines and plum trees, and he estimated plaintiff's damages from the gas during those years at $500.

This gas did not continually escape during the burning of a kiln, but only during the last two days, and was carried into and over plaintiff's land only when the wind was from the south.

It is a general rule that every person may exercise exclusive dominion over his own property, and subject it to such uses as will best subserve his private interests. Generally, no other person can say how he shall use or what he shall do with his property. But this general right of property has its exceptions and qualifications. *Sic utere tuo ut alienum non laedas* is an old maxim which has a broad application. It does not mean that one must never use his own so as to do any injury to his neighbor or his property. Such a rule could not be enforced in civilized society. Persons living in organized communities must suffer some damage, annoyance and inconvenience from each other. For these they are compensated by all the advantages of civilized society. If one lives in the city he must expect to suffer the dirt, smoke, noisome odors, noise and confusion incident to city life. . . .

But every person is bound to make a reasonable use of his property so as to occasion no unnecessary damage or annoyance to his neighbor. If he make an unreasonable, unwarrantable or unlawful use of it, so as to produce material annoyance, inconvenience, discomfort or hurt to his neighbor, he will be guilty of a nuisance to his neighbor. And the law will hold him responsible for the consequent damage. As to what is a reasonable use of one's own property cannot be defined by any certain general rules, but must depend upon the circumstances of each case. A use of property in one locality and under some circumstances may be lawful and reasonable, which, under other circumstances, would be unlawful, unreasonable and a nuisance. To constitute a nuisance, the use must be such as to produce a tangible and appreciable injury to neighboring property, or such as to render its enjoyment specially uncomfortable or inconvenient.

Within the rules thus referred to, that defendant's brick burning was a nuisance to plaintiffs cannot be doubted. . . .

Without further citation of authority I think it may safely be said that no definition of nuisance can be found in any text book or reported decision which will not embrace this case.

But the claim is made that although the brick burning in this case is a nuisance, a court of equity will not and ought not to restrain it, and the plaintiffs should be left to their remedy at law to recover damages, and this claim must now be examined.

. . . .

Here the remedy at law was not adequate. The mischief was substantial and, within the principle laid down in the cases above cited and others to which our attention has been called, irreparable.

The plaintiffs had built a costly mansion and had laid out their grounds and planted them with ornamental and useful trees and vines, for their comfort and enjoyment. How can one be compensated in damages for the destruction of his ornamental trees, and the flowers and vines which surrounded his home? How can a jury estimate their value in dollars and cents? The fact that trees and vines are for ornament or luxury entitles them no less to the protection of the law. Every one has the right to surround himself with articles of luxury, and he will be no less protected than one who provides himself only with articles of necessity. The law will protect a flower or a vine as well as an oak. (*Cook v. Forbes,* L. R., 5 Eq. Ca., 166; *Broadbent v. Imperial Gas Co.,* 7 DeG., McN. & G., 436.) These damages are irreparable too, because the trees and vines cannot be replaced, and the law will not compel a person to take money rather than the objects of beauty and utility which he places around his dwelling to gratify his taste or to promote his comfort and his health.

Here the injunction also prevents a multiplicity of suits. The injury is a recurring one, and every time the poisonous breath from defendant's brick-kiln sweeps over plaintiffs' land they have a cause of action. Unless the nuisance be restrained the litigation would be interminable. The policy of the law favors, and the peace and good order of society are best promoted by the termination of such litigations by a single suit.

The fact that this nuisance is not continual, and that the injury is only occasional, furnishes no answer to the claim for an injunction. The nuisance has occurred often enough within two years to do the plaintiffs large damage. Every time a kiln is burned some injury may be expected, unless the wind should blow the poisonous gas away from plaintiffs' lands. Nuisances causing damage less frequently have been restrained.

It matters not that the brick-yard was used before plaintiffs bought their lands or built their houses. One cannot erect a nuisance upon his land adjoining vacant lands owned by another and thus measurably control the uses to which his neighbor's land may in the future be subjected. He may make a reasonable and lawful use of his land and thus cause his neighbor some inconvenience, and probably some damage which the law would regard as *damnum absque injuria*. But he cannot place upon his land any thing which the law would pronounce a nuisance, and thus compel his neighbor to leave his land vacant, or to use it in such way only as the neighboring nuisance will allow.

. . . .

Where the damage to one complaining of a nuisance is small or trifling, and the damage to the one causing the nuisance will be large in case he be restrained, the courts will sometimes deny an injunction. But such is not this case; here the damage to the plaintiffs, as found by the referee, is large and substantial. It does not appear how much damage the defendant will suffer from the restraint of the injunction. He does not own the only piece of ground where bricks can be made. We know that material for brick making exists in all parts of our State, and particularly at various points along the Hudson river. An injunction need not therefore destroy defendant's business or interfere materially with the useful and necessary trade of brick making. It does not appear how valuable defendant's land is for a brick-yard, nor how expensive are his erections for brick making. I think we may infer that they are not expensive. For aught that appears, his land may be put to other use just as profitable to him. It does not appear that defendant's damage from an abatement of the nuisance will be as great as plaintiffs' damages from its continuance. Hence this is not a case within any authority to which our attention has been called, where an injunction should be denied on account of the serious consequences to the defendant.

We cannot apprehend that our decision in this case can improperly embarrass those engaged in the useful trade of brick making. Similar decisions in England, where population and human habitations are more dense, do not appear to have produced any embarrassment. In this country there can be no trouble to find places where brick can be made without damage to persons living in the vicinity. It certainly cannot be necessary to make them in the heart of a village or in the midst of a thickly settled community.

HENDRICKS V. STALNAKER

Supreme Court of Appeals of West Virginia
181 W.Va. 31 (1989)

NEELY, JUSTICE:

Walter S. Stalnaker, defendant below, appeals from a decision by the Circuit Court of Lewis County declaring a water well drilled on his property to be a private nuisance to Harry L. Hendricks and Mary Hendricks, plaintiffs below. The Hendrickses, owners of the property adjacent to that of Mr. Stalnaker, were refused a Health Department permit for a septic system located within 100 feet of Mr. Stalnaker's water well. The Circuit Court of Lewis County, based on a jury verdict, found the water well to be a private nuisance and ordered its abatement. On appeal, Mr. Stalnaker argues that because his water well was not an unreasonable use of his land, he is not liable for the effects on the Hendrickses' property. We agree and, therefore, reverse the decision of the circuit court.

Mr. Stalnaker owns approximately 10 acres of land situated on Glady Fork Road, Lewis County. In 1985, Mr. Stalnaker constructed his home on a 2.493 acre portion of the tract, and had two water wells dowsed. One well was located behind his house and the other, near the Hendrickses' property. The rear well was near land disturbed by a former strip mine and, therefore, the well produced poor quality water. Except for a small section of land near the Hendrickses' property—the location of the second "dowsed" well—most of Mr. Stalnaker's home tract had been disturbed by a strip mine. In August 1985, Mr. Stalnaker spent approximately $3,000 in an unsuccessful attempt to treat the water from the rear well.

In 1984, the Hendrickses purchased approximately 2.95 acres adjacent to Mr. Stalnaker's property for a home site or a trailer development. On 31 December 1985, Mr. Hendricks met with the Lewis County sanitarian to determine locations for a water well and a septic system. The Health Department requires a distance of 100 feet between water wells and septic systems before it will issue permits. Because the Hendrickses' land was too hilly or had been disturbed in order to build a pond, the only location for a septic system on the tract was near Mr. Stalnaker's property. . . .

I

In the past we have broadly described what constitutes a nuisance:

> A nuisance is anything which annoys or disturbs the free use of one's property, or which renders its ordinary use or physical occupation uncomfortable. . . . A nuisance is anything which interferes with the rights of a citizen, either in person, property, the enjoyment of his property, or his comfort. . . . A condition is a nuisance when it clearly appears that enjoyment of property is materially lessened, and physical comfort of persons in their homes is materially interfered with thereby. (Citations omitted).

This definition of nuisance includes acts or conditions that affect either the general public or a limited number of persons. . . .

. . .The definition of private nuisance includes conduct that is intentional and unreasonable, negligent or reckless, or that results in an abnormally dangerous conditions or activities in an inappropriate place. *See* W. Prosser, *Handbook of the Law of Torts* § 87 at 580, § 89 at 593 (4th ed. 1971); *Restatement (Second) of Torts* §§ 821D, 821F, 822 (1979); W. Keeton, *Prosser and Keeton on the Law of Torts* § 87 (5th ed. 1984). Recovery for a private nuisance is limited to plaintiffs who have suffered a significant harm to their property rights or privileges caused by the interference. *Restatement (Second) of Torts* §§ 821E, 821F (1979).

Early West Virginia cases indicate that the existence of a private nuisance was determined primarily by the harm caused. Gradually the focus included an examination of the reasonableness of the property's use.

The unreasonableness of an intentional interference must be determined by a balancing of the landowners' interests. An interference is unreasonable when the gravity of the harm outweighs the social value of the activity alleged to cause the harm. *See* W. Prosser, *supra* § 87, at 581, § 89 at 596; *Restatement (Second) of Torts* § 826 (1979); W. Keeton, *supra* § 88, at 629. *Restatement (Second) of Torts* §§ 827 and 828 (1979) list some of the factors to be considered in determining the gravity of the harm and the social value of the activity alleged to cause the harm. However, this balancing to determine unreasonableness is not absolute. Additional consideration might include the malicious or indecent conduct of the actor. *Restatement (Second) of Torts* § 829.

. . . .

The critical question is whether the interference, the installation of a water well, was unreasonable. Unreasonableness is determined by balancing the competing landholders' interests. We note that either use, well or septic system, burdens the adjacent property. Under Health Department regulations, a water well merely requires non-interference within 100 feet of its location. In the case of a septic system, however, the 100 foot safety zone, extending from the edge of the absorption field, may intrude on adjacent property. Thus, the septic system, with its potential for drainage, places a more invasive burden on adjacent property. Clearly both uses present similar considerations of gravity of harm and social value of the activity alleged to cause the harm. Both a water well and a septic system are necessary to use this land for housing; together they constitute the in and out of many water systems. Neither party has an inexpensive and practical alternative. The site of the water well means quality water for Mr. Stalnaker and the Hendrickses have only one location available for their septic system.

In the case before us, we are asked to determine if the water well is a private nuisance. But if the septic system were operational, the same question could be asked about the septic system. Because of the similar competing interests, the balancing of these landowners' interests is at least equal or, perhaps, slightly in favor of the water well. Thus, the Hendrickses have not shown that the balancing of interests favors their septic system. We find that the evidence presented clearly does not demonstrate that the water well is an unreasonable use of land and, therefore, does not constitute a private nuisance.

SPUR INDUSTRIES, INC. V. DEL E. WEBB DEVELOPMENT CO.

Supreme Court of Arizona
108 Ariz. 178 (1972)

CAMERON, VICE CHIEF JUSTICE.

From a judgment permanently enjoining the defendant, Spur Industries, Inc., from operating a cattle feedlot near the plaintiff Del E. Webb Development Company's Sun City, Spur appeals. Webb cross-appeals. Although numerous issues are raised, we feel that it is necessary to answer only two questions. They are:

1. Where the operation of a business, such as a cattle feedlot is lawful in the first instance, but becomes a nuisance by reason of a nearby residential area, may the feedlot operation be enjoined in an action brought by the developer of the residential area?

2. Assuming that the nuisance may be enjoined, may the developer of a completely new town or urban area in a previously agricultural area be required to indemnify the operator of the feedlot who must move or cease operation because of the presence of the residential area created by the developer?

. . . .

In 1956, Spur's predecessors in interest, H. Marion Welborn and the Northside Hay Mill and Trading Company, developed feed-lots, about 1/2 mile south of Olive Avenue, in an area between the confluence of the usually dry Agua Fria and New Rivers. The area is well suited for cattle feeding and in 1959, there were 25 cattle feeding pens or dairy operations within a 7 mile radius of the location developed by Spur's predecessors. In April and May of 1959, the Northside Hay Mill was feeding between 6,000 and 7,000 head of cattle and Welborn approximately 1,500 head on a combined area of 35 acres.

In May of 1959, Del Webb began to plan the development of an urban area to be known as Sun City. . . . By September 1959, Del Webb had started construction of a golf course south of Grand Avenue and Spur's predecessors had started to level ground for more feedlot area. In 1960, Spur purchased the property in question and began a rebuilding and expansion program extending both to the north and south of the original facilities. By 1962, Spur's expansion program was completed and had expanded from approximately 35 acres to 114 acres. . . .

Accompanied by an extensive advertising campaign, homes were first offered by Del Webb in January 1960 and the first unit to be completed was south of Grand Avenue and approximately 2 1/2 miles north of Spur. By 2 May 1960, there were 450 to 500 houses completed or under construction. At this time, Del Webb did not consider odors from the Spur feed pens a problem and Del Webb continued to develop in a southerly direction, until sales resistance became so great that the parcels were difficult if not impossible to sell.

. . . .

By December 1967, Del Webb's property had extended south to Olive Avenue and Spur was within 500 feet of Olive Avenue to the north. Del Webb filed its original complaint alleging that in excess of 1,300 lots in the southwest portion were unfit for development for sale as residential lots because of the operation of the Spur feedlot.

Del Webb's suit complained that the Spur feeding operation was a public nuisance because of the flies and the odor which were drifting or being blown by the prevailing south to north wind over the southern portion of Sun City. At the time of the suit, Spur was feeding between 20,000 and 30,000 head of cattle, and the facts amply support the finding of the trial court that the feed pens had become a nuisance to the people who resided in the southern part of Del Webb's development. The testimony indicated that cattle in a commercial feedlot will produce 35 to 40 pounds of wet manure per day, per head, or over a million pounds of wet manure per day for 30,000 head of cattle, and that despite the admittedly good feedlot management and good housekeeping practices by Spur, the resulting odor and flies produced an annoying if not unhealthy situation as far as the senior citizens of southern Sun City were concerned. There is no doubt that some of the citizens of Sun City were unable to enjoy the outdoor living which Del Webb had advertised and that Del Webb was faced with sales resistance from prospective purchasers as well as strong and persistent complaints from the people who had purchased homes in that area.

. . . .

It is clear that as to the citizens of Sun City, the operation of Spur's feedlot was both a public and a private nuisance. They could have successfully maintained an action to abate the nuisance. Del Webb, having shown a special injury in the loss of sales, had a standing to bring suit to enjoin the nuisance. Engle v. Clark, 53 Ariz. 472, 90 P.2d 994 (1939); City of Phoenix v. Johnson, supra. The judgment of the trial court permanently enjoining the operation of the feedlot is affirmed.

. . .

In the so-called 'coming to the nuisance' cases, the courts have held that the residential landowner may not have relief if he knowingly came into a neighborhood reserved for industrial or agricultural endeavors and has been damaged thereby:

'Plaintiffs chose to live in an area uncontrolled by zoning laws or restrictive covenants and remote from urban development. In such an area plaintiffs cannot complain that legitimate agricultural pursuits are being carried on in the vicinity, nor can plaintiffs, having chosen to build in an agricultural area, complain that the agricultural pursuits carried on in the area depreciate the value of their homes. The area being Primarily agricultural, and opinion reflecting the value of such property must take this factor into account. The standards affecting the value of residence property in an urban setting, subject to zoning controls and controlled planning techniques, cannot be the standards by which agricultural properties are judged.

'People employed in a city who build their homes in suburban areas of the county beyond the limits of a city and zoning regulations do so for a reason. Some do so to avoid the high taxation rate imposed by cities, or to avoid special assessments for street, sewer and water projects. They usually build on improved or hard surface highways, which have been built either at state or county expense and thereby avoid special assessments for these improvements. It may be that they desire to get away from the congestion of traffic, smoke, noise, foul air and the many other annoyances of city life. But with all these advantages in going beyond the area which is zoned and restricted to protect them in their homes, they must be prepared to take the disadvantages.' Dill v. Excel Packing Company, 183 Kan. 513, 525, 526, 331 P.2d 539, 548, 549 (1958).

. . . .

Were Webb the only party injured, we would feel justified in holding that the doctrine of 'coming to the nuisance' would have been a bar to the relief asked by Webb, and, on the other hand, had Spur located the feedlot near the outskirts of a city and had the city grown toward the feedlot, Spur would have to suffer the cost of abating the nuisance as to those people locating within the growth pattern of the expanding city:

'The case affords, perhaps, an example where a business established at a place remote from population is gradually surrounded and becomes part of a populous center, so that a business which formerly was not an interference with the rights of others has become so by the encroachment of the population' City of Ft. Smith v. Western Hide & Fur Co., 153 Ark. 99, 103, 239 S.W. 724, 726 (1922).

. . . .

There was no indication in the instant case at the time Spur and its predecessors located in western Maricopa County that a new city would spring up, full-blown, alongside the feeding operation and that the developer of that city would ask the court to order Spur to move because of the new city. Spur is required to move not because of any wrongdoing on the part of Spur, but because of a proper and legitimate regard of the courts for the rights and interests of the public.

Del Webb, on the other hand, is entitled to the relief prayed for (a permanent injunction), not because Webb is blameless, but because of the damage to the people who have been encouraged to purchase homes in Sun City. It does not equitable or legally follow, however, that Webb, being entitled to the injunction, is then free of any liability to Spur if Webb has in fact been the cause of the damage Spur has sustained. It does not seem harsh to require a developer, who has taken advantage of the lesser land values in a rural area as well as the availability of large tracts of land on which to build and develop a new town or city in the area, to indemnify those who are forced to leave as a result.

Having brought people to the nuisance to the foreseeable detriment of Spur, Webb must indemnify Spur for a reasonable amount of the cost of moving or shutting down. It should be noted that this relief to Spur is limited to a case wherein a developer has, with foreseeability, brought into a previously agricultural or industrial area the population which makes necessary the granting of an injunction against a lawful business and for which the business has no adequate relief.

It is therefore the decision of this court that the matter be remanded to the trial court for a hearing upon the damages sustained by the defendant Spur as a reasonable and direct result of the granting of the permanent injunction.

DISCUSSION PROBLEMS

1. Electronic Interference

In 1980, Central Travel Services leased a new Honeywell computer terminal, specifically designed for the needs of retail travel agencies, from ITT Electronic Travel Services. Two storefronts away, the Page County Appliance Center noticed that its televisions, displayed for customers, suddenly could not get reception "fit to watch" on two of the three local television stations. The interference was traced to radiation emanating from the Travel Service's computers.

Honeywell engineers were able to make adjustments to the computer that improved the Appliance Center's television reception by 70%, but they could not completely alleviate the interference. According to Honeywell, the interference was an unavoidable consequence of the computer's design and, although it would have been possible to design this type of product in a way that would avoid such interference, it would have been prohibitively expensive to do so. The Appliance Center sued Central Travel, ITT, and Honeywell for nuisance. Should it prevail?

2. Hog Waste

In the late 1960s, Clark Helmkamp purchased a house on the east side of U.S. Highway 71 in Carroll, Iowa. In 1970, the Clark Ready Mix Company purchase an adjacent plot of land on the west side of the highway and "began operating a cement ready-mix plant with a silo, bins for storing sand, gravel, and crushed limestone, a diesel-powered front-end loader to transport this aggregate, and driveways for trucks," roughly 375 feet from the plant. A significant amount of concrete powder escaped from the plant, and when the wind blew toward the east, dust coated Helmkamp's property and penetrated his home. Cement loaders and jackhammers caused significant noise and expelled diesel smoke while in operation. Helmkamp sued Clark and sought an injunction prohibiting the operation of the plant.

In 1977, Dennis and Ruth Weinhold purchased a four-acre farm in Buena Vista County, Iowa. In 1990, their neighbors, Norman and Pam Wolff, turned a portion of their 80-acre farm into a commercial hog feeding facility that included a 500,000-gallon, uncovered waste collection basin that was 130 feet long, 110-feet wide, and 14.5 feet deep. Waste ran from under the slatted floor of the hog pens into the basin, which was emptied twice a year.

In 1991, the Iowa Legislature passed a statute that provided that, after that date, "a farm or farm operation located in an agricultural area shall not be found to be nuisance."

The Weinholds kept a diary for two years, which chronicled the "terrible stink," "burning eyes and phlegmonous irritation," and difficulty sleeping that was sometimes so bad that it drove them away from their home, depending on the season and which way the wind blew. The Weinholds and other witnesses distinguished the odor emanating from the Wolffs' collection basin from the "normal hog smell" that came from other hog confinement operations that did not feature outdoor waste storage. The Weinholds sued the Wolffs for nuisance and sought money damages for the harm suffered and an injunction ordering the Wolffs to abate the nuisance.

Should the plaintiffs in either or both cases prevail? If so, should they be entitled to money damages, an injunction prohibiting the defendants from continuing to operate their businesses, or both? Are there any material differences between the two cases that would justify inconsistent outcomes?

3. The Dog Trainer

Donald Wiggins moved to his rural property on a dead-end road in order to train bird dogs. His dog-training business earned close to $140,000, and Wiggins had won numerous awards. Wiggins kept 69 dogs or more at a time.

Larry Dobbs, a neighbor, complained about constant barking on Wiggins's property, which he said forced him to keep his windows closed and made it impossible for him to enjoy his yard. Wiggins bought shock collars for the dogs, relocated "troublemaker" dogs, stored hay so as to dampen noise, installed a sprinkler system to douse the dogs once they barked, and even tried playing music to calm the dogs. These measures helped to abate the noise but did not entirely eliminate the barking.

Dobbs sued. The trial court, sitting as trier of fact, found for Dobbs and ordered Wiggins to cap the number of dogs in his kennel to six. Wiggins appealed both the trial court's finding that his dogs created a nuisance and the scope of the injunction. Who should prevail?

CHAPTER 4

THE RIGHT TO EXCLUDE (TRESPASS)

■ ■ ■

INTRODUCTION

A popular metaphor is that "property" is a "bundle of sticks"—a collection of loosely related rights that is not identical in every case. The law of property might provide a person who possesses land or chattels some or even many of the possible "sticks" (or rights) available in the bundle but also restrict or take away others. For example, as the prior chapter demonstrated, if you own a plot of land in a densely populated area, you may certainly use it to plant a garden and probably to build a house, but you almost certainly may not use it to construct a dynamite factory. The fact that your bundle might not include every conceivable stick does not mean that you do not in fact have "property." No one would claim, for example, that the fact that you may not use your land to build a dynamite factory, or that you may not use your car to run over a pedestrian on the sidewalk, means that your land or your car are not your property.

Are there any rights that are so fundamental to the notion of property that they must be part of any bundle of sticks? Some theorists claim that the right to exclude others from the use or enjoyment of a particular thing is the right that comes the closest to being so essential to the notion of property that one cannot exist without the other. After all, in a crowded world, there must be some limits to the uses to which you can put your land or your car, but, at least in theory, there need not be any limits on the rights of a possessor to exclude others.

Should owners of property have an absolute right to exclude? This Chapter considers whether and when the fundamental right to exclude should yield to the demands of potential intruders. The law of trespass generally establishes the right of a landowner to exclude others, but the exception for intruders possessing a "legal privilege" signals that the right is not entirely absolute. Rest. (3d) Torts § 50. *Ploof v. Putnam* considers when, if ever, the needs of a non-owner to invade physical property are so substantial that the law should prioritize them over the desires of the landowner. In *Uston v. Resorts Int'l Hotel, Inc.* and *Brooks v. Chicago Downs, Assoc.,* courts reach different conclusions as to whether a landowner may exclude certain members of the public when others are granted a right of access. Consider which court has the stronger argument, or if the cases can be distinguished on their facts.

As you read the materials, consider also what remedies should be available to a landowner who is the victim of an impermissible intrusion. Does the choice of remedies available affect the value of the right to exclude?

Restatement (Third) of Torts
§ 50. Trespasser Defined

A trespasser is a person who enters or remains on land in the possession of another without the possessor's consent or other legal privilege.

Comment:

c. *Other legal privilege.* A person may have legal privilege to enter on the land of another despite lack of consent by the land possessor. The circumstances providing for such privilege include the right to enter to avoid an imminent public disaster; to prevent serious harm to oneself, a land possessor, or a third person; to reclaim goods; to abate a public nuisance; and to permit certain law-enforcement activities. In addition, if a landowner withdraws consent to enter from others, including lessees, suddenly and without advance notice, those whose right to enter has been rescinded have legal privilege to remain for a reasonable time and to remove personal property before leaving the land.

Restatement (Second) of Torts
§ 197. Private Necessity

1) One is privileged to enter or remain on land in the possession of another if it is or reasonably appears to be necessary to prevent serious harm to

a) the actor, or his land or chattels, or

b) the other or a third person, or the land or chattels of either, unless the actor knows or has reason to know that the one for whose benefit he enters is unwilling that he shall take such action.

Restatement (Second) of Torts § 77. Defense of Possession by Force Not Threatening Death or Serious Bodily Harm

An actor is privileged to use reasonable force, not intended or likely to cause death or serious bodily harm, to prevent or terminate another's intrusion upon the actor's land or chattels, if:

(a) the intrusion is not privileged or the other intentionally or negligently causes the actor to believe that it is not privileged, and

(b) the actor reasonably believes that the intrusion can be prevented or terminated only by the force used, and

(c) the actor has first requested the other to desist and the other has disregarded the request, or the actor reasonably believes that a request will be useless or that substantial harm will be done before it can be made.

Restatement (Second) of Torts § 163 Intended Intrusions Causing No Harm

One who intentionally enters land in the possession of another is subject to liability to the possessor for a trespass, although his presence on the land causes no harm to the land, its possessor, or to any thing or person in whose security the possessor has a legally protected interest.

CASES

PLOOF V. PUTNAM

Supreme Court of Vermont
81 Vt. 471 (1908)

MUNSON, J.

It is alleged as the ground on recovery that on the 13th day of November 1904, the defendant was the owner of a certain island in Lake Champlain, and of a certain dock attached thereto, which island and dock were then in charge of the defendant's servant; that the plaintiff was then possessed of and sailing upon said lake a certain loaded sloop, on which were the plaintiff and his wife and two minor children; that there then arose a sudden and violent tempest, whereby the sloop and the property and persons therein were placed in great danger of destruction; that, to save these from destruction or injury, the plaintiff was compelled to, and did, moor the sloop to defendant's dock; that the defendant, by his servant, unmoored the sloop, whereupon it was driven upon the shore by the tempest, without the plaintiff's fault; and that the sloop and its contents were thereby destroyed, and the plaintiff and his wife and children cast into the lake and upon the shore, receiving injuries. This claim is set forth in two counts-one in trespass, charging that the defendant by his servant with force and arms willfully and designedly unmoored the sloop; the other in case, alleging that it was the duty of the defendant by his servant to permit the plaintiff to moor his sloop to the dock, and to permit it to remain so moored during the continuance of the tempest, but that the defendant by his servant, in disregard of this duty, negligently, carelessly, and wrongfully unmoored the sloop. Both counts are demurred to generally.

There are many cases in the books which hold that necessity, and an inability to control movements inaugurated in the proper exercise of a strict right, will justify entries upon land and interferences with personal property that would otherwise have been trespasses. A reference to a few of these will be sufficient to illustrate the doctrine. In Miller v. Fandrye, Poph. 161, trespass was brought for chasing sheep, and the defendant pleaded that the sheep were trespassing upon his land, and that he with a little dog chased them out, and that, as soon as the sheep were off his land, he called in the dog. It was argued that, although the defendant might lawfully drive the sheep from his own ground with a dog, he had no right to pursue them into the next ground; but the court considered that the defendant might drive the sheep from his land with a dog, and that the nature of a dog is such that he cannot be withdrawn in an instant, and that, as the defendant had done his best to recall the dog, trespass would not lie. In trespass of cattle taken in A., defendant pleaded that he was seised of C. and found the cattle there damage feasant, and chased them towards the pound, and they escaped from him and went into A., and he presently retook them; and this was held a good plea. 21 Edw. IV, 64; Vin. Ab. Trespass, H. a, 4, pl. 19. If one have a way over the land of another for his beasts to pass, and the beasts, being properly driven, feed the grass by morsels in passing, or run out of the way and are promptly pursued and brought back, trespass will not lie. See Vin. Ab. Trespass, K. a, pl. 1. A traveler on a highway who finds it obstructed from a sudden and temporary cause may pass upon the adjoining land without becoming a trespasser because of the necessity. Henn's Case, W. Jones, 296; Campbell v. Race, 7 Cush. (Mass.) 408, 54 Am. Dec. 728; Hyde v. Jamaica, 27 Vt. 443 (459); Morey v. Fitzgerald, 56 Vt. 487, 48 Am. Rep. 811. An entry upon land to save goods which are in danger of being lost or destroyed by water or fire is not a trespass. 21 Hen. VII, 27; Vin. Ab. Trespass, H. a, 4, pl. 24, K. a, pl. 3. In Proctor v. Adams, 113 Mass. 376, 18 Am. Rep. 500, the defendant went upon the plaintiff's beach for the purpose of saving and restoring to the lawful owner a boat which had been driven ashore, and was in danger of being carried off by the sea; and it was held no trespass. See, also, Dunwich v. Sterry, 1 B. & Ad. 831.

This doctrine of necessity applies with special force to the preservation of human life. One assaulted and in peril of his life may run through the close of another to escape from his assailant. 37 Hen. VII, pl. 26. One may sacrifice the personal property of another to save his life or the lives of his fellows. In Mouse's Case, 12 Co. 63, the defendant was sued for taking and carrying away the plaintiff's casket and its contents. It appeared that the ferryman of Gravesend took 47 passengers into his barge to pass to London, among whom were the plaintiff and defendant; and the barge being upon the water a great tempest happened, and a strong wind, so that the barge and all the passengers were in danger of being lost if certain ponderous things were not cast out, and the defendant thereupon cast out the plaintiff's casket. It was resolved that in case of necessity, to save the lives of the passengers, it was lawful for the defendant, being a passenger, to cast the plaintiff's casket out of the barge; that, if the ferryman surcharge the barge, the owner shall have his remedy upon the surcharge against the ferryman, but that if there be no surcharge, and the danger accrue only by the act of God, as by tempest, without fault of the ferryman, every one ought to bear his loss to safeguard the life of a man.

It is clear that an entry upon the land of another may be justified by necessity, and that the declaration before us discloses a necessity for mooring the sloop. But the defendant questions the sufficiency of the counts because they do not negative the existence of natural objects to which the plaintiff could have moored with equal safety. The allegations are, in substance, that the stress of a sudden and violent tempest compelled the plaintiff to moor to defendant's dock to save his sloop and the people in it. The averment of necessity is complete, for it covers not only the necessity of mooring to the dock; and the details of the situation which created this necessity, whatever the legal requirements regarding them, are matters of proof, and need not be alleged. It is certain that the rule suggested cannot be held applicable irrespective of circumstance, and the question must be left for adjudication upon proceedings had with reference to the evidence or the charge.

The defendant insists that the counts are defective, in that they fail to show that the servant in casting off the rope was acting within the scope of his employment. It is said that the allegation that the island and dock were in charge of the servant does not imply authority to do an unlawful act, and that the allegations as a whole fairly indicate that the servant unmoored the sloop for a wrongful purpose of his own, and not by virtue of any general authority or special instruction received from the defendant. But we think the counts are sufficient in this respect. The allegation is that the defendant did this by his servant. The words "willfully, and designedly" in one count, and "negligently, carelessly, and wrongfully" in the other, are not applied to the servant, but to the defendant acting through the servant. The necessary implication is that the servant was acting within the scope of his employment.

Judgment affirmed and cause remanded.

USTON V. RESORTS INTERNATIONAL HOTEL, INC.

Supreme Court of New Jersey
89 N.J. 163 (1982)

PASHMAN, J.

Since January 30, 1979, appellant Resorts International Hotel, Inc. (Resorts) has excluded respondent, Kenneth Uston, from the blackjack tables in its casino because Uston's strategy increases his chances of winning money. Uston concedes that his strategy of card counting can tilt the odds in his favor under the current blackjack rules promulgated by the Casino Control Commission (Commission). However, Uston contends that Resorts has no common law or statutory right to exclude him because of his strategy for playing blackjack.

. . . .

I

Kenneth Uston is a renowned teacher and practitioner of a complex strategy for playing blackjack known as card counting. Card counters keep track of the playing cards as they are dealt and adjust their betting patterns when the odds are in their favor. When used over a period of time, this method allegedly ensures a profitable encounter with the casino.

Uston first played blackjack at Resorts' casino in November 1978. Resorts took no steps to bar Uston at that time, apparently because the Commission's blackjack rules then in operation minimized the advantages of card counting.

On January 5, 1979, however, a new Commission rule took effect that dramatically improved the card counter's odds. *N.J.A.C.* 19:47–2.5. The new rule, which remains in effect, restricted the reshuffling of the deck in ways that benefitted card counters. Resorts concedes that the Commission could promulgate blackjack rules that virtually eliminate the advantage of card counting. However, such rules would slow the game, diminishing the casino's "take" and consequently its profits from blackjack gaming.

. . . .

The Commission upheld Resorts' decision to exclude Uston. Relying on *Garifine v. Monmouth Park Jockey Club*, 29 *N.J.* 47, 148 *A.*2d 1 (1959), the Commission held that Resorts enjoys a common law right to exclude anyone it chooses, as long as the exclusion does not violate state and federal civil rights laws. The Appellate Division reversed, 179 *N.J.Super.* 223, 431 *A.*2d 173 (1981). . . . We hold that the common law right to exclude is substantially limited by a competing common law right of reasonable access to public places.

. . . .

III

Resorts claimed that it could exclude Uston because it had a common law right to exclude anyone at all for any reason. While we hold that the Casino Control Act precludes Resorts from excluding Uston for the reasons stated, it is important for us to address the asserted common law right for two reasons. First, Resorts' contentions and the Commission's position concerning the common law right are incorrect. Second, the act has not completely divested Resorts of its common law right to exclude.

The right of an amusement place owner to exclude unwanted patrons and the patron's competing right of reasonable access both have deep roots in the common law. *See* Arterburn, "The Origin and First Test of Public Callings," 75 *U.Pa.L.Rev.* 411 (1927); Wyman, "The Law of Public Callings as a Solution of the Trust Problem," 17 *Harv.L.Rev.* 156 (1904). In this century, however, courts have disregarded the right of reasonable access in the common law of some jurisdictions at the time the Civil War Amendments and Civil Rights Act of 1866 were passed.

As Justice Goldberg noted in his concurrence in *Bell v. Maryland*, 378 *U.S.* 226, 84 *S.Ct.* 1814, 12 *L.Ed.*2d 822 (1964):

> Underlying the congressional discussions and at the heart of the Fourteenth Amendment's guarantee of equal protection, was the assumption that the State by statute or by "the good old common law" was obligated to guarantee all citizens access to places of public accommodation. [378 *U.S.* at 296, 84 *S.Ct.* at 1852, 12 *L.Ed.*2d at 839, Goldberg, J., joined by Warren, C. J. and Douglas, J., concurring]

[This did not eliminate the ability of "amusement place" owners to exclude patrons, but the owners had to do so in a non-discriminatory manner, consistent with state and federal civil rights laws.]

At one time, an absolute right of exclusion prevailed in this state, though more for reasons of deference to the noted English precedent of *Wood v. Leadbitter*, 13 *M&W* 838, 153 *Eng.Rep.* 351, (Ex.1845), than for reasons of policy. In *Shubert v. Nixon Amusement Co.*, 83 *N.J.L.* 101, 83 *A.* 369 (Sup.Ct.1912), the former Supreme Court dismissed a suit for damages resulting from plaintiff's ejection from defendants' theater. Noting that plaintiff made no allegation of exclusion on the basis of race, color or previous condition of servitude, the Court concluded:

> In view of the substantially uniform approval of, and reliance on, the decision in *Wood v. Leadbitter* in our state adjudications, it must fairly be considered to be adopted as part of our jurisprudence, and whatever views may be entertained as to the natural justice or injustice of ejecting a theater patron without reason after he has paid for his ticket and taken his seat, we feel

constrained to follow that decision as the settled law. [83 *N.J.L.* at 106, 83 *A.* 369]

It hardly bears mention that our common law has evolved in the intervening 70 years. In fact, *Leadbitter* itself was disapproved three years after the *Shubert* decision by *Hurst v. Picture Theatres Limited*, (1915) 1 *K.B.* 1 (1914). Of far greater importance, the decisions of this Court have recognized that "the more private property is devoted to public use, the more it must accommodate the rights which inhere in individual members of the general public who use that property." *State v. Schmid*, 84 *N.J.* 535, 562, 423 *A.*2d 615 (1980).

State v. Schmid involved the constitutional right to distribute literature on a private university campus. The Court's approach in that case balanced individual rights against property rights. It is therefore analogous to a description of the common law right of exclusion. Balancing the university's interest in controlling its property against plaintiff's interest in access to that property to express his views, the Court clearly refused to protect unreasonable exclusions. Justice Handler noted that

> Regulations . . . devoid of reasonable standards designed to protect both the legitimate interests of the University as an institution of higher education and the individual exercise of expressional freedom cannot constitutionally be invoked to prohibit the otherwise noninjurious and reasonable exercise of [First Amendment] freedoms." [*Id.* at 567, 423 *A.*2d 615]

In *State v. Shack*, 58 *N.J.* 297, 277 *A.*2d 369 (1971), the Court held that although an employer of migrant farm workers "may reasonably require" those visiting his employees to identify themselves, "the employer may not deny the worker his privacy or interfere with his opportunity to live with dignity and to enjoy associations customary among our citizens." *Id.* at 308, 277 *A.*2d 369. The Court reversed the trespass convictions of an attorney and a social services worker who had entered the property to assist farmworkers there.

Schmid recognizes implicitly that when property owners open their premises to the general public in the pursuit of their own property interests, they have no right to exclude people unreasonably. On the contrary, they have a duty not to act in an arbitrary or discriminatory manner toward persons who come on their premises. That duty applies not only to common carriers, *Messenger v. Pennsylvania Railroad Co.*, 37 *N.J.L.* 531 (E. & A. 1874), innkeepers, *see Garifine, supra*, owners of gasoline service stations, *Streeter v. Brogan*, 113 *N.J.Super.* 486, 274 *A.*2d 312 (Ch.Div.1971), or to private hospitals, *Doe v. Bridgeton Hospital Ass'n, Inc.*, 71 *N.J.* 478, 366 *A.*2d 641 (1976), *cert.* den., 433 *U.S.* 914, 97 *S.Ct.* 2987, 53 *L.Ed.*2d 1100 (1977), but to all property owners who open their premises to the public. Property owners have no legitimate interest in unreasonably excluding particular members of the public when they open their premises for public use.

No party in this appeal questions the right of property owners to exclude from their premises those whose actions "disrupt the regular and essential operations of the premises." In some circumstances, proprietors have a duty to remove disorderly or otherwise dangerous persons from the premises. These common law principles enable the casino to bar from its entire facility, for instance, the disorderly, the intoxicated, and the repetitive petty offender.

Whether a decision to exclude is reasonable must be determined from the facts of each case. Respondent Uston does not threaten the security of any casino occupant. Nor has he disrupted the functioning of any casino operations. Absent a valid contrary rule by the Commission, Uston possesses the usual right of reasonable access to Resorts International's blackjack tables.

. . . .

V

In sum, absent a valid Commission regulation excluding card counters, respondent Uston will be free to employ his card-counting strategy at Resorts' blackjack tables. There is currently no Commission rule banning Uston, and Resorts has no authority to exclude him for card counting.

BROOKS V. CHICAGO DOWNS ASSOCIATION, INC.

United States Court of Appeals, Seventh Circuit
791 F.2d 512 (1986)

FLAUM, CIRCUIT JUDGE.

This is a case of first impression on whether under Illinois law the operator of a horse race track has the absolute right to exclude a patron from the track premises for any reason, or no reason, except race, color, creed, national origin, or sex. We find that Illinois follows the common law rule and would allow the exclusion. The court below is thus affirmed.

I

Plaintiffs are citizens of Pennsylvania who have formed a Pennsylvania partnership whose sole purpose is to pool the assets of the partners in order to place bets at horse racing tracks throughout the country. The plaintiffs are self-proclaimed expert handicappers, even though on the approximately 140 days they have bet at various race tracks they have ended up with net losses on 110 of those days. This case is about a bet they were not allowed to make.

The defendant is a private Illinois corporation licensed by the State of Illinois to conduct harness racing at Sportsman's Park race track in Cicero,

Illinois. At various times during the racing season, Sportsman's Park conducts a parimutual pool known as "Super Bet." In order to win the Super Bet pool, one must select the first two finishers of the fifth and sixth races and the first three finishers of the seventh race. The Super Bet pool is able to increase quickly and substantially because if the pool is not won on any given day, the total amount wagered is rolled over and added to the Super Bet purse for the next racing date. For example, in April of 1985 the plaintiffs, using their method for handicapping horses, placed bets on the Super Bet totalling $60,000. They picked the right horses and took home approximately $600,000.

In late July, 1985 the president of Chicago Downs ordered two of the plaintiffs (Jeffrey Yass and Kenneth Brodie) barred from Sportsman's Park just as they were seeking to place a $250,000 wager in the Super Bet. After the plaintiffs had been barred from Sportsman's Park, the Park's counsel informed them that they would be denied entry to all future racing dates at the Park. The plaintiffs then filed suit seeking injunctive relief that would prohibit the defendant from barring them from entering the race track premises. Sportsman's Park filed a motion to dismiss the complaint on the ground that under Illinois law the operator of a proprietary race track has the absolute right to exclude a patron from the track premises for any reason except race, creed, color, national origin, or sex. The trial court agreed with the defendants and granted their motion to dismiss, from which the plaintiffs now appeal. We affirm.

II

. . .

The parties do not contest the Illinois Supreme Court's holding that a race track operator has the right to exclude patrons *for good cause. Phillips v. Graham*, 86 Ill.2d 274, 56 Ill.Dec. 355, 427 N.E.2d 550 (1981). But in this case, the race track argues that it should be able to exclude a patron absent any cause at all, as long as it does not do so on the basis of race, color, creed, national origin, or sex. Under the defendant's theory, because the race track is a privately owned place of amusement it may exclude someone simply for wearing a green hat or a paisley tie. It need give no reason for excluding the patron, under its version of the common law, because it is not a state-granted monopoly, but a state-regulated licensee operating on private property.

. . .

Of the cases cited by the Illinois courts as demonstrating the common law rule, *Madden v. Queens County Jockey Club,* 296 N.Y. 249, 72 N.E.2d 697 (Ct.App.), is the most explicit and most cited. The plaintiff, "Coley" Madden, who claimed to be a professional "patron of the races," was barred from the defendant's Aqueduct Race Track under the mistaken belief that he was "Owney" Madden, reputed to be the fabled Frank Costello's bookmaker. Coley Madden brought suit for declaratory judgment and contended that as a citizen and taxpayer he had the right to enter the track and patronize the races. The defendant moved to dismiss on the ground that it had an unlimited right of exclusion. The trial court granted plaintiff's motion and entered an order enjoining the defendant from barring Coley Madden from its race track. The appellate division reversed, and the New York Court of Appeals affirmed the appellate division's reversal of the trial court. The Court of Appeals framed the question: "Whether the operator of a race track can, without reason or sufficient excuse, exclude a person from attending its races." Its answer: "In our opinion he can; he has the power to admit as spectators only those whom he may select, and to exclude others solely of his own [volition,] as long as the exclusion is not founded on race, creed, color or national origin."

The court went on to explain the common law:

> At common law a person engaged in a public calling, such as innkeeper or common carrier, was held to be under a duty to the general public and was obliged to serve, without discrimination, all who sought service. [Citations omitted.] On the other hand, proprietors of private enterprises, such as places of amusement and resort, were under no such obligation, enjoying an absolute power to serve whom they pleased. [Citations omitted.] *A race track, of course, falls within that classification.*

. . .

In holding that Illinois follows the traditional common law rule we are not unmindful that several other states have questioned that rule as a matter both of law and of policy. For example, many of the states that follow the common law rule have used language broader than the facts in the case before them required. While these cases state that a proprietor has the absolute right to exclude, the facts of the case show that just cause existed to exclude the patron. *See, e.g., Silbert v. Ramsey,* 301 Md. 96, 482 A.2d 147 (1984) (patron excluded on the basis of his prior conviction for violation of state lottery laws); *James v. Churchill Downs, Inc.,* 620 S.W.2d 323 (Ky.App.1981) (excluded patron was a convicted bookmaker); *Tropical Park, Inc. v. Jack,* 374 So.2d 639 (Fla.App.1979) (patron alleged to have "known underworld connections" was rightfully excluded); *Burrillville Racing Association v. Garabedian,* 113 R.I. 134, 318 A.2d 469 (1974) (excluded patron had prior conviction for income tax evasion in connection with a wager messenger operation); *People v. Licata,* 28 N.Y.2d 113, 268 N.E.2d 787 (1971) (defendant had prior convictions for bookmaking); *Flores v. Los Angeles Turf Club, Inc.,* 55 Cal.2d 736, 13 Cal.Rptr. 201, 361 P.2d 921 (1961) (plaintiff was a convicted bookmaker). But that fact only demonstrates that proprietors of amusement facilities, whose very survival depends on bringing the public into their place of amusement, are reasonable people who usually do not exclude their customers unless they have a reason to do so. What the proprietor of a race track does not want to have to do is *prove* or *explain* that his reason for exclusion is a *just* reason. He doesn't want to be liable to Coley Madden solely because he mistakenly believed he was a mobster. The proprietor wants to be able to keep someone off his private property even if they only *look like* a mobster. As long as the proprietor is not excluding the mobster look-a-like because of his national origin (or because of race, color, creed, or sex), then the common law, and the law of Illinois, allows him to do just that.

We also choose not to follow the arguable—but not clear—abandonment of the common law rule in New Jersey in the case of *Uston v. Resorts International Hotel, Inc.,* 89 N.J. 163, 445 A.2d 370 (1982). In 1959 the New Jersey Supreme Court decided *Garifine v. Monmouth Park Jockey Club,* 29 N.J. 47, 148 A.2d 1 (Sup.Ct.1959), which was an appeal from the trial court's refusal to grant the plaintiff injunctive relief from his exclusion from Monmouth Park race track. The defendant race track, relying on *Madden,* moved to dismiss the complaint on the ground that it had "an absolute right" to exclude the plaintiff. On appeal, the plaintiff contended that the operator of a race track should not have the common law right to exclude a patron without reasonable cause and that under the New Jersey Civil Rights Act the operator did not have such authority. In a scholarly opinion the court traced the genesis of the right of race tracks to exclude patrons without justifying the exclusion:

> There was a time in English history when the common law recognized in many callings the duty to serve the public without discrimination. [Citations omitted.] With the passing of time and the changing of conditions, the common law confined this duty to exceptional callings where the needs of the public urgently called for its continuance. Innkeepers and common carriers may be said to be the most notable illustrations of business operators who, both under early principles and under the common law today, are obliged to serve the public without discrimination. [Citations omitted.] On the other hand, operators of most businesses, including places of amusement such as race tracks, have never been placed under any such common-law obligation, for no comparable considerations of public policy have ever so dictated.

However, in 1982 the New Jersey Supreme Court decided *Uston* in which the plaintiff was a practitioner of a strategy of playing blackjack known as "card counting." The defendant operated a gambling casino licensed pursuant to the New Jersey Casino Control Act. The defendant excluded Uston from the blackjack tables in its casino because of Uston's strategy of "card counting." The New Jersey Supreme Court held that the Casino Control Act gave the Casino Control Commission the exclusive authority to exclude patrons based upon their strategies for playing licensed casino games and that any common law right the defendant may have had to exclude Uston for these reasons was abrogated by the Act and outweighed by Uston's right of access. *Uston,* 445 A.2d at 372.

. . .

[T]he New Jersey decisions do paint the wider policy picture of which our decision today is a part. As a policy matter, it is arguably unfair to allow a place of amusement to exclude for any reason or no reason, and to be free of accountability, except in cases of obvious discrimination. In this case, the general public is not only invited but, through advertising, is encouraged to come to the race track and wager on the races' outcome. But the common law allows the race track to exclude patrons, no matter if they come from near or far, or in reasonable reliance on representations of accessibility. We may ultimately believe that market forces would preclude any outrageous excesses—such as excluding anyone who has blond hair, or (like the plaintiffs) who is from Pennsylvania, or (even more outrageous) who has $250,000 to spend in one day of betting. But the premise of the consumer protection laws that the New Jersey Supreme Court alluded to in *Uston* and *Marzocca* recognizes that the reality of an imperfect market allows numerous consumer depredations. Excluding a patron simply because he is named Adam Smith arguably offends the very precepts of equality and fair dealing expressed in everything from the antitrust statutes to the Illinois Consumer Fraud and Deceptive Business Practice Act. Ill.Rev.Stat. ch. 121 ½, ¶¶ 262–72.

But the market here is not so demonstrably imperfect that there is a monopoly or any allegation of consumer fraud. Consequently, there is no such explicit legislative directive in the context of patrons attending horse races in Illinois—so the common law rule, relic though it may be, still controls. . . .

III

For the foregoing reasons the court below is affirmed.

DISCUSSION PROBLEMS

1. Fracking

Southwestern Energy Production Company operated a series of wells on leased land in Pennsylvania that they used to extract natural gas from the Marcellus Shale formation using hydraulic fracturing. By pumping large quantities of liquids and solids into the ground, Southwestern created subsurface rock fractures that ran horizontally from their leased land under to beneath the adjoining property owned by the Briggs family. This activity caused natural gas previously locked in rock formations under the

Briggs's property to flow across the property line into Southwestern's wells. Southwestern did not drill into land beneath the Briggs's property, nor did any of their liquid or solid fracking materials cross the property line.

The Briggs sued for trespass and conversion. Should they prevail?

2. Dock Damage

The steamship Reynolds, owned by Lake Erie Transportation Company, unloaded its cargo in November, 1905, while moored to a docked owned by R.C. Vincent. When the Reynolds had concluded its delivery and was scheduled to depart, a storm with violent, 50 mile-per-hour winds had developed, navigation had become extremely difficult, and no tugs were willing to tow the ship away from the dock. The ship remained moored, and the storm caused the boat to smash into the dock repeatedly, damaging the dock.

Vincent sought compensation for the damage, and Lake Erie Transportation refused to pay. Should Vincent be entitled to collect?

3. The Mobile Home

Steenberg Homes, Inc. needed to deliver a mobile home for use as a summer cottage to land adjacent to the property of Harvey and Lois Jacque. The only road to the property was covered in seven feet of snow and contained a sharp curve, which would complicate the delivery and require Steenberg to use special technology. The easiest and least costly solution would be to transport the mobile home across the Jacques' snow-covered farm field. Steenberg asked for permission, but the Jacques refused. Steenberg proceeded to haul the mobile home across the Jacques' field anyway. The activity caused no damage to the Jacques' property.

The Jacques sued Steenberg for trespass and sought damages. Should they be entitled to recover? If so, how much?

4. The Shopping Center

Lloyd Corporation, Ltd., owned a retail shopping mall in Portland, Oregon. Approximately 20 acres of the mall's 50 total acres consisted of open and covered parking areas, which together accommodated 1000 vehicles. The entire area was generally open to the public and, in fact, the mall owners exerted considerable effort to encourage potential shoppers to come. The owners permitted the American Legion to sell poppies for disabled veterans on the property and permitted the Salvation Army and the Volunteers of America to solicit donations during the winter holiday season, but it denied permission to other charitable organizations.

In 1968, five people entered the mall property and distributed printed leaflets that invited the public to attend a protest against the military draft and the Vietnam War. The distribution of the leaflets was quiet and orderly and there was no litter. Nonetheless, mall security guards informed the five that they were trespassing and ordered them to leave the property. Did the mall have the right to exclude the leaflet distributors from the property?

CHAPTER 5

THE RIGHT TO EXCLUDE PART II (INTANGIBLE PROPERTY)

■ ■ ■

INTRODUCTION

When physical property is at issue, the problem of incompatible uses means that, in the absence of the right to exclude, a possessor might be limited in the uses he can make of things. In *Ploof v. Putnam*, for example, the property owner's use and enjoyment of the dock is compromised if he is not permitted to exclude the sloop from docking during the storm. When intellectual property and other intangible interests that are non-rivalrous are at issue, this problem does not arise. A possessor's right to exclude will often have economic value, and an argument in favor of that right might be persuasive on this basis, but the right to exclude is not strictly necessary to enable a possessor to use a thing as he sees fit. Should this difference affect the extent of a possessor's property rights?

This chapter first considers this issue in the context of copyright law. *Campbell v. Acuff-Rose Music* considers whether one musical artist may prevent another from making use of the former's creative work in the latter's creative work. If musician Roy Orbison (actually, his estate) cannot prevent the band "2 Live Crew" from using portions of "Oh, Pretty Woman," this would have no direct effect on Orbison's ability to use his creative work, but it might reduce the economic value or undermine the artistic value of that work. The relevant legal doctrine in the dispute is known as "fair use": if a use qualifies as a fair use, the copyright holder cannot exclude the would-be user; if it does not, the copyright holder may exclude, and unauthorized use constitutes actionable copyright infringement. 17 U.S.C. § 107. Do the limits on exclusion provided by the fair use doctrine intrude too much on the property rights of creators, or not enough?

As a side point, notice that the multi-factor balancing test for what constitutes fair use is an excellent example of a legal "standard" (i.e., a court is called upon to make nuanced, highly factual judgments to render a decision in the case of a dispute), although it is a different type of than the standard of "reasonableness" deployed in nuisance law. Compare the nature of the fair use standard in 17 U.S.C. § 107 to the "first sale" doctrine of 17 U.S.C. § 109, which is a legal "rule." What are the advantages and disadvantages of multi-factor balancing tests like the fair use doctrine?

Doe v. TCI Cablevision concerns a different type of intangible property interest: the right to preclude others from using one's name and likeness for commercial gain. Rest. (3d) Unfair Competition § 46. Should hockey player Tony Twist be able to prohibit an author from using his persona in a story portrayed in a comic book? Why or why not?

Intel v. Hamidi grapples with a question, increasingly common in the information economy, of whether one party's use of another's digital infrastructure should be treated, for purposes of analyzing the right to exclude, like physical property or like intellectual property. Is a distinction between these two categories even meaningful?

---

17 U.S. Code § 107. Limitations on Exclusive Rights: Fair use

Notwithstanding the provisions of sections 106 and 106A, the fair use of a copyrighted work, including such use by reproduction in copies or phonorecords or by any other means specified by that section, for purposes such as criticism, comment, news reporting, teaching (including multiple copies for classroom use), scholarship, or research, is not an infringement of copyright. In determining whether the use made of a work in any particular case is a fair use the factors to be considered shall include—

(1) the purpose and character of the use, <u>including</u> whether such use is of a commercial nature or is for nonprofit educational purposes;

(2) the nature of the copyrighted work;

(3) the amount and substantiality of the portion used in relation to the copyrighted work as a whole; and

(4) the effect of the use upon the potential market for or value of the copyrighted work.

The fact that a work is unpublished shall not itself bar a finding of fair use if such finding is made upon consideration of all the above factors.

17 U.S. Code § 109. Limitations on exclusive rights: Effect of transfer of particular copy or phonorecord

(a) . . .The owner of a particular copy or phonorecord lawfully made under this title, or any person authorized by such owner, is entitled, without the authority of the copyright owner, to sell or otherwise dispose of the possession of that copy or phonorecord.

Restatement (Third) Unfair Competition § 46. Appropriation of the Commercial Value of a Person's Identity: The Right of Publicity

One who appropriates the commercial value of a person's identity by using without consent the person's name, likeness, or other indicia of identity for purposes of trade is subject to liability for the relief appropriate under the rules [concerning injunctions] and [damages].

Restatement (Second) Torts § 217. Ways of Committing Trespass to Chattel

A trespass to a chattel may be committed by intentionally by

(a) dispossessing another of the chattel, or

(b) using or intermeddling with a chattel in the possession of another.

CASES

CAMPBELL V. ACUFF-ROSE MUSIC, INC.

Supreme Court of the United States
510 U.S. 569 (1994)

JUSTICE SOUTER delivered the opinion of the Court.

We are called upon to decide whether 2 Live Crew's commercial parody of Roy Orbison's song, "Oh, Pretty Woman," may be a fair use within the meaning of the Copyright Act of 1976, 17 U.S.C. § 107 (1988 ed. and Supp. IV). Although the District Court granted summary judgment for 2 Live Crew, the Court of Appeals reversed, holding the defense of fair use barred by the song's commercial character and excessive borrowing. Because we hold that a parody's commercial character is only one element to be weighed in a fair use enquiry, and that insufficient consideration was given to the nature of parody in weighing the degree of copying, we reverse and remand.

I

In 1964, Roy Orbison and William Dees wrote a rock ballad called "Oh, Pretty Woman" and assigned their rights in it to respondent Acuff-Rose Music, Inc. See Appendix A, *infra,* at 1179. Acuff-Rose registered the song for copyright protection.

Petitioners Luther R. Campbell, Christopher Wongwon, Mark Ross, and David Hobbs are collectively known as 2 Live Crew, a popular rap music group. In 1989, Campbell wrote a song entitled "Pretty Woman," which he later described in an affidavit as intended, "through comical lyrics, to satirize the original work. . . ." App. to Pet. for Cert. 80a. On July 5, 1989, 2 Live Crew's manager informed Acuff-Rose that 2 Live Crew had written a parody of "Oh, Pretty Woman," that they would afford all credit for ownership and authorship of the original song to Acuff-Rose, Dees, and Orbison, and that they were willing to pay a fee for the use they wished to make of it. Enclosed with the letter were a copy of the lyrics and a recording of 2 Live Crew's song. See Appendix B, *infra,* at 1179–80. Acuff-Rose's agent refused permission, stating that "I am aware of the success enjoyed by 'The 2 Live Crews', but I must inform you that we cannot permit the use of a parody of 'Oh, Pretty Woman.' " App. to Pet. for Cert. 85a. Nonetheless, in June or July 1989, 2 Live Crew released records, cassette tapes, and compact discs of "Pretty Woman" in a collection of songs entitled "As Clean As They Wanna Be." The albums and compact discs identify the authors of "Pretty Woman" as Orbison and Dees and its publisher as Acuff-Rose.

Almost a year later, after nearly a quarter of a million copies of the recording had been sold, Acuff-Rose sued 2 Live Crew and its record company, Luke Skyywalker Records, for copyright infringement. The District Court granted summary judgment for 2 Live Crew, reasoning that the commercial purpose of 2 Live Crew's song was no bar to fair use; that 2 Live Crew's version was a parody, which "quickly degenerates into a play on words, substituting predictable lyrics with shocking ones" to show "how bland and banal the Orbison song" is; that 2 Live Crew had taken no more than was necessary to "conjure up" the original in order to parody it; and that it was "extremely unlikely that 2 Live Crew's song could adversely affect the market for the original." 754 F.Supp. 1150, 1154–1155, 1157–1158 (MD Tenn.1991). The District Court weighed these factors and held that 2 Live Crew's song made fair use of Orbison's original. *Id.,* at 1158–1159.

The Court of Appeals for the Sixth Circuit reversed and remanded. 972 F.2d 1429, 1439 (1992). Although it assumed for the purpose of its opinion that 2 Live Crew's song was a parody of the Orbison original, the Court of Appeals thought the District Court had put too little emphasis on the fact that "every commercial use . . . is presumptively . . . unfair," *Sony Corp. of America v. Universal City Studios, Inc.,* 464 U.S. 417, 451, 104 S.Ct. 774, 792, 78 L.Ed.2d 574 (1984), and it held that "the admittedly commercial nature" of the parody "requires the conclusion" that the first of four factors relevant under the statute weighs against a finding of fair use. 972 F.2d, at 1435, 1437. Next, the Court of Appeals determined that, by "taking the heart of the original and making it the heart of a new work," 2 Live Crew had, qualitatively, taken too much. *Id.,* at 1438. Finally, after noting that the effect on the potential market for the original (and the market for derivative works) is "undoubtedly the single most important element of fair use," *Harper & Row, Publishers, Inc. v. Nation Enterprises,* 471 U.S. 539,

566, 105 S.Ct. 2218, 2233, 85 L.Ed.2d 588 (1985), the Court of Appeals faulted the District Court for "refus[ing] to indulge the presumption" that "harm for purposes of the fair use analysis has been established by the presumption attaching to commercial uses." 972 F.2d, at 1438–1439. In sum, the court concluded that its "blatantly commercial purpose . . . prevents this parody from being a fair use." *Id.,* at 1439.

We granted certiorari, 507 U.S. 1003, 113 S.Ct. 1642, 123 L.Ed.2d 264 (1993), to determine whether 2 Live Crew's commercial parody could be a fair use.

II

It is uncontested here that 2 Live Crew's song would be an infringement of Acuff-Rose's rights in "Oh, Pretty Woman," under the Copyright Act of 1976, 17 U.S.C. § 106 (1988 ed. and Supp. IV), but for a finding of fair use through parody. From the infancy of copyright protection, some opportunity for fair use of copyrighted materials has been thought necessary to fulfill copyright's very purpose, "[t]o promote the Progress of Science and useful Arts. . . ." U.S. Const., Art. I, § 8, cl. 8. For as Justice Story explained, "[i]n truth, in literature, in science and in art, there are, and can be, few, if any, things, which in an abstract sense, are strictly new and original throughout. Every book in literature, science and art, borrows, and must necessarily borrow, and use much which was well known and used before." *Emerson v. Davies,* 8 F.Cas. 615, 619 (No. 4,436) (CCD Mass.1845). Similarly, Lord Ellenborough expressed the inherent tension in the need simultaneously to protect copyrighted material and to allow others to build upon it when he wrote, "while I shall think myself bound to secure every man in the enjoyment of his copy-right, one must not put manacles upon science." *Carey v. Kearsley,* 4 Esp. 168, 170, 170 Eng.Rep. 679, 681 (K.B.1803). In copyright cases brought under the Statute of Anne of 1710, English courts held that in some instances "fair abridgements" would not infringe an author's rights, see W. Patry, The Fair Use Privilege in Copyright Law 6–17 (1985) (hereinafter Patry); Leval, Toward a Fair Use Standard, 103 Harv.L.Rev. 1105 (1990) (hereinafter Leval), and although the First Congress enacted our initial copyright statute, Act of May 31, 1790, 1 Stat. 124, without any explicit reference to "fair use," as it later came to be known, the doctrine was recognized by the American courts nonetheless.

In *Folsom v. Marsh,* 9 F.Cas. 342 (No. 4,901) (CCD Mass. 1841), Justice Story distilled the essence of law and methodology from the earlier cases: "look to the nature and objects of the selections made, the quantity and value of the materials used, and the degree in which the use may prejudice the sale, or diminish the profits, or supersede the objects, of the original work." *Id.,* at 348. Thus expressed, fair use remained exclusively judge-made doctrine until the passage of the 1976 Copyright Act, in which Justice Story's summary is discernible:

"§ 107. Limitations on exclusive rights: Fair use

"Notwithstanding the provisions of sections 106 and 106A, the fair use of a copyrighted work, including such use by reproduction in copies or phonorecords or by any other means specified by that section, for purposes such as criticism, comment, news reporting, teaching (including multiple copies for classroom use), scholarship, or research, is not an infringement of copyright. In determining whether the use made of a work in any particular case is a fair use the factors to be considered shall include—

"(1) the purpose and character of the use, including whether such use is of a commercial nature or is for nonprofit educational purposes;

"(2) the nature of the copyrighted work;

"(3) the amount and substantiality of the portion used in relation to the copyrighted work as a whole; and

"(4) the effect of the use upon the potential market for or value of the copyrighted work.

"The fact that a work is unpublished shall not itself bar a finding of fair use if such finding is made upon consideration of all the above factors." 17 U.S.C. § 107 (1988 ed. and Supp. IV).

Congress meant § 107 "to restate the present judicial doctrine of fair use, not to change, narrow, or enlarge it in any way" and intended that courts continue the common-law tradition of fair use adjudication. H.R.Rep. No. 94–1476, p. 66 (1976) (hereinafter House Report); S.Rep. No. 94–473, p. 62 (1975) U.S.Code Cong. & Admin.News 1976, pp. 5659, 5679 (hereinafter Senate Report). The fair use doctrine thus "permits [and requires] courts to avoid rigid application of the copyright statute when, on occasion, it would stifle the very creativity which that law is designed to foster." *Stewart v. Abend,* 495 U.S. 207, 236, 110 S.Ct. 1750, 1767, 109 L.Ed.2d 184 (1990) (internal quotation marks and citation omitted).

The task is not to be simplified with bright-line rules, for the statute, like the doctrine it recognizes, calls for case-by-case analysis. *Harper & Row,* 471 U.S., at 560, 105 S.Ct., at 2230; *Sony,* 464 U.S., at 448, and n. 31, 104 S.Ct., at 792, & n. 31; House Report, pp. 65–66; Senate Report, p. 62. The text employs the terms "including" and "such as" in the preamble paragraph to indicate the "illustrative and not limitative" function of the examples given, § 101; see *Harper & Row, supra,* 471 U.S., at 561, 105 S.Ct., at 2230, which thus provide only general guidance about the sorts of copying that courts and Congress most commonly had found to be fair uses.

Nor may the four statutory factors be treated in isolation, one from another. All are to be explored, and the results weighed together, in light of the purposes of copyright. See Leval 1110–1111; Patry & Perlmutter, Fair Use Misconstrued: Profit, Presumptions, and Parody, 11 Cardozo Arts & Ent.L.J. 667, 685–687 (1993) (hereinafter Patry & Perlmutter).

A

The first factor in a fair use enquiry is "the purpose and character of the use, including whether such use is of a commercial nature or is for nonprofit educational purposes." § 107(1). This factor draws on Justice Story's formulation, "the nature and objects of the selections made." *Folsom v. Marsh, supra,* at 348. The enquiry here may be guided by the examples given in the preamble to § 107, looking to whether the use is for criticism, or comment, or news reporting, and the like, see § 107. The central purpose of this investigation is to see, in Justice Story's words, whether the new work merely "supersede[s] the objects" of the original creation, *Folsom v. Marsh, supra,* at 348; accord, *Harper & Row, supra,* 471 U.S., at 562, 105 S.Ct., at 2231 ("supplanting" the original), or instead adds something new, with a further purpose or different character, altering the first with new expression, meaning, or message; it asks, in other words, whether and to what extent the new work is "transformative." Leval 1111. Although such transformative use is not absolutely necessary for a finding of fair use, *Sony, supra,* 464 U.S., at 455, n. 40, 104 S.Ct., at 795, n. 40, the goal of copyright, to promote science and the arts, is generally furthered by the creation of transformative works. Such works thus lie at the heart of the fair use doctrine's guarantee of breathing space within the confines of copyright, see, *e.g., Sony, supra,* at 478–480, 104 S.Ct., at 807–808 (BLACKMUN, J., dissenting), and the more transformative the new work, the less will be the significance of other factors, like commercialism, that may weigh against a finding of fair use.

. . .

While we might not assign a high rank to the parodic element here, we think it fair to say that 2 Live Crew's song reasonably could be perceived as commenting on the original or criticizing it, to some degree. 2 Live Crew juxtaposes the romantic musings of a man whose fantasy comes true, with degrading taunts, a bawdy demand for sex, and a sigh of relief from paternal responsibility. The later words can be taken as a comment on the naiveté of the original of an earlier day, as a rejection of its sentiment that ignores the ugliness of street life and the debasement that it signifies. It is this joinder of reference and ridicule that marks off the author's choice of parody from the other types of comment and criticism that traditionally have had a claim to fair use protection as transformative works.

The Court of Appeals, however, immediately cut short the enquiry into 2 Live Crew's fair use claim by confining its treatment of the first factor essentially to one relevant fact, the commercial nature of the use. The court then inflated the significance of this fact by applying a presumption ostensibly culled from *Sony,* that "every commercial use of copyrighted material is presumptively . . . unfair. . . ." *Sony,* 464 U.S., at 451, 104 S.Ct., at 792. In giving virtually dispositive weight to the commercial nature of the parody, the Court of Appeals erred.

The language of the statute makes clear that the commercial or nonprofit educational purpose of a work is only one element of the first factor enquiry into its purpose and character. . . .

Sony itself called for no hard evidentiary presumption. There, we emphasized the need for a "sensitive balancing of interests,"464 U.S., at 455, n. 40, 104 S.Ct., at 795, n. 40, noted that Congress had "eschewed a rigid, bright-line approach to fair use," *id.,* at 449, n. 31, 104 S.Ct., at 792, n. 31, and stated that the commercial or nonprofit educational character of a work is "not conclusive," *id.,* at 448–449, 104 S.Ct., at 792, but rather a fact to be "weighed along with other[s] in fair use decisions," *id.,* at 449, n. 32, 104 S.Ct. at 792, n. 32, (quoting House Report, p. 66) U.S.Code Cong. & Admin.News 1976, pp. 5659, 5679. The Court of Appeals's elevation of one sentence from *Sony* to a *per se* rule thus runs as much counter to *Sony* itself as to the long common-law tradition of fair use adjudication. Rather, as we explained in *Harper & Row, Sony* stands for the proposition that the "fact that a publication was commercial as opposed to nonprofit is a separate factor that tends to weigh against a finding of fair use."471 U.S., at 562, 105 S.Ct., at 2231. But that is all, and the fact that even the force of that tendency will vary with the context is a further reason against elevating commerciality to hard presumptive significance. . . .

The second statutory factor, "the nature of the copyrighted work," § 107(2), draws on Justice Story's expression, the "value of the materials used." *Folsom v. Marsh,* 9 F.Cas., at 348. This factor calls for recognition that some works are closer to the core of intended copyright protection than others, with the consequence that fair use is more difficult to establish when the former works are copied. See, *e.g., Stewart v. Abend,* 495 U.S., at 237–238, 110 S.Ct., at 1768–1769 (contrasting fictional short story with factual works); *Harper & Row,* 471 U.S., at 563–564, 105 S.Ct., at 2231–2233 (contrasting soon-to-be-published memoir with published speech); *Sony,* 464 U.S., at 455, n. 40, 104 S.Ct., at 792, n. 40 (contrasting motion pictures with news broadcasts); *Feist,* 499 U.S., at 348–351, 111 S.Ct., at 1289–1291 (contrasting creative works with bare factual compilations); 3 M. Nimmer & D. Nimmer, Nimmer on Copyright § 13.05[A][2] (1993) (hereinafter Nimmer); Leval 1116. We agree with both the District Court and the Court of Appeals that the Orbison original's creative expression for public dissemination falls within the core of the copyright's protective purposes. 754 F.Supp., at 1155–1156; 972 F.2d, at 1437. This fact, however, is not much help in this case, or ever likely to help much in separating the fair use sheep from the infringing goats in a parody case, since parodies almost invariably copy publicly known, expressive works.

C

The third factor asks whether "the amount and substantiality of the portion used in relation to the copyrighted work as a whole," § 107(3) (or, in Justice Story's words, "the quantity and value of the materials used," *Folsom v. Marsh, supra,* at 348) are reasonable in relation to the purpose of the copying. . . .

We think the Court of Appeals was insufficiently appreciative of parody's need for the recognizable sight or sound when it ruled 2 Live Crew's use unreasonable as a matter of law. It is true, of course, that 2 Live Crew copied the characteristic opening bass riff (or musical phrase) of the original, and true that the words of the first line copy the Orbison lyrics. But if quotation of the opening riff and the first line may be said to go to the "heart" of the original, the heart is also what most readily conjures up the song for parody, and it is the heart at which parody takes aim. Copying does not become excessive in relation to parodic purpose merely because the portion taken was the original's heart. If 2 Live Crew had copied a significantly less memorable part of the original, it is difficult to see how its parodic character would have come through. See *Fisher v. Dees, supra,* at 439.

This is not, of course, to say that anyone who calls himself a parodist can skim the cream and get away scot free. In parody, as in news reporting, see *Harper & Row, supra,* context is everything, and the question of fairness asks what else the parodist did besides go to the heart of the original. It is significant that 2 Live Crew not only copied the first line of the original, but thereafter departed markedly from the Orbison lyrics for its own ends. 2 Live Crew not only copied the bass riff and repeated it, but also produced otherwise distinctive sounds, interposing "scraper" noise, overlaying the music with solos in different keys, and altering the drum beat. See 754 F.Supp., at 1155. This is not a case, then, where "a substantial portion" of the parody itself is composed of a "verbatim" copying of the original. It is not, that is, a case where the parody is so insubstantial, as compared to the copying, that the third factor must be resolved as a matter of law against the parodists.

. . .

D

The fourth fair use factor is "the effect of the use upon the potential market for or value of the copyrighted work." § 107(4). . . .

. . .[A]s to parody pure and simple, it is more likely that the new work will not affect the market for the original in a way cognizable under this factor, that is, by acting as a substitute for it ("supersed[ing] [its] objects").

See Leval 1125; Patry & Perlmutter 692, 697–698. This is so because the parody and the original usually serve different market functions. Bisceglia, ASCAP, Copyright Law Symposium, No. 34, at 23.

We do not, of course, suggest that a parody may not harm the market at all, but when a lethal parody, like a scathing theater review, kills demand for the original, it does not produce a harm cognizable under the Copyright Act. Because "parody may quite legitimately aim at garroting the original, destroying it commercially as well as artistically," B. Kaplan, An Unhurried View of Copyright 69 (1967), the role of the courts is to distinguish between "[b]iting criticism [that merely] suppresses demand [and] copyright infringement[, which] usurps it." *Fisher v. Dees,* 794 F.2d, at 438.

Although 2 Live Crew submitted uncontroverted affidavits on the question of market harm to the original, neither they, nor Acuff-Rose, introduced evidence or affidavits addressing the likely effect of 2 Live Crew's parodic rap song on the market for a nonparody, rap version of "Oh, Pretty Woman." And while Acuff-Rose would have us find evidence of a rap market in the very facts that 2 Live Crew recorded a rap parody of "Oh, Pretty Woman" and another rap group sought a license to record a rap derivative, there was no evidence that a potential rap market was harmed in any way by 2 Live Crew's parody, rap version. The fact that 2 Live Crew's parody sold as part of a collection of rap songs says very little about the parody's effect on a market for a rap version of the original, either of the music alone or of the music with its lyrics. The District Court essentially passed on this issue, observing that Acuff-Rose is free to record "whatever version of the original it desires," 754 F.Supp., at 1158; the Court of Appeals went the other way by erroneous presumption. Contrary to each treatment, it is impossible to deal with the fourth factor except by recognizing that a silent record on an important factor bearing on fair use disentitled the proponent of the defense, 2 Live Crew, to summary judgment. The evidentiary hole will doubtless be plugged on remand.

III

It was error for the Court of Appeals to conclude that the commercial nature of 2 Live Crew's parody of "Oh, Pretty Woman" rendered it presumptively unfair. No such evidentiary presumption is available to address either the first factor, the character and purpose of the use, or the fourth, market harm, in determining whether a transformative use, such as parody, is a fair one. The court also erred in holding that 2 Live Crew had necessarily copied excessively from the Orbison original, considering the parodic purpose of the use. We therefore reverse the judgment of the Court of Appeals and remand the case for further proceedings consistent with this opinion.

It is so ordered.

APPENDIX A TO OPINION OF THE COURT

"Oh, Pretty Woman" by Roy Orbison and William Dees

Pretty Woman, walking down the street,
Pretty Woman, the kind I like to meet,
Pretty Woman, I don't believe you, you're not the truth,
No one could look as good as you
Mercy
Pretty Woman, won't you pardon me,
Pretty Woman, I couldn't help but see,
Pretty Woman, that you look lovely as can be
Are you lonely just like me?
Pretty Woman, stop a while,
Pretty Woman, talk a while,
Pretty Woman give your smile to me
Pretty Woman, yeah, yeah, yeah
Pretty Woman, look my way,
Pretty Woman, say you'll stay with me
'Cause I need you, I'll treat you right
Come to me baby, Be mine tonight
Pretty Woman, don't walk on by,
Pretty Woman, don't make me cry,
Pretty Woman, don't walk away,
Hey, O.K.
If that's the way it must be, O.K.
I guess I'll go on home, it's late
There'll be tomorrow night, but wait!
What do I see
Is she walking back to me?
Yeah, she's walking back to me!
Oh, Pretty Woman.

APPENDIX B TO OPINION OF THE COURT

"Pretty Woman" as Recorded by 2 Live Crew

Pretty woman walkin' down the street
Pretty woman girl you look so sweet
Pretty woman you bring me down to that knee
Pretty woman you make me wanna beg please
Oh, pretty woman
Big hairy woman you need to shave that stuff
Big hairy woman you know I bet it's tough
Big hairy woman all that hair it ain't legit
'Cause you look like 'Cousin It'
Big hairy woman
Bald headed woman girl your hair won't grow
Bald headed woman you got a teeny weeny afro
Bald headed woman you know your hair could look nice
Bald headed woman first you got to roll it with rice
Bald headed woman here, let me get this hunk of biz for ya
Ya know what I'm saying you look better than rice a roni
Oh bald headed woman
Big hairy woman come on in
And don't forget your bald headed friend
Hey pretty woman let the boys
Jump in
Two timin' woman girl you know you ain't right
Two timin' woman you's out with my boy last night
Two timin' woman that takes a load off my mind
Two timin' woman now I know the baby ain't mine
Oh, two timin' woman
Oh pretty woman

DOE, A/K/A TONY TWIST V. TCI CABLEVISION

Supreme Court of Missouri
110 S.W.3d 363 (Mo. 2003)

STEPHEN N. LIMBAUGH, JR., JUDGE.

Appellant Anthony Twist, also known as Tony Twist, is a former professional hockey player in the National Hockey League. After learning of the existence of a comic book, titled *Spawn,* that contained a villainous character sharing his name, Twist brought misappropriation of name and defamation claims against respondents, the creators, publishers and marketers of *Spawn* and related promotional products. Respondents defended on First Amendment grounds. The circuit court dismissed the defamation count, but allowed the misappropriation of name count to go to trial, which resulted in a jury verdict in favor of Twist in the amount of $24,500,000. The circuit court, however, granted respondents' motion for judgment notwithstanding the verdict. . . .

I.

Tony Twist began his NHL career in 1988 playing for the St. Louis Blues, later to be transferred to the Quebec Nordiques, only to return to St. Louis where he finished his career in 1999, due to injuries suffered in a motorcycle accident. During his hockey career, Twist became the League's preeminent "enforcer," a player whose chief responsibility was to protect goal scorers from physical assaults by opponents. In that role, Twist was notorious for his violent tactics on the ice. Describing Twist, a *Sports Illustrated* writer said: "It takes a special talent to stand on skates and beat someone senseless, and no one does it better than the St. Louis Blues left winger." Austin Murphy, *Fighting For A Living: St. Louis Blues Enforcer Tony Twist, Whose Pugilistic Talents Appear To Run In The Family, Doesn't Pull Any Punches On The Job,* SPORTS ILLUSTRATED, Mar. 16, 1998, at 42. The article goes on to quote Twist as saying, "I want to hurt them. I want to end the fight as soon as possible and I want the guy to remember it." *Id.*

Despite his well-deserved reputation as a tough-guy "enforcer," or perhaps because of that reputation, Twist was immensely popular with the hometown fans. He endorsed products, appeared on radio and television, hosted the "Tony Twist" television talk show for two years, and became actively involved with several children's charities. It is undisputed that Twist engaged in these activities to foster a positive image of himself in the community and to prepare for a career after hockey as a sports commentator and product endorser.

Respondent Todd McFarlane, an avowed hockey fan and president of Todd McFarlane Productions, Inc. (TMP), created *Spawn* in 1992. TMP employs the writers, artists and creative staff responsible for production of the comic book. *Spawn* is marketed and distributed monthly by Image Comics, Inc., which was formed by McFarlane and others.

Spawn is "a dark and surreal fantasy" centered on a character named Al Simmons, a CIA assassin who was killed by the Mafia and descended to hell upon death. Simmons, having made a deal with the devil, was transformed into the creature Spawn and returned to earth to commit various violent and sexual acts on the devil's behalf. In 1993, a fictional character named "Anthony 'Tony Twist' Twistelli" was added to the *Spawn* storyline. The fictional "Tony Twist" is a Mafia don whose list of evil deeds includes multiple murders, abduction of children and sex with prostitutes. The fictional and real Tony Twist bear no physical resemblance to each other and, aside from the common nickname, are similar only in that each can be characterized as having an "enforcer" or tough-guy persona.

Each issue of the *Spawn* comic book contains a section entitled "Spawning Ground" in which fan letters are published and McFarlane responds to fan questions. In the September 1994 issue, McFarlane admitted that some of the *Spawn* characters were named after professional hockey players, including the "Tony Twist" character: "Antonio Twistelli, a/k/a Tony Twist, is actually the name of a hockey player of the Quebec Nordiques." And, again, in the November 1994 issue, McFarlane stated that the name of the fictional character was based on Twist, a real hockey player, and further promised the readers that they "will continue to see current and past hockey players' names in my books."

In April 1996, *Wizard,* a trade magazine for the comic book industry, interviewed McFarlane. In the published article, "Spawning Ground: A Look at the Real Life People Spawn Characters Are Based Upon," McFarlane is quoted as saying that he uses the names of real-life people to create the identities of the characters. Brief biographies and drawings of the *Spawn* characters follow the McFarlane interview. The paragraph devoted to the "Tony Twist" character contained a drawing of the character accompanied by the following description:

First Appearance: Spawn # 6

Real-Life Persona: Tony Twist.

Relation: NHL St. Louis Blues right winger.

The Mafia don that has made life exceedingly rough for Al Simmons and his loved ones, in addition to putting out an ill-advised contract on the Violator, is named for former Quebec Nordiques hockey player Tony Twist, now a renowned enforcer (i.e. "Goon") for the St. Louis Blues of the National Hockey League.

Below the character description was a photo of a Tony Twist hockey trading card, in which Twist was pictured in his St. Louis Blues hockey jersey.

In 1997, Twist became aware of the existence of *Spawn* and of the comic book's use of his name for that of the villainous character. On one occasion, several young hockey fans approached Twist's mother with Spawn trading cards depicting the Mafia character "Tony Twist." Subsequently, at an autograph session Twist was asked to sign a copy of the *Wizard* article in which McFarlane was interviewed and Twist's hockey trading card was pictured.

In October 1997, Twist filed suit against McFarlane and various companies associated with the *Spawn* comic book (collectively "respondents"), seeking an injunction and damages for, *inter alia,* misappropriation of name and defamation, the latter claim being later dismissed. McFarlane and the other defendants filed motions for summary judgment asserting First Amendment protection from a prosecution of the misappropriation of name claim, but the motions were overruled.

At trial, McFarlane denied that the comic book character was "about" the real-life Tony Twist despite the fact that the names were the same. McFarlane also denied that he or the other defendants had attained any benefit by using Twist's name. Twist, however, presented evidence that McFarlane and the other defendants had indeed benefited by using his name. For example, Twist introduced evidence suggesting that in marketing Spawn products, McFarlane directly targeted hockey fans—Twist's primary fan base—by producing and licensing Spawn logo hockey pucks, hockey jerseys and toy zambonis. On cross-examination, McFarlane admitted that on one occasion defendants sponsored "Spawn Night" at a minor league hockey game, where McFarlane personally appeared and distributed Spawn products, including products containing the "Tony Twist" character. Another "Spawn Night" was planned to take place at a subsequent NHL game, but the event never occurred. On the issue of damages, Twist, through purported expert testimony, offered a formula for determining the fair market value that McFarlane and the other defendants should have paid Twist to use his name. In addition, Twist introduced evidence that his association with the *Spawn* character resulted in a diminution in the commercial value of his name as an endorser of products. To that end, Sean Philips, a former executive of a sports nutrition company, testified that his company withdrew a $100,000 offer to Twist to serve as the company's product endorser after Philips learned that Twist's name was associated with the evil Mafia don in the *Spawn* comic book.

As noted, at the conclusion of the trial, the jury returned a verdict in favor of Twist and against the defendants jointly in the amount of $24,500,000. On motions for a judgment notwithstanding the verdict or in the alternative a new trial, the circuit court overturned the verdict finding that Twist had failed to make a submissible case on the misappropriation of name count. The court further held that in the event the judgment notwithstanding the verdict was reversed on appeal, the motion for new trial was granted for evidentiary and instructional errors. Finally, the circuit court denied Twist's request for injunctive relief.

II.

The tort of misappropriation of name is one of four recognized torts falling under the general heading of invasion of privacy. *Sullivan v. Pulitzer Broadcasting Co.,* 709 S.W.2d 475, 477 (Mo. banc 1986). The interest protected by the misappropriation of name tort "is the interest of the individual in the exclusive use of his own identity, in so far as it is represented by his name or likeness, and in so far as the use may be of benefit to him or others." RESTATEMENT (SECOND) OF TORTS sec. 652C cmt. a (1977). Recently, development of the misappropriation of name tort has given rise to a separate yet similar tort termed the "right of publicity," which is said to "protect a person from losing the benefit of their [sic] work in creating a publicly recognizable persona." *Bear Foot, Inc. v. Chandler,* 965 S.W.2d 386, 389 (Mo.App.1998). Though facially similar, the protections afforded by each tort are slightly different: "the [misappropriation of name tort] protects against intrusion upon an individual's private self-esteem and dignity, while the right of publicity protects against commercial loss caused by appropriation of an individual's [identity] for commercial exploitation." 4 J. THOMAS MCCARTHY, MCCARTHY ON TRADEMARKS AND UNFAIR COMPETITION sec. 28.6 (4th ed.2003); *see also Bear Foot,* 965 S.W.2d at 389 ("In contrast to the [misappropriation of name tort], the right of publicity is not intended to protect the person's feelings. . . .")

Because the two torts differ in the type of protection that each seeks to provide, there are corresponding differences between the types of damages that may be recovered. In a misappropriation of name action, a plaintiff may recover damages not only for pecuniary loss, but also for mental or emotional distress and suffering. *See Haith v. Model Cities Health Corp. of Kansas City,* 704 S.W.2d 684, 688 (Mo.App.1986); RESTATEMENT (THIRD) OF UNFAIR COMPETITION sec. 49 cmt. b (1995); MCCARTHY, TRADEMARKS sec. 28.6 (explaining that in misappropriation of name actions, damages are "measured by 'mental distress'—some bruising of the human psyche.") By contrast, in a right of publicity action, "the measure of damages properly focuses on the pecuniary loss to the plaintiff or the unjust pecuniary gain to the defendant." RESTATEMENT (THIRD) OF UNFAIR COMPETITION sec. 49 cmt. b; *see also Bear Foot,* 965 S.W.2d at 389; *Haith,* 704 S.W.2d at 688.

In this case, Twist seeks to recover the amount of the fair market value that respondents should have paid to use his name in connection with Spawn products and for damage done to the commercial value—in effect the endorsement value—of his name. Therefore, Twist's case, though brought as a misappropriation of name action, is more precisely labeled a right of publicity action—a point that both parties appear to concede in their briefs.

Despite the differences in the types of damages that may be recovered, the elements of the two torts are essentially the same. To establish the misappropriation tort, the plaintiff must prove that the defendant used the plaintiff's name without consent to obtain some advantage. *Nemani v. St. Louis Univ.,* 33 S.W.3d 184, 185 (Mo. banc 2000); *Haith,* 704 S.W.2d at 687. In a right of publicity action, the plaintiff must prove the same elements as in a misappropriation suit, with the minor exception that the plaintiff must prove that the defendant used the name to obtain a *commercial* advantage. RESTATEMENT (THIRD) OF UNFAIR COMPETITION sec. 46; *see also* RESTATEMENT (SECOND) OF TORTS sec. 652C cmt. b (explaining that, in contrast, the misappropriation of name tort applies when plaintiff's name is used for commercial *or* non-commercial advantage). Given the similarity of elements of the two actions, Missouri cases analyzing the tort of misappropriation of name are pertinent to our recognition of a right of publicity claim.

. . .[I]n view of *Nemani* and the earlier precedent of *Bear Foot,* and consistent with the RESTATEMENT (THIRD) OF UNFAIR COMPETITION, the elements of a right of publicity action include: (1) That defendant used plaintiff's name as a symbol of his identity (2) without consent (3) and with the intent to obtain a commercial advantage.

. . .

A.

Respondents' initial contention that Twist did not prove that his name was used as a "symbol of his identity" is spurious. . . .

Here, all parties agree that the "Tony Twist" character is not "about" him, in that the character does not physically resemble Twist nor does the *Spawn* story line attempt to track Twist's real life. Instead, Twist maintains that the sharing of the same (and most unusual) name and the common persona of a tough-guy "enforcer" create an unmistakable correlation between Twist the hockey player and Twist the Mafia don that, when coupled with Twist's fame as a NHL star, conclusively establishes that respondents used his name and identity. This Court agrees. Indeed, respondent McFarlane appears to have conceded the point by informing his readers in separate issues of *Spawn* and in the *Wizard* article that the hockey player Tony Twist was the basis for the comic book character's name.

. . .

III.

Having determined that Twist made a submissible case at trial, we next address whether the right of publicity claim is nevertheless prohibited by the First Amendment. Courts throughout the country have struggled with this issue. . . .

Right to publicity cases . . . focus . . . on the threshold legal question of whether the use of a person's name and identity is "expressive," in which case it is fully protected, or "commercial," in which case it is generally not protected. For instance, the use of a person's identity in news, entertainment, and creative works for the purpose of communicating information or expressive ideas about that person is protected "expressive" speech. On the other hand, the use of a person's identity for purely commercial purposes, like advertising goods or services or the use of a person's name or likeness on merchandise, is rarely protected.

. . .

As discussed, Twist made a submissible case that respondents' use of his name and identity was for a commercial advantage. Nonetheless, there is still an expressive component in the use of his name and identity as a metaphorical reference to tough-guy "enforcers." And yet, respondents agree (perhaps to avoid a defamation claim) that the use was not a parody or other expressive comment or a fictionalized account of the real Twist. As such, the metaphorical reference to Twist, though a literary device, has very little literary value compared to its commercial value. On the record here, the use and identity of Twist's name has become predominantly a ploy to sell comic books and related products rather than an artistic or literary expression, and under these circumstances, free speech must give way to the right of publicity.

. . .

VI.

For the foregoing reasons, the circuit court's judgment notwithstanding the verdict is reversed, the judgment granting a new trial is affirmed, the judgment denying injunctive relief is affirmed, and the case is remanded.

(Unanimous)

INTEL CORP. V. HAMIDI

Supreme Court of California
30 Cal. 4th 1342 (2003)

WERDEGAR, J.

Intel Corporation (Intel) maintains an electronic mail system, connected to the Internet, through which messages between employees and those outside the company can be sent and received, and permits its employees to make reasonable nonbusiness use of this system. On six occasions over almost two years, Kourosh Kenneth Hamidi, a former Intel employee, sent e-mails criticizing Intel's employment practices to numerous current employees on Intel's electronic mail system. Hamidi breached no computer security barriers in order to communicate with Intel employees. He offered to, and did, remove from his mailing list any recipient who so wished. Hamidi's communications to individual Intel employees caused neither physical damage nor functional disruption to the company's computers, nor did they at any time deprive Intel of the use of its computers. The contents of the messages, however, caused discussion among employees and managers.

On these facts, Intel brought suit, claiming that by communicating with its employees over the company's e-mail system Hamidi committed the tort of trespass to chattels. The trial court granted Intel's motion for summary judgment and enjoined Hamidi from any further mailings. A divided Court of Appeal affirmed.

After reviewing the decisions analyzing unauthorized electronic contact with computer systems as potential trespasses to chattels, we conclude that under California law the tort [of trespass] does not encompass, and should not be extended to encompass, an electronic communication that neither damages the recipient computer system nor impairs its functioning. Such an electronic communication does not constitute an actionable trespass to personal property, i.e., the computer system, because it does not interfere with the possessor's use or possession of, or any other legally protected interest in, the personal property itself. . . .

DISCUSSION

I. Current California Tort Law

Dubbed by Prosser the "little brother of conversion," the tort of trespass to chattels allows recovery for interferences with possession of personal property "not sufficiently important to be classed as conversion, and so to compel the defendant to pay the full value of the thing with which he has interfered." (Prosser & Keeton, Torts (5th ed.1984) § 14, pp. 85–86.)

Though not amounting to conversion, the defendant's interference must, to be actionable, have caused some injury to the chattel or to the plaintiff's rights in it. Under California law, trespass to chattels "lies where an intentional interference with the possession of personal property *has proximately caused injury.*" In cases of interference with possession of personal property not amounting to conversion, "the owner has a cause of action for trespass or case, *and may recover only the actual damages suffered by reason of the impairment of the property or the loss of its use.*" In modern American law generally, "[t]respass remains as an occasional remedy for minor interferences, *resulting in some damage,* but not sufficiently serious or sufficiently important to amount to the greater tort" of conversion. (Prosser & Keeton, Torts, *supra,* § 15, p. 90, italics added.)

The Restatement, too, makes clear that some actual injury must have occurred in order for a trespass to chattels to be actionable. Under section 218 of the Restatement Second of Torts, dispossession alone, without further damages, is actionable (see *id.,* par. (a) & com. d, pp. 420–421), but other forms of interference require some additional harm to the personal property or the possessor's interests in it. (*Id.,* pars. (b)–(d).) "The interest of a possessor of a chattel in its inviolability, unlike the similar interest of a possessor of land, is not given legal protection by an action for nominal damages for harmless intermeddlings with the chattel. In order that an actor who interferes with another's chattel may be liable, his conduct must affect some other and more important interest of the possessor. *Therefore, one who intentionally intermeddles with another's chattel is subject to liability only if his intermeddling is harmful to the possessor's materially valuable interest in the physical condition, quality, or value of the chattel, or if the possessor is deprived of the use of the chattel for a substantial time, or some other legally protected interest of the possessor is affected as stated in Clause (c).* Sufficient legal protection of the possessor's interest in the mere inviolability of his chattel is afforded by his privilege to use reasonable force to protect his possession against even harmless interference." (*Id.,* com. e, pp. 421–422, italics added.)

. . . .

Intel suggests that the requirement of actual harm does not apply here because it sought only injunctive relief, as protection from future injuries. But as Justice Kolkey, dissenting below, observed, "[t]he fact the relief sought is injunctive does not excuse a showing of injury, whether actual or threatened." Indeed, in order to obtain injunctive relief the plaintiff must ordinarily show that the defendant's wrongful acts threaten to cause *irreparable* injuries, ones that cannot be adequately compensated in damages. (5 Witkin, Cal. Procedure (4th ed. 1997) Pleading, § 782, p. 239.)

. . . .

The dispositive issue in this case, therefore, is whether the undisputed facts demonstrate Hamidi's actions caused or threatened to cause damage to Intel's computer system, or injury to its rights in that personal property, such as to entitle Intel to judgment as a matter of law. To review, the undisputed evidence revealed no actual or threatened damage to Intel's computer hardware or software and no interference with its ordinary and intended operation. Intel was not dispossessed of its computers, nor did Hamidi's messages prevent Intel from using its computers for any measurable length of time. Intel presented no evidence its system was slowed or otherwise impaired by the burden of delivering Hamidi's electronic messages. Nor was there any evidence transmission of the messages imposed any marginal cost on the operation of Intel's computers. In sum, no evidence suggested that in sending messages through Intel's Internet connections and internal computer system Hamidi used the system in any manner in which it was not intended to function or impaired the system in any way. . . .

Intel relies on language in the *eBay* decision suggesting that unauthorized use of another's chattel is actionable even without any showing of injury: "Even if, as [defendant] BE argues, its searches use only a small amount of eBay's computer system capacity, BE has nonetheless deprived eBay of the ability to use that portion of its personal property for its own purposes. The law recognizes no such right to use another's personal property." (*eBay, supra,* 100 F.Supp.2d at p. 1071.) But as the *eBay* court went on immediately to find that the defendant's conduct, if widely replicated, *would* likely impair the functioning of the plaintiff's system (*id.* at pp. 1071–1072), we do not read the quoted remarks as expressing the court's complete view of the issue. In isolation, moreover, they would not be a correct statement of California or general American law on this point. While one may have no *right* temporarily to use another's personal property, such use is actionable as a trespass only if it "has proximately caused injury."

. . . .

Writing on behalf of several industry groups appearing as amici curiae, Professor Richard A. Epstein of the University of Chicago urges us to excuse the required showing of injury to personal property in cases of unauthorized electronic contact between computers, "extending the rules of trespass to real property to all interactive Web sites and servers." The court is thus urged to recognize, for owners of a particular species of personal property, computer servers, the same interest in inviolability as is generally accorded a possessor of land. In effect, Professor Epstein suggests that a company's server should be its castle, upon which any unauthorized intrusion, however harmless, is a trespass.

. . . .

Other scholars are less optimistic about such a complete propertization of the Internet. Professor Mark Lemley of the University of California, Berkeley, writing on behalf of an amici curiae group of professors of intellectual property and computer law, observes that under a property rule of server inviolability, "each of the hundreds of millions of [Internet] users must get permission in advance from anyone with whom they want to communicate and anyone who owns a server through which their message may travel." The consequence for e-mail could be a substantial reduction in the freedom of electronic communication, as the owner of each computer through which an electronic message passes could impose its own limitations on message content or source. As Professor Dan Hunter of the University of Pennsylvania asks rhetorically: "Does this mean that one must read the 'Terms of Acceptable Email Usage' of every email system that one emails in the course of an ordinary day? If the University of Pennsylvania had a policy that sending a joke by email would be an unauthorized use of their system, then under the logic of [the lower court decision in this case], you commit 'trespass' if you emailed me a . . . cartoon." (Hunter, *Cyberspace as Place, and the Tragedy of the Digital Anticommons* (2003) 91 Cal. L.Rev. 439, 508–509.)

. . . .

A leading scholar of Internet law and policy, Professor Lawrence Lessig of Stanford University, has criticized Professor Epstein's theory of the computer server as quasi-real property, previously put forward in the *eBay* case (*eBay, supra,* 100 F.Supp.2d 1058), on the ground that it ignores the costs to society in the loss of network benefits: "eBay benefits greatly from a network that is open and where access is free. It is this general feature of the Net that makes the Net so valuable to users and a source of great innovation. And to the extent that individual sites begin to impose their own rules of exclusion, the value of the network as a network declines. If machines must negotiate before entering any individual site, then the costs of using the network climb." (Lessig, The Future of Ideas: The Fate of the Commons in a Connected World (2001) p. 171; see also Hunter, *Cyberspace as Place, and the Tragedy of the Digital Anticommons, supra,* 91 Cal. L.Rev. at p. 512 ["If we continue to mark out anticommons claims in cyberspace, not only will we preclude better, more innovative uses of cyberspace resources, but we will lose sight of what might be possible"].)

We discuss this debate among the amici curiae and academic writers only to note its existence and contours, not to attempt its resolution. Creating an absolute property right to exclude undesired communications from one's e-mail and Web servers might help force spammers to internalize the costs they impose on ISP's and their customers. But such a property rule might also create substantial new costs, to e-mail and e-commerce users and to society generally, in lost ease and openness of communication and in lost network benefits. In light of the unresolved controversy, we would be acting rashly to adopt a rule treating computer servers as real property for purposes of trespass law.

WE CONCUR: KENNARD, MORENO and PERREN, JJ.

Concurring Opinion by KENNARD, J.

I concur.

Does a person commit the tort of trespass to chattels by making occasional personal calls to a mobile phone despite the stated objection of the person who owns the mobile phone and pays for the mobile phone service? Does it matter that the calls are not made to the mobile phone's owner, but to another person who ordinarily uses that phone? Does it matter that the person to whom the calls are made has not objected to them? Does it matter that the calls do not damage the mobile phone or reduce in any significant way its availability or usefulness?

The majority concludes, and I agree, that using another's equipment to communicate with a third person who is an authorized user of the equipment and who does not object to the communication is trespass to chattels only if the communications damage the equipment or in some significant way impair its usefulness or availability.

Intel has my sympathy. Unsolicited and unwanted bulk e-mail, most of it commercial, is a serious annoyance and inconvenience for persons who communicate electronically through the Internet, and bulk e-mail that distracts employees in the workplace can adversely affect overall productivity. But, as the majority persuasively explains, to establish the tort of trespass to chattels in California, the plaintiff must prove either damage to the plaintiff's personal property or actual or threatened impairment of the plaintiff's ability to use that property. Because plaintiff Intel has not shown that defendant Hamidi's occasional bulk e-mail messages to Intel's employees have damaged Intel's computer system or impaired its functioning in any significant way, Intel has not established the tort of trespass to chattels.

Dissenting Opinion of BROWN, J.

. . . .

Intel has invested millions of dollars to develop and maintain a computer system. It did this not to act as a public forum but to enhance the productivity of its employees. Kourosh Kenneth Hamidi sent as many as 200,000 e-mail messages to Intel employees. The time required to review and delete Hamidi's messages diverted employees from productive tasks and undermined the utility of the computer system. "There may . . . be situations in which the value to the owner of a particular type of chattel may be impaired by dealing with it in a manner that does not affect its physical condition." (Rest.2d Torts, § 218, com. h, p. 422.) This is such a case.

The majority refuses to protect Intel's interest in maintaining the integrity of its own system, contending that (1) Hamidi's mailings did not physically injure the system; (2) Intel receives many unwanted messages, of which Hamidi's are but a small fraction; (3) Intel must have contemplated that it would receive some unwanted messages; and (4) Hamidi used the e-mail system for its intended purpose, to communicate with employees.

. . . .

Because I do not share the majority's antipathy toward property rights and believe the proper balance between expressive activity and property protection can be achieved without distorting the law of trespass, I respectfully dissent.

Intel had the right to exclude the unwanted speaker from its property, which Hamidi does not dispute; he does not argue that he has a to right force unwanted messages on Intel. The instant case thus turns on the question of whether Intel deserves a remedy for the continuing violation of its rights. I believe it does, and as numerous cases have demonstrated, an injunction to prevent a trespass to chattels is an appropriate means of enforcement.

The majority denies relief on the theory that Intel has failed to establish the requisite actual injury. As discussed, *post,* however, the injunction was properly granted because the rule requiring actual injury pertains to damages, not equitable relief, and thus courts considering comparable intrusions have provided injunctive relief without a showing of actual injury. Furthermore, there was actual injury as (1) Intel suffered economic loss; (2) it is sufficient for the injury to impair the chattel's utility to the owner rather than the chattel's market value; and (3) even in the absence of any injury to the owner's utility, it is nevertheless a trespass where one party expropriates for his own use the resources paid for by another.

Harmless Trespasses to Chattels May be Prevented

Defendant Hamidi used Intel's server in violation of the latter's demand to stop. This unlawful use of Intel's system interfered with the use of the system by Intel employees. This misconduct creates a cause of action. "[I]t is a trespass to damage goods or destroy them, *to make an unpermitted use of them,* or to move them from one place to another." (Prosser & Keeton on Torts (5th ed. 1984) Trespass to Chattels, § 14, p. 85, fns. omitted & italics added.) "[T]he unlawful taking away of another's personal property, the seizure of property upon a wrongful execution, and *the appropriation of another's property to one's own use, even for a temporary purpose,* constitute trespasses, although a mere removal of property without injuring it is not a trespass *when done by one acting rightfully.*" (7 Speiser et al., American Law of Torts (1990) Trespass, § 23:23, p. 667 (Speiser) fns. omitted & italics added.)

The law's special respect for land ownership supports liability for damages even without actual harm. (Speiser, *supra,* § 23:1, p. 592.) By contrast, one who suffers interference with a chattel may *prevent* the interference before or during the fact, *or recover actual damages* (corresponding to the harm suffered), but at least according to the Restatement, may not recover damages in excess of those suffered. But the Restatement expressly refutes defendant's assertion that only real property is inviolable. From the modest distinction holding that only victims of a trespass to land may profit in the form of damages exceeding actual harm, defendant offers the position that only trespasses to land may be *prevented.* The law is to the contrary; numerous cases have authorized injunctive relief to safeguard the inviolability of personal property.

. . . .

Hamidi concedes Intel's legal entitlement to block the unwanted messages. The problem is that although Intel has resorted to the cyberspace version of reasonable force, it has so far been unsuccessful in determining how to resist the unwanted use of its system. Thus, while Intel has the legal right to exclude Hamidi from its system, it does not have the physical ability. It *may* forbid Hamidi's use, but it *cannot* prevent it.

To the majority, Hamidi's ability to outwit Intel's cyber defenses justifies denial of Intel's claim to exclusive use of its property. Under this reasoning, it is not right but might that determines the extent of a party's possessory interest. Although the world often works this way, the legal system should not.

. . . .

The principles of both personal liberty and social utility should counsel us to usher the common law of property into the digital age.

Dissenting Opinion by MOSK, J.

. . . .

The Restatement Second of Torts explains that a trespass to a chattel occurs if "the chattel is impaired as to its *condition, quality, or value*" or if "harm is caused to some . . . thing in which the possessor has a legally protected interest." (Rest.2d Torts, § 218, subds. (b) & (d), p. 420, italics added.) As to this tort, a current prominent treatise on the law of torts explains that "[t]he defendant may interfere with the chattel by interfering with the plaintiff's access or use" and observes that the tort has been applied so as "to protect computer systems from electronic invasions by way of unsolicited email or the like." (1 Dobbs, The Law of Torts (2001) § 60, pp. 122 123.) Moreover, "[t]he harm necessary to trigger liability for trespass to chattels can be . . . harm to something other than the chattel itself." (*Id.*, pp. 124–125; see also 1 Harper et al., The Law of Torts (3d ed.1996 & 2003 supp.) § 2.3, pp. 2:14–2:18.) The Restatement points out that, unlike a possessor of land, a possessor of a chattel is not given legal protection from harmless invasion, but "the actor" may be liable if the conduct affects "some other and more important *interest* of the possessor." (Rest.2d Torts, § 218, com. (e), p. 421, italics added.)

. . . .

The common law tort of trespass to chattels does not require physical disruption to the chattel. It also may apply when there is impairment to the "quality" or "value" of the chattel. (Rest.2d Torts, § 218, subd. (b), p. 420; see also *id.,* com. (e), pp. 421–422 [liability if "intermeddling is harmful to the possessor's materially valuable interest in the physical condition, quality, or value of the chattel"].) Moreover, as we held in *Zaslow v. Kroenert* (1946) 29 Cal.2d 541, 551, 176 P.2d 1, it also applies "[w]here the conduct complained of does not amount to a substantial interference with possession or the right thereto, but consists of intermeddling with or use of or damages to the personal property."

Here, Hamidi's deliberate and continued intermeddling, and threatened intermeddling, with Intel's proprietary computer system for his own purposes that were hostile to Intel, certainly impaired the quality and value of the system as an internal business device for Intel and forced Intel to incur costs to try to maintain the security and integrity of its server—efforts that proved ineffective. These included costs incurred to mitigate injuries that had already occurred. . . . Indeed, part of the value of the proprietary computer system is the ability to exclude intermeddlers from entering it for significant uses that are disruptive to its owner's business operations.

DISCUSSION PROBLEMS

1. A Perfect 10

A "Google Image Search" provides search results as a webpage of small images called "thumbnails," which are stored in Google's servers. The thumbnail images are reduced, lower-resolution versions of full-sized images stored on third-party computers. When a user clicks on a thumbnail image, he is given the option of connecting his browser to the website publisher's computer, which then downloads the full-size image, and makes the image appear at the bottom of the window on the user's screen. Google does not store the images that fill this lower part of the window and does not communicate the images to the user; Google simply provides HTML instructions directing a user's browser to access a third-party website. However, the top part of the window (containing the information from the Google webpage) appears to frame and comment on the bottom part of the window. Thus, the user's window appears to be filled with a single integrated presentation of the full-size image, but it is actually an image from a third-party website framed by information from Google's website. The process by which the webpage directs a user's browser to incorporate content from different computers into a single window is referred to as "in-line linking."

Perfect 10 publishes a magazine and operates a website that features nude photographs of models. It objected to Google creating thumbnail images of its photos and linking to the full-size images on Perfect 10's website. Can it prevent Google from using its photographs in these ways?

2. Ceramic Tiles

Annie Lee is an artist who sells her designs in the form of notecards of small lithographs. A.R.T. Company purchased some of Lee's cards and prints, mounted them on ceramic tiles, covered the artwork with a transparent epoxy resin, and sold the tiles to third parties. Lee contends that A.R.T. violated her copyright by creating derivative works from her original art without her permission. According to the Copyright Act:

> A "derivative work" is a work based upon one or more preexisting works, such as a translation, musical arrangement, dramatization, fictionalization, motion picture version, sound recording, art reproduction, abridgment, condensation, or any other form in which a work may be recast, transformed, or adapted. A work consisting of editorial revisions, annotations, elaborations, or other modifications, which, as a whole, represent an original work of authorship, is a "derivative work."

17 U.S.C. 101. The Act provides copyright owners with exclusive rights to "prepare derivative works based upon the copyrighted work." 17 U.S.C. 106(2).

If Lee sues A.R.T., should she prevail?

3. The Wheel of Fortune

In the 1980s, Samsung Electronics designed an advertising campaign that emphasized the durability of its products by suggesting that those products would last far into the future. In what it internally referred to as the "Vanna White" ad, one advertisement depicted a robot wearing a wig, gown, and jewelry that resembled White's hair and dress, posed next to a game board recognizable as the board used on the television game show "Wheel of Fortune," with a caption reading "Longest-Running game show. 2012 A.D." Vanna White, the long-time hostess of "Wheel of Fortune," objected and filed suit against Samsung for violating her common law right of publicity. Can White prevent Samsung from using elements of her likeness without her permission?

CHAPTER 6

BATTERY

■ ■ ■

INTRODUCTION

The law of property can be understood as the set of legal principles that governs the rights that people have relative to other people concerning things. The law of torts (i.e., harms) can be understood as the legal principles that provide a remedy for intrusions of property rights (assuming that we understand our bodies as a form of property, since tort law protects against physical harm, in addition to interference with rights in land, chattels, and intellectual creations). Whether an act that intrudes upon a property right constitutes a tort, and thus gives rise to a remedy, usually depends not only on whether an actor causes a harm, but also on that actor's mental state, or *mens rea*. In some circumstances, the law requires that the actor intend to cause the harm, although the actor sometimes need not intend the extent of the injury or desire any injury at all. Trespass, nuisance, and battery are all *intentional* torts in this sense.

The law of battery raises several interesting doctrinal questions that similarly arise in many areas of law. For a battery to occur, an actor must have intended to cause a harmful or offensive contact (or threat thereof), and a harmful or offensive contact must actually have occurred. Rest. (2d) §§ 13, 18. One issue is what, precisely, must be "intended" in the subjective mind of the defendant: merely the contact, or contact of a certain variety? *Reynolds v. MacFarlane* explores this question, along with the question of what interference satisfies the doctrine's "contact" requirement. A second issue, with implications beyond the law of battery, is from what point of view should the question of whether contact is harmful or offensive be judged. An "objective" standard calls for the contact to be evaluated from a neutral perspective, or one of a "reasonable person"; that is, was the contact objectively harmful or offensive. In contrast, a "subjective" standard calls for the contact to be evaluated from the perspective of the claimant; that is, was the contact actually harmful or offensive to the purported victim. *Wishnatsky v. Huey* explores this distinction.

At a higher level of principle, there is an unaddressed question in the law concerning why battery law is not usually understood as a means of resolving a type of incompatible use problem, in the way that nuisance is. Physical contact is the result of two people trying to make use of the same space; is it always obvious which party should bear the consequences of this conflict? For example, if Reynolds' and MacFarlane's hands come into contact with each other during a scuffle over a $10 bill, why is it that the law privileges Reynolds' claim to that space?

Restatement (Second) of Torts § 13. Battery: Harmful Contact

An actor is subject to liability to another for battery if

(a) He acts intending to cause a harmful or offensive contact with the person of the other or a third person, or an imminent apprehension of such a contact, and

(b) A harmful contact with the person of the other directly or indirectly results.

Comment:

c. . . . If an act is done with the intention described in this Section, it is immaterial that the actor is not inspired by any personal hostility to the other, or a desire to injure him. . . .

Restatement (Second) of Torts § 18. Battery: Offensive Contact

(1) An actor is subject to liability to another for battery if

(a) he acts intending to cause a harmful or offensive contact with the person of the other or a third person, or an imminent apprehension of such a contact, and

(b) an offensive contact with the person of the other directly or indirectly results

Comment:

c. *Meaning of "contact with another's person."* In order to make the actor liable under the rule stated in this Section, it is not necessary that he should bring any part of his own body in contact with another's person. It is enough that he intentionally cause his clothing or anything held or attached to him to come into such contact. So too, he is liable under the rule stated in this Section if he throws a substance, such as water, upon the other or if he sets a dog upon him. It is not necessary that the contact with the other's person be directly caused by some act of the actor. All that is necessary is that the actor intend to cause the other, directly or indirectly, to come in contact with a foreign substance in a manner which the other will reasonably regard as offensive.

Restatement (Second) of Torts § 19. What Constitutes Offensive Contact

A bodily contact is offensive if it offends a reasonable sense of personal dignity.

Comment:

a. In order that a contact be offensive to a reasonable sense of personal dignity, it must be one which would offend the ordinary person and as such one not unduly sensitive as to his personal dignity. It must, therefore, be a contact which is unwarranted by the social usages prevalent at the time and place at which it is inflicted.

CASES

REYNOLDS V. MACFARLANE

Court of Appeals of Utah
322 P.3d 755 (2014)

BENCH, SENIOR JUDGE:

John Reynolds appeals from the trial court's dismissal of his intentional tort claims against Bret MacFarlane. We affirm in part, reverse in part, and remand to the trial court.

On August 5, 2009, MacFarlane walked into the break room at his workplace where his coworker, Reynolds, was standing in front of the microwave oven. Reynolds was holding a ten dollar bill somewhat loosely in his hand. Reynolds was unaware of MacFarlane's presence. MacFarlane approached Reynolds from behind and, without touching Reynolds, quickly snatched the ten dollar bill. Reynolds immediately spun around and faced MacFarlane. MacFarlane then stated, "That was too easy," and returned the ten dollar bill to Reynolds. As MacFarlane began to walk away, Reynolds struck MacFarlane, splitting his lip. MacFarlane asked why he hit him. Reynolds replied, "You pissed me off."

. . .

Nearly one year later, Reynolds filed a complaint against MacFarlane . . . for battery. The court granted Reynolds's motion. After hearing the evidence, the trial court found MacFarlane "to be more credible in that [his] testimony was more consistent and was corroborated by multiple parties." Accordingly, the court based its findings of fact largely on MacFarlane's testimony. The trial court concluded that Reynolds had not met his burden of proof to show that MacFarlane had committed an assault or a battery against him and then dismissed the case with prejudice. Reynolds appeals.

. . .

II. Battery

Reynolds . . . challenges the trial court's determination that he failed to establish the elements of a battery. We review the trial court's legal conclusions for correctness.

Utah has adopted the Restatement (Second) of Torts to define the elements of the intentional tort of battery. Consequently, an actor is liable for battery if " '(a) he acts intending to cause a harmful or offensive contact with the person of the other . . . or an imminent apprehension of such a contact, and (b) a harmful contact with the person of the other directly or indirectly results.' " *Id.* (quoting Restatement (Second) of Torts § 13 (1965)).

In this case, the trial court found that MacFarlane did not touch Reynolds when he grabbed the ten dollar bill from Reynolds's hand. Because "MacFarlane never touched or came into contact with Reynolds," the trial court concluded that Reynolds did not meet his burden of proof to show that a harmful contact resulted from MacFarlane's action. Reynolds asserts that the trial court's conclusion is erroneous because MacFarlane's grabbing of an object—the ten dollar bill—from his hand was sufficient contact with his person to constitute a battery.

For the intentional tort of battery, harmful or offensive contact "includes all physical contacts that the individual either expressly communicates are unwanted, or those contacts to which no reasonable person would consent."

But "it is not necessary that the plaintiff's actual body be disturbed." Restatement (Second) of Torts § 18 cmt. c (1965). Rather, "[p]rotection of the interest in freedom from intentional and unpermitted contacts with the plaintiff's person extends to any part of the body, or to anything which is attached to it and practically identified with it." W. Page Keeton et al., *Prosser and Keeton on the Law of Torts* § 9, at 39 (5th ed.1984) (footnote omitted). "Thus, if all other requisites of a battery against the plaintiff are satisfied, contact with the plaintiff's clothing, or with a cane, a paper, or any other object held in the plaintiff's hand, will be sufficient" to support a battery claim because the "interest in the integrity of [a] person includes all those things which are in contact or connected with the person." *Id.* § 9, at 39–40 (footnotes omitted); *see also Morgan v. Loyacomo*, 190 Miss. 656, 1 So.2d 510, 511 (1941) ("[T]o constitute assault and battery, it is not necessary to touch the plaintiff's body or even his clothing; knocking or snatching anything from [the] plaintiff's hand or touching anything connected with his person, when done in a rude or insolent manner, is sufficient."); *Picard v. Barry Pontiac-Buick, Inc.*, 654 A.2d 690, 694 (R.I.1995) ("[D]efendant's offensive contact with an object attached to or identified with plaintiff's body was sufficient to constitute a battery.");

Fisher v. Carrousel Motor Hotel, Inc., 424 S.W.2d 627, 629 (Tex.1967) ("The intentional snatching of an object from one's hand is as clearly an offensive invasion of his person as would be an actual contact with the body."). *But see Workman v. United Fixtures Co.*, 116 F.Supp.2d 885, 896–97 (W.D.Mich.2000) (concluding that even if the defendant removed a paper from the plaintiff's hand, "nothing in the record suggests that [the defendant's] alleged actions amounted to an offensive contact battery"). We consider the above authorities as persuasive and not inconsistent with our supreme court's battery analysis.

In this case, MacFarlane's act of taking the ten dollar bill held loosely in Reynolds's hand was sufficient contact to constitute the contact element of battery, *see Wagner*, 2005 UT 54, ¶ 16, 122 P.3d 599, notwithstanding the fact that MacFarlane did not touch Reynolds's body. When held in his hand, the ten dollar bill was connected to Reynolds such that when MacFarlane snatched the bill from Reynolds, MacFarlane's act resulted in offensive contact with Reynolds's person. The intent element of battery was also met in this case because the trial court found that MacFarlane intended to take the bill from Reynolds's hand when he acted. *See id.* ¶ 29 ("[T]he only intent required to commit a battery is the intent to make a contact, not an intent to harm, injure, or offend through that contact."). Accordingly, we conclude that the trial court erred in dismissing Reynolds's battery claim because the court's factual findings establish both elements of the claim.

The trial court determined that Reynolds suffered no damages as a result of the August 5, 2009 incident. The Utah Supreme Court has explained that "[a] harmful or offensive contact is simply one to which the recipient of the contact has not consented either directly or by implication." "[H]armful or offensive contact is *not limited to that which is medically injurious* or perpetrated with the intent to cause some form of psychological or physical injury." *Id.* (emphasis added). Instead, harmful or offensive contact "includes all physical contacts that the individual either expressly communicates are unwanted, or those contacts to which no reasonable person would consent." *Id.* Moreover, "[c]ommon law battery does not require that the nonconsensual contact be injurious. Rather, proof of an unauthorized invasion of the plaintiff's person, even if harmless, *entitles him to at least nominal damages.*" *Lounsbury v. Capel*, 836 P.2d 188, 192–93 (Utah Ct.App.1992) (emphasis added); *see also id.* at 196 ("[A plaintiff] need not prove injury to sustain his battery claim; if he proves no more than the 'offense' of the nonconsensual touching, he is entitled to nominal damages."); Keeton et al. § 9, at 41 ("[T]he defendant is liable not only for contacts which do actual physical harm, but also for those relatively trivial ones which are merely offensive and insulting."). "Damages for pain, suffering, 'psychological problems' and the like, however, may . . . be recovered only to the extent that [the plaintiff] proves they were a proximate result" of the nonconsensual touching. *Lounsbury,* 836 P.2d at 196.

Here, the trial court found that "no injury resulted to Reynolds as a direct and proximate cause of MacFarlane's actions." Thus, the trial court ruled that Reynolds's claimed damages—the one-day suspension and his medical issues following the break-room incident with MacFarlane—were not proximately caused by MacFarlane's act. Reynolds has not effectively challenged this ruling on appeal. However, because we have concluded that MacFarlane committed a battery, Reynolds is entitled to nominal damages. Accordingly, we remand to the trial court for an award of nominal damages to Reynolds for battery.

WISHNATSKY V. HUEY

Court of Appeals of North Dakota
584 N.W.2d 859 (1998)

PER CURIAM.

Martin Wishnatsky appealed a summary judgment dismissing his battery action against David W. Huey, and an order denying his motion for an altered judgment. We conclude, as a matter of law, that no battery occurred, and we affirm the judgment and the order.

On January 10, 1996, Huey, an assistant attorney general, was engaged in a conversation with attorney Peter B. Crary in Crary's office. Without knocking or announcing his entry, Wishnatsky, who performs paralegal work for Crary, attempted to enter the office. Huey pushed the door closed, thereby pushing Wishnatsky back into the hall. Wishnatsky reentered the office and Huey left.

Wishnatsky brought an action against Huey, seeking damages for battery. Huey moved for summary judgment of dismissal. The trial court granted Huey's motion and a judgment of dismissal was entered. . . .

. . . .

"In its original conception [battery] meant the infliction of physical injury." VIII Sir William Holdsworth, *A History of English Law* 422 (2d Impression 1973). By the Eighteenth Century, the requirement of an actual physical injury had been eliminated:

> At Nisi Prius, upon evidence in trespass for assault and battery, Holt, C.J. declared,
>
> > 1. That the least touching of another in anger is a battery. 2. If two or more meet in a narrow passage, and without any violence or design of harm, the one touches the other gently, it is no battery. 3. If any of them use violence against the other, to force his way in a rude inordinate manner, it is a

> battery; or any struggle about the passage, to that degree as may do hurt, is a battery. Vid.Bro.Tresp. 236. 7 E. 4, 26. 22 Ass. 60. 3 H. 4, 9.

Cole v. Turner, Pasch. 3 Ann., 63 Ann., 6 Mod. 149, 90 Eng.Rep. 958 (1704). Blackstone explained:

> The least touching of another's person willfully, or in anger, is a battery; for the law cannot draw the line between different degrees of violence, and therefore totally prohibits the first and lowest stage of it: every man's person being sacred, and no other having a right to meddle with it, in any the slightest manner.

3 William Blackstone, *Commentaries*. On the other hand, "in a crowded world, a certain amount of personal contact is inevitable, and must be accepted." W. Page Keeton et al., *Prosser and Keeton on the Law of Torts* § 9, at 42 (5th ed.1984).

The American Law Institute has balanced the interest in unwanted contacts and the inevitable contacts in a crowded world in *Restatement (Second) of Torts* §§ 18, 19 (1965):

> 18. Battery: Offensive Contact
>
> (1) An actor is subject to liability to another for battery if
>
> (a) he acts intending to cause a harmful or offensive contact with the person of the other or a third person, or an imminent apprehension of such a contact, and
>
> (b) an offensive contact with the person of the other directly or indirectly results.
>
> (2) An act which is not done with the intention stated in Subsection (1,a) does not make the actor liable to the other for a mere offensive contact with the other's person although the act involves an unreasonable risk of inflicting it and, therefore, would be negligent or reckless if the risk threatened bodily harm.
>
> . . . .
>
> 19. What Constitutes Offensive Contact
>
> A bodily contact is offensive if it offends a reasonable sense of personal dignity.

Comment *c* to § 18 notes that the contact need not be "directly caused by some act of the actor" and also notes that "the essence of the plaintiff's grievance consists in the offense to the dignity involved in the unpermitted and intentional invasion of the inviolability of his person and not in any physical harm done to his body." Comment *a* to § 19 explains what kind of conduct offends a reasonable sense of personal dignity:

> In order that a contact be offensive to a reasonable sense of personal dignity, it must be one which would offend the ordinary person and as such one not unduly sensitive as to his personal dignity. It must, therefore, be a contact which is unwarranted by the social usages prevalent at the time and place at which it is inflicted.
>
> . . . .

Wishnatsky responded to Huey's motion for summary judgment with an affidavit of Crary and with his own affidavit stating in part:

> 1. I am a born-again Christian and cultivate holiness in my life. [A]s a result I am very sensitive to evil spirits and am greatly disturbed by the demonic. However, in Christ there is victory.
>
> 2. On January 9, 1996, Mr. David Huey of the North Dakota Attorney General's office, visited the ministry where I was working at 16 Broadway in Fargo, North Dakota with an ex parte court order.
>
> 3. The following morning I entered the office of Peter Crary, an attorney for whom I do paralegal work, to give him certain papers that had been requested. Mr. Crary was speaking with Mr. David Huey at the time. As I began to enter the office Mr Huey threw his body weight against the door and forced me out into the hall. I had not said a word to him. At the same time, he snarled: "You get out of here." This was very shocking and frightening to me. In all the time I have been working as an aide to Mr. Crary, I have never been physically assaulted or spoken to in a harsh and brutal manner. My blood pressure began to rise, my heart beat accelerated and I felt waves of fear in the pit of my stomach. My hands began to shake and my body to tremble. Composing myself, I reentered the office, whereupon Mr. Huey began a half-demented tirade against me and stormed out into the hall. I looked at Mr. Crary in wonder.

We certainly agree with the Supreme Court's determination that when Wishnatsky attempted to enter the room in which Huey was conversing with Crary, "Huey apparently reacted in a rude and abrupt manner in attempting to exclude Wishnatsky from that conversation." *Wishnatsky v. Huey,* 1997 ND 35, ¶ 15, 560 N.W.2d 878. As a matter of law, however, Huey's "rude and abrupt" conduct did not rise to the level of battery.

The evidence presented to the trial court demonstrates Wishnatsky is "unduly sensitive as to his personal dignity." *Restatement (Second) of Torts* § 19 cmt. a (1965). Without knocking or otherwise announcing his intentions, Wishnatsky opened the door to the office in which Huey and Crary were having a private conversation and attempted to enter. Huey closed the door opened by Wishnatsky, thereby stopping Wishnatsky's forward progress and pushing him back into the hall. The bodily contact was momentary, indirect, and incidental. Viewing the evidence in the light most favorable to Wishnatsky, and giving him the benefit of all favorable inferences which can reasonably be drawn from the evidence, we conclude Huey's conduct in response to Wishnatsky's intrusion into his private conversation with Crary, while "rude and abrupt," would not "be offensive to a reasonable sense of personal dignity." In short, an "ordinary person . . . not unduly sensitive as to his personal dignity" intruding upon a private conversation in Wishnatsky's manner would not have been offended by Huey's response to the intrusion. We conclude that Huey's conduct did not constitute an offensive-contact-battery, as a matter of law, and the trial court did not err in granting Huey's motion for summary judgment dismissing Wishnatsky's action.

Affirmed.

DISCUSSION PROBLEMS

1. The Great American Smokeout

The year was 1990. Radio talk show host Bill Cunningham invited an anti-smoking advocate, Ahron Leichtman, on his show on the date of an event called "The Great American Smokeout," purportedly to discuss the harmful effects of second-hand smoke. During the show, Cunningham encouraged his side-kick, Andy Furman, another employee of the radio station, to light a cigar and blow smoke repeatedly in Leichtman's face. Leichtman sued Cunningham, Furman, and the station for battery. Should he prevail?

2. Smoking in an Office

William McCracken, a postal service employee, visited the office of O.B. Sloan, the postmaster of Charlotte, North Carolina, on two occasions to discuss his application for sick leave because of his allergies to tobacco smoke. According to McCracken's physician, he suffered allergies of "3+ on a scale of one to four." The two men agreed that, at a 1975 meeting, Sloan said, "Bill, I know you claim to have an allergy to tobacco smoke and you have presented statements from your doctor stating this, but there is no law against smoking, so I'm going to smoke," and that Sloan then smoked a cigar in McCracken's presence. Does McCracken have a valid battery claim against Sloan?

3. The Shoulder Massage

Paul Holbrook and Meredith Paul were co-workers at a medical supply company in the mid-1990s who worked alone together on occasion. According to Paul, Holbrook asked her to wear revealing clothing and suggested that they engage in sexual relations. On two occasions in which they were alone, Holbrook tried to massage Paul's shoulders. On both occasions, Paul pulled away and told Holbrook to leave, which he did. After these events, Paul complained to management, and the two never again worked the same shifts and his behavior toward her ceased. Do these events constitute a battery?

CHAPTER 7

STRICT LIABILITY

■ ■ ■

INTRODUCTION

Intentional torts, such as battery, require the *mens rea* of "intent." The tort of negligence, which we examine in Chapters 8–10, requires the lesser *mens rea* of "negligence." Rest. (3d) Torts § 3. Other torts, known as "strict liability" torts, have no *mens rea* requirement at all, meaning that all that is needed for liability to attach is for an actor's action to cause an injury. In American law, liability for harm is strict in a limited range of circumstances, most notably in the case of "abnormally dangerous activities." Rest. (3d) Torts § 20.

Rylands v. Fletcher and *Brown v. Collins* are seminal 19th century cases from Great Britain and the United States (New Hampshire), respectively, that grapple with the choice between strict liability and fault-based liability and reach different conclusions. What arguments support strict liability? What arguments support a requirement of fault? Which court offers the more convincing analysis?

When negligence is the standard for liability, damages are reduced if the negligence of the injured party contributes to the injury. But to what extent? *McIntire v. Ballentine* exemplifies the modern shift away from a rule of "contributory negligence," which precludes recovery if the plaintiff is partially at fault, to "comparative fault," which reduces the plaintiff's recovery (but does not preclude it) to the extent both parties share fault.

Restatement (Third) of Torts § 1. Intent

A person acts with the intent to produce a consequence if:

(a) the person acts with the purpose of producing that consequence; or

(b) the person acts knowing that the consequence is substantially certain to result.

Comment:

d. Relationship between intent and negligence. The conclusion that a person's conduct is not intentionally harmful leaves open the possibility that the conduct is tortious under some other theory. An intentional tort requires that the actor desires the harm to occur or knows that the harm is substantially certain to occur. In a negligence case the defendant does not desire to cause harm, and in a typical negligence case harm is a possibility but not a certainty. For purposes of finding negligence, under § 3, it suffices if the actor knows or can foresee the possibility of harm and can eliminate or reduce that possibility by adopting reasonable precautions.

Restatement (Third) of Torts § 4. Physical Harm

"Physical harm" means the physical impairment of the human body ("bodily harm") or of real property or tangible personal property ("property damage"). Bodily harm includes physical injury, illness, disease, impairment of bodily function, and death.

Comment:

b. Bodily harm and emotional harm. The definition of bodily harm is meant to preserve the ordinary distinction between bodily harm and emotional harm. Accordingly, if the defendant's negligent conduct (for example, negligent driving) frightens the plaintiff (for example, a pedestrian crossing the street), the harm to the plaintiff's nerve centers caused by this fear does not constitute bodily harm. This distinction is not precise and may be difficult to make in certain cases, but the more restrictive rules for recovery for emotional harm require that such determinations be made. . . .

Restatement (Third) of Torts § 20. Abnormally Dangerous Activities

(a) An actor who carries on an abnormally dangerous activity is subject to strict liability for physical harm resulting from the activity.

(b) An activity is abnormally dangerous if:

(1) the activity creates a foreseeable and highly significant risk of physical harm even when reasonable care is exercised by all actors; and

(2) the activity is not one of common usage.

Restatement (Third) of Torts § 21. Intrusion by Livestock or Other Animals

An owner or possessor of livestock or other animals, except for dogs and cats, that intrude upon the land of another is subject to strict liability for physical harm caused by the intrusion.

Comment:

d. Rationale. This Section accepts the traditional English rule, which is itself accepted by a significant number of American jurisdictions. . . .On balance, . . .in livestock-trespass cases it is wiser to place upon the livestock owner the primary obligation of avoiding harm by building fences. Moreover, in the large majority of cases, if the livestock owner does exercise reasonable care in erecting and maintaining a fence, that fence will suffice in restraining the livestock. Nevertheless, in a limited number of cases in which a fence proves inadequate despite reasonable care, the choice between strict liability and negligence liability for the livestock owner becomes relevant. Overall, strict liability is desirable. Because in most instances a reasonable, nonnegligent fence will succeed in restraining the defendant's livestock, the added burden that strict liability places on the livestock owner is itself limited. In addition, strict liability sets forth a rule that is administratively easy to apply. . . .

Restatement (Third) of Torts § 3. Negligence

A person acts negligently if the person does not exercise reasonable care under all the circumstances. Primary factors to consider in ascertaining whether the person's conduct lacks reasonable care are the foreseeable likelihood that the person's conduct will result in harm, the foreseeable severity of any harm that may ensue, and the burden of precautions to eliminate or reduce the risk of harm.

CASES

RYLANDS V. FLETCHER

House of Lords (G.B)
3 LR HL 330 (1868)

THE LORD CHANCELLOR (Lord *Cairns*):

[Plaintiff] is the occupier of a mine and works under a close of land. The Defendants are the owners of a mill in his neighbourhood, and they proposed to make a reservoir for the purpose of keeping and storing water to be used about their mill upon another close of land, which, for the purposes of this case, may be taken as being adjoining to the close of the Plaintiff, although, in point of fact, some intervening land lay between the two. Underneath the close of land of the Defendants on which they proposed to construct their reservoir there were certain old and disused mining passages and works. There were five vertical shafts, and some horizontal shafts communicating with them. The vertical shafts had been filled up with soil and rubbish, and it does not appear that any person was aware of the existence either of the vertical shafts or of the horizontal works communicating with them. In the course of the working by the Plaintiff of his mine, he had gradually worked through the seams of coal underneath the close, and had come into contact with the old and disused works underneath the close of the Defendants.

In that state of things the reservoir of the Defendants was constructed. . . .[W]hen the reservoir was constructed, and filled, or partly filled, with water, the weight of the water bearing upon the disused and imperfectly filled-up vertical shafts, broke through those shafts. The water passed down them and into the horizontal workings, and from the horizontal workings under the close of the Defendants it passed on into the workings under the close of the Plaintiff, and flooded his mine, causing considerable damage, for which this action was brought.

The Court of Exchequer, when the special case stating the facts to which I have referred, was argued, was of opinion that the Plaintiff had established no cause of action. The Court of Exchequer Chamber, before which an appeal from this judgment was argued, was of a contrary opinion, and the Judges there unanimously arrived at the conclusion that there was a cause of action, and that the Plaintiff was entitled to damages.

My Lords, the principles on which this case must be determined appear to me to be extremely simple. The Defendants, treating them as the owners or occupiers of the close on which the reservoir was constructed, might lawfully have used that close for any purpose for which it might in the ordinary course of the enjoyment of land be used; and if, in what I may term the natural user of that land, there had been any accumulation of water, either on the surface or underground, and if, by the operation of the laws of nature, that accumulation of water had passed off into the close occupied by the Plaintiff, the Plaintiff could not have complained that that result had taken place. If he had desired to guard himself against it, it would have lain upon him to have done so, by leaving, or by interposing, some barrier between his close and the close of the Defendants in order to have prevented that operation of the laws of nature.

. . .

On the other hand if the Defendants, not stopping at the natural use of their close, had desired to use it for any purpose which I may term a non-natural use, for the purpose of introducing into the close that which in its natural condition was not in or upon it, for the purpose of introducing water either above or below ground in quantities and in a manner not the result of any work or operation on or under the land,—and if in consequence of their doing so, or in consequence of any imperfection in the mode of their doing so, the water came to escape and to pass off into the close of the Plaintiff, then it appears to me that that which the Defendants were doing they were doing at their own peril; and, if in the course of their doing it, the evil arose to which I have referred, the evil, namely, of the escape of the water and its passing away to the close of the Plaintiff and injuring the Plaintiff, then for the consequence of that, in my opinion, the Defendants would be liable. . . .

The same result is arrived at on the principles referred to by Mr. Justice *Blackburn* in his judgment, in the Court of Exchequer Chamber, where he states the opinion of that Court as to the law in these words: "We think that the true rule of law is, that the person who, for his own purposes, brings on his land and collects and keeps there anything likely to do mischief if it escapes, must keep it in at his peril; and if he does not do so, is *primâ facie* answerable for all the damage which is the natural consequence of its escape. He can excuse himself by shewing that the escape was owing to the Plaintiff's default; or, perhaps, that the escape was the consequence of *vis major*, or the act of God; but as nothing of this sort exists here, it is unnecessary to inquire what excuse would be sufficient. The general rule, as above stated, seems on principle just. The person whose grass or corn is eaten down by the escaping cattle of his neighbour, or whose mine is flooded by the water from his neighbour's reservoir, or whose cellar is invaded by the filth of his neighbour's privy, or whose habitation is made unhealthy by the fumes and noisome vapours of his neighbour's alkali works, is damnified without any fault of his own; and it seems but reasonable and just that the neighbour who has brought something on his own property (which was not naturally there), harmless to others so long as it is confined to his own property, but which he knows will be mischievous if it gets on his neighbour's, should be obliged to make good the damage which ensues if he does not succeed in confining it to his own property. But for his act in bringing it there no mischief could have accrued, and it seems but just that he should at his peril keep it there, so that no mischief may accrue, or answer for the natural and anticipated consequence. And upon authority this we think is established to be the law, whether the things so brought be beasts, or water, or filth, or stenches."

My Lords, in that opinion, I must say I entirely concur. . . .

LORD CRANWORTH:

My Lords, I concur. . . . If a person brings, or accumulates, on his land anything which, if it should escape, may cause damage to his neighbour, he does so at his peril. If it does escape, and cause damage, he is responsible, however careful he may have been, and whatever precautions he may have taken to prevent the damage.

In considering whether a Defendant is liable to a Plaintiff for damage which the Plaintiff may have sustained, the question in general is not whether the Defendant has acted with due care and caution, but whether his acts have occasioned the damage. . . .For when one person, in managing his own affairs, causes, however innocently, damage to another, it is obviously only just that he should be the party to suffer.

BROWN V. COLLINS

Supreme Court of New Hampshire
53 N.H. 442 (1873)

DOE, J.

It is agreed that the defendant was in the use of ordinary care and skill in managing his horses, until they were frightened; and that they then became unmanageable, and ran against and broke a post on the plaintiff's land. It is not explicitly stated that the defendant was without actual fault,—that he was not guilty of any malice, or unreasonable unskilfulness or negligence; but it is to be inferred that the fact was so: and we decide the case on that ground. We take the case as one where, without actual fault in the defendant, his horses broke from his control, ran away with him, went upon the plaintiff's land, and did damage there, against the will, intent, and desire of the defendant.

. . .

In *Fletcher v. Rylands*, L. R. 3 H. L. 330), Lord CRANWORTH said,—"In considering whether a defendant is liable to a plaintiff for damage which the plaintiff may have sustained, the question in general is not whether the defendant has acted with due care and caution, but whether his acts have occasioned the damage. This is all well explained in the old case of *Lambert v. Bessey*, reported by Sir Thomas Raymond (Sir T. Raym. 421). And the doctrine is founded on good sense. For when one person, in managing his own affairs, causes, however innocently, damage to another, it is obviously only just that he should be the party to suffer."

. . .But the drift of the ancient English authorities on the law of torts seems to differ materially from the view now prevailing in this country. Formerly, in England, there seems to have been no well-defined test of an actionable tort. Defendants were often held liable "because," as Raymond says, "he that is damaged ought to be recompensed;" and not because, upon some clearly stated principle of law founded on actual culpability, public policy, or natural justice, he was entitled to compensation from the defendant. The law was supposed to regard "the loss and damage of the party suffering," more than the negligence and blameworthiness of the defendant: but how much more it regarded the former than the latter, was a question not settled, and very little investigated. "The loss and damage of the party suffering," if without relief, would be a hardship to him; relief compulsorily furnished by the other party would often be a hardship to him: when and why the "loss and damage" should, and when and why they should not, be transferred from one to the other, by process of law, were problems not solved in a philosophical manner. There were precedents, established upon superficial, crude, and undigested notions; but no application of the general system of legal reason to this subject.

Mr. Holmes says, "It may safely be stated that all the more ancient examples are traceable to conceptions of a much ruder sort (than actual fault), and in modern times to more or less definitely thought-out views of public policy. The old writs in trespass did not allege, nor was it necessary to show, anything savoring of culpability. It was enough that a certain event had happened, and it was not even necessary that the act should be done intentionally, though innocently. An accidental blow was as good a cause of action as an intentional one. On the other hand, when, as in *Rylands v. Fletcher,* modern courts hold a man liable for the escape of water from a reservoir which he has built upon his land, or for the escape of cattle, although he is not alleged to have been negligent, they do not proceed upon the ground that there is an element of culpability in making such a reservoir, or in keeping cattle, sufficient to charge the defendant as soon as a *damnum* occurs, but on the principle that it is politic to make those who go into extra-hazardous employments take the risk on their own shoulders." He alludes to the fact that "there is no certainty what will be thought extra-hazardous in a certain jurisdiction at a certain time," but suggests that many particular instances point to the general principle of liability for the consequences of extra-hazardous undertakings as the tacitly assumed ground of decision. If the hazardous nature of things or of acts is adopted as the test, or one of the tests, and the English authorities are taken as the standard of what is to be regarded as hazardous, "it will be necessary to go the length of saying that an owner of real property is liable for all damage resulting to his neighbour's property from anything done upon his own land" (Mellish's argument in *Fletcher v. Rylands,* L. R. 1 Ex. 272), and that an individual is answerable "who, for his own benefit, makes an improvement on his own land, according to his best skill and diligence, and not foreseeing it will produce any injury to his neighbor, if he thereby unwittingly injure his neighbor. If danger is adopted as a test, and the English authorities are abandoned, the fact of danger, controverted in each case, will present a question for the jury, and expand the issue of tort or no tort, into a question of reasonableness in a form much broader than has been generally used; or courts will be left to devise tests of peril, under varying influences of time and place that may not immediately produce a uniform, consistent, and permanent rule.

It would seem that some of the early English decisions were based on a view as narrow as that which regards nothing but the hardship "of the party suffering;" disregards the question whether, by transferring the hardship to the other party, anything more will be done than substitute one suffering party for another; and does not consider what legal reason can be given for relieving the party who has suffered, by making another suffer the expense of his relief. For some of those decisions, better reasons may now be given than were thought of when the decisions were announced: but whether a satisfactory test of an actionable tort can be extracted from the ancient authorities, and whether the few modern cases that carry out the doctrine of those authorities as far as it is carried in *Fletcher v. Rylands* can be sustained, is very doubtful. The current of American authority is very strongly against some of the leading English cases.

. . .*[Fletcher v. Rylands]* seems to be substantially an adoption of the early authorities, and an extension of the ancient practice of holding the defendant liable, in some cases, on the partial view that regarded the misfortune of the plaintiff upon whom a damage had fallen, and required no legal reason for transferring the damage to the defendant. The ancient rule was, that a person in whose house, or on whose land, a fire accidentally originated, which spread to his neighbor's property and destroyed it, must make good the loss. No inquiry was made into the reason of putting upon him his neighbor's loss as well as his own. The rule of such cases is applied, by BLACKBURN, to everything which a man brings on his land, which will, if it escape, naturally do damage. One result of such a doctrine is, that every one building a fire on his own hearth, for necessary purposes, with the utmost care, does so at the peril, not only of losing his own house, but of being irretrievably ruined if a spark from his chimney starts a conflagration which lays waste the neighborhood. "In conflict with the rule, as laid down in the English cases, is a class of cases in reference to damage from fire communicated from the adjoining premises. Fire, like water or steam, is likely to produce mischief if it escapes and goes beyond control; and yet it has never been held in this country that one building a fire upon his own premises can be made liable if it escapes upon his neighbor's premises, and does him damage without proof of negligence." *Losee v. Buchanan,* 51 N. Y. 476, 487.

Everything that a man can bring on his land is capable of escaping,—against his will, and without his fault, with or without assistance, in some form, solid, liquid, or gaseous, changed or unchanged by the transforming processes of nature or art,—and of doing damage after its escape. Moreover, if there is a legal principle that makes a man liable for the natural consequences of the escape of things which he brings on his land, the application of such a principle cannot be limited to those things: it must be applied to all his acts that disturb the original order of creation; or, at least, to all things which he undertakes to possess or control anywhere, and which were not used and enjoyed in what is called the natural or primitive condition of mankind, whatever that may have been. This is going back a long way for a standard of legal rights, and adopting an arbitrary test of responsibility that confounds all degrees of danger, pays no heed to the essential elements of actual fault, puts a clog upon natural and reasonably necessary uses of matter, and tends to embarrass and obstruct much of the work which it seems to be man's duty carefully to do. The distinction made by Lord CAIRNS—*Rylands v. Fletcher,* L. R. 3 H. L. 330—between a natural and a non-natural use of land, if he meant anything more than the difference between a reasonable use and an unreasonable one, is not established in the law. Even if the arbitrary test were applied only to things which a man brings on his land, it would still recognize the peculiar rights of savage life in a wilderness, ignore the rights growing out of a civilized state of society, and make a distinction not warranted by the enlightened spirit of the common law: it would impose a penalty upon efforts, made in a reasonable, skilful, and careful manner, to rise above a condition of barbarism. It is impossible that legal principle can throw so serious an obstacle in the way of progress and improvement. Natural rights are, in general, legal rights; and the rights of civilization are, in a legal sense, as natural as any others. "Most of the rights of property, as well as of person, in the social state, are not absolute but relative"—*Losee v. Buchanan,* 51 N. Y. 485; and, if men ever were in any other than the social state, it is neither necessary nor expedient that they should now govern themselves on the theory that they ought to live in some other state. The common law does not usually establish tests of responsibility on any other basis than the propriety of their living in the social state, and the relative and qualified character of the rights incident to that state.

In *Fletcher v. Rylands* Mr. Justice BLACKBURN, commenting upon the remark of Mr. Baron MARTIN, "that, when damage is done to personal property, or even to the person, by collision, either upon land or at sea, there must be negligence in the party doing the damage to render him legally responsible," says,—"This is no doubt true; and, as was pointed out by Mr. Mellish during his argument before us, this is not confined to cases of collision, for there are many cases in which proof of negligence is essential, as, for instance, where an unruly horse gets on the footpath of a public street and kills a passenger; or where a person in a dock is struck by the falling of a bale of cotton which the defendant's servants are lowering; and many other similar cases may be found. But we think these cases distinguishable from the present. Traffic on the highways, whether by land or sea, cannot be conducted without exposing those whose persons or property are near it to some inevitable risk; and that being so, those who go on the highway, or have their property adjacent to it, may well be held to do so subject to their taking upon themselves the risk of injury from that inevitable danger; and persons who, by the license of the owner, pass near to warehouses where goods are being raised or lowered, certainly do so subject to the inevitable risk of accident. In neither case, therefore, can they recover without proof of want of care or skill occasioning the accident; and it is believed that all the cases in which inevitable accident has been held an excuse for what, *prima facie,* was a trespass, can be explained on the same principle, viz., that the circumstances were such as to show that the plaintiff had taken that risk upon himself." This would be authority for holding, in the present case, that the plaintiff, by having his post near the street, took upon himself the risk of its being broken by an inevitable accident carrying a traveller off the street. But such a doctrine would open more questions, and more difficult ones, than it would settle. At what distance from a highway would an object be near it? What part of London is not near a street? And then, as the defendant had as good a right to be at home with his horses as to be in the highway, why might not his neighbor, by electing to live in an inhabited country, as well be held to take upon himself the risk of an inevitable accident happening by reason of the country being inhabited, as to assume a highway risk by living near a road? If neighborhood is the test, who are a man's neighbors but the whole human race? If a person, by remaining in England, is held to take upon himself one class of the inevitable dangers of that country because he could avoid that class by migrating to a region of solitude, why should he not, for a like reason, also be held to expose himself voluntarily to other classes of the inevitable dangers of that country? And where does this reasoning end?

. . .

The difficulty under which the plaintiff might labor in proving the culpability of the defendant,—which is sometimes given as a reason for imposing an absolute liability without evidence of negligence—or changing the burden of proof—seems not to have been given in the English cases relating to damage done by brutes or fire. And, however large or small the class of cases in which such a difficulty may be the foundation of a rule of law, since the difficulty has been so much reduced by the abolition of witness disabilities,—the present case is not one of that class.

. . .

[T]he occurrence complained of in this case was one for which the defendant is not liable, unless every one is liable for all damage done by superior force overpowering him, and using him or his property as an instrument of violence. The defendant, being without fault, was as innocent as if the pole of his wagon had been hurled on the plaintiff's land by a whirlwind, or he himself, by a stronger man, had been thrown through the plaintiff's window. Upon the facts stated, taken in the sense in which we understand them, the defendant is entitled to judgment.

Case discharged.

MCINTYRE V. BALENTINE

Supreme Court of Tennessee
833 S.W.2d 52 (1992)

DROWOTA, JUSTICE.

In this personal injury action, we granted Plaintiff's application for permission to appeal in order to decide whether to adopt a system of comparative fault in Tennessee. . . .We now replace the common law defense of contributory negligence with a system of comparative fault. . . .

In the early morning darkness of November 2, 1986, Plaintiff Harry Douglas McIntyre and Defendant Clifford Balentine were involved in a motor vehicle accident resulting in severe injuries to Plaintiff. The accident occurred in the vicinity of Smith's Truck Stop in Savannah, Tennessee. As Defendant Balentine was traveling south on Highway 69, Plaintiff entered the highway (also traveling south) from the truck stop parking lot. Shortly after Plaintiff entered the highway, his pickup truck was struck by Defendant's Peterbilt tractor. At trial, the parties disputed the exact chronology of events immediately preceding the accident.

Both men had consumed alcohol the evening of the accident. After the accident, Plaintiff's blood alcohol level was measured at .17 percent by weight. Testimony suggested that Defendant was traveling in excess of the posted speed limit.

Plaintiff brought a negligence action against Defendant Balentine and Defendant East-West Motor Freight, Inc. Defendants answered that Plaintiff was contributorily negligent, in part due to operating his vehicle while intoxicated. After trial, the jury returned a verdict stating: "We, the jury, find the plaintiff and the defendant equally at fault in this accident; therefore, we rule in favor of the defendant."

After judgment was entered for Defendants, Plaintiff brought an appeal alleging the trial court erred by refusing to instruct the jury regarding the doctrine of comparative negligence. . . . The Court of Appeals affirmed, holding that (1) comparative negligence is not the law in Tennessee. . . .

I.

The common law contributory negligence doctrine has traditionally been traced to Lord Ellenborough's opinion in *Butterfield v. Forrester,* 11 East 60, 103 Eng.Rep. 926 (1809). There, plaintiff, "riding as fast as his horse would go," was injured after running into an obstruction defendant had placed in the road. Stating as the rule that "[o]ne person being in fault will not dispense with another's using ordinary care," plaintiff was denied recovery on the basis that he did not use ordinary care to avoid the obstruction.

The contributory negligence bar was soon brought to America as part of the common law and proceeded to spread throughout the states. This strict bar may have been a direct outgrowth of the common law system of issue pleading; issue pleading posed questions to be answered "yes" or "no," leaving common law courts, the theory goes, no choice but to award all or nothing. A number of other rationalizations have been advanced in the attempt to justify the harshness of the "all-or-nothing" bar. Among these:

the plaintiff should be penalized for his misconduct; the plaintiff should be deterred from injuring himself; and the plaintiff's negligence supersedes the defendant's so as to render defendant's negligence no longer proximate.

In Tennessee, the rule as initially stated was that "if a party, by his own gross negligence, brings an injury upon himself, or contributes to such injury, he cannot recover;" for, in such cases, the party "must be regarded as the author of his own misfortune." In subsequent decisions, we have continued to follow the general rule that a plaintiff's contributory negligence completely bars recovery.

Equally entrenched in Tennessee jurisprudence are exceptions to the general all-or-nothing rule: contributory negligence does not absolutely bar recovery where defendant's conduct was intentional, where defendant's conduct was "grossly" negligent, where defendant had the "last clear chance" with which, through the exercise of ordinary care, to avoid plaintiff's injury, or where plaintiff's negligence may be classified as "remote."

. . .

Between 1920 and 1969, a few states began utilizing the principles of comparative fault in all tort litigation. Then, between 1969 and 1984, comparative fault replaced contributory negligence in 37 additional states. In 1991, South Carolina became the 45th state to adopt comparative fault, leaving Alabama, Maryland, North Carolina, Virginia, and Tennessee as the only remaining common law contributory negligence jurisdictions.

. . .[W]e conclude that it is time to abandon the outmoded and unjust common law doctrine of contributory negligence and adopt in its place a system of comparative fault. Justice simply will not permit our continued adherence to a rule that, in the face of a judicial determination that others bear primary responsibility, nevertheless completely denies injured litigants recompense for their damages.

. . .

Two basic forms of comparative fault are utilized by 45 of our sister jurisdictions, these variants being commonly referred to as either "pure" or "modified." In the "pure" form[2], a plaintiff's damages are reduced in proportion to the percentage negligence attributed to him; for example, a plaintiff responsible for 90 percent of the negligence that caused his injuries nevertheless may recover 10 percent of his damages. In the "modified" form[3], plaintiffs recover as in pure jurisdictions, but only if the

---

[2] The 13 states utilizing pure comparative fault are Alaska, Arizona, California, Florida, Kentucky, Louisiana, Mississippi, Missouri, Michigan, New Mexico, New York, Rhode Island, and Washington.

[3] The 21 states using the "50 percent" modified form: Connecticut, Delaware, Hawaii, Illinois, Indiana, Iowa, Massachusetts, Minnesota, Montana, Nevada, New Hampshire, New

plaintiff's negligence either (1) does not exceed ("50 percent" jurisdictions) or (2) is less than ("49 percent" jurisdictions) the defendant's negligence.

Although we conclude that the all-or-nothing rule of contributory negligence must be replaced, we nevertheless decline to abandon totally our fault-based tort system. We do not agree that a party should necessarily be able to recover in tort even though he may be 80, 90, or 95 percent at fault. We therefore reject the pure form of comparative fault.

We recognize that modified comparative fault systems have been criticized as merely shifting the arbitrary contributory negligence bar to a new ground. However, we feel the "49 percent rule" ameliorates the harshness of the common law rule while remaining compatible with a fault-based tort system. We therefore hold that so long as a plaintiff's negligence remains less than the defendant's negligence the plaintiff may recover; in such a case, plaintiff's damages are to be reduced in proportion to the percentage of the total negligence attributable to the plaintiff.

Turning to the case at bar, the jury found that "the plaintiff and defendant [were] equally at fault." Because the jury, without the benefit of proper instructions by the trial court, made a gratuitous apportionment of fault, we find that their "equal" apportionment is not sufficiently trustworthy to form the basis of a final determination between these parties. Therefore, the case is remanded for a new trial in accordance with the dictates of this opinion.

* * *

Suggested Jury Instructions

[The following instructions should be preceded by instructions on negligence, proximate cause, damages, etc.]

1. If you find that defendant was not negligent or that defendant's negligence was not a proximate cause of plaintiff's injury, you will find for defendant.

2. If you find that defendant was negligent and that defendant's negligence was a proximate cause of plaintiff's injury, you must then determine whether plaintiff was also negligent and whether plaintiff's negligence was a proximate cause of his/her injury.

3. In this state, negligence on the part of a plaintiff has an impact on a plaintiff's right to recover damages. Accordingly, if you find that each party was negligent and that the negligence of each party was a proximate

---

Jersey, Ohio, Oklahoma, Oregon, Pennsylvania, South Carolina, Texas, Vermont, Wisconsin, and Wyoming. The 9 states using the "49 percent" form: Arkansas, Colorado, Georgia, Idaho, Kansas, Maine, North Dakota, Utah, and West Virginia. Two states, Nebraska and South Dakota, use a slight-gross system of comparative fault.

cause of plaintiff's damages, then you must determine the degree of such negligence, expressed as a percentage, attributable to each party.

4. If you find from all the evidence that the percentage of negligence attributable to plaintiff was equal to, or greater than, the percentage of negligence attributable to defendant, then you are instructed that plaintiff will not be entitled to recover any damages for his/her injuries. If, on the other hand, you determine from the evidence that the percentage of negligence attributable to plaintiff was less than the percentage of negligence attributable to defendant, then plaintiff will be entitled to recover that portion of his/her damages not caused by plaintiff's own negligence.

5. The court will provide you with a special verdict form that will assist you in your duties. This is the form on which you will record, if appropriate, the percentage of negligence assigned to each party and plaintiff's total damages. The court will then take your findings and either (1) enter judgment for defendant if you have found that defendant was not negligent or that plaintiff's own negligence accounted for 50 percent or more of the total negligence proximately causing his/her injuries or (2) enter judgment against defendant in accordance with defendant's percentage of negligence.

SPECIAL VERDICT FORM

We, the jury, make the following answers to the questions submitted by the court:

1. Was the defendant negligent?

Answer: ____ (Yes or No)

(If your answer is "No," do not answer any further questions. Sign this form and return it to the court.)

2. Was the defendant's negligence a proximate cause of injury or damage to the plaintiff?

Answer: ____ (Yes or No)

(If your answer is "No," do not answer any further questions. Sign this form and return it to the court.)

3. Did the plaintiff's own negligence account for 50 percent or more of the total negligence that proximately caused his/her injuries or damages?

Answer: ____ (Yes or No)

(If your answer is "Yes," do not answer any further questions. Sign this form and return it to the court.)

4. What is the total amount of plaintiff's damages, determined without reference to the amount of plaintiff's negligence?

Amount in dollars: $______

5. Using 100 percent as the total combined negligence which proximately caused the injuries or damages to the plaintiff, what are the percentages of such negligence to be allocated to the plaintiff and defendant?

Plaintiff______%

Defendant______%

(Total must equal 100%)

____

______

DISCUSSION PROBLEMS

1. Dog Bite

Ellen Pingaro was a meter reader for the New Jersey Natural Gas Company. When she approached Joseph Rossi's house to read his gas meter for the first time, her hand-held computer beeped her a message: "Bad dog, knock." Pingaro knocked on Rossi's door but received no answer. For a decade prior, the Gas Company had accommodated Rossi's request to not enter the yard without him. If he was not home when the meter reader arrived, the reader would estimate his bill or return at a later date. Pingaro was not aware of this history and had received no instructions from the company as to how she should proceed if Rossi were not home.

Pingaro proceeded to the fenced-in backyard, rattled the gate and her keys and yelled "gas company." There was no response. She looked around the backyard for dogs or other animals. After satisfying herself that the yard was clear, she unhooked the gate—on which was posted a large "Beware of Dog" sign—and walked towards the meter. Immediately upon entering the backyard two dogs approached her. One dog, a large German Shepard, jumped up, knocked her down and bit her on both arms, legs and head. She subdued the dog by hitting it with her flashlight, exited the yard and called for help. After a trip to the emergency room for stiches, Pingaro required physical therapy and was out of work for six months.

New Jersey has a "dog bite" statute, that provides:

> The owner of any dog which shall bite a person while such person is on or in a public place, or lawfully on or in a private place, including the property of the owner of the dog, shall be liable for such damages as may be suffered by the person bitten, regardless

of the former viciousness of such dog or the owner's knowledge of such viciousness.

Pingaro sued Rossi. Should she be able to recover? How should her behavior factor into the amount of any award?

2. Broken Collarbone.

Anne Hockema was speeding down Hanawalt Road when 8-year-old Jacob Secrest darted out into the street in front of her car. The car struck Jacob, who required surgery for a broken elbow and collarbone and subsequent physical therapy. Jacob's parents sued Hockema on behalf of Jacob for his pain and suffering, and on their own behalf for Jacob's medical bills, for which they were responsible. The jury determined that Jacob was 66.75% at fault for the accident, and that Hockema was 33.25% responsible.

What percentage of the damages should Jacob and his parents recover?

CHAPTER 8

NEGLIGENCE (BREACH OF THE STANDARD OF CARE)

■ ■ ■

INTRODUCTION

The tort of negligence has four elements. First, the defendant must owe a duty of care to the plaintiff. All individuals have a general duty to exercise "ordinary care" or "reasonable care" toward the person and property of others. (Whether and when individuals have a duty to protect others from harms directly caused by third parties is more complicated and contested, but we will not have time in this course to examine this branch of negligence law.) Second, the defendant must have "breached" the duty of care, by acting "negligently." (Note: it means the same thing to say that the defendant acted negligently as it does to say that the defendant breached the duty of care.) Third, the negligent act must have "caused" the plaintiff's injury. Fourth, the harm must fall within the "scope of liability" of negligence law. This Chapter examines breach of the duty of care; the next two chapters will consider the "causation" requirement and "scope of liability" limitations.

When evaluating breach of the duty of care, there are two primary issues, one substantive and one procedural. First, the procedural issue: who decides whether an actor breached the standard of care, judge or jury? Generally speaking, breach of the duty of care is a question for the jury, but there are definite limits to jury discretion. How should decision-making responsibility be allocated? Do *Adams v. Bullock* and *Martin v. Evans* provide consistent guidance concerning when a judge should and should not take the question of breach away from a jury and resolve it as a "matter of law?"

Second, the substantive issue: what behavior fails the requirement to exercise reasonable care? In the famous case of *United States v. Carroll Towing* (not included here), Judge Learned Hand articulated a cost-benefit test for negligence, which is often known as the "Hand Test" or "Hand Rule": an act or omission is negligent if the probability of harm to the victim multiplied by the damage that would be caused exceeds the cost to the actor of taking precautions necessary to mitigate the risk. The Hand Test reflects economic logic—the law should encourage people to act when the expected social benefits exceed the expected social costs and discourage action when costs exceed benefits—and is reflected in the substantive description of negligence provided by the Restatement. Rest. (3d.) Torts § 3. But it is unclear how much, if at all, the Hand Test actually reflects the law of negligence in action, as juries typically determine whether an act or omission breaches the standard of care and there is little evidence that judges instruct juries to apply the Hand Test when reaching their determination. How should a judge or jury determine whether an act or omission is "negligent," and what evidence should be required? *McCourt v. Abernethy* explores the difference in the way the law treats the question of negligence on the part of a professional, bound to abide by professional standards, from the way it treats the question of negligence on the part of an ordinary individual.

Restatement (Third) Torts § 3. Negligence

A person acts negligently if the person does not exercise reasonable care under all the circumstances. Primary factors to consider in ascertaining whether the person's conduct lacks reasonable care are the foreseeable likelihood that the person's conduct will result in harm, the foreseeable severity of any harm that may ensue, and the burden of precautions to eliminate or reduce the risk of harm.

Comment:

e. Balancing risks and benefits. . . .Conduct is negligent if its disadvantages outweigh its advantages, while conduct is not negligent if its advantages outweigh its disadvantages. The disadvantage in question is the magnitude of risk that the conduct occasions; as noted, the phrase "magnitude of the risk" includes both the foreseeable likelihood of harm and the foreseeable severity of harm that might ensue. The "advantages" of the conduct relate to the burden of risk prevention that is avoided when the actor declines to incorporate some precaution. The actor's conduct is hence negligent if the magnitude of the risk outweighs the burden of risk prevention.

Restatement (Third) of Torts § 13. Custom

(a) An actor's compliance with the custom of the community, or of others in like circumstances, is evidence that the actor's conduct is not negligent but does not preclude a finding of negligence.

(b) An actor's departure from the custom of the community, or of others in like circumstances, in a way that increases risk is evidence of the actor's negligence but does not require a finding of negligence.

Comment:

a. *Background*. . . In tort law, negligence is often defined as the lack of "ordinary care." Because complying with custom confirms that the actor has behaved in the ordinary way, one might suppose that proof of compliance with custom would be a complete defense against an allegation of negligence. In this respect, however, the negligence standard, concerned with "reasonable care," is more demanding than a standard understood solely in terms of ordinary care. While the actor is entitled to present to the jury evidence showing that the actor complied with custom, the other party is free to present other evidence. . .and in doing so seek to establish that the actor's conduct lacks reasonable care.

Restatement (Third) of Torts § 14. Statutory Violations as Negligence Per Se

An actor is negligent if, without excuse, the actor violates a statute that is designed to protect against the type of accident the actor's conduct causes, and if the accident victim is within the class of persons the statute is designed to protect.

Comment:

c. *Rationale*. . . .[I]n ordinary tort cases, so long as reasonable minds can differ, the responsibility for determining whether a person's conduct is negligent is vested in the jury. One major reason for this is to take advantage of community assessments in making the negligence determination. Yet when the legislature has addressed the issue of what conduct is appropriate, the judgment of the legislature, as the authoritative representative of the community, takes precedence over the views of any one jury. [It also] must be recognized that the negligence standard encounters difficulty in dealing with problems of recurring conduct. When each jury makes up its own mind as to the negligence of that conduct, there are serious disadvantages in terms of inequality, high litigation costs, and failing to provide clear guidance to persons engaged in primary activity. . . .In general, statutes address conduct that conspicuously recurs in a way that brings it to the attention of the legislature. Negligence per se hence replaces decisionmaking by juries in categories of cases where the operation of the latter may be least satisfactory.

Restatement (Third) of Torts § 16. Statutory Compliance

(a) An actor's compliance with a pertinent statute, while evidence of nonnegligence, does not preclude a finding that the actor is negligent under § 3 for failing to adopt precautions in addition to those mandated by the statute.

(b) If an actor's adoption of a precaution would require the actor to violate a statute, the actor cannot be found negligent for failing to adopt that precaution.

CASES

ADAMS V. BULLOCK

Court of Appeals of New York
227 N.Y. 208 (1919)

CARDOZO, J.

The defendant runs a trolley line in the city of Dunkirk, employing the overhead wire system. At one point, the road is crossed by a bridge or culvert which carries the tracks of the Nickle Plate and Pennsylvania Railroads. Pedestrians often use the bridge as a short cut between streets, and children play on it. On April 21, 1916, the plaintiff, a boy of 12 years, came across the bridge, swinging a wire about 8 feet long. In swinging it, he brought it in contact with the defendant's trolley wire, which ran beneath the structure. The side of the bridge was protected by a parapet 18 inches wide. Four feet 7 3/4 inches below the top of the parapet, the trolley wire was strung. The plaintiff was shocked and burned when the wires came together. He had a verdict at Trial Term, which has been affirmed at the Appellate Division by a divided court.

We think the verdict cannot stand. The defendant in using an overhead trolley was in the lawful exercise of its franchise. Negligence, therefore, cannot be imputed to it because is used that system and not another. There was, of course, a duty to adopt all reasonable precautions to minimize the resulting perils. We think there is no evidence that this duty was ignored. The trolley wire was so placed that no one standing on the bridge or even bending over the parapet could reach it. Only some extraordinary casualty, not fairly within the area of ordinary prevision, could make it a thing of danger. Reasonable care in the use of a destructive agency imports a high degree of vigilance. But no vigilance, however alert, unless fortified by the gift of prophecy, could have predicted the point upon the route where such an accident would occur. It might with equal reason have been expected anywhere else. At any point upon the route a mischievous or thoughtless boy might touch the wire with a metal pole, or fling another wire across it. If unable to reach it from the walk, he might stand upon a wagon or climb upon a tree. No special danger at this bridge warned the defendant that there was need of special measures of precaution. No like accident had occurred before. No custom had been disregarded. We think that ordinary caution did not involve forethought of this extraordinary peril. It has been so ruled in like circumstances by courts in other jurisdictions.

. . .

The judgment should be reversed, and a new trial granted, with costs to abide the event.

MARTIN V. EVANS

Supreme Court of Pennsylvania
551 Pa. 496 (1998)

NEWMAN, JUSTICE.

. . .This personal injury suit arose from an accident in which [Weldon] Evans' tractor-trailer backed into Appellee Anthony Martin (Martin). The parties presented conflicting testimony relating directly to the issue of Evans' negligence, and the jury concluded that Evans was not negligent. Because the verdict rested on a credibility determination, we hold that the trial court usurped the jury's responsibility by disregarding its finding that Evans was not negligent. Accordingly, we reverse and reinstate the jury's verdict.

FORC Company employed Evans as a truck driver. On May 24, 1989, Evans was driving a tractor-trailer that was forty-five feet long, eight feet wide and thirteen feet, six inches tall. He was proceeding southbound on Interstate 79 when he pulled into the Canonsburg rest stop. Along the left-hand side of the parking lot, there were parallel parking spots for trucks. Evans pulled his truck into what he believed to be the last parallel parking spot in that row. Notes of Testimony (N.T.), May 6, 1994, at 261. Because it was the last spot, he had to angle the cab of the truck to the trailer to maneuver the truck into the space. *Id.* at 262.

Evans left the truck running, and went to the restrooms. When he returned, he looked in back of the truck before he got into the cab and noticed that no one was parked behind him. N.T. at 264–65. He recorded the stop in his logbook, which took approximately two minutes, then he prepared to back up. N.T. at 265–66. Evans testified that he put the truck into reverse and released both the emergency brake for the cab and the emergency brake for the tractor. When released, the emergency brakes emit a hissing sound that lasts for about two seconds. N.T. at 270–71. He activated his four-way flashers, which are similar to an automobile's hazard lights. Then he looked through the side-view mirrors, but because of the angle of the truck and the length of the trailer, he could not see directly behind him. He reversed the truck "[s]lower than you could walk" until he felt a nudge and saw someone waving at him to stop. N.T. at 272–73. He stopped the truck and through his right-hand rear view mirror he saw someone fall just to the right, rear of his truck. When he got out of his truck to investigate, Evans saw Martin lying on the ground. *Id.*

Martin and Rochester Steverson (Steverson) were driving southbound on Interstate 79 on May 24, 1989, when they, too, stopped at the Canonsburg rest area. Their truck was an Isuzu box truck that was about twenty feet long and ten feet wide. N.T., May 5, 1994, at 70. The driver of the truck parked approximately seven to ten feet directly behind Evans' tractor-trailer. Martin was either walking or standing between the Isuzu truck and Evans' tractor-trailer when the tractor-trailer began to back into him. He claimed that he tried to get out of the way but was unable to do so. He became pinned between the two vehicles. Once he realized what was happening, Steverson put the Isuzu truck into reverse to free Martin, who fell to the ground. Martin suffered injuries to his right arm and back. As result, Martin brought a negligence action against Evans, his employer FORC Company, Lend-Lease, Inc., and National Rental Systems.

A jury trial took place from May 5, 1994 to May 11, 1994. The parties presented conflicting testimony concerning the circumstances surrounding the accident. The trial court instructed the jury on negligence, contributory negligence, and comparative negligence. The court presented the following interrogatories to the jury for its consideration:

Question 1a

Do you find that defendant Weldon R. Evans was negligent?

Yes ____ No ____

If you answered "Yes" to Question 1a, go on to Question 1b. If you answered "No" to Question 1a, the plaintiff cannot recover and you should not answer any further questions and should return to the courtroom.

Question 1b

Was the defendant's negligence a substantial factor in bringing about the plaintiff's harm?

Yes ____ No ____

If you answered "Yes" to Question 1b, go on to Question 2a. If you answered "No" to Question 1b, the plaintiff cannot recover and you should not answer any further questions and should return to the courtroom.

Question 2a

Do you find that plaintiff Anthony Martin was contributorily negligent?

Yes ____ No ____

If you answered "Yes" to Question 2a, go on to Question 2b. If you answered "No" to Question 2a, go on to Question 4.

Question 2b

Was plaintiff's contributory negligence a substantial factor in bringing about his harm?

Yes ____ No ____

If you answered "Yes" to Question 2b, go on to Question 3. If you answered "No" to Question 2b, go on to Question 4.

* * *

The jury answered "No" to Question 1a, therefore, did not answer the remaining questions. The trial court molded the jury's answer into a verdict in favor of Appellants.

Martin moved for a new trial. The trial court granted the motion on the grounds that the jury's verdict "shocked the Court's sense of justice." Slip Op. at 8. The court reasoned that because Evans sat in his truck for "a couple [of] minutes" before backing up, he was aware that there were blind spots in his mirrors such that he was unable to see directly behind his vehicle, and it was a busy rest area and likely that a pedestrian or vehicle could stand or park directly behind him, the jury's verdict that Evans was not negligent was unacceptable. Slip Op. at 7–8.

Evans appealed to the Superior Court, which concluded in a Memorandum Opinion that the trial court properly granted a new trial, and thus affirmed. This Court granted Evans' Petition for Allowance of Appeal to determine whether the trial court abused its discretion in granting a new trial where the parties presented conflicting testimony that required a credibility determination. We now reverse.

. . .To establish a cause of action in negligence, the plaintiff must demonstrate that the defendant owed a duty of care to the plaintiff, the defendant breached that duty, the breach resulted in injury to the plaintiff, and the plaintiff suffered an actual loss or damage. Negligence is the absence of ordinary care that a reasonably prudent person would exercise in the same or similar circumstances. The mere occurrence of an accident does not establish negligent conduct. Rather, the plaintiff has the burden of establishing, by a preponderance of the evidence, that the defendant engaged in conduct that deviated from the general standard of care expected under the circumstances, and that this deviation proximately caused actual harm.

The trial court instructed the jury with regard to the definition of negligence as follows:

> The legal term, negligence, otherwise known as carelessness, is the absence of ordinary care which a reasonably prudent person would exercise in the circumstances here presented.
>
> Negligent conduct may consist either of an act or an omission to act when there is a duty to do so. In other words, negligence is the failure to do something which a reasonably careful person would do, or the doing of something which a reasonably careful person would not do in light of all the surrounding circumstances established by the evidence in this case. It is for you to determine how a reasonably careful person would act in those circumstances.
>
> Now, I told you in defining negligence that part of that definition was absence of ordinary care.
>
> I want to define ordinary care for you. Ordinary care is the care a reasonably careful person would use under the circumstances presented in this case. It is the duty of every person to use ordinary care not only for his own safety and the protection of his property, but also to avoid injury to others. What constitutes ordinary care varies according to the particular circumstances and conditions existing then and there. The amount of care required by law must be in keeping with the degree of danger involved. . . .

N.T., May 11, 1994, at 417–18. Thus, the trial court called upon the jury to evaluate the testimony and decide whether Evans exercised ordinary care under the circumstances.

. . .

Evans testified that when he pulled into the Canonsburg rest area, he parked in what he believed to be the last legal parking space in that particular row. N.T., May 6, 1994, at 261. As proof of this, he stated that he had to park at an angle to fit his tractor-trailer into the lines. N.T. at 262. When he returned from the restrooms, he claimed that no one was parked behind him. N.T. 264–65. He knew that he only had to back up a couple of feet to be able to pull out of the space. After he made a recording in his logbook, he put in the clutch, put the truck into low reverse, activated his four-way flashers, and checked his mirrors. N.T. at 265–72. Evans further stated that although he could not see directly behind him at that moment, he kept his eye on the right mirror because he knew he would be able to see out of that side first. N.T. at 272. According to Evans, he moved his tractor-trailer backwards "[s]lower than you could walk." N.T. at 273. When he felt a nudge and saw someone waving at him to stop in his rear view mirror, he stopped instantly. N.T. at 272.

Martin testified . . . that he did not hear the truck's engine or the release of the emergency brakes, nor did he see any flashing lights from the back of the tractor-trailer. *Id.* After the tractor-trailer pushed him up against the Isuzu truck, he claimed that Steverson jumped into the truck, started it, and put it in reverse, at which point Martin fell to the ground. Neil Martin corroborated this version of the events.

. . .

Steverson testified that he parked the truck approximately ten feet behind the tractor-trailer and turned off the ignition. N.T. at 230. According to Steverson, Martin got out of the passenger's seat, and walked in front of the Isuzu truck and leaned against it while talking to his brother, Neil, for a couple of minutes. N.T. at 231. When Steverson realized that the tractor-trailer was moving towards them and that Martin was caught between the two, he started the truck and put it in reverse. N.T. at 234.

State Police Trooper Dennis Spirk, who arrived at the scene of the accident to investigate, testified . . . Evans stated that when he returned from the restrooms he walked around the back of his truck before he got into the cab, N.T., May 6, 1994, at 305, and that from the cab he did not see anything behind him. N.T. at 300. Trooper Spirk stated that Steverson indicated that he was the driver of the smaller truck. N.T. at 298. In response to questioning, Anthony Martin told Trooper Spirk that he was standing between the two trucks, with his back to the tractor-trailer and facing the truck he had just exited, when the tractor-trailer backed up and hit him. N.T. at 299.

Credibility determinations are within the sole province of the jury. "A jury is entitled to believe all, part or none of the evidence presented. . . . A jury can believe any part of a witness' testimony that they choose, and may disregard any portion of the testimony that they disbelieve." *Randt,* at 234, 671 A.2d at 233 (citation omitted). . . .

However, the trial court concluded that "[u]nder all of the facts and circumstances of this case, even when viewed most favorably to the verdict winner, this Court cannot accept the jury's conclusion that Evans was not negligent." In support of its conclusion, the trial court cited evidence supporting the fact that Evans made no effort during the two minutes after he entered his cab and prior to putting his truck in motion, to determine if there was anyone or anything behind his vehicle. This, coupled with the facts that the rest area was busy and there were "blind spots" in the mirrors, caused the trial court to reach its conclusion.

However, the evidence equally supports a finding that Evans exercised ordinary care under the circumstances. Evans testified that he parked in what he believed to be the last legal parking space in the row. In fact, he stated that he had to park his tractor-trailer with the cab at an angle to the trailer because it was the last spot and there was barely enough room for his vehicle. When he returned to his truck, no one was parked behind him. Before backing up, he activated his four-way flashers and released his emergency brakes, which he knew made a loud hissing sound. Then, he proceeded to move the truck backwards "slower than you could walk." N.T. at 273. Therefore, if the jury were to believe Evans' account of the events, he took the necessary precautions required by the circumstances and proceeded with care.

A resolution of whether Evans was negligent relied upon a credibility determination and the jury's assessment of what constituted ordinary care under the circumstances. Because this assessment was solely within the province of the jury, *Randt,* the trial court was not at liberty to reassess the evidence and make its own credibility determinations simply because it would have reached a different conclusion. *Thompson.* Accordingly, we hold that the trial court abused its discretion by disregarding the jury's credibility determination and substituting its own. The verdict was not so contrary to the evidence so as to shock one's sense of justice.

We reverse and reinstate the jury's verdict.

MCCOURT V. ABERNATHY

Supreme Court of South Carolina
318 S.C. 301 (1995)

SHAW, ACTING ASSOCIATE JUSTICE:

Respondent, Steven McCourt, as personal representative of the estate of his wife, Wendy Marie McCourt, brought wrongful death and survival causes of action against appellants, Glenn Abernathy, M.D., J.D. Clyde, M.D., and Family Medicine Associates, P.A. The jury returned a verdict in favor of respondent for both actual and punitive damages against Dr. Abernathy and Dr. Clyde. The doctors appeal the denial of their motions for new trial and new trial *nisi*. We affirm.

The record discloses as follows. Twenty-three year old Wendy McCourt first sought treatment from the appellants in December, 1987. At that time, Dr. Abernathy obtained a history from Wendy revealing past liver problems and subsequently sought medical records from Dr. Truss, who had been Wendy's treating physician in Alabama. On Wednesday or Thursday, March 9 or 10, 1988 Wendy was injured while working with horses. There is evidence Wendy was seen by Dr. Abernathy in his office at that time and was treated for a pulled muscle. On Sunday, March 13, her condition worsened and Wendy went to the Anderson Memorial Hospital emergency room. She was experiencing greater pain and had difficulty breathing. Dr. Clyde examined Wendy at that time and treated her for a pulled chest muscle. There is evidence Dr. Clyde treated the puncture wound to Wendy's finger at that time. She was given prescriptions for Motrin and Co-Tylenol. She returned to her home.

The following day, March 14, Wendy's condition became significantly worse and she again sought treatment at the emergency room. She was examined by an emergency room physician who ran some blood tests. This physician indicated an immediate need to admit Wendy to the hospital. He telephoned Dr. Abernathy and was given permission to admit Wendy. At 6:30 that evening, Dr. Abernathy examined Wendy and observed the injured finger, for which he prescribed Keflex, an oral antibiotic.

At 9:00 the following morning, both Dr. Abernathy and Dr. Clyde saw Wendy while making rounds at the hospital. By that time, Wendy's condition had worsened yet more and the doctors consulted Dr. Kovaz, an internist. Although appellants requested a consult from Dr. Kovaz, they did not express any urgency in his seeing her. After examining Wendy, Dr. Kovaz immediately moved her to the intensive care unit with a diagnosis of sepsis, a bacterial infection. Although treatment with intravenous antibiotics was begun at that time, her condition continued to deteriorate. Over the next 4 days, her skin began to slough off, her eyes filled with blood, her feet turned black, she bled from her nose, mouth and pores, and she became bloated beyond recognition. On March 19, 1988, Wendy McCourt died from beta strep septicemia with multiple organ system failure secondary to the sepsis.

Respondent presented expert testimony from Dr. Neal Craine and Dr. Kenneth DeHart. Dr. Craine stated Wendy's illness was caused by "an unfortunate circumstance where transient bacteria in the bloodstream landed in an area already traumatized by the injury with the horse." He testified, assuming, as the "Death Summary" indicates, Dr. Abernathy saw Wendy on the 9th, she had a puncture wound to the finger and it was known she was working around horses, he should have put her on preventive antibiotics on that day. He stated it would also have been below the standard of care for Dr. Clyde to have observed an infected finger on the 13th and not treat her with antibiotics nor order laboratory tests. He stated he felt Wendy had a 100% chance of survival on the 13th had she been started on antibiotics at that time. Based on the test results received on the afternoon of the 14th, he stated that a doctor should know the patient was seriously ill and should have suspected sepsis. He concluded Wendy's life could have been saved if antibiotics had been started on the 9th, which would have prevented or treated an early infection of the finger. He also stated, more likely than not, Wendy could have been saved on the 13th by treatment with antibiotics as well as on the 14th with aggressive antibiotic therapy. He stated it was also below the standard of care to wait until the 15th to call in a specialist.

Dr. DeHart likewise testified, assuming Wendy presented with an infected finger on the 9th, failure to treat that prophylactically fell below the standard of care. He stated, assuming Wendy presented with an infected finger on the 13th, Dr. Clyde's treatment fell below the standard of care by failing to order lab tests, failing to immobilize the finger, and in failing to start antibiotics. As to Dr. Abernathy's treatment on the 14th, he testified it was "profoundly below the standard of care", not because he missed the diagnosis, but because he failed to order aggressive observation and failed to request consultation intervention.

This matter was tried to a jury and on January 7, 1993 the jury returned the following verdicts for appellant:

> Wrongful death action: Actual damages—$200,000 against Dr. Abernathy and $100,000 against Dr. Clyde; Punitive damages—$500,000 against Dr. Abernathy and $250,000 against Dr. Clyde.
>
> . . .

[The defendants challenged the verdict on the ground that the trial court provided improper jury instructions.]

In instructing the jury on the burden of proof of the plaintiff and the standard of care required of the defendants, the trial judge gave the following relevant charges.

> The material elements of a medical malpractice action require the plaintiff to prove to your satisfaction as jurors by the greater weight or preponderance of the evidence and present evidence of the generally recognized practices and procedures which would be exercised by ordinary competent practitioners in a defendant doctor's field of medicine under the same or similar circumstances, and then to present evidence that a defendant doctor negligently departed from those recognized and generally accepted standards, practices, and procedures in the manner alleged by the plaintiff; and, in addition, to proving that a physician was in some way negligent, the plaintiff must also prove that a physician's negligence was a proximate cause of the plaintiff's injuries and/or death.
>
> . . . .
>
> The mere fact that the plaintiff's expert may use a different approach is not considered a deviation from the recognized standard of medical care. Nor is the standard violated because the expert disagrees with a defendant as to what is the best or better approach in treating a patient. Medicine is an inexact science, and generally qualified physicians may differ as to what constitutes a preferable course of treatment. Such differences to preference under our law do not amount to malpractice.
>
> I further charge you that the degree of skill and care that a physician must use in diagnosing a condition is that which would

> be exercised by competent practitioners in the defendant doctor's field of medicine. In South Carolina the question of whether a physician, in making a diagnosis deviated from the applicable standard of care either by not employing a particular procedure or by not ordering a particular test is to be determined by what an ordinary careful and prudent physician would have done under the same or similar circumstances.
>
> . . . .
>
> Negligence may not be inferred from a bad result. Our law says that a physician is not an insurer of health, and a physician is not required to guarantee results. He undertakes only to meet the standard of skill possessed generally by others practicing in his field under similar circumstances.

. . .[W]e find no error.

Appellants next contend . . .the punitive damages awards are excessive and, because there was no evidence of conduct rising to the level of recklessness, the verdict was the result of passion and prejudice. We disagree.

In order for a plaintiff to recover punitive damages, there must be evidence the defendant's conduct was wilful, wanton, or in reckless disregard of the plaintiff's rights. A conscious failure to exercise due care constitutes wilfulness.

. . .

We find the record before us contains evidence that both Dr. Abernathy and Dr. Clyde consciously failed to exercise due care in treating Wendy. This evidence includes, but is not limited to: (1) failure to properly diagnose and treat Wendy within the standard of care on three separate occasions; (2) failure to order timely diagnostic tests in light of continual complaints and no improvement of Wendy's condition; (3) failure to appreciate the seriousness of Wendy's deteriorating condition in the face of highly abnormal blood work; (4) failure to aggressively monitor Wendy's deteriorating condition; and (5) failure to promptly seek the immediate aid of a specialist once the seriousness of Wendy's condition became apparent. While the evidence indicates a more severe degree of culpability on the part of Dr. Abernathy than Dr. Clyde, the record contains sufficient evidence of conduct on the part of both doctors to support the awards of punitive damages. The jury's determination of damages is entitled to substantial deference. *Rush* at 805. We find no abuse of the trial judge's discretion in this respect.

AFFIRMED.

DISCUSSION PROBLEMS

1. Telephone Wire

In the 1930s, the New York Telephone Company had a contract that allowed it to place bare telephone wires on the top of wooden poles originally built to carry electricity lines. By installing the wire on the poles, it could later provide telephone service to local residents. In one location, the telephone wire was 75 feet long, but it was coiled and tied to the pole under the electricity line, such that the entire wire was 12–14 feet off of the ground. Several years later, the wire had come loose from the coil, and it hung down within the reach of a person standing on the ground. In need of wire to fix a swing, and believing the telephone wire was not live, Kendrick Morrison used a pair of scissors to cut off a length of the wire. Unbeknownst to Morrison, a tree branch had broken and landed on the live electrical line, which was in turn pushed into contact with the telephone wire higher up on the pole, enabling the wire to conduct electricity. Because the line was not providing phone service, however, the company did not know the wire was, in fact, "live." Morrison was electrocuted and died.

Morrison's estate sued the phone company for negligence. Should it be entitled to present its case to a jury?

2. Lawnmower Accident

Steven and Julie Kovich hired a local teenager, Ashton Minish, to mow their lawn. As Minish was mowing, the lawn mower expelled a foreign object, which flew through the air 75 feet and struck Karie Campbell in the eye. The parties agreed that Minish inspected the lawnmower for "a couple of minutes" before beginning the task, that "he was not doing anything usual" but merely pushing the mower across the lawn, that he did not appear to be in a hurry, and that he appeared to be watching where he was walking. Campbell alleged that the Koviches did not know how old Minish was, and that they knew nothing about the equipment he would be using.

Campbell sued Minish and the Koviches for negligence. Is Campbell entitled to have a jury determine whether the parties breached their respective duties of care?

3. The T.J. Hooper

In March 1928, the owner of two barges contracted to have two tugboats, the Montrose and the T.J. Hooper, tow the barges, loaded with coal, from Norfolk, Virginia, up the Atlantic coast to New York. At the beginning of the journey, weather conditions were good, but a storm arose when the barges were off the coast of New Jersey. Both barges sprung leaks and sank. Although there were issues with the seaworthiness of the barges, they would have been saved if they had been towed into the Delaware

Breakwater rather than continuing northward in the Atlantic Ocean when the storm hit. Weather reports broadcast over the radio led other tugs in the area to enter the Breakwater, and the captains of the two tugs indicated they would have taken the same action had they received those reports. The Montrose and the Hooper, however, were not equipped with radio receivers, so they did not receive the warnings.

The barge owners sued the tugboat company for negligence, pointing out, as the court described, that "an adequate receiving set suitable for a coastwise tug can now be got at small cost and is reasonably reliable if kept up," and would have allowed the tugs access to the weather reports broadcast twice a day along the Atlantic coast. The court found, however, that there was not a general custom among coastal tug companies to outfit their boats with radio receiving sets. One line did so; the rest did not.

Does the evidence justify a finding of negligence on the part of the tugboat company?

4. The Missing Guardrail

Larry Bayne, a truck driver, was unloading goods at Todd Shipyards Corporation's loading dock, when he fell more than four feet off the loading platform and suffered injuries. Bayne sued, alleging that the defendant was negligent because it had failed to install a guardrail on the side of the platform.

Pursuant to its statutory authority to promulgate workplace safety regulations, the state of Washington's Department of Labor and Industries had adopted a regulation that provided: "All elevated walks, runways or platforms, if four feet or more from the floor level, shall be provided with a standard railing." How, if at all, should this regulation affect the outcome of the lawsuit?

CHAPTER 9

CAUSATION

■ ■ ■

INTRODUCTION

It is not enough for the imposition of liability that a defendant acts negligently; the negligent act must cause the damage to the plaintiff's person or property. This requirement is usually understood to mean that the negligent act must be a "but-for" cause of the victim's harm; in other words, in the absence of the negligent act, there would have been no injury. Rest. (3d) Torts § 26.

The basic concept is obvious enough: if I drive my car unsafely but I don't run into you, no plausible view of private law would suggest that you should be able to sue me and collect damages (although we might think it justified for the state to fine or jail me). But difficult questions of causation can arise when an individual acts negligently and a victim suffers harm but the causal link is not entirely clear. The law needs to determine what type and amount of evidence is necessary to establish that causal link.

As is the case with the negligence determination, the causation determination is generally a question for the jury, but there are limits. Consequently, in litigation, the legal issue often concerns the state of the evidence: specifically, whether the evidence of causation presented by the plaintiff is sufficient for a jury to conclude, if it chooses to do so, that the defendant's negligent act or omission caused the plaintiff's injury. *Muckler v. Buchl* grapples with this problem in the context of fall that might have been caused by the defendant's negligence but might not have been. *Summers v. Tice* asks whether a victim should ever be permitted to recover when the evidence presented does not prove that the defendant's negligent act was more likely than not the cause of the plaintiff's injury.

Restatement (Third) of Torts § 6. Liability for Negligence Causing Physical Harm

An actor whose negligence is a factual cause of physical harm is subject to liability for any such harm within the scope of liability, unless the court determines that the ordinary duty of reasonable care is inapplicable.

Comment:

d. Rationales. One justification for imposing liability for negligent conduct that causes physical harm is corrective justice; imposing liability remedies an injustice done by the defendant to the plaintiff. An actor who permits conduct to impose a risk of physical harm on others that exceeds the burden the actor would bear in avoiding that risk impermissibly ranks personal interests ahead of the interests of others. This, in turn, violates an ethical norm of equal consideration when imposing risks on others. Imposing liability remedies this violation.

Another justification for imposing liability for negligence is to give actors appropriate incentives to engage in safe conduct. The actor's adoption of appropriate precautions improves overall social welfare and thereby advances broad economic goals.

e. Implications. A general rule imposing negligence liability for physical harm has affirmative and negative implications. Affirmatively, an actor bears liability for physical harm caused by the actor's negligence. Negatively, an actor does not bear liability for harm caused by the actor unless the harm was caused by the actor's failure to exercise reasonable care. Despite the general rule, other rules of law, such as various rules of strict liability, do sometimes impose liability in the absence of negligence.

Restatement (Third) of Torts § 26. Factual Cause

Tortious conduct must be a factual cause of harm for liability to be imposed. Conduct is a factual cause of harm when the harm would not have occurred absent the conduct. . . .

Comment:

b. "But-for" standard for factual cause. The standard for factual causation in this Section is familiarly referred to as the "but-for" test, as well as a *sine qua non* test. Both express the same concept: an act is a factual cause of an outcome if, in the absence of the act, the outcome would not have occurred. With recognition that there are multiple factual causes of an event, see Comment *c*, a factual cause can also be described as a necessary condition for the outcome. . . .

c. Tortious conduct need only be one of the factual causes of harm. An actor's tortious conduct need only be *a* factual cause of the other's harm. The existence of other causes of the harm does not affect whether specified tortious conduct was a necessary condition for the harm to occur. Those other causes may be innocent or tortious, known or unknown, influenced by the tortious conduct or independent of it, but so long as the harm would not have occurred absent the tortious conduct, the tortious conduct is a factual cause. Recognition of multiple causes does not require modifying or abandoning the but-for standard in this Section. Tortious conduct by an actor need be only one of the causes of another's harm. . . .

e. Counterfactual inquiry for factual cause. The requirement that the actor's tortious conduct be necessary for the harm to occur requires a counterfactual inquiry. One must ask what would have occurred if the actor had not engaged in the tortious conduct. . . .

CASES

MUCKLER V. BUCHL

Supreme Court of Minnesota
276 Minn. 490 (1967)

SHERAN, JUSTICE.

Appeal from a district court judgment.

About 8:30 p.m., on August 11, 1962, plaintiff's decedent, a 55-year-old woman, fell down a flight of stairs extending from the landing between the first and second floors down to the first floor of the Minneapolis apartment house in which she had been a tenant for 7 years. She broke her hip in the fall and was taken to a hospital where she died less than 4 months later.

On March 15, 1963, decedent's husband commenced an action for death by wrongful act against the apartment-house owner. At trial which commenced August 9, 1965, plaintiff claimed the accident was caused by defendant's negligence in having the stairs too dimly lit for safety contrary to a relevant ordinance and to his common-law duty. Pursuant to a verdict in favor of plaintiff, judgment for $17,000 was entered on October 26, 1965, and defendant appealed therefrom on January 24, 1966.

. . .

Does the evidence justify a finding that the fall which caused injuries resulting in the death of plaintiff's decedent was caused by the negligence of defendant in failing properly to light the stairway in the apartment building where the fall occurred?

. . .

1. Were it not for our decision in Majerus v. Guelsow, 262 Minn. 1, 113 N.W.2d 450, we would be hesitant to affirm the jury's implicit finding that decedent was caused to fall because of the darkness of the stairway, there being no direct evidence on the issue.

Just before she fell, decedent was walking down the stairs directly behind a departing guest who had been visiting her in the second-floor apartment occupied by decedent and her husband. The guest gave the following description of the events occurring between the time she left decedent's apartment and the time the critical injury was sustained:

'Q. As you went out into the hallway and as the door of the apartment was closed, how can you describe the condition of the light at that time?

'The Witness: It was dark. I could distinguish the hand rail and I hung onto that because I could not tell where the steps were.

'Q. I believe there is one flight of steps there from that second floor landing down about five or six steps to a landing between floors; is that your recollection?

'A. Yes, sir.

'Q. Right at that landing, between the floors there are two little windows adjacent to the landing; is that right?

'A. I believe so.

'Mr. Green (plaintiff's attorney): Now, you got down to the first floor landing, or the landing between floors, without any particular incident?

'A. Yes.

'Q. Did you then make the turn to go down the second flight to the landing on the first floor?

'A. Yes, sir.

'Q. Tell us what happened as you went down that second flight of stairs?

'A. I was being very careful. I couldn't tell where the steps were so I had to feel my way down, and then I don't know how far I was from the bottom, probably three or four steps, and I heard something behind me and I imagined it was Mrs. Muckler tripping or falling—I couldn't tell then—so I instinctively put my hand out and there was nothing there, and I heard the scream and the thump and there she was.

'Q. At this point where you heard this noise, had Mrs. Muckler been behind you?

'A. Yes, she was behind me.

'Q. And the rest of the people you described were all on down ahead of you?

'A. Some place ahead.

'Q. Did you see her go past you when this occurred or feel her or anything? Were you aware of her going past?

'A. No.

'Q. Why was that?

'A. I don't know why it was. I suppose the excitement, it happened so fast, I can't really tell.

'Q. Where did Mrs. Muckler then finally wind up?

'A. I heard the thump and the scream almost simultaneously and then the doors from the first floor opened so then I could see her.

'Q. Where was she?

'A. Lying on the floor, on the landing.'

If decedent ever said what caused her to fall, the record does not disclose it.

An electrical engineer who measured the light at the place of the accident at a time when, according to the evidence, conditions were substantially the same as those prevailing at the time of the event gave testimony from which the jury could infer that the light at and near the place of the occurrence measured one-tenth of a foot-candle or less-significantly below the two foot-candles required by an ordinance of the city of Minneapolis.

At the time of the accident the stairway was not lighted by artificial illumination. Defendant's agent was in exclusive control of the switch to the lights which could have been used for this purpose.

Except for the inadequacy of the lighting, the evidence shows that there was no defect in the stairway to which the fall could be attributed. A handrail was in place.

Decedent, about 55 years of age, was in good health except for a diabetic condition which under the evidence the jury could have found to be controlled. Also there was evidence from which the jury could have found that decedent did not consume intoxicating liquors on the day of the accident or at any other time. There is no evidence indicating that decedent had fallen while descending the steps of the apartment building on any prior occasion during the 7 years she lived there as a tenant.

The evidence is consistent with the theory that decedent fell on the stairway because of the darkness. But it is also consistent with the possibility that the fall would have occurred no matter what the lighting condition might have been. We can eliminate the diabetic condition as a probable explanation of the occurrence in view of the testimony of competent witnesses that decedent was not suffering observable symptoms before and as she started down the stairway. The possibility that the fall was attributable to intoxication can be eliminated on the basis of testimony to the effect that decedent never used intoxicants. But experience tells us that people sometimes fall on stairways even though fully alert and in the best of health. We cannot say with certitude that this was not one of those instances.

Construing the evidence in the light most favorable to the prevailing party, as we must, we are still working in the field of probability. And the degree of probability of a connection between an alleged cause and a given result needed to sustain an affirmative jury finding cannot be defined with mathematical certainty. The line separating fact situations where an inference of causation is permissible from those in which it is not must, of necessity, reflect the general practical experience of the court called upon to make the demarcation. So considered, it seems reasonable that one attempting to descend a stairway so dark that the steps are barely discernible would be likely to fall because of the darkness. And, the accident having happened, it seems to us more probable that the darkened state of the stairway was the precipitating factor for the accident than otherwise. The minimum standards for lighting for stairways set by Minneapolis ordinance also suggest an experience-tested relationship between lack of adequate lighting on stairs and accidents of the type with which we are here concerned.

Admittedly, the case is a close one. In such a situation, while precedents from other jurisdictions involving an assessment of similar facts are not compelling, we must of necessity be guided by our own prior decisions in comparable situations.

. . .

Affirmed.

SUMMERS V. TICE

Supreme Court of California
33 Cal.2d 80 (1948)

CARTER, JUSTICE.

Each of the two defendants appeals from a judgment against them in an action for personal injuries. Pursuant to stipulation the appeals have been consolidated.

Plaintiff's action was against both defendants for an injury to his right eye and face as the result of being struck by bird shot discharged from a shotgun. The case was tried by the court without a jury and the court found that on November 20, 1945, plaintiff and the two defendants were hunting quail on the open range. Each of the defendants was armed with a 12 gauge shotgun loaded with shells containing 7 1/2 size shot. Prior to going hunting plaintiff discussed the hunting procedure with defendants, indicating that they were to exercise care when shooting and to 'keep in line.' In the course of hunting plaintiff proceeded up a hill, thus placing the hunters at the points of a triangle. The view of defendants with reference to plaintiff was unobstructed and they knew his location. Defendant Tice flushed a quail which rose in flight to a ten foot elevation and flew between plaintiff and defendants. Both defendants shot at the quail, shooting in plaintiff's direction. At that time defendants were 75 yards from plaintiff. One shot struck plaintiff in his eye and another in his upper lip. Finally it was found by the court that as the direct result of the shooting by defendants the shots struck plaintiff as above mentioned and that defendants were negligent in so shooting and plaintiff was not contributorily negligent.

. . .

[The trial court] found that both defendants were negligent and 'That as a direct and proximate result of the shots fired by defendants, and each of them, a birdshot pellet was caused to and did lodge in plaintiff's right eye and that another birdshot pellet was caused to and did lodge in plaintiff's upper lip.' . . .[T]he court was unable to ascertain whether the shots were from the gun of one defendant or the other or one shot from each of them. The one shot that entered plaintiff's eye was the major factor in assessing damages and that shot could not have come from the gun of both defendants. It was from one or the other only.

It has been held that where a group of persons are on a hunting party, or otherwise engaged in the use of firearms, and two of them are negligent in firing in the direction of a third person who is injured thereby, both of those so firing are liable for the injury suffered by the third person, although the negligence of only one of them could have caused the injury. [I]n Oliver v. Miles, there two persons were hunting together. Both shot at some partridges and in so doing shot across the highway injuring plaintiff who was travelling on it. The court stated they were acting in concert and thus both were liable. The court then stated (110 So. 668): 'We think that each is liable for the resulting injury to the boy, although no one can say definitely who actually shot him. *To hold otherwise would be to exonerate both from liability, although each was negligent, and the injury resulted from such negligence.*' (Emphasis added.) 110 So. p. 668. It is said in the Restatement: 'For harm resulting to a third person from the tortious conduct of another, a person is liable if he (b) knows that the other's conduct constitutes a breach of duty and gives substantial assistance or encouragement to the other so to conduct himself, or (c) gives substantial assistance to the other in accomplishing a tortious result and his own conduct, separately considered, constitutes a breach of duty to the third person.' (Rest., Torts, sec. 876(b)(c).) Under subsection (b) the example is given: 'A and B are members of a hunting party. Each of them in the presence of the other shoots across a public road at an animal this being negligent as to persons on the road. A hits the animal. B's bullet strikes C, a traveler on the road. A is liable to C.' (Rest., Torts, Sec. 876(b), Com.,

Illus. 3.) An illustration given under subsection (c) is the same as above except the factor of both defendants shooting is missing and joint liability is not imposed. It is further said that: 'If two forces are actively operating, one because of the actor's negligence, the other not because of any misconduct on his part, and each of itself sufficient to bring about harm to another, the actor's negligence may be held by the jury to be a substantial factor in bringing it about.' (Rest., Torts, sec. 432.) Dean Wigmore has this to say: 'When two or more persons by their acts are possibly the sole cause of a harm, or when two or more acts of the same person are possibly the sole cause, and the plaintiff has introduced evidence that the one of the two persons, or the one of the same person's two acts, is culpable, then the defendant has the burden of proving that the other person, or his other act, was the sole cause of the harm. (b) The real reason for the rule that each joint tortfeasor is responsible for the whole damage is the practical unfairness of denying the injured person redress simply because he cannot prove how much damage each did, when it is certain that between them they did all; let them be the ones to apportion it among themselves. Since, then, the difficulty of proof is the reason, the rule should apply whenever the harm has plural causes, and not merely when they acted in conscious concert. ' (Wigmore, Select Cases on the Law of Torts, sec. 153.) Similarly Professor Carpenter has said: '(Suppose) the case where A and B independently shoot at C and but one bullet touches C's body. In such case, such proof as is ordinarily required that either A or B shot C, of course fails. It is suggested that there should be a relaxation of the proof required of the plaintiff where the injury occurs as the result of one where more than one independent force is operating, and it is impossible to determine that the force set in operation by defendant did not in fact constitute a cause of the damage, and where it may have caused the damage, but the plaintiff is unable to establish that it was a cause.' (20 Cal.L.Rev. 406.)

When we consider the relative position of the parties and the results that would flow if plaintiff was required to pin the injury on one of the defendants only, a requirement that the burden of proof on that subject be shifted to defendants becomes manifest. They are both wrongdoers both negligent toward plaintiff. They brought about a situation where the negligence of one of them injured the plaintiff, hence it should rest with them each to absolve himself if he can. The injured party has been placed by defendants in the unfair position of pointing to which defendant caused the harm. If one can escape the other may also and plaintiff is remediless. Ordinarily defendants are in a far better position to offer evidence to determine which one caused the injury. This reasoning has recently found favor in this Court. In a quite analogous situation this Court held that a patient injured while unconscious on an operating table in a hospital could hold all or any of the persons who had any connection with the operation even though he could not select the particular acts by the particular person which led to his disability. Ybarra v. Spangard, 25 Cal.2d 486, 154 P.2d

687, 162 A.L.R. 1258. There the Court was considering whether the patient could avail himself of res ipsa loquitur, rather than where the burden of proof lay, yet the effect of the decision is that plaintiff has made out a case when he has produced evidence which gives rise to an inference of negligence which was the proximate cause of the injury. It is up to defendants to explain the cause of the injury. It was there said: 'If the doctrine is to continue to serve a useful purpose, we should not forget that 'the particular force and justice of the rule, regarded as a presumption throwing upon the party charged the duty of producing evidence, consists in the circumstance that the chief evidence of the true cause, whether culpable or innocent, is practically accessible to him but inaccessible to the injured person." 25 Cal.2d at page 490, 154 P.2d at page 689, 162 A.L.R. 1258. Similarly in the instant case plaintiff is not able to establish which of defendants caused his injury.

The foregoing discussion disposes of the authorities cited by defendants such as Kraft v. Smith, 24 Cal.2d 124, 148 P.2d 23, and Hernandez v. Southern California Gas Co., 213 Cal. 384, 2 P.2d 360, stating the general rule that one defendant is not liable for the independent tort of the other defendant, or that ordinarily the plaintiff must show a causal connection between the negligence and the injury. There was an entire lack of such connection in the Hernandez case and there were not several negligent defendants, one of whom must have caused the injury.

Defendants rely upon Christensen v. Los Angeles Electrical Supply Co., 112 Cal.App. 629, 297 P. 614, holding that a defendant is not liable where he negligently knocked down with his car a pedestrian and a third person then ran over the prostrate person. That involves the question of intervening cause which we do not have here. Moreover it is out of harmony with the current rule on that subject and was properly questioned in Hill v. Peres, 136 Cal.App. 132, 28 P.2d 946 (hearing in this Court denied), and must be deemed disapproved. See, Mosley v. Arden Farms Co., 26 Cal.2d 213, 157 P.2d 372, 158 A.L.R. 872; Sawyer v. Southern California Gas Co., 206 Cal. 366, 274 P. 544; 6 Cal.Jur. Ten Yr.Supp., Automobiles, sec. 349; 19 Cal.Jur. 570–572.

Cases are cited for the proposition that where two or more tort feasors acting independently of each other cause an injury to plaintiff, they are not joint tort feasors and plaintiff must establish the portion of the damage caused by each, even though it is impossible to prove the portion of the injury caused by each. See, Slater v. Pacific American Oil Co., 212 Cal. 648, 300 P. 31; Miller v. Highland Ditch Co., 87 cal. 430, 25 P. 550, 22 Am.St.Rep. 254; People v. Gold Run D. & M. Co., 66 Cal. 138, 4 P. 1152, 56 Am.Rep. 80; Wade v. Thorsen, 5 Cal.App.2d 706, 43 P.2d 592; California Orange Co. v. Riverside P. C. Co., 50 Cal.App. 522, 195 P. 694; City of Oakland v. Pacific Gas & E. Co., 47 Cal.App.2d 444, 118 P.2d 328. In view of the foregoing discussion it is apparent that defendants in cases like the present one may be treated as liable on the same basis as joint tort feasors, and hence the last cited cases are distinguishable inasmuch as they involve independent tort feasors.

In addition to that, however, it should be pointed out that the same reasons of policy and justice shift the burden to each of defendants to absolve himself if he can—relieving the wronged person of the duty of apportioning the injury to a particular defendant, apply here where we are concerned with whether plaintiff is required to supply evidence for the apportionment of damages. If defendants are independent tort feasors and thus each liable for the damage caused by him alone, and, at least, where the matter of apportionment is incapable of proof, the innocent wronged party should not be deprived of his right to redress. The wrongdoers should be left to work out between themselves any apportionment. See, Colonial Ins. Co., v. Industrial Acc. Com., 29 Cal.2d 79, 172 P.2d 884. Some of the cited cases refer to the difficulty of apportioning the burden of damages between the independent tort feasors, and say that where factually a correct division cannot be made, the trier of fact may make it the best it can, which would be more or less a guess, stressing the factor that the wrongdoers are not a position to complain of uncertainty. California Orange Co. v. Riverside P. C. Co., supra.

It is urged that plaintiff now has changed the theory of his case in claiming a concert of action; that he did not plead or prove such concert. From what has been said it is clear that there has been no change in theory. The joint liability, as well as the lack of knowledge as to which defendant was liable, was pleaded and the proof developed the case under either theory. We have seen that for the reasons of policy discussed herein, the case is based upon the legal proposition that, under the circumstances here presented, each defendant is liable for the whole damage whether they are deemed to be acting in concert or independently.

The judgment is affirmed.

DISCUSSION PROBLEMS

1. Flood

In August 2010, a major rainstorm struck Ottumwa, Iowa. Water overflowed the banks of Little Cedar Creek and then over U.S. Highway 63/149 flooding the house of David and Julie Garr, rising to the level of the doorknob on the front door and causing $145,000 in damage. The Garrs sued the city, alleging that the city was negligent in managing storm water by (1) approving an adjacent residential development, the Quail Creek Addition, which resulted in increased water in the creek and frequent flooding, (2) failing to establish appropriate storm water control to protect the Garrs and other downstream residents from increased water flows that resulted from the addition, and (3) failing to comply with applicable storm water management policies.

At the trial, the Garrs presented the expert testimony of Dr. Stewart Melvin, an expert in hydrology, the study of water's movement in the environment, on the issue of causation. Dr. Melvin testified that water from the Quail Creek Addition discharges into Little Cedar Creek, and that the addition had "some" effect on the amount of water traveling through the creek during storms. On cross examination, Dr. Melvin stated that he had not performed exact calculations supporting his conclusion that developing Quail Creek Addition had an effect on the creek's water levels; rather, Dr. Melvin relied on his estimations of water depths and flow in the area.

Dr. Melvin prepared a report, which was admitted into evidence, which estimated "peak flows from different sized storms in the 2000-acre watershed." According to the report, if a rainstorm dropped 5.5 inches of rain in twenty-four hours, which according to the report would result in a twenty-five-year flood, flooding would occur to the first floor of the Garrs' home. If it rained 6.1 inches in twenty-four hours, which according to the report would result in a fifty-year flood, the first floor of the Garrs' home would be flooded with three feet of water. In the report, Dr. Melvin acknowledged his understanding that the flood underlying the Garrs' lawsuit "put approximately 4 [feet] of water above the floor of the Garr residence and water was running over the road."

The report made clear that 6.8 inches of rain in twenty-four hours would have caused water from the creek to flow over U.S. Highway 63/149. On cross-examination, Dr. Melvin said he had heard reports that as much as ten inches of rain fell on the 2000-acre watershed on August 20, 2010. He admitted that "if there was 10 inches of rainfall in that period, probably when you get that kind of a quantity, the effects of hardly anything makes any difference. It's just the rainfall."

Was there sufficient evidence for a jury to conclude that the City's negligence caused the damage to the Garrs' house?

2. Medical Error

Nena Falcon suffered a respiratory and cardiac arrest after giving birth in a Michigan hospital. The autopsy report indicated that amniotic fluid embolism, a rare and unpreventable complication, was the cause of death. If Falcon's physician had inserted an intravenous line in Falcon prior to the onset of the embolism, that line could have been used to infuse life-saving fluids into her circulatory system. Falcon's expert testified that the physician's failure to do so failed to satisfy the standard of care. But the intervention would not have necessarily saved her life. Falcon's expert witness testified that that the use of an intravenous line would have provided her with a 37.5% chance of survival.

Should Falcon be entitled to recover from her physician for medical malpractice?

3. The DES Litigation

In 1947, the Food and Drug Administration authorized the marketing of diethylstilbesterol (DES), as a miscarriage preventative medication. The drug was administered to Judith Sindell's mother, and between 1.5 million and 3 million other women, for the purpose of preventing miscarriage. Unfortunately, DES can cause cancerous vaginal and cervical growths in the daughters exposed to it before birth, because their mothers took the drug during pregnancy. During the period that DES was marketed, the approximately 200 pharmaceutical companies that produced and sold it knew or should have known that it was a carcinogenic substance, that there was a grave danger after varying periods of latency it would cause cancerous and precancerous growths in the daughters of the mothers who took it, and that it was ineffective to prevent miscarriage. Nevertheless, the companies continued to advertise and market the drug as a miscarriage preventative.

Sindell suffered a particular form of cancer known to be caused by DES, but all manufacturers produced their drugs from an identical formula, and Sindell could not identify which company caused her injury. She sued five large drug companies that had manufactured DES at the time that her mother took the drug, alleging that they were jointly liable for her injuries. None of the companies had produced a majority of the DES sold at the relevant time, but the five together produced most (but not all) of the DES sold. Should Sindell be entitled to recover damages from any or all of the defendants?

CHAPTER 10

SCOPE OF LIABILITY

■ ■ ■

INTRODUCTION

In some situations, harm caused by the defendant's negligence seems so remote or out of proportion to the defendant's fault that the law declines to impose liability. Traditionally, courts have used two different doctrines to establish limits on the scope of liability. Some courts have considered the remoteness of harm under the rubric of causation, concluding that although a negligent act might have been a "but for" cause of the harm, the remoteness of the negligence to the harm can mean that the negligence was not a "proximate cause" of the harm. Other courts have addressed the problem as an element of the duty requirement, holding that actors lack a duty of care to victims in the case of remote harms.

Whichever doctrinal hook a court uses, the consequence is that a particular harm will sometimes be found to be non-compensable because it is beyond the scope of liability of negligence law. Where this boundary lies is one of the most inscrutable issues in tort law. If you find yourself scratching your head after studying this chapter, you will not be alone!

In *Union Pump Co. v. Albritton,* the Texas Supreme Court frames the question as one of proximate cause. In *Palsgraf v. Long Island R.R. Co.*—one of the most famous opinions in tort law—Judge Cardozo, writing for the New York Court of Appeals describes the issue as one of duty (although the equally famous dissent of Judge Andrews prefers the proximate cause frame). Does this matter? Both courts seem to believe the fundamental question is whether the harm was "foreseeable." Is this helpful? The Restatement tries to sharpen the inquiry by enunciating a harm-within-the-risk test: "An actor's liability is limited to those harms that result from the risks that made the actor's conduct tortious." Rest. (3d) Torts § 29. Does this help clarify the rule beyond stating that what matters is the foreseeability of the injury?

Restatement (Third) of Torts § 7. Duty

(a) An actor ordinarily has a duty to exercise reasonable care when the actor's conduct creates a risk of physical harm.

(b) In exceptional cases, when an articulated countervailing principle or policy warrants denying or limiting liability in a particular class of cases, a court may decide that the defendant has no duty or that the ordinary duty of reasonable care requires modification.

Comment:

a. The proper role for duty. . . .[A]ctors engaging in conduct that creates risks to others have a duty to exercise reasonable care to avoid causing physical harm. . . .Nevertheless, in some categories of cases, reasons of principle or policy dictate that liability should not be imposed. In these cases, courts use the rubric of duty to apply general categorical rules withholding liability.

There are two different legal doctrines for withholding liability: no-duty rules and scope-of-liability doctrines (often called "proximate cause"). An important difference between them is that no-duty rules are matters of law decided by the courts, while the defendant's scope of liability is a question of fact for the factfinder. When liability depends on factors specific to an individual case, the appropriate rubric is scope of liability. On the other hand, when liability depends on factors applicable to categories of actors or patterns of conduct, the appropriate rubric is duty. No-duty rules are appropriate only when a court can promulgate relatively clear, categorical, bright-line rules of law applicable to a general class of cases.

Restatement (Third) of Torts § 29. Limitations on Liability for Tortious Conduct

An actor's liability is limited to those harms that result from the risks that made the actor's conduct tortious.

Comment:

f. Relationship with duty limitations. This Chapter is about limits on the liability of an actor whose tortious conduct is a factual cause of harm. There are two primary legal doctrines for limiting liability: duty and scope of liability. Some courts use duty in situations in which other courts would use proximate cause. . . .

One significant difference between these two doctrines is helpful in determining their appropriate spheres of application. Duty is a question of law for the court . . . while scope of liability, although very much an evaluative matter, is treated as a question of fact for the factfinder. . . .

j. Connection with reasonable foreseeability as a limit on liability. Many jurisdictions employ a "foreseeability" test for proximate cause, and in negligence actions such a rule is essentially consistent with the standard set forth in this Section. Properly understood, both the risk standard and a foreseeability test exclude liability for harms that were sufficiently unforeseeable at the time of the actor's tortious conduct that they were not among the risks—potential harms—that made the actor negligent. Negligence limits the requirement of reasonable care to those risks that are foreseeable. . . .Thus, when scope of liability arises in a negligence case, the risks that make an actor negligent are limited to foreseeable ones, and the factfinder must determine whether the type of harm that occurred is among those reasonably foreseeable potential harms that made the actor's conduct negligent.

Although the risk standard in this Section is comparable to the foreseeability standard in actions based on negligence, the risk standard contained in this Section is preferable because it provides greater clarity, facilitates clearer analysis in a given case, and better reveals the reason for its existence. The risk standard provides greater clarity and facilitates analysis because it focuses attention on the particular circumstances that existed at the time of the actor's conduct and the risks that were posed by that conduct. Risks may be foreseeable in context, as when an extraordinary storm is forecast, requiring precautions against the risks posed by it, that might otherwise be thought of, out of context, as exceedingly unlikely and therefore unforeseeable. The risk standard focuses on the appropriate context, although a foreseeability standard, properly explained, could do this also. The risk standard provides better understanding about the reasons for its existence by appealing to the intuition that it is fair for an actor's liability to be limited to those risks that made the conduct wrongful. Thus, factfinders can apply the risk standard with more sensitivity to the underlying rationale than they might muster with an unadorned foreseeable-harm standard.

A foreseeability test for negligence cases risks being misunderstood because of uncertainty about what must be foreseen, by whom, and at what time. When courts pose the foreseeability inquiry as whether the harm was foreseeable at the time the defendant acted or as whether an intervening act was foreseeable, attention is deflected from the crux of the risk-standard inquiry. Moreover, the risk standard deals more comfortably with scope of liability when the defendant is an actor for whom the law modifies the objective standard of care. Thus, the risk standard would adapt the scope of liability for a child who is not expected to anticipate the same scope of harms as an adult.

Restatement (Third) of Torts § 34. Intervening Acts and Superseding Causes

When a force of nature or an independent act is also a factual cause of harm, an actor's liability is limited to those harms that result from the risks that made the actor's conduct tortious.

Comment:

e. Unforeseeable, unusual, or highly culpable intervening acts. In some cases, the risk that makes conduct tortious is one created by another person's conduct. . . . In such cases, the intervening act and the attendant harm are within the scope of the defendant's liability, and those cases are not addressed in this Comment. However, in other cases, the risk is one that exists independently of human intervention, although causes in addition to the defendant's tortious conduct are required for the harm to occur. When those other causes—intervening acts—are unforeseeable, unusual, or highly culpable they may bear on whether the harm is within the scope of the risk.

CASES

UNION PUMP CO. V. ALLBRITTON

Supreme Court of Texas
898 S.W.2d 773 (Tx. 1995)

OWEN, JUSTICE.

The issue in this case is whether the condition, act, or omission of which a personal injury plaintiff complains was, as a matter of law, too remote to constitute legal causation.

. . .

On the night of September 4, 1989, a fire occurred at Texaco Chemical Company's facility in Port Arthur, Texas. A pump manufactured by Union Pump Company caught fire and ignited the surrounding area. This particular pump had caught on fire twice before. Sue Allbritton, a trainee employee of Texaco Chemical, had just finished her shift and was about to leave the plant when the fire erupted. She and her supervisor Felipe Subia, Jr., were directed to and did assist in abating the fire.

Approximately two hours later, the fire was extinguished. However, there appeared to be a problem with a nitrogen purge valve, and Subia was instructed to block in the valve. Viewing the facts in a light most favorable to Allbritton, there was some evidence that an emergency situation existed at that point in time. Allbritton asked if she could accompany Subia and was allowed to do so. To get to the nitrogen purge valve, Allbritton followed Subia over an aboveground pipe rack, which was approximately two and one-half feet high. . . . Allbritton was injured when she hopped or slipped off the pipe rack. There is evidence that the pipe rack was wet because of the fire and that Allbritton and Subia were still wearing fireman's hip boots and other firefighting gear when the injury occurred.

. . .

Allbritton sued Union Pump, alleging negligence. . . . But for the pump fire, she asserts, she would never have walked over the pipe rack, which was wet with water or firefighting foam.

Following discovery, Union Pump moved for summary judgment. To be entitled to summary judgment, the movant has the burden of establishing that there is no genuine issue of material fact and that it is entitled to judgment as a matter of law. *Nixon v. Mr. Property Management Co.,* 690 S.W.2d 546, 548 (Tex.1985). A defendant who moves for summary judgment must conclusively disprove one of the elements of each of the plaintiff's causes of action. *Lear Siegler, Inc. v. Perez,* 819 S.W.2d 470, 471 (Tex.1991). All doubts must be resolved against Union Pump and all evidence must be viewed in the light most favorable to Allbritton.

. . .

Negligence requires a showing of proximate cause. . . . Proximate cause consists of both cause in fact and foreseeability. Cause in fact means that the defendant's act or omission was a substantial factor in bringing about the injury which would not otherwise have occurred.

. . .

At some point in the causal chain, the defendant's conduct or product may be too remotely connected with the plaintiff's injury to constitute legal causation. As this Court noted in *City of Gladewater v. Pike,* 727 S.W.2d 514, 518 (Tex.1987), defining the limits of legal causation "eventually mandates weighing of policy considerations." *See also Springall v. Fredericksburg Hospital and Clinic,* 225 S.W.2d 232, 235 (Tex.Civ.App.—San Antonio 1949, no writ), in which the court of appeals observed:

> [T]he law does not hold one legally responsible for the remote results of his wrongful acts and therefore a line must be drawn between immediate and remote causes. The doctrine of "proximate cause" is employed to determine and fix this line and "is the result of an effort by the courts to avoid, as far as possible the metaphysical and philosophical niceties in the age-old discussion of causation, and to lay down a rule of general application which will, as nearly as may be done by a general rule, apply a practical test, the test of common experience, to human conduct when determining legal rights and legal liability.

Drawing the line between where legal causation may exist and where, as a matter of law, it cannot, has generated a considerable body of law. Our Court has considered where the limits of legal causation should lie in the factually analogous case of *Lear Siegler, Inc. v. Perez, supra*. . . . Perez, an employee of the Texas Highway Department, was driving a truck pulling a flashing arrow sign behind a highway sweeping operation to warn traffic of the highway maintenance. The sign malfunctioned when wires connecting it to the generator became loose, as they had the previous day. Perez got out of the truck to push the wire connections back together, and an oncoming vehicle, whose driver was asleep, struck the sign, which in turn struck Perez. Perez's survivors brought suit against the manufacturer of the sign. In holding that any defect in the sign was not the legal cause of Perez's injuries, we found a comment to the *Restatement (Second) of Torts,* section 431, instructive on the issue of legal causation:

> In order to be a legal cause of another's harm, it is not enough that the harm would not have occurred had the actor not been negligent. . . . The negligence must also be a substantial factor in bringing about the plaintiff's harm. The word "substantial" is used to denote the fact that the defendant's conduct has such an effect in producing the harm as to lead reasonable men to regard it as a cause, using that word in the popular sense, in which there always lurks the idea of responsibility, rather than in the so-called "philosophic sense," which includes every one of the great number of events without which any happening would not have occurred.

As this Court explained in *Lear Siegler,* the connection between the defendant and the plaintiff's injuries simply may be too attenuated to constitute legal cause. 819 S.W.2d at 472. Legal cause is not established if the defendant's conduct or product does no more than furnish the condition that makes the plaintiff's injury possible. *Id.* This principle applies with equal force to proximate cause and producing cause. *Id.* at 472 n. 1.

This Court similarly considered the parameters of legal causation in *Bell v. Campbell,* 434 S.W.2d 117, 122 (Tex.1968). In *Bell,* two cars collided, and a trailer attached to one of them disengaged and overturned into the opposite lane. A number of people gathered, and three of them were attempting to move the trailer when they were struck by another vehicle. *Id.* at 119. This Court held that the parties to the first accident were not a proximate cause of the plaintiffs' injuries, reasoning:

> All acts and omissions charged against respondents had run their course and were complete. Their negligence did not actively contribute in any way to the injuries involved in this suit. It simply created a condition which attracted [the plaintiffs] to the scene, where they were injured by a third party.
>
> *Id.* at 122.

In *Bell,* this Court examined at some length decisions dealing with intervening causes and decisions dealing with concurring causes. The principles underlying the various legal theories of causation overlap in many respects, but they are not coextensive. While in *Bell,* this Court held "the injuries involved in this suit were not proximately caused by any negligence of [defendants] but by an independent and intervening agency," *id.*, we also held "[a]ll forces involved in or generated by the first collision had come to rest, and no one was in any real or apparent danger therefrom[,]" *id.* at 120, and accordingly, that the "[defendants'] negligence was not a concurring cause of [the plaintiffs'] injuries." *Id.* at 122. This reasoning applies with equal force to Allbritton's claims.

Even if the pump fire were in some sense a "philosophic" or "but for" cause of Allbritton's injuries, the forces generated by the fire had come to rest when she fell off the pipe rack. The fire had been extinguished, and Allbritton was walking away from the scene. Viewing the evidence in the light most favorable to Allbritton, the pump fire did no more than create the condition that made Allbritton's injuries possible. We conclude that the circumstances surrounding her injuries are too remotely connected with Union Pump's conduct or pump to constitute a legal cause of her injuries. *See Lear Siegler*, 819 S.W.2d at 472.

Accordingly, we reverse the judgment of the court of appeals and render judgment that plaintiff take nothing.

PHILLIPS, CHIEF JUSTICE, and GONZALEZ, HIGHTOWER, HECHT, GAMMAGE and ENOCH, JUSTICES, join.

CORNYN, JUSTICE, concurring.

. . . The pump defect clearly was a "but for" cause of Allbritton's injuries: assuming the truth of Allbritton's allegations, as we must in this summary judgment case, if the pump had not been defective, there would have been no fire, and Allbritton would have gone home uninjured at the end of her shift. Assuming the substantial factor test from Section 432(2) of the *Restatement (Second)* applies, the pump defect was also a substantial factor in her injury.

. . .In proximate cause, this other element is foreseeability, but it also incorporates policy driven decisions such as when subsequent events will be treated as intervening causes. In this case, the injury to Allbritton was not foreseeable. . . .Holding Union Pump liable . . .is akin to holding it liable for an auto accident she suffered on the way home, even though the accident probably would not have occurred had she left after her normal shift. Foreseeability allows us to cut off Union Pump's liability at some point; I would do so at the point the crisis had abated or at the point that Allbritton and Subia departed from their usual, safe path.

SPECTOR, JUSTICE, dissenting.

The summary judgment evidence in this case does not negate causation as a matter of law.

The record reflects that at the time Sue Allbritton's injury occurred, the forces generated by the fire in question had *not* come to rest. Rather, the emergency situation was continuing. The whole area of the fire was covered in water and foam; in at least some places, the water was almost knee-deep. Allbritton was still wearing hip boots and other gear, as required to fight the fire. Viewing all the evidence in the light most favorable to Allbritton, I agree with Justice Cornyn that the pump defect was both a "but-for" cause and a substantial factor in bringing about Allbritton's injury. . . .

This case is markedly different from the two main cases on which the majority relies. In each of those cases, a defendant's negligence simply created a condition that attracted an individual to the scene, where a negligent third party inflicted an injury. Here, in contrast, there was no negligent third party. To whatever extent Allbritton's own negligence may have contributed to her injury, a jury should be allowed to allocate comparative responsibility.

Because Union Pump has failed to establish its right to summary judgment as a matter of law, I dissent.

PALSGRAF V. LONG ISLAND R.R. CO.

Court of Appeals of New York
248 N.Y. 339 (1928)

CARDOZO, C.J.

Plaintiff was standing on a platform of defendant's railroad after buying a ticket to go to Rockaway Beach. A train stopped at the station, bound for another place. Two men ran forward to catch it. One of the men reached the platform of the car without mishap, though the train was already moving. The other man, carrying a package, jumped aboard the car, but seemed unsteady as if about to fall. A guard on the car, who had held the door open, reached forward to help him in, and another guard on the platform pushed him from behind. In this act, the package was dislodged, and fell upon the rails. It was a package of small size, about fifteen inches long, and was covered by a newspaper. In fact it contained fireworks, but there was nothing in its appearance to give notice of its contents. The fireworks when they fell exploded. The shock of the explosion threw down some scales at the other end of the platform many feet away. The scales struck the plaintiff, causing injuries for which she sues.

The conduct of the defendant's guard, if a wrong in its relation to the holder of the package, was not a wrong in its relation to the plaintiff, standing far away. Relatively to her it was not negligence at all. Nothing in the situation gave notice that the falling package had in it the potency of peril to persons thus removed. Negligence is not actionable unless it involves the invasion of a legally protected interest, the violation of a right. 'The plaintiff, as she stood upon the platform of the station, might claim to be protected against intentional invasion of her bodily security. Such invasion is not charged. She might claim to be protected against unintentional invasion by conduct involving in the thought of reasonable men an unreasonable hazard that such invasion would ensue. These, from the point of view of the law, were the bounds of her immunity, with perhaps some rare exceptions, survivals for the most part of ancient forms of liability, where conduct is held to be at the peril of the actor. If no hazard was apparent to the eye of ordinary vigilance, an act innocent and harmless, at least to outward seeming, with reference to her, did not take to itself the quality of a tort because it happened to be a wrong, though apparently not one involving the risk of bodily insecurity, with reference to some one else. . . .The plaintiff sues in her own right for a wrong personal to her, and not as the vicarious beneficiary of a breach of duty to another.

. . .One who jostles one's neighbor in a crowd does not invade the rights of others standing at the outer fringe when the unintended contact casts a bomb upon the ground. The wrongdoer as to them is the man who carries the bomb, not the one who explodes it without suspicion of the danger. Life will have to be made over, and human nature transformed, before prevision so extravagant can be accepted as the norm of conduct, the customary standard to which behavior must conform.

The argument for the plaintiff is built upon the shifting meanings of such words as 'wrong' and 'wrongful,' and shares their instability. What the plaintiff must show is 'a wrong' to herself; i. e., a violation of her own right, and not merely a wrong to some one else, nor conduct 'wrongful' because unsocial, but not 'a wrong' to any one. We are told that one who drives at reckless speed through a crowded city street is guilty of a negligent act and therefore of a wrongful one, irrespective of the consequences. Negligent the act is, and wrongful in the sense that it is unsocial, but wrongful and unsocial in relation to other travelers, only because the eye of vigilance perceives the risk of damage. If the same act were to be committed on a speedway or a race course, it would lose its wrongful quality. The risk reasonably to be perceived defines the duty to be obeyed, and risk imports relation; it is risk to another or to others within the range of apprehension. . . .The range of reasonable apprehension is at times a question for the court, and at times, if varying inferences are possible, a question for the jury. Here, by concession, there was nothing in the situation to suggest to the most cautious mind that the parcel wrapped in newspaper would spread wreckage through the station. If the guard had thrown it down knowingly and willfully, he would not have threatened the plaintiff's safety, so far as appearances could warn him. His conduct would not have involved, even then, an unreasonable probability of invasion of her bodily security. Liability can be no greater where the act is inadvertent.

The judgment of the Appellate Division and that of the Trial Term should be reversed, and the complaint dismissed, with costs in all courts.

. . .

ANDREWS, J. (dissenting).

Assisting a passenger to board a train, the defendant's servant negligently knocked a package from his arms. It fell between the platform and the cars. Of its contents the servant knew and could know nothing. A violent explosion followed. The concussion broke some scales standing a considerable distance away. In falling, they injured the plaintiff, an intending passenger.

Upon these facts, may she recover the damages she has suffered in an action brought against the master? The result we shall reach depends upon our theory as to the nature of negligence. Is it a relative concept—the breach of some duty owing to a particular person or to particular persons? Or, where there is an act which unreasonably threatens the safety of others, is the doer liable for all its proximate consequences, even where they result in injury to one who would generally be thought to be outside the radius of danger? . . .

Should we drive down Broadway at a reckless speed, we are negligent whether we strike an approaching car or miss it by an inch. The act itself is wrongful. It is a wrong not only to those who happen to be within the radius of danger, but to all who might have been there—a wrong to the public at large.

. . .

The proposition is this: Every one owes to the world at large the duty of refraining from those acts that may unreasonably threaten the safety of others. Such an act occurs. Not only is he wronged to whom harm, might reasonably be expected to result, but he also who is in fact injured, even if he be outside what would generally be thought the danger zone. There needs be duty due the one complaining, but this is not a duty to a particular individual because as to him harm might be expected. Harm to some one being the natural result of the act, not only that one alone, but all those in fact injured may complain. We have never, I think, held otherwise. Indeed in the Di Caprio Case we said that a breach of a general ordinance defining the degree of care to be exercised in one's calling is evidence of negligence as to every one. We did not limit this statement to those who might be expected to be exposed to danger. Unreasonable risk being taken, its consequences are not confined to those who might probably be hurt.

. . .

The right to recover damages rests on additional considerations. The plaintiff's rights must be injured, and this injury must be caused by the negligence. We build a dam, but are negligent as to its foundations. Breaking, it injures property down stream. We are not liable if all this happened because of some reason other than the insecure foundation. But, when injuries do result from out unlawful act, we are liable for the consequences. It does not matter that they are unusual, unexpected, unforeseen, and unforeseeable. But there is one limitation. The damages must be so connected with the negligence that the latter may be said to be the proximate cause of the former.

. . .

There are some hints that may help us. The proximate cause, involved as it may be with many other causes, must be, at the least, something without which the event would not happen. The court must ask itself whether there was a natural and continuous sequence between cause and effect. Was the one a substantial factor in producing the other? Was there a direct connection between them, without too many intervening causes? Is the effect of cause on result not too attenuated? Is the cause likely, in the usual judgment of mankind, to produce the result? Or, by the exercise of prudent foresight, could the result be foreseen? Is the result too remote from the cause, and here we consider remoteness in time and space.

. . .

The act upon which defendant's liability rests is knocking an apparently harmless package onto the platform. The act was negligent. For its proximate consequences the defendant is liable. If its contents were broken, to the owner; if it fell upon and crushed a passenger's foot, then to him; if it exploded and injured one in the immediate vicinity, to him also as to A in the illustration. Mrs. Palsgraf was standing some distance away. How far cannot be told from the record—apparently 25 or 30 feet, perhaps less. Except for the explosion, she would not have been injured. We are told by the appellant in his brief, 'It cannot be denied that the explosion was the direct cause of the plaintiff's injuries.' So it was a substantial factor in producing the result—there was here a natural and continuous sequence—direct connection. The only intervening cause was that, instead of blowing her to the ground, the concussion smashed the weighing machine which in turn fell upon her. There was no remoteness in time, little in space. And surely, given such an explosion as here, it needed no great foresight to predict that the natural result would be to injure one on the platform at no greater distance from its scene than was the plaintiff. Just how no one might be able to predict. Whether by flying fragments, by broken glass, by wreckage of machines or structures no one could say. But injury in some form was most probable.

Under these circumstances I cannot say as a matter of law that the plaintiff's injuries were not the proximate result of the negligence. That is all we have before us. The court refused to so charge. No request was made to submit the matter to the jury as a question of fact, even would that have been proper upon the record before us.

The judgment appealed from should be affirmed, with costs.

POUND, LEHMAN, and KELLOGG, JJ., concur with CARDOZO, C. J.

ANDREWS, J., dissents in opinion in which CRANE and O'BRIEN, JJ., concur.

DISCUSSION PROBLEMS

1. The Drawbridge Collision

The Buffalo River flows through Buffalo from east to west, with many turns and bends, until it empties into Lake Erie. Its navigable western portion is lined with docks, grain elevators, and industrial installations; during the winter, lake vessels tie up there, pending resumption of navigation on the Great Lakes. The current occasionally propels broken ice down the river, which sometimes overflows its banks. About a mile from the mouth, the City of Buffalo maintains a drawbridge that is raised and lowered by a bridge operator to permit ships to pass through to the lake.

On January 21, 1959, rain and thaw followed a period of freezing weather, an ice jam upriver broke and an ice flow headed through town toward Lake Erie. A ship called the Shiras, owned by the Kinsman Transit Company, was moored on the side of the river, but the mooring cable pulled out of the ground when the pressure of the flowing ice built up on the ship. Once pried loose from its mooring, the Shiras careened down the river. Careening down the river, the Shiras struck the bow of another ship, the Tewksbury, pried it loose from its mooring, and carried it down the river. The trial judge found that the owner of the Shiras was negligent in its inspection of the ship's mooring cable, that the shipkeeper was negligent for not deploying the ship's anchors, and that the ship would not have been pried loose absent these errors.

As the ice and the ships headed down the river, observers called for the bridge to be raised, but the bridge operator had negligently left his post to visit a tavern and did not heed the warning in time. At 11:17 P.M., the Shiras and the Tewksbury crashed into the center of the bridge. The two vessels and bridge debris created a dam, causing water and ice to back up, flooding and damaging property on the banks of the river as far as three miles upstream.

Should the Kinsman Transit Company (as owner of the Shiras) and/or the City of Buffalo (as the operator of the bridge) be liable for the upstream property damage?

2. The Manhattan Building Collapse

In 1997, a section of the south wall of 540 Madison Avenue, a 39-story office tower, partially collapsed and bricks, mortar and other material fell onto Madison Avenue at 55th Street, a prime commercial location crammed with stores and skyscrapers. New York City officials directed the closure of 15 heavily trafficked blocks on Madison Avenue—from 42nd to 57th Street—as well as adjacent side streets between Fifth and Park Avenues to all vehicular and pedestrian traffic. The closure lasted for approximately two weeks, but some businesses nearest to 540 Madison remained closed for a longer period.

532 Madison Avenue Gourmet Foods, a delicatessen located one-half block south of 540 Madison, suffered no physical damage from the building collapse, but it was subsequently closed for five weeks, losing substantial income. Assuming that the owners of the collapsed building were negligent, should the delicatessen be entitled to recover from the owner of 540 Madison for its lost profits?

3. The Oklahoma City Bombing

In April 1995, Timothy McVeigh set off a truck bomb at the Alfred P. Murrah Federal Building in Oklahoma City that killed 168 people and injured hundreds of others. McVeigh and his accomplice, Terry Nichols, built the bomb using 4000 pounds of ammonium nitrate, which they purchased from the Mid-Kansas Cooperative Association, mixed with fuel oil.

The victims and their families filed a class action lawsuit against ICI Explosives, the chemical company that manufactured the ammonium nitrate, alleging that ICI acted negligently by mislabeling the ammonium nitrate that it sold to the Mid-Kansas Co-op as "fertilizer grade," which is of lower density and would not have been combustible enough to build a bomb capable of bringing down the Murrah Building, what was actually "explosive grade" ammonium nitrate that was capable of the destruction.

The plaintiffs also alleged that ICI sold the ammonium nitrate to Mid-Kansas without first verifying that the Cooperative had the required permits to receive it and without registering the sale, as was required by state law for all explosives, defined as "any chemical compound, mixture or device, of which the primary purpose is to function by explosion, and includes but is not limited to dynamite and other high explosives, black powder, pellet powder, initiating explosives, detonators, safety fuses, squibs, detonating cord, igniter cord and igniters."

Assuming that they can prove the facts alleged, should the plaintiffs be able to recover damages from ICI?

CHAPTER 11

GIFT, ABANDONMENT, AND FOUND PROPERTY

■ ■ ■

INTRODUCTION

In the 21st century, virtually no property is "unowned." To acquire property, we almost always enter into transactions (i.e., contracts). For most of us, most of the time, we sell our labor for money, and then we use money to purchase goods, services, land, or intellectual property. Beginning with Chapter 12, we will delve deeply into the subject of contract law. But there are other ways that property is transferred. This Chapter briefly considers these methods of property acquisition.

The most important non-contract method of property transfer is gift, either *inter vivos* (while alive) or testamentary (at death). Gifts require donative intent accompanied by a transfer. Rest. (3d) Property (Wills & Don. Trans.) § 6.1. The most complicated question concerns the extent to which the donor may control the donee's use of the gift, an issue explored in *Adler v. Save.*

Less significant but occasionally important is the transfer as a consequence of finding abandoned, lost or mislaid property. "Abandonment" by an owner requires both an intent to disclaim ownership and an act that furthers this intent. 1 Am. Jur. 2d Abandoned, Lost, and Unclaimed Property § 8. What evidence is sufficient to establish the necessary intent to abandon? *C&H Manufacturing, LLC v. Harland Co. Industrial Development Authority, Inc.* considers.

Title to abandoned property is transferred to the finder who is first to establish possession. 1 Am. Jur. 2d Abandoned, Lost, and Unclaimed Property § 25. The recipient of title to property that is found but not previously abandoned depends on whether the item is considered "lost" or "mislaid." 1 Am. Jur. 2d Abandoned, Lost, and Unclaimed Property §§ 13, 15. Should this distinction matter? Consider *Benjamin v. Lidner Aviation, Inc.*

Restatement (Third) of Property (Wills & Don. Trans.) § 6.1. Requirements Applicable to All Gifts of Property

(a) To make a gift of property, the donor must transfer an ownership interest to the donee without consideration and with donative intent.

(b) Acceptance by the donee is required for a gift to become complete. Acceptance is presumed, subject to the donee's right to refuse or disclaim.

Comment:

b. *Donative intent.* To be a gift, a transfer must be made with donative intent. The requirement of donative intent is the essence of a gift. . . .

p. *Donative promises.* A statement by the donor that he or she will give property to the donee sometime in the future generally is not enforceable. Such a transaction is normally analyzed under contract doctrine as being unenforceable because it lacks consideration. . . .

Restatement (Third) of Property (Wills & Don. Trans.) § 6.2. Gifts of Personal Property

The transfer of personal property, necessary to perfect a gift, may be made

(1) by delivering the property to the donee or

(2) by *inter vivos* donative document.

1 Am. Jur. 2d Abandoned, Lost, and Unclaimed Property

§ 8. Elements; Act or Omission

The primary elements of an abandonment of property are the intention to abandon and the external act or omission to act by which that intention is manifested or carried into effect. "Abandonment" of property requires a manifest act, an unmistakable affirmative act, that expresses the intent of the owner to forsake his or her property. In other words, abandonment of property requires intent plus an act that effectuates the intention.

An abandonment may arise from a single act or from a series of acts. The act or acts must be clear, unequivocal, and decisive. A sufficient act is one that manifests a conscious purpose and intention of the owner of personal property neither to use nor to retake the property into his or her possession. The property rights must also be voluntarily relinquished.

§ 13. Lost Property

"Lost property" is property which the owner has involuntarily parted with through neglect, carelessness, or inadvertence. Lost property is property which the owner has unwittingly suffered to pass out of his or her possession, and of whose whereabouts the owner has no knowledge, or property which has passed out of the owner's possession unintentionally and involuntarily. Only if the owner parted with the possession of the property involuntarily and does not know thereafter where to find it may the property be deemed to be "lost property."

Goods or chattels are lost in the legal sense of the word only when possession has been casually and involuntarily parted with so that the mind has no impress of, and can have no recourse to, the event. Articles which are accidentally dropped in any public place, public thoroughfare, or street are lost in the legal sense. If property is deliberately placed somewhere and then forgotten, it is not "lost."

§ 15. Mislaid Property

"Mislaid property" is that which is intentionally put into a certain place and later forgotten. The place where property was found, the length of time property remained unclaimed, and the surrounding circumstances are all evidence as to whether the item was or was not dropped by inadvertence, negligence, or carelessness, which factors tend to establish that the property in question has been mislaid rather than lost.

§ 25. Finders

The principle of common law abandonment allows a finder to claim possession of abandoned property. Thus, property which is abandoned becomes subject to appropriation by the first taker or finder who reduces it to possession.

A finder does not acquire title merely by the strength of his or her discovery of abandoned property. One who seeks to acquire abandoned property must take possession of the property with an intent to acquire title. Stated another way, title to abandoned personal property vests in the first person lawfully reducing the same to possession.

To establish a claim under the law of finds, a common law doctrine, a finder must show:

(1) intent to reduce property to possession,

(2) actual or constructive possession of the property, and

(3) that the property is either unowned or abandoned.

The law of finds dictates that the finder of abandoned property must continuously possess, or be in the process of reducing to possession, the property which he or she has found. The law, however, does not require one who discovers abandoned property to have it actually in hand. The law protects the rights of persons who discover abandoned property, and who are actually engaged in reducing it to possession, to complete this project without interference. The law of finds also dictates that the prerequisites for divesting title must be satisfied.

§ 28. Owner of Land Where Property Found

Traditionally, the rights of the finder of abandoned property would prevail as against the person upon whose land the property was found and any person upon whose land it happens to have been left. That is, the determination of the finder's right to abandoned property is unaffected by the ownership of the land on which the property is found.

§ 29. Finder's Rights

Lost property belongs to the first finder as against all persons but the loser. That is, the finder of lost property does not acquire absolute ownership but acquires such property interest or right as will enable him or her to keep it against all the world but the rightful owner. The finder of lost property holds it as a bailee for the true owner. As to all others, the finder's rights are tantamount to ownership, giving him or her the right to possess and hold the found goods. This rule is not affected by the place of finding as the owner or occupier of the premises on which lost property is found does not acquire title to the lost property. Thus, the finder of lost property has a right to possession of the article superior to that of the owner or occupant of the premises where it is found but not against the lost property's true owner.

§ 37. Finders

A finder of mislaid property acquires no ownership rights in it. Where such property is found upon another's premises, the finder has no right to its possession but is required to turn it over to the owner of the premises, who has the duty to safeguard the property for the true owner. This is true whether the finder is an employee or occupier of the premises on which the mislaid article is found or a customer of the owner or occupant. If the finder of mislaid property is the employee of another, and he or she finds it in his or her status as an employee, then the right of custody of the property is in the employer and not in the employee or agent who recovers its physical possession.

CASES

ADLER V. SAVE

Superior Court of New Jersey, Appellate Division
432 N.J.Super. 101 (2013)

FUENTES, P.J.A.D.

This appeal requires us to address the enforceability of a conditional inter vivos gift. Guided by the facts presented here, we hold that a charity that solicits and accepts a gift from a donor, knowing that the donor's expressed purpose for making the gift was to fund a particular aspect of the charity's mission, is bound to return the gift when the charity unilaterally decides not to honor the donor's originally expressed purpose.

Absent the donor's consent, the recipient of the gift is not at liberty to ignore or materially modify the expressed purpose underlying the donor's decision to give, even if the conditions that existed at the time of the gift may have materially changed, making the fulfillment of the donor's condition either impossible or highly impractical. When, as here, the donor is alive and able to prove the conditional nature of the gift through his or her testimony and other corroborative evidence, a reviewing court's duty is to enforce the donor's original intent, by directing the charity to either fulfill the condition or return the gift.

Here, Judge Thomas W. Sumners, Jr., sitting also as the trier of fact, came to the same legal conclusion after hearing the evidence presented by the parties over a two-day period. The following facts, derived from the evidence presented in this bench trial, will inform our legal analysis.

I

Defendant SAVE, n/k/a SAVE, A Friend to Homeless Animals (SAVE), was founded in 1941 as a non-profit animal shelter located in the greater Princeton area. Recognized as a charitable organization under 26 *U.S.C.A.* § 501(c)(3), defendant's self-proclaimed mission is to provide for the rescue, shelter, veterinary care, and adoption of stray companion animals in the region. Plaintiffs Bernard and Jeanne Adler shared defendant's concern for the welfare of animals, especially for larger dogs and older cats.

. . .

At the time of trial in 2010, plaintiffs had recently "rescued" a "120-pound Bernese Mountain Dog and a 105-pound Newfoundland, both that wouldn't have been adopted from shelters because they were too wild." The total number of animals they have had living with them at any one time include three dogs and four cats; one of their sons also had a Bernese Mountain Dog that stayed with them "close to half a year." The smallest dog weighed 82 pounds; the heaviest was the then recently rescued 120-pound Bernese Mountain Dog.

Plaintiffs' first involvement with SAVE began in the early 1990s, when a trainer they knew introduced them to the organization. At first, their involvement with SAVE was limited to bringing extra animal food and toys to SAVE's facility and spending time with wayward and feral cats. Mr. Adler in particular spent time attempting to humanize feral cats because, otherwise, there is "little hope" of adoption. In addition to these personal acts of kindness, commencing around 1992, plaintiffs began making financial donations to SAVE.

Mr. Adler testified that the financial contributions were relatively small at first. "It would be anywhere from a couple of hundred dollars to a thousand, fifteen hundred dollars." They also began attending fundraisers, "getting as many things as [they] could to get involved with, and give [SAVE] extra donations that way." Plaintiffs made these financial donations without specific conditions, expecting only that the funds would be used "for the general maintenance of the animals. To buy them food, shelter." . . .

II

Sara Nicolls served as SAVE's Executive Director from May 1999 to 2005. At the time the SAVE board of trustees hired her, its main concern was how to address the problems associated with renovating an antiquated facility that was constructed in the 1940s. . . .

After discussing the expansion of services required and the limitations associated with operating within an urban environment, the board retained an architectural firm to design a new shelter facility. . . .

. . . The fundraising campaign next focused on a select group of historically loyal and generous supporters. This elite class of donors was invited to a spring benefit event, where Ms. Nicolls personally solicited their support for the proposed new facility at Herrontown Road.

Plaintiffs were among the guests at this event. Ms. Nicolls testified that plaintiffs approached her and "said that they were very interested in the project." After she explained all of the various features of the project, she showed them the proposed plans and gave them a DVD that talked about the challenge grants. Ms. Nicolls testified that plaintiffs, whom she described as long time "very generous donors," told her that

> they had adopted several animals and have a couple of large dogs so they were very specifically interested in the dog living rooms and helping for the large dogs and then they have elderly cats and they were interested in a cat living room as well.

Ms. Nicolls testified as follows in response to questions posed by plaintiffs' counsel:

> Q. Did you show them when you met with them where on the proposed plans you had special accommodations for large dogs?
>
> A. Correct. We went over the plans in great detail, and those are the areas they were looking to be interested in.

. . .

. . .Mr. Adler agreed to donate a total of $50,000. As he explained, "[t]he purpose was to have rooms for large dogs and older cats that are not easily adopted and specifically for the naming rights for those rooms at that facility on Herrontown Road."

. . .

On December 23, 2002, plaintiffs issued a personal check to SAVE in the amount of $5000. The memo of the check simply stated: "Donation." A SAVE staff member issued a receipt to plaintiffs with the caption: "General Donation." However, under her signature, the staff person who acknowledged receipt of the check wrote: "restricted for expansion."

Plaintiffs issued another personal check to SAVE on December 30, 2003, in the amount of $10,000; the memo of the check again merely stated: "Donation." On December 31, 2003, plaintiffs issued a third personal check to SAVE in the amount of $10,000; unlike the other two checks, however, this check did not have a memo notation.

Plaintiffs made their final donation installment in the form of a gift of shares of stock.

. . .

In February 2006, defendant announced to its donors, including plaintiffs, that it was merging with another charitable foundation. As a result, SAVE would not construct its new shelter at its original Herrontown Road location. The newly formed "merged charity" was transferring all operations formerly housed at Herrontown Road to a location in Montgomery Township, where it planned to construct a new animal shelter, significantly smaller than the facility originally proposed to be built at Herrontown Road.

This announcement came as a total surprise to plaintiffs.

. . .

Mr. Adler . . . characterized the facility proposed to be built in Montgomery Township as a "substantially" lesser facility than the one originally proposed at Herrontown Road. The first phase of the Montgomery facility called for the construction of a 3000 square foot shelter, which is one tenth the size of the 30,000 square foot facility Ms. Nicolls showed the Adlers at the spring capital fundraising event.

III

On October 12, 2007, plaintiffs filed suit in the Law Division in Mercer County, seeking the return of the donation they had made to SAVE. Plaintiffs alleged that SAVE accepted their donation fully aware that plaintiffs expected the funds to be specifically earmarked for the stated purpose of constructing two rooms exclusively designated for the care of large dogs and older cats. These rooms were to be part of a larger facility to be constructed at Herrontown Road, in Princeton.

Plaintiffs maintained that SAVE violated this material aspect of their gift by deciding, without their knowledge or approval, to use the funds plaintiffs donated to construct a facility that did not meet plaintiffs' expressed animal-care conditions and would be located in an area outside its original service region. According to plaintiffs, despite several good faith attempts to convince defendant to voluntarily return their funds, SAVE steadfastly and wrongfully refused to do so.

IV

After considering the testimony of the witnesses, documentary exhibits admitted into evidence, and the arguments of counsel, Judge Sumners held in plaintiffs' favor, finding that they were entitled to the full return of their charitable gift.

. . .

In this appeal, defendant argues that Judge Sumners erred in finding that plaintiffs' donation was a conditional gift. Alternatively, defendant argues that, even if the gift was conditional, returning the funds to plaintiffs is not warranted because "the condition has been or will be met." Finally, assuming arguendo the absence of merit in these arguments, defendant maintains that the trial court should have reformed plaintiffs' gifts under the doctrine of equitable deviation.

Stated differently, in lieu of returning the funds to plaintiffs, defendant maintains the trial court should have crafted a remedy that would have permitted the charity to spend the funds in order "to effectuate the original purpose of the gift as close as possible." According to defendant, public policy demands that we reverse the trial court because, if we permit this decision to stand, it would be detrimental to charities throughout this State.

For plaintiffs, their most important preoccupation was to provide a space for large dogs and older cats. Because they believed these types of animals were highly unlikely to be adopted, they wanted to provide a humane environment for their long-term care. Their moral commitment to these animals was so strong that they were willing to donate $50,000 to make this a reality. In the words of Mrs. Adler: "That's what we do. That's who we are."

Ms. Nicolls's uncontroverted testimony established, beyond a rational doubt, that SAVE accepted plaintiffs' generosity, fully aware that it was expressly conditioned upon fulfilling these material conditions. Ms. Nicolls's testimony was corroborated by the letters she wrote, as SAVE's executive director, acknowledging the conditional nature of plaintiffs' donations.

Equally clear is SAVE's unilateral decision not to honor plaintiffs' conditions and rededicate their donations to serve a purpose unrelated to plaintiffs' expressed wishes. To be clear, the record shows that SAVE: (1) decided to construct a substantially smaller facility; (2) outside the Princeton area; (3) without any specifically designated rooms to serve the needs of large dogs and older cats; and (4) without any mention of plaintiffs' names.

Citing 15 *Am.Jur.*2d *Charities* § 145 (2000), SAVE argues that "[c]onditions with a right of reverter or right to demand forfeiture 'will not be implied unless the intendment is clear.' " Accepting, arguendo, this statement to be a correct articulation of New Jersey law, a notion we do not implicitly endorse, the record here makes it clear that plaintiffs expressly announced their conditions at the time they made their gift, and defendant expressly acknowledged those conditions at the time it accepted plaintiffs' gift. . . .

. . .Based on the unquestioned realization that the recipient accepted the gift fully aware of the donor's conditions and did not express any reservation to the donor about its ability to meet those conditions, we conclude that this created a reasonable expectation in the donor's mind that: (1) the recipient would attempt to meet those conditions in good faith; (2) absent the donor's consent, the recipient did not have the right to ignore or disregard any of the material conditions of the gift; and (3) if the recipient of the gift decides to unilaterally disregard the donor's expressed condition, basic fairness dictates that the gift must be returned to the donor.

. . .

Relying on . . . ancient principles of probate law, SAVE argues that the trial court "should not have allowed plaintiffs' gift to fail." According to SAVE, Judge Sumners should have applied plaintiffs' donation to a charitable purpose "as nearly as possible to the particular purpose." SAVE's argument in this respect crumbles under the weight of its own logic. As emphasized repeatedly by the court in *MacKenzie,* in the law of charitable trusts, where the gift has been made for a charitable purpose, and either originally or in the course of time cannot be literally executed, the gift will be administered, as nearly as may be, "*according to the donor's intentions.*" *Ibid.* (emphasis added).

Under the facts presented here, it would be a perversion of these equitable principles to permit a modern charity like SAVE to aggressively solicit funds from plaintiffs, accept plaintiffs' unequivocally expressed conditional gift, and thereafter disregard those conditions and rededicate the gift to a purpose materially unrelated to plaintiffs' original purpose, without even attempting to ascertain from plaintiffs what, in their view, would be "a charitable purpose as nearly possible" to their particular original purpose.

. . .

Affirmed.

C&H MANUFACTURING, LLC V. HARLAN COUNTY INDUSTRIAL DEVELOPMENT AUTHORITY, INC.

Court of Appeals of Kentucky
600 S.W.3d 740 (2020)

JONES, JUDGE:

Appellant, C&H Manufacturing, LLC ("C&H"), initiated the underlying action against Hurberries, Inc. ("Hurberries") and Harlan County Industrial Development Authority, Inc. ("HCIDA") on several claims of conversion. The circuit court entered summary judgment for both Hurberries and HCIDA on June 20, 2018, upon finding that C&H had effectively abandoned the equipment on the premises leased by Hurberries from HCIDA. C&H now appeals this judgment. Following our review of the record and applicable law, we affirm.

I. BACKGROUND

. . .

Appellant, C&H, was involved in the manufacturing of metal parts, some of which were sold for use in the coal mining industry. On June 19, 2001, C&H sought and obtained its first loan, [which] provided for the construction of a manufacturing facility on property owned by Kingdom Come in Lynch, Kentucky ("the Lynch property") to be operated by C&H.

. . .

C&H . . . abandoned its lease of the Lynch property altogether in 2007 due to declining business, leaving the three items [a press brake, a shear, and a cutting system] in the facility. After C&H left, . . . Kingdom Come's business dissolved. At this point, HCIDA assumed control of the Lynch property and facility. . . .

. . . Hurberries entered into a verbal agreement with HDIDA [Harlan County Industrial Development Authority] to lease the Lynch property. In approximately March of 2007, a few weeks after C&H left the facility, Hurberries began using the real property under its lease. Hurberries also made use of the equipment left behind by C&H.

Despite vacating the premises and leaving behind the equipment, C&H never made a demand to HCIDA or Hurberries for the return of the equipment, nor did it attempt to collect the equipment. C&H's owner, Herman McKnight, testified that he left the equipment behind believing that Hurberries' rent payments would be applied to his debt on the equipment [that C&H still owed to its bank]. He explained that he planned to retrieve the equipment only after the debt on the equipment had been satisfied. There was never a formal agreement reached between C&H and HCIDA and/or Hurberries in this regard. . . .

It was not until 2017 that C&H, motivated to recoup rental payments in hopes that it would be able to reclaim the equipment, initiated this claim against HCIDA and Hurberries, alleging conversion of the manufacturing equipment at the Lynch property. C&H claimed that HCIDA had converted the equipment by leasing the facility, and thereby the equipment contained therein, to Hurberries and receiving lease payment for its use. In the alternative, C&H contended that Hurberries converted the equipment by using it at the Lynch facility.

. . .

The parties undertook considerable discovery, and on February 28, 2017, the circuit court set a trial for February 6, 2018. During this discovery period, Mr. McKnight admitted in deposition that at no point did he, in either his personal or professional capacity for C&H, make a demand for the return of the equipment or the check.

Following these admissions, Hurberries filed a motion for summary judgment on May 24, 2017. Hurberries argued that C&H's claim failed because C&H could not prove an essential element of conversion—the demand for the return of the equipment. HCIDA also filed a motion for summary judgment on September 18, 2017, adding that C&H was barred from asserting a claim for conversion because it abandoned the equipment at the Lynch property. HCIDA also asserted laches and statute of limitation defenses.

The circuit court heard the parties' arguments for summary judgment on January 11, 2018. C&H argued that because Hurberries had originally attempted to purchase the equipment from C&H and then continued to use the equipment after negotiations failed, Hurberries had intentionally and unlawfully converted the equipment. The circuit court, however, viewed C&H's failure to collect the equipment from the Lynch factory as abandonment and additionally noted that C&H never made any demand for the equipment's return. Consequently, the circuit court granted summary judgment to both Hurberries and HCIDA. This appeal followed.

II. ANALYSIS

. . .

Conversion is an intentional tort defined as "the wrongful exercise of dominion and control over property of another[.]"

. . .

. . .[T]he doctrine of abandonment precludes any claim for conversion. Abandoned property is defined as property "to which the owner has voluntarily relinquished all right, title, claim[,] and possession with the intention of terminating his ownership, but without vesting it in any other person[.]" *Goss v. Bisset*, 411 S.W.2d 50, 53 (Ky. 1967). Abandoned property may be "appropriated by anyone, if it has not been reclaimed by the former owner, and ownership of it vests by operation of law, in the person first lawfully appropriating it and reducing it to possession with the intention to become its owner, provided such taking is fair."

Our Court has previously recognized a presumption of abandonment when a commercial tenant turns over its lease to another commercial tenant in the same business and leaves behind equipment or personal property. *Goss*, 411 S.W.2d at 53. In *Goss*, a lessor and her lessee disputed ownership of several items of property that a previous tenant left behind at its former lease when it moved to an adjacent building. *Id.* at 52. The items of property originally belonged to another company which abandoned the property when it assigned its lease to the company that eventually became the lessee company. *Id.* When confronted with these facts, the *Goss* Court made two findings of particular relevance to the appeal at hand.

First, the Court found that the lessor did not obtain "any possession, actual or constructive, of property not covered by the lease," as there was nothing in the record to suggest that either tenant intended to hold the equipment on the landlord's behalf. *Id.* at 53. As our Court pointed out in a later case, "[p]roperty which is abandoned becomes subject to appropriation by the first taker or finder who reduces it to possession. Such person thereupon acquires absolute ownership in the property abandoned, as against both the former owner and any person upon whose land it happens to have been left." *Greer*, 330 S.W.3d at 765 (quoting *Kelley*, 246 S.W.3d at 473). Thus, it stands that a landlord does not assert an ownership interest in property left behind at a leased premises when reletting the premises.

Second, the Court held that possession of such chattels left behind on commercial property by one lessee "passe[s] directly and immediately from one tenant to the other[.]" *Goss*, 411 S.W.2d at 53.

> Unless there is evidence to the contrary, we think it must be presumed that when the owner of a [ ] business has turned his lease over to another tenant whose purpose is to engage in the same type of business, and has left major items of equipment without returning for them within a reasonable time thereafter, his intention was either to abandon the property or pass title to the successor. . . .

Id.

Under Kentucky law, abandonment is the voluntary relinquishment of possession along with an intent to repudiate ownership. *Ellis v. McCormack*, 309 Ky. 576, 218 S.W.2d 391, 392 (1949). "[C]onduct on the part of the owner inconsistent with an intention to continue to claim the property or right may, in fact, raise a presumption or inference of abandonment." 1 C.J.S. *Abandonment* § 12 (2020) (footnote omitted). When considering intent, the question is not focused on the parties' internal objective but what can be gathered from their external conduct. The intent to repudiate ownership may be inferred from the facts; for example, the lapse of a long period of time following relinquishment of possession constitutes significant evidence of the intention to abandon the property. *Greer*, 330 S.W.3d at 765 (citing *Ellis*, 218 S.W.2d at 392). The use of abandoned property therefore cannot be deemed unlawful from the outset if the previous owner is presumed to have relinquished all rights and title to the property.

Under the holding of *Goss*, we agree with the circuit court that C&H abandoned its equipment, thereby invalidating its conversion claims. At the time that Hurberries began its lease, C&H had already effectively abandoned the equipment under *Goss* and passed possession of it to Hurberries "directly and immediately." *Goss*, 411 S.W.2d at 53. C&H was aware that Hurberries began to lease the same premises for the same business purpose shortly thereafter, particularly in light of their failed sales negotiations. C&H's failure to even attempt to collect the equipment in the weeks prior to any sales negotiations or after the failed negotiations demonstrates an intent to abandon the equipment, which was heavily burdened with unpaid debt. C&H additionally failed to request relief at this time from the court to recover the equipment at the Lynch property. Moreover, C&H did not make any demand for the return of any property during the eight or nine years between the time C&H left its lease and the time it filed the underlying action, nor did it make any attempts to remove the subject equipment from the property or make payments on it. There was nothing about C&H's outward behavior to suggest that C&H did not intend to abandon its equipment.

Likewise, we find no error in the circuit court's granting summary judgment to HCIDA. C&H claimed that HCIDA asserted ownership and "exercised dominion over" the equipment by leasing the factory containing the equipment to Hurberries, thereby committing conversion against C&H's secured creditor. It is clear under *Goss* that a lessor is never in constructive possession of a tenant's property, preventing a lessor from claiming prior possession over any chattels left behind on leased property against any future lessee. 411 S.W.2d at 54. As lessor, HCIDA had neither possession nor the right to interfere with Hurberries' possession of C&H's abandoned equipment. HCIDA leased out the Lynch property, as was its right as owner of the premises, which happened to contain the equipment C&H left behind. This is not an exercise of dominion over the property in a manner denying C&H's rights to use and enjoy the property it abandoned. To hold otherwise would prevent lessors from leasing facilities in which lessees left behind property for fear of ensuing litigation.

BENJAMIN V. LINDNER AVIATION, INC.

Supreme Court of Iowa
534 N.W.2d 400 (1995)

TERNUS, JUSTICE.

Appellant, Heath Benjamin, found over $18,000 in currency inside the wing of an airplane. At the time of this discovery, appellee, State Central Bank, owned the plane and it was being serviced by appellee, Lindner Aviation, Inc. All three parties claimed the money as against the true owner. After a bench trial, the district court held that the currency was mislaid property and belonged to the owner of the plane. The court awarded a finder's fee to Benjamin. Benjamin appealed and Lindner Aviation and State Central Bank cross-appealed. We reverse on the bank's cross-appeal and otherwise affirm the judgment of the district court.

I. *Background Facts and Proceedings.*

In April of 1992, State Central Bank became the owner of an airplane when the bank repossessed it from its prior owner who had defaulted on a loan. In August of that year, the bank took the plane to Lindner Aviation for a routine annual inspection. Benjamin worked for Lindner Aviation and did the inspection.

As part of the inspection, Benjamin removed panels from the underside of the wings. Although these panels were to be removed annually as part of the routine inspection, a couple of the screws holding the panel on the left wing were so rusty that Benjamin had to use a drill to remove them. Benjamin testified that the panel probably had not been removed for several years.

Inside the left wing Benjamin discovered two packets approximately four inches high and wrapped in aluminum foil. He removed the packets from the wing and took off the foil wrapping. Inside the foil was paper currency, tied in string and wrapped in handkerchiefs. The currency was predominately twenty-dollar bills with mint dates before the 1960s, primarily in the 1950s. The money smelled musty.

Benjamin took one packet to his jeep and then reported what he had found to his supervisor, offering to divide the money with him. However, the supervisor reported the discovery to the owner of Lindner Aviation, William Engle. Engle insisted that they contact the authorities and he called the Department of Criminal Investigation. The money was eventually turned over to the Keokuk police department.

Two days later, Benjamin filed an affidavit with the county auditor claiming that he was the finder of the currency under the provisions of Iowa Code chapter 644 (1991). Lindner Aviation and the bank also filed claims to the money. The notices required by chapter 644 were published and posted. *See* Iowa Code § 644.8 (1991). No one came forward within twelve months claiming to be the true owner of the money. *See id.* § 644.11 (if true owner does not claim property within twelve months, the right to the property vests in the finder).

Benjamin filed this declaratory judgment action against Lindner Aviation and the bank to establish his right to the property. The parties tried the case to the court. The district court held that chapter 644 applies only to "lost" property and the money here was mislaid property. The court awarded the money to the bank, holding that it was entitled to possession of the money to the exclusion of all but the true owner. . . .

Benjamin appealed. . . . He claims that the trial court should have found that the property was treasure trove or was lost or abandoned rather than mislaid, thereby entitling the finder to the property.

The bank and Lindner Aviation cross-appealed. Lindner Aviation claims that if the money is mislaid property, it is entitled to the money as the owner of the premises on which the money was found, the hangar where the plane was parked. It argues in the alternative that it is the finder, not Benjamin, because Benjamin discovered the money during his work for Lindner Aviation. The bank asserts in its cross-appeal that it owns the premises where the money was found—the airplane. . . .

II. *Standard of Review.*

Whether the money found by Benjamin was treasure trove or was mislaid, abandoned or lost property is a fact question. 1 Am.Jur.2d *Abandoned, Lost, and Unclaimed Property* § 41, at 49 (2d ed. 1994) (hereinafter "1 Am.Jur.2d *Abandoned Property*"); *cf. Bennett v. Bowers*, 238 Iowa 702, 706, 28 N.W.2d 618, 620 (1947) (whether realty has been abandoned is a question of fact); *Roberson v. Ellis,* 58 Or. 219, 114 P. 100, 103 (1911) (whether money was hidden long enough to be classified as treasure trove was a fact question for the jury). Therefore, the trial court's finding that the money was mislaid is binding on us if supported by substantial evidence. Iowa R.App.P. 14(f)(1); *see Eldridge,* 291 N.W.2d at 323 (affirming trial court's finding that property was lost property because supported by substantial evidence).

. . .

IV. *Classification of Found Property.*

Under the common law, there are four categories of found property: (1) abandoned property, (2) lost property, (3) mislaid property, and (4) treasure trove. The rights of a finder of property depend on how the found property is classified.

A. *Abandoned property.* Property is abandoned when the owner no longer wants to possess it. Abandonment is shown by proof that the owner intends to abandon the property and has voluntarily relinquished all right, title and interest in the property. 1 Am.Jur.2d *Abandoned Property* §§ 11–14, at 15–20. Abandoned property belongs to the finder of the property against all others, including the former owner.

B. *Lost property.* "Property is lost when the owner unintentionally and involuntarily parts with its possession and does not know where it is." 1 Am.Jur.2d *Abandoned Property* § 4, at 9–10. Stolen property found by someone who did not participate in the theft is lost property. 1 Am.Jur.2d *Abandoned Property* § 5, at 11. Under chapter 644, lost property becomes the property of the finder once the statutory procedures are followed and the owner makes no claim within twelve months. Iowa Code § 644.11 (1991).

C. *Mislaid property.* Mislaid property is voluntarily put in a certain place by the owner who then overlooks or forgets where the property is. It differs from lost property in that the owner voluntarily and intentionally places mislaid property in the location where it is eventually found by another. 1 Am.Jur.2d *Abandoned Property* § 10, at 14. In contrast, property is not considered lost unless the owner parts with it involuntarily. 1 Am.Jur.2d *Abandoned Property* § 10, at 14.

The finder of mislaid property acquires no rights to the property. 1 Am.Jur.2d *Abandoned Property* § 24, at 30. The right of possession of mislaid property belongs to the owner of the premises upon which the property is found, as against all persons other than the true owner.

D. *Treasure trove.* Treasure trove consists of coins or currency concealed by the owner. *Id.* It includes an element of antiquity. *Id.* To be classified as treasure trove, the property must have been hidden or concealed for such a length of time that the owner is probably dead or undiscoverable. 1 Am.Jur.2d *Abandoned Property* § 8, at 13. Treasure trove belongs to the finder as against all but the true owner. *Zornes,* 223 Iowa at 1145, 274 N.W. at 879.

V. *Is There Substantial Evidence to Support the Trial Court's Finding That the Money Found by Benjamin Was Mislaid?*

We think there was substantial evidence to find that the currency discovered by Benjamin was mislaid property. In the *Eldridge* case, we examined the location where the money was found as a factor in determining whether the money was lost property. Similarly, in *Ritz,* we considered the manner in which the money had been secreted in deciding that it had not been abandoned.

The place where Benjamin found the money and the manner in which it was hidden are also important here. The bills were carefully tied and wrapped and then concealed in a location that was accessible only by removing screws and a panel. These circumstances support an inference that the money was placed there intentionally. This inference supports the conclusion that the money was mislaid. *Jackson v. Steinberg,* 186 Or. 129, 200 P.2d 376, 378 (1948) (fact that $800 in currency was found concealed beneath the paper lining of a dresser indicates that money was intentionally concealed with intention of reclaiming it; therefore, property was mislaid, not lost); *Schley v. Couch,* 155 Tex. 195, 284 S.W.2d 333, 336 (1955) (holding that money found buried under garage floor was mislaid property as a matter of law because circumstances showed that money was placed there deliberately and court presumed that owner had either forgotten where he hid the money or had died before retrieving it).

The same facts that support the trial court's conclusion that the money was mislaid prevent us from ruling as a matter of law that the property was lost. Property is not considered lost unless considering the place where and the conditions under which the property is found, there is an inference that the property was left there unintentionally. 1 Am.Jur.2d *Abandoned Property* § 6, at 12; *see Sovern,* 20 P. at 105 (holding that coins found in a jar under a wooden floor of a barn were not lost property because the circumstances showed that the money was hidden there intentionally); *see Farrare v. City of Pasco,* 68 Wash.App. 459, 843 P.2d 1082, 1084 (1993) (where currency was deliberately concealed, it cannot be characterized as lost property). Contrary to Benjamin's position the circumstances here do not support a conclusion that the money was placed in the wing of the airplane unintentionally. Additionally, as the trial court concluded, there was no evidence suggesting that the money was placed in the wing by someone other than the owner of the money and that its location was unknown to the owner. For these reasons, we reject Benjamin's argument that the trial court was obligated to find that the currency Benjamin discovered was lost property.

We also reject Benjamin's assertion that as a matter of law this money was abandoned property. Both logic and common sense suggest that it is unlikely someone would voluntarily part with over $18,000 with the intention of terminating his ownership. The location where this money was found is much more consistent with the conclusion that the owner of the property was placing the money there for safekeeping. *See Ritz*, 467 N.W.2d at 269 (property not abandoned where money was buried in jars and tin cans, indicating a desire by the owner to preserve it); *Jackson*, 200 P.2d at 378 (because currency was concealed intentionally and deliberately, the bills could not be regarded as abandoned property); 1 Am.Jur.2d *Abandoned Property* § 13, at 17 (where property is concealed in such a way that the concealment appears intentional and deliberate, there can be no abandonment). We will not presume that an owner has abandoned his property when his conduct is consistent with a continued claim to the property. Therefore, we cannot rule that the district court erred in failing to find that the currency discovered by Benjamin was abandoned property.

Finally, we also conclude that the trial court was not obligated to decide that this money was treasure trove. Based on the dates of the currency, the money was no older than thirty-five years. The mint dates, the musty odor and the rusty condition of a few of the panel screws indicate that the money may have been hidden for some time. However, there was no evidence of the age of the airplane or the date of its last inspection. These facts may have shown that the money was concealed for a much shorter period of time.

Moreover, it is also significant that the airplane had a well-documented ownership history. The record reveals that there were only two owners of the plane prior to the bank. One was the person from whom the bank repossessed the plane; the other was the original purchaser of the plane when it was manufactured. Nevertheless, there is no indication that Benjamin or any other party attempted to locate and notify the prior owners of the plane, which could very possibly have led to the identification of the true owner of the money. Under these circumstances, we cannot say as a matter of law that the money meets the antiquity requirement or that it is probable that the owner of the money is not discoverable.

We think the district court had substantial evidence to support its finding that the money found by Benjamin was mislaid. The circumstances of its concealment and the location where it was found support inferences that the owner intentionally placed the money there and intended to retain ownership. We are bound by this factual finding.

VI. *Is the Airplane Or the Hangar the "Premises" Where the Money Was Discovered?*

Because the money discovered by Benjamin was properly found to be mislaid property, it belongs to the owner of the premises where it was found. Mislaid property is entrusted to the owner of the premises where it is found rather than the finder of the property because it is assumed that the true owner may eventually recall where he has placed his property and return there to reclaim it.

We think that the premises where the money was found is the airplane, not Lindner Aviation's hangar where the airplane happened to be parked when the money was discovered. The policy behind giving ownership of mislaid property to the owner of the premises where the property was mislaid supports this conclusion. If the true owner of the money attempts to locate it, he would initially look for the plane; it is unlikely he would begin his search by contacting businesses where the airplane might have been inspected. Therefore, we affirm the trial court's judgment that the bank, as the owner of the plane, has the right to possession of the property as against all but the true owner.

. . .

We conclude that the district court's finding that the money discovered by Benjamin was mislaid property is supported by substantial evidence. Therefore, we affirm the district court's judgment that the bank has the right to the money as against all but the true owner.

SNELL, Justice (dissenting).

. . .

After considering the four categories of found money, the majority decides that Benjamin found mislaid money. The result is that the bank gets all the money; Benjamin, the finder, gets nothing. Apart from the obvious unfairness in result, I believe this conclusion fails to come from logical analysis.

Mislaid property is property voluntarily put in a certain place by the owner who then overlooks or forgets where the property is. The property here consisted of two packets of paper currency totalling $18,910, three to four inches high, wrapped in aluminum foil. Inside the foil, the paper currency, predominantly twenty dollar bills, was tied with string and wrapped in handkerchiefs. Most of the mint dates were in the 1950s with one dated 1934. These packets were found in the left wing of the Mooney airplane after Benjamin removed a panel held in by rusty screws.

These facts satisfy the requirement that the property was voluntarily put in a certain place by the owner. But the second test for determining that property is mislaid is that the owner "overlooks or forgets where the property is." I do not believe that the facts, logic, or common sense lead to a finding that this requirement is met. It is not likely or reasonable to suppose that a person would secrete $18,000 in an airplane wing and then forget where it was.

. . .

The scenario unfolded in this case convinces me that the money found in the airplane wing was abandoned. Property is abandoned when the owner no longer wants to possess it. The money had been there for years, possibly thirty. No owner had claimed it in that time. No claim was made by the owner after legally prescribed notice was given that it had been found. Thereafter, logic and the law support a finding that the owner has voluntarily relinquished all right, title, and interest in the property. Whether the money was abandoned due to its connection to illegal drug trafficking or is otherwise contraband property is a matter for speculation. In any event, abandonment by the true owner has legally occurred and been established.

I would hold that Benjamin is legally entitled to the entire amount of money that he found in the airplane wing as the owner of abandoned property.

HARRIS and ANDREASEN, JJ., join this dissent.

DISCUSSION PROBLEMS

1. The Engagement Ring

On the occasion of their engagement, Jerod Heiman presented Heather Parrish with a ring that he had purchased for $9033. The parties stipulated that the ring was given "in contemplation of marriage between the parties." One year later, Heiman terminated the engagement and sought the return of the ring. He made no allegations that Parrish was in any way at "fault" for causing the relationship to terminate. Is he legally entitled to recover the ring?

2. The Spleen

In 1976, 32-year-old John Moore was diagnosed with hairy cell leukemia, which caused his spleen to balloon in size. Dr. David Golde at UCLA performed a splenectomy that saved Moore's life. The spleen was kept in UCLA's tissue bank, as is typical when organs are removed during surgery.

Golde subsequently used Moore's spleen to create the "Mo" cell line, for which he obtained a patent, without ever discussing his research plans with Moore or obtaining his consent. In return for the patent and his consulting services, Golde received stock from a Massachusetts biotech firm that became worth $2.25 million when the company issued an initial public offering in 1986. Moore sued Golde and the University of California for conversion, alleging that the doctor had an undisclosed research and economic interest in his spleen at the time of the operation. Should Moore prevail?

3. More Biological Samples

Over 27 years, Dr. William Catalona, a urologist at Washington University in St. Louis, collected thousands of blood and tissue samples from his patients for prostate cancer research. He was instrumental in establishing the university's biological materials repository to house these and other tissue samples.

The individuals who contributed specimens were required to read and sign a form indicating their consent to have their samples used for research. The form described the patient's contribution as a "donation," indicated that the samples might be used for research with collaborators at other universities, and agreed to "waive any claim" the donor might have to the donated tissues or any materials or treatments they could be used to develop. The form also indicated that the patient could request the destruction of their samples if they changed their mind about participating but noted that it would not be possible to destroy or recall any research results already obtained. An accompanying genetic research information brochure, which donors also were required to sign, indicated that the tissue samples would be used by Washington University researchers, "may" be shared with other researchers, and may be used in studies conducted 10–20 years in the future. The brochure stated that "by agreeing to participate, you are making a free and generous gift of your tissue" and also informed the patients of their right to have their samples destroyed upon request should they change their mind and no longer wish to participate.

In 2003, Dr. Catalona left Washington University for Northwestern University, where he planned to continue his research. He sent a letter to his former patients informing them of his move and requesting that they sign and return a form requesting that Washington University "release all of my samples to Dr. Catalona at Northwestern University upon his request." Approximately 6000 individuals signed and returned the forms. What legal obligations did Washington University have with regard to those 6,000 tissue donors?

CHAPTER 12

CONTRACT FORMATION

■ ■ ■

INTRODUCTION

According to the Restatement (Second) of Contracts, "the formation of a contract requires a bargain in which there is a manifestation of mutual assent to the exchange and a consideration." Rest. (2d) Contracts § 17. Without both mutual assent and consideration, then there is no agreement that the law recognizes as a contract.

The "consideration" requirement means that a contract must be based on an exchange of items of value. If A promises B $1,000, B must promise to provide or presently provide something in return (goods, services, labor, land, etc.). See Rest. (2d) Contracts § 71. Whether the consideration requirement is met can pose a difficult question in cases involving family, friends, or other close associates, when a question arises as to whether a transfer of property or a promised transfer should be classified as a gift or as part of a bargain. But in arms-length transactions conducted in a business environment, the presence of consideration is rarely at issue, so we will not delve deeper into this requirement here.

The "mutual assent" requirement leads to more disputes. Contractual obligations, unlike obligations under tort law or criminal law, are fundamentally voluntary. But what words or conduct are necessary and sufficient to show that a party has assented to being bound to a contract?

A foundational question, harkening back to our discussion of battery law in Chapter 6, is whether courts should employ an "objective" or a "subjective" standard to judge the presence of assent: that is, should the operative question be whether an actor believed that she was agreeing to be bound to a contract, or whether her words and actions would suggest to a reasonable person that she assented? A subjective standard would best protect the autonomy interests of individuals to enter (or not to enter) into contracts, but an objective standard best protects parties' reliance on a counterpart's words or actions and encourages clarity of communication. Contract law clearly adopts the objective approach. As Judge Learned Hand wrote:

> A contract has, strictly speaking, nothing to do with the personal, or individual, intent of the parties. A contract is an obligation attached by the mere force of law to certain acts of the parties,

> usually words, which ordinarily accompany and represent a known intent. If, however, it were proved by twenty bishops that either party, when he used the words, intended something else than the usual meaning which the law imposes upon them, he would still be held.

Hotchkiss v. National City Bank of N.Y., 200 F. 287, 293 (S.D.N.Y. 1911).

Arguably, the most difficult problem that arises when courts must determine the presence or absence of mutual assent is determining when contract negotiations have moved past mere expressions of interest by the parties to expressions of commitment to a transaction. *Compare* Rest. (2d) Contracts § 26 (Preliminary Negotiations) *with* § 27 (Existence of Contract Where Written Memorial is Contemplated). *Empro Manufacturing Co. v. Ball-Co Manufacturing Inc.* considers when a document labeled as a "Letter of Intent" satisfies the mutual assent requirement. *International Casings Group, Inc. v. Premium Standard Farms, Inc.* explores whether and when an e-mail exchange crosses the line from negotiation to contract.

Writing down the terms of a contract is always good practice. Documentation increases the predictability of the outcome if conflict arises and results in litigation, and it can reduce the likelihood of outright fraud by one of the parties. Even more importantly, reducing terms to writing lessens the likelihood that contemporaneous misunderstandings or imprecise memories will lead to later disputes between parties who are acting in good faith, which can ruin relationships even if they do not wind up in court. But, in this area at least, the law does not mirror what constitutes good practice. Oral contracts are *generally* enforceable in the American legal system, although the rule known as the "statute of frauds" provides a significant exception to this rule.

In 1677, the British Parliament enacted the original version, entitled "An Act for the Prevention of Frauds and Perjuries." Most American legislatures later adopted similar statutes, with some variations, and these statutes continue to exist in most American jurisdictions today. The Restatement identifies five categories of contracts commonly subject to state statutes of frauds: (1) contracts that call for an executor or administrator of an estate to answer for the debts of the decedent (known as executorships); (2) contracts that call for one person to answer for the duties of another (known as suretyships); (3) contracts for which marriage provides consideration; (4) contracts for the sale of interests in land; and (5) contracts "not to be performed within one year" of their making. Rest. (2d) Contracts § 110. The Uniform Commercial Code, adopted in every state, adds contracts for the sale of goods that exceed $500 in value (U.C.C. § 2–201), and leases of goods where total payments exceed $1,000. U.C.C. § 2A–201.

An important subtlety is that a contract covered by the statute of frauds (often described as one that "falls within" the statute) need not be a written *contract* to be enforceable. It is sufficient that a written memorandum of some sort establishes the existence of a contract (consideration and mutual assent) as well as its essential terms and is signed by the party seeking to avoid enforcement (known as "the party to be charged"). Rest. (2d) Contracts § 131. *Waddle v. Elrod* explores the requirements for satisfying the statute of frauds when a contract falls within the statute.

Restatement (Second) of Contracts § 3. Agreement Defined; Bargain Defined

An agreement is a manifestation of mutual assent on the part of two or more persons. A bargain is an agreement to exchange promises or to exchange a promise for a performance or to exchange performances.

Restatement (Second) of Contracts § 17. Requirement of a Bargain

. . .[T]he formation of a contract requires a bargain in which there is a manifestation of mutual assent to the exchange and a consideration.

Restatement (Second) of Contracts § 26. Preliminary Negotiations

A manifestation of willingness to enter into a bargain is not an offer if the person to whom it is addressed knows or has reason to know that the person making it does not intend to conclude a bargain until he has made a further manifestation of assent.

Restatement (Second) of Contracts § 27. Existence of Contract Where Written Memorial Is Contemplated

Manifestations of assent that are in themselves sufficient to conclude a contract will not be prevented from so operating by the fact that the parties also manifest an intention to prepare and adopt a written memorial thereof; but the circumstances may show that the agreements are preliminary negotiations.

Restatement (Second) of Contracts § 71. Requirement of Exchange; Types of Exchange

(1) To constitute consideration, a performance or a return promise must be bargained for.

(2) A performance or return promise is bargained for if it is sought by the promisor in exchange for his promise and is given by the promisee in exchange for that promise.

(3) The performance may consist of

(a) an act other than a promise, or

(b) a forbearance, or

(c) the creation, modification, or destruction of a legal relation.

(4) The performance or return promise may be given to the promisor or to some other person. It may be given by the promisee or by some other person.

Restatement (Second) of Contracts § 110. Classes of Contracts Covered

(1) The following classes of contracts are subject to a statute, commonly called the Statute of Frauds, forbidding enforcement unless there is a written memorandum or an applicable exception:

(a) a contract of an executor or administrator to answer for a duty of his decedent (the executor-administrator provision);

(b) a contract to answer for the duty of another (the suretyship provision);

(c) a contract made upon consideration of marriage (the marriage provision);

(d) a contract for the sale of an interest in land (the land contract provision);

(e) a contract that is not to be performed within one year from the making thereof (the one-year provision).

(2) The following classes of contracts, which were traditionally subject to the Statute of Frauds, are now governed by Statute of Frauds provisions of the Uniform Commercial Code:

(a) a contract for the sale of goods for the price of $500 or more (Uniform Commercial Code § 2–201);

(b) a contract for the sale of securities (Uniform Commercial Code § 8–319);

(c) a contract for the sale of personal property not otherwise covered, to the extent of enforcement by way of action or defense beyond $5,000 in amount or value of remedy (Uniform Commercial Code § 1–206).

CASES

EMPRO MANUFACTURING CO. V. BALL-CO MANUFACTURING, INC.

United States Court of Appeals, Seventh Circuit
870 F.2d 423 (1989)

EASTERBROOK, J.

We have a pattern common in commercial life. Two firms reach concord on the general terms of their transaction. They sign a document, captioned "agreement in principle" or "letter of intent," memorializing these terms but anticipating further negotiations and decisions—an appraisal of the assets, the clearing of a title, the list is endless. One of these terms proves divisive, and the deal collapses. The party that perceives itself the loser then claims that the preliminary document has legal force independent of the definitive contract. Ours is such a dispute.

Ball-Co Manufacturing, a maker of specialty valve components, floated its assets on the market. Empro Manufacturing showed interest. After some preliminary negotiations, Empro sent Ball-Co a three-page "letter of intent" to purchase the assets of Ball-Co and S.B. Leasing, a partnership holding title to the land under Ball-Co's plant. Empro proposed a price of $2.4 million, with $650,000 to be paid on closing and a 10-year promissory note for the remainder, the note to be secured by the "inventory and equipment of Ballco." The letter stated "[t]he general terms and conditions of such proposal (which will be subject to and incorporated in a formal, definitive Asset Purchase Agreement signed by both parties)." Just in case Ball-Co might suppose that Empro had committed itself to buy the assets, paragraph four of the letter stated that "Empro's purchase shall be subject to the satisfaction of certain conditions precedent to closing including, but not limited to" the definitive Asset Purchase Agreement and, among five other conditions, "[t]he approval of the shareholders and board of directors of Empro."

Although Empro left itself escape hatches, as things turned out Ball-Co was the one who balked. The parties signed the letter of intent in November 1987 and negotiated through March 1988 about many terms. Security for the note proved to be the sticking point. Ball-Co wanted a security interest in the land under the plant; Empro refused to yield.

When Empro learned that Ball-Co was negotiating with someone else, it filed this diversity suit. Contending that the letter of intent obliges Ball-Co to sell only to it, Empro asked for a temporary restraining order. The district judge. . .concluded that the statement, appearing twice in the letter, that the agreement is "subject to" the execution of a definitive contract meant that the letter has no independent force.

. . .

Because letters of intent are written without the care that will be lavished on the definitive agreement, it may be a bit much to put dispositive weight on "subject to" in every case. . . .[These terms] might have been used carelessly, and if the full agreement showed that the formal contract was to be nothing but a memorial of an agreement already reached, the letter of intent would be enforceable. *Borg-Warner Corp. v. Anchor Coupling Co.,* 16 Ill. 2d 234, 156 N.E.2d 513 (1958). . . .

A canvass of the terms of the letter Empro sent does not assist it, however. "Subject to" a definitive agreement appears twice. The letter also recites, twice, that it contains the "general terms and conditions," implying that each side retained the right to make (and stand on) additional demands. Empro insulated itself from binding effect by listing, among the conditions to which the deal was "subject," the "approval of the shareholders and board of directors of Empro." The board could veto a deal negotiated by the firm's agents for a reason such as the belief that Ball-Co had been offered too much (otherwise the officers, not the board, would be the firm's final decisionmakers, yet state law vests major decisions in the board). The shareholders could decline to give their assent for any reason (such as distrust of new business ventures) and could not even be required to look at the documents, let alone consider the merits of the deal. See Earl Sneed, *The Shareholder May Vote As He Pleases: Theory and Fact,* 22 U. Pittsburgh L. Rev. 23, 31–36, 40–42 (1960) (collecting cases). Empro even took care to require the return of its $5,000 in earnest money "without set off, in the event this transaction is not closed," although the seller usually gets to keep the earnest money if the buyer changes its mind. So Empro made clear that it was free to walk.

Neither the text nor the structure of the letter suggests that it was to be a one-sided commitment, an option in Empro's favor binding only Ball-Co. From the beginning Ball-Co assumed that it could negotiate terms in addition to, or different from, those in the letter of intent. The cover letter from Ball-Co's lawyer returning the signed letter of intent to Empro stated that the "terms and conditions are generally acceptable" but that "some clarifications are needed in Paragraph 3(c) (last sentence)," the provision concerning Ball-Co's security interest. "Some clarifications are needed" is an ominous noise in a negotiation, foreboding many a stalemate. Although we do not know what "clarifications" counsel had in mind, the specifics are not important. It is enough that even on signing the letter of intent Ball-Co proposed to change the bargain, conduct consistent with the purport of the letter's text and structure.

The shoals that wrecked this deal are common hazards in business negotiations. Letters of intent and agreements in principle often, and here, do no more than set the stage for negotiations on details. Sometimes the details can be ironed out; sometimes they can't. Illinois, as *Chicago Investment, Interway,* and *Feldman* show, allows parties to approach agreement in stages, without fear that by reaching a preliminary understanding they have bargained away their privilege to disagree on the specifics. . . . AFFIRMED.

INTERNATIONAL CASINGS GROUP, INC. V. PREMIUM STANDARD FARMS, INC.

United States District Court, Western District of Missouri
358 F.Supp.2d 863 (2005)

LAUGHREY, J.

Pending before the Court is Plaintiff International Casing Group's ("ICG") Motion for Preliminary Injunction. For the reasons set forth below, the Court grants ICG's Motion.

I. BACKGROUND

Defendant Premium Standard Farms ("PSF") is a pork producer that has sold its hog casings to ICG for over six years. The two PSF facilities that supply their hog casings to ICG are located in Milan, Missouri ("Milan facility"), and Clinton, North Carolina ("Clinton facility"). ICG has its own equipment and employees on site at the Clinton and Milan facilities to harvest and process the casings.

Prior to May 2002, PSF and ICG had long term output contracts for both facilities. In May 2002, PSF and ICG terminated these contracts. However, the parties continued performing under the terms of their contracts, and in June 2002, they resumed negotiations regarding new terms for both facilities. The parties negotiated a myriad of issues, including, but not limited to, an electrical room that needed re-wiring at the Clinton facility, pricing adjustments related to quality control issues (frequently referred to as the bloody guts issue) and a blower pipe at the Clinton facility. Many of these negotiations occurred via e-mail between the parties and both entities consistently relayed negotiation terms and positions to one another via electronic correspondence. The negotiations were protracted.

In early 2004, Kent Pummill ("Pummill") represented PSF in its negotiations with ICG and Tom Sanecki ("Sanecki") represented ICG. In a series of e-mails from March and April 2004, Pummill and Sanecki discussed several open issues. Because of the importance of these e-mails, the Court includes them verbatim. All of the following e-mails were sent in 2004. . . .

02/19 Sender: Kent Pummill Recipient: Tom Sanecki

Here is where we are at. We agree that there is some blood in the casings as with all CO2 systems. We don't agree it is an 8 cent discount. We would like to offer the following: 2 cent discount on the Clinton contract; we [PSF] will pay 100% of the electrical that was completed last year; you pay for putting in the stainless steel pipe going to your building. . . .Where are your sticking points, so we can get both plants under contract and behind us?

Thanks, Kent

02/26 Sender: Kent Pummill Recipient: Tom Sanecki

Did you get my e-mail. What is your counter-offer? I agree, we have gone too long. Lets get this cleaned up.

Thanks, Kent

02/26 Sender: Tom Sanecki Recipient: Kent Pummill

I am in LA this week, I will call you next week to discuss, or would you prefer Eric and I come to KC for a quick meeting next week. We would be available Tuesday–Thursday.

02/26 Sender: Kent Pummill Recipient: Tom Sanecki

Bo is traveling. Shoot me your counter offer next week, and lets get this moving.

03/18 Sender: Tom Sanecki Recipient: Kent Pummill

I will be out of the office thru 03/29/04.

I have the following questions and I think we should schedule a meeting in KC to get this resolved. . . .Electrical room and blow pipe—not to beat a dead horse but, I think getting the guts, undamaged, to the casing department should be PSF's responsibility. ICG paid for the blow system and it has worked for years. It has only been since it has been disassembled by your maintenance department for cleaning that we have been having problems with damaged guts.

The quote we have is for $25,000, I expect this to go up due to the increases in the cost of steel, my guess is an additional $8,000–$10,000. We also need to make sure that the finish is not going to cause damage. My suggestion is that ICG will pay for the pipe and turn the blower system over to PSF, if PSF will extend both contracts an additional two years.

The remaining issue is the compensation for the bloody guts. $0.02 is not enough to compensate for the additional processing required. I suggest that we schedule a meeting for either 04/06/04 or 04/07/04 in KC. Please let me know your thoughts.

03/23 Sender: Kent Pummill Recipient: Tom Sanecki

We might as well schedule a meeting then, because if you want more than 2 cents, then our plan is to put it back out to bid. . . .We have paid for the electrical room. You pay for the pipe. Sounds like it just comes down to the discount #. We will do a 2 cent discount at Clinton and will go 5 years on a new contract for both plants. Your choice, this or us putting both plants back out to bid. Let me know, we would be glad to meet.

Thanks, Kent

04/19 Sender: Tom Sanecki Recipient: Kent Pummill

I am not happy about the $0.02. . . .The pipe vs. the electrical room is ok, and the sooner we get this contract signed the better, we need to get this pipe replaced. It is [a]ffecting our yields. Do we agree that when ICG pays for the pipe replacement and we have the 5 year contract that PSF will take responsibility and ownership of the pipe?

Can we do something about the costs we have incurred with the bloody guts we have already processed? This started in January 15, 2003, so for 16+ months. Can we get an additional $0.02 for the next 16 months or an additional $0.005 off for the 5 year contract?

Please call me when you get a chance [phone number deleted].

04/20 Sender: Kent Pummill Recipient: Tom Sanecki

Send the new contracts with a decrease of $0.025 for the next 5 years at Clinton. We will take ownership of the new pipe installed by ICG after it is installed.

Thanks, Kent

04/27 Sender: Tom Sanecki Recipient: Kent Pummill

I have sent you 4 copies of each contract. I have initialed and signed each. Please have Bo sign and initial and return 2 copies to ICG.

I put the effective date of the $0.025 reduction at Clinton for 05/03/2004. ICG will get the blow pipe replaced ASAP after receiving the signed contracts. PSF will maintain the blow system and at the end of the new contract it will become PSF's property.

PSF will pay for the electrical room upgrades at Clinton. Thanks for your help.

04/27 Sender: Kent Pummill Recipient: Tom Sanecki

Will do. Thank you. Kent

05/10 Sender: Tom Sanecki Recipient: Kent Pummill

How are the contracts going? ? ? ? ?

05/10 Sender: Kent Pummill Recipient: Tom Sanecki

Legal has them. I will double check this morning.

06/07 Sender: Kent Pummill Recipient: Tom Sanecki

Finally got them back from Legal and Bo Manly.

Bo is adamant about not going 5 years. He turned 180 degrees on me. He wants just 3. If you can agree with me on 3 years, then I will mark through and initial the "2G" section and change and initial the term to 3 years, and get Bo to sign and send them on their way. I thought we were home free; we are real close. Will this work for you? I will take another penny off the price for Clinton to get this signed and off my desk. I think you and I are both tired and want this off our desks. Let me know.

Kent

06/21 Sender: Tom Sanecki Recipient: Kent Pummill

OK, but as you can imagine I am surprised by this change. Do you want to mark-up your contract and mark the price schedule, then sign and send to me. We will get the blow pipe done ASAP. Thanks.

06/21 Sender: Kent Pummill Recipient: Tom Sanecki

We will mark up the contract and send it to you. Thanks, Kent.

Send me a new pricing schedule, and I will attach the new one to Clinton's contracts.

06/21 Sender: Tom Sanecki Recipient: Kent Pummill

Shall we make these prices effective 06/28/2004?

06/21 Sender: Kent Pummill Recipient: Tom Sanecki

That is fine.

The "contracts"[1] referred to in Sanecki's April 27, 2004, e-mail outlined the payment mechanism for the casings and provided that the price of the casings would be based on a price benchmark contained in the Pratt Report, which is a trade publication used by the casings industry. The pricing schedule was attached to each "contract," incorporated by reference, signed by Sanecki and sent to PSF. The pricing schedule reflected that ICG was paying less for the casings from the Clinton facility than those from the Milan facility. These "contracts" were for five years.

In his June 7 e-mail to Sanecki, Pummill agrees to take off another penny for the Clinton casings in exchange for a three instead of a five year contract. After receiving Sanecki's agreement to the three year duration, Pummill marked up the contracts and gave them to Robert W. (Bo) Manly ("Manly") for Manly's signature. Manly is the president of PSF. While awaiting Manly's signature on the contracts, ICG and PSF implemented the new pricing schedules as of June 28, 2004. In July 2004, Sanecki inquired a few times about obtaining the written contracts and Pummill responded that Manly still had them.

On August 2, 2004, Pummill e-mailed Sanecki to tell him that Calvin Held ("Held") was now supervising both the Milan and Clinton facilities and that Manly wanted Held to "approve" the contracts for the two facilities. Pummill also indicated that Held was inquiring about why ICG was paying less money for the casings from the Clinton facility than the casings from the Milan facility. In September 2004, Sanecki met with Held to discuss the price disparity between the two facilities. It appears that Held did not notify Sanecki at that meeting that PSF would not honor the pricing arrangement. The new prices continued to be paid even after the meeting.

---

1 Sanecki referred to these documents as contracts. The Court does not believe a contract was reached as of April 27, 2004; hence, the use of quotation marks.

On November 17, 2004, PSF sent ICG written notice of its intent to terminate the parties' business relationship. . . .On January 7, 2005, the Court held an evidentiary hearing regarding ICG's Motion for Preliminary Injunction. Pending resolution of that Motion, the parties are performing under the terms reached as of June 21, 2004. . . .

II. DISCUSSION

In determining whether to grant a preliminary injunction, courts weigh four factors: (1) the probability that the movant will succeed on the merits; (2) the threat of irreparable harm to the movant; (3) the balance between the harm to the movant and any harm that granting the injunction will cause to other parties to the litigation; and (4) the public interest. *Dataphase Sys., Inc. v. C L Sys., Inc.,* 640 F.2d 109 (8th Cir. 1981). [Only subpart 1 is included here.—EDS.]

A. Success on the Merits

1. Meeting of the Minds

To be successful, ICG must establish that it has a contract with PSF. The parties agree that this transaction is controlled by the UCC which provides:

> (1) A contract for sale of goods may be made in any manner sufficient to show agreement, including conduct by both parties which recognizes the existence of such a contract.
>
> . . .
>
> (3) Even though one or more terms are left open, a contract for sale does not fail for indefiniteness if the parties have intended to make a contract and there is a reasonably certain basis for giving an appropriate remedy.

Mo. Rev. Stat. § 400.2–204. PSF contends that it has no agreement with ICG because there was never a "meeting of the minds," particularly, with reference to price.

PSF is correct that ICG must establish that there was a "meeting of the minds" between ICG and PSF. . . .Whether a meeting of the minds exists, however, "is determined objectively by looking at the intent of the parties as expressed by their actual words or acts." *Paul's Rod & Bearing, Ltd. v. Kelly,* 847 S.W.2d 68 (Mo. Ct. App. 1991). A meeting of the minds cannot be "determined on the undisclosed assumption or secret surmise of either party." *Computer Network, Ltd. v. Purcell Tire & Rubber Co.,* 747 S.W.2d 669 (Mo. Ct. App. 1988). This is because Missouri follows the objective theory of contracts. "The objective theory lays stress on the outward manifestation of assent made to the other party in contrast to the older idea that a contract was a true 'meeting of the minds.' " *Id.* (quoting J. Calamari & J. Perillo, Contracts § 2–13, at 23 (2d ed. 1977)).

There is substantial evidence to show that PSF and ICG did reach a meeting of the minds on June 21, 2004 for a new three year, hog casing, output contract for the Milan and Clinton facilities. The parties had been negotiating since 2002 and had resolved most of the issues in dispute by April of 2004. Price, the bloody guts issue and the defective pipe at the Clinton facility were still being discussed. On March 23, Kent Pummill, who had authority to negotiate on behalf of PSF, said: "We have paid for the electrical room. You pay for the [Clinton] pipe. Sounds like it just comes down to the discount #. We will do a 2 cent discount at Clinton and will go 5 years on a new contract for both plants. Your choice, this or us putting both plants back out to bid. Let me [k]now, we would be glad to meet."

Tom Sanecki, who had authority to negotiate for ICG, responded by accepting some of Pummill's proposal and raising additional issues. The following day, Pummill instructs Sanecki to send the new contracts with a decrease of $.025. Mr. Sanecki does so and there is no response from PSF until June 7, 2004 when Mr. Pummill writes: "Finally got them [contracts] back from legal and Bo Manly. . . .Bo is adamant about not going 5 years. He turned 180 degrees on me. He wants just 3. If you can agree with me on 3 years, then I will mark through and initial the '2G' section and change and initial the term to 3 years, and get Bo to sign and send them on their way. I thought we were home free; we are real close. Will this work for you? I will take another penny off the price for Clinton to get this signed and off my desk."

Mr. Sanecki responds OK. At that point, both parties had agreed on all the essential terms of the contract. While PSF now contends that the price issue was unresolved, that argument is inconsistent with its agreement to implement the new prices effective June 28, 2004 pursuant to an e-mail exchange between Sanecki and Pummill on June 21, 2004. That agreement occurred on the same day that both sides had resolved all outstanding issues under discussion and Pummill had offered a lower price for the Clinton facility and Sanecki had accepted it.

. . .

Sometime after June 21, 2004, and before August 2, 2004, PSF placed Calvin Held over both the Clinton and Milan facilities. August 2 is the first time that PSF notifies ICG that Held is "approving both contracts." An inquiry is made by PSF on that date as to why there is a difference between the price at Milan and the price at Clinton. A meeting is arranged with Held and at that meeting he is told by Sanecki the reason for the price differential. It does not appear that PSF told ICG at that meeting that the price being paid pursuant to the June 21 agreement was unacceptable or notified ICG that it would no longer pay that price. In fact, the price was paid by PSF through 2004. Indeed, the new prices remained in effect even after PSF notified ICG that it must vacate the Milan and Clinton facilities.

While it is possible that a jury may conclude differently, it is more likely that a jury will believe that Held, the new PSF manager, didn't like the deal that had been struck for his facilities and PSF was back tracking on an agreement that had already been made.

Finally, PSF contends that there was no meeting of the minds on June 21, 2004, because the agreement was never reduced to writing and signed by both parties. However, merely because parties intend a written memorialization of the agreed upon terms does not demonstrate that they intend the writing to be a condition precedent to the formation of a contract. "Mutual manifestations of assent that are in themselves sufficient to make a contract will not be prevented from so operating by the mere fact that the parties also manifest an intention to prepare and adopt a written memorial thereof. . . ." 1 Restatement of the Law of Contracts, Ch. 3, § 26. The real question is whether the parties intended a written document to be a condition precedent to the formation of a binding contract. . . .

Considering the evidence presented at the preliminary injunction hearing, the Court concludes that a jury is likely to find that the parties intended that their agreement be reduced to writing as a memorialization. They did not intend the writing to be a condition precedent to the formation of the contract. Pummill's e-mail on June 7, 2004, said that everything looked fine except two things. Sanecki then agreed to PSF's proposal concerning those two things. The parties then implemented the new pricing structure which was the major stumbling block to the formation of the contract. In his June 21 e-mail, Pummill says that "we" will mark up the contracts to conform to the agreement and PSF was then to send them to ICG. At no time does Pummill say "I" will mark them up and then give them to Manley for his approval, and if Manly approves them, we will send them to you. There is nothing in the communications or the actions of the parties that suggest that no contract was formed until the paper documents were formally signed by both Sanecki and Manly. . . .

Nor is there objective evidence to indicate that Pummill did not have the authority to enter into the agreement on behalf of PSF. The evidence strongly suggests that he had authority to bind PSF. While there is evidence that suggests that Sanecki did not want to make repairs required by the terms of the agreement until there was a writing, this does not mean that the parties intended the written documents be a condition precedent to the formation of a contract. Sanecki was obviously concerned about making the repairs on the defendant's property in the event that PSF attempted to backtrack on its agreement. It was also a minor issue in comparison to the implementation of the new pricing structure which was done as of June 28, 2004. It is probable that a jury will find that a written document with a formal signature was not a condition precedent to the formation of the contract. . . .

Because the parties' writings in April and June 2004 manifest a meeting of the minds regarding their intentions to enter into an agreement and because those writings are authenticated in a way that satisfies the Statute of Frauds, the Court finds that ICG is more likely to succeed on the merits of its claim. Although ICG's success is not guaranteed because some of the issues are factual in nature and reserved for juries, the Court finds that it is more likely than not based on the evidence before the Court at this juncture. Additionally, the Court finds that ICG cannot obtain cover goods that are of the same quality and degree as those produced by PSF and that ICG will suffer the greater harm if the Court does not grant ICG's pending Motion. Finally, the Court finds that the public interest weighs in favor of enforcing the parties' agreement. Therefore, the four factors outlined in *Dataphase*, 640 F.2d at 114, weigh in favor of granting ICG's Motion for Injunction.

III. CONCLUSION

Accordingly, it is hereby ORDERED that International Casing Group, Inc.'s Motion for Preliminary Injunction is GRANTED.

WADDLE V. ELROD

Supreme Court of Tennessee
367 S.W.3d 217 (2012)

CLARK, C.J.

. . .

[Earline Waddle sued Lorene Elrod over a prior land transaction.] The day before trial, Ms. Elrod's attorney, Mr. Gregory Reed, advised Ms. [Mary Beth] Hagan, counsel for Ms. Waddle, that Ms. Elrod was willing to return her one-half interest to avoid going to trial if Ms. Waddle would settle the case and release all other claims against her. Through her attorney, Ms. Waddle agreed to settle the case on the condition that she would not be responsible for any of the court costs. Around 4:00 p.m., Mr. Reed advised Ms. Hagan that Ms. Elrod had agreed to settle the case with Ms. Waddle's condition. At 4:34 p.m., Ms. Hagan sent the following email to Mr. Reed:

> Greg,
>
> This confirms that we have settled this case on the following terms:
>
> Elrod deeds property interest back to Waddle, Both [sic] parties sign full release, Waddle bears no court costs.
>
> Let me know if I have correctly stated our agreement.
>
> Thanks,
>
> Mary Beth

At 5:02 p.m., Mr. Reed responded:

> That is the agreement. I understand that you will draft the deed and take a shot at the court's order. No admission of guilt is to be included.
>
> Greg Reed

Approximately three weeks later, however, Ms. Elrod advised her attorney that she had changed her mind and no longer wanted to settle the case. Ms. Waddle filed a motion asking the trial court to enforce the settlement agreement. Ms. Elrod argued that the Statute of Frauds bars enforcement of the settlement agreement because it was not evidenced by a writing signed by Ms. Elrod or her attorney describing with specificity the terms of the agreement and the property at issue. Ms. Waddle argued in response that the email from Ms. Elrod's attorney, which confirmed the terms of the settlement and included Mr. Reed's typewritten name, constituted a writing signed by an agent of the party to be charged and satisfied the Statute of Frauds.

Following a hearing, the trial court entered an order enforcing the settlement agreement. Ms. Elrod appealed. The Court of Appeals affirmed the trial court's judgment enforcing the settlement agreement, reasoning that the Statute of Frauds applies only to "any contract for the *sale* of lands," Tenn.Code Ann. § 29–2–101(a)(4) (emphasis added), and does not apply to a settlement agreement requiring the transfer of an interest in real property. We granted Ms. Elrod's application for permission to appeal.

ANALYSIS

As the Court of Appeals recognized, Ms. Elrod does not dispute that the parties reached an agreement; rather, she argues that the Statute of Frauds applies and precludes enforcement of the settlement agreement because it required the transfer of an interest in real property.

The settlement agreement in the present case requires a conveyance of real property. With respect to real property, Tennessee's Statute of Frauds provides:

> No action shall be brought. . .[u]pon any contract for the sale of lands, tenements, or hereditaments,. . .unless the promise or agreement, upon which such action shall be brought, or some memorandum or note thereof, shall be in writing, and signed by the party to be charged therewith, or some other person lawfully authorized by such party. In a contract for the sale of lands, tenements, or hereditaments, the party to be charged is the party against whom enforcement of the contract is sought.
>
> . . .

The primary purpose of the Statute of Frauds is to reduce the risk of fraud and perjury associated with oral testimony. The Statute of Frauds also fosters certainty in transactions by ensuring that contract formation is not "based upon loose statements or innuendoes long after witnesses have become unavailable or when memories of the precise agreement have been dimmed by the passage of time." *Price,* 682 S.W.2d at 932. Another purpose of the Statute of Frauds is to protect property owners against "hasty or inconsiderate agreements concerning a valuable species of property" and "misunderstandings as to the nature and extent of such agreements." *Brandel v. Moore Mortg. & Inv. Co.,* 774 S.W.2d 600, 604 (Tenn. Ct. App.1989).

While this Court has long emphasized that the Statute of Frauds should be strictly adhered to and construed to accomplish its intended purposes, the Statute of Frauds is an affirmative defense. In other words, parol agreements within the Statute of Frauds are not *void ab initio,* and enforcement of such agreements may be barred only if a party pleads the Statute of Frauds. Parties may choose to abide by parol contracts for the sale of land. Indeed, the Statute of Frauds "was not enacted for the purpose of permitting a person to avoid a contract. Its object was not to grant a privilege to a person to refuse to perform what he has agreed to do. It was not enacted as a shield to the dishonest. . . ." *Cobble,* 230 S.W.2d at 196.

. . .

Consistent with the rule applied by a majority of jurisdictions, we hereby hold that the Statute of Frauds applies to any settlement agreement requiring a transfer of an interest in real property. We emphasize, however, that in determining whether the Statute of Frauds applies, courts must consider the terms of the settlement agreement, not the subject matter of the litigation. Settlement agreements arising from litigation that involves real property are subject to the Statute of Frauds only if the terms of the settlement agreement require the transfer of an interest in real property. *See, e.g., Meyer v. Lipe,* 14 S.W.3d 117, 120 (Mo. Ct. App. 2000) (explaining that the Statute of Frauds does not apply to settlements which fix a disputed or uncertain boundary line because no conveyance of land or passage of title is involved, only an effort to clarify and give effect to the title the parties already possess). Because the settlement agreement herein required Ms. Elrod to transfer her one-half interest in the property to Ms. Waddle, the Statute of Frauds applies.

We next consider whether the Statute of Frauds bars enforcement of the settlement agreement at issue in this appeal. As already explained, parol contracts are enforceable if "some memorandum or note thereof, shall be in writing and signed by the party to be charged therewith, or some other person lawfully authorized by such party." Tenn. Code Ann. § 29–2–101(a)(4). The Statute of Frauds does not require a written contract, only a written memorandum or note evidencing the parties' agreement. Additionally, while the writing required by the Statute of Frauds must contain the essential terms of the contract, it need not be in a single document.

Of course, even if one or more memoranda are produced sufficiently describing the terms of a parol agreement, the Statute of Frauds also requires that one of the writings be signed by the party to be charged or by some other person authorized to act on that party's behalf. The authority of the agent or the evidence of his agency need not be in writing, however. While the Statute of Frauds does not define "signed," many years ago the Court of Appeals considered whether a party's printed name on a bill of sale satisfied the signature requirement. In holding that the printed name was sufficient, the Court of Appeals stated:

> The [S]tatute [of Frauds] does not specify any particular form of signing. It merely requires that the party to be charged shall have signed the memorandum. It has been held that a cross mark is a good signature; also initials; even numerals, when used with the intention of constituting a signature; and a typewritten name or imprint made by a rubber stamp has the same effect; and this is equally true, though the typewriting or stamp impression be made by another, if the person to be charged has directed it. This has been the law in England for more than a century, and has been followed quite generally in this country.

While *Gessler* predates email, its holding appears broad enough to encompass typed names appearing in emails. However, we need not rely upon *Gessler* to determine whether the email that includes the name of Ms. Elrod's attorney satisfies the Statute of Frauds requirement of a writing signed by the party to be charged. In 2001 the General Assembly enacted the [Uniform Electronic Transactions Act ("UETA")].

The UETA "applies to electronic records and electronic signatures relating to a transaction." Tenn. Code Ann. § 47–10–103(a). The UETA governs "transactions between parties each of which has agreed to conduct transactions by electronic means. Whether the parties agree to conduct a transaction by electronic means is determined from the context and surrounding circumstances, including the parties' conduct." "Transaction means an action or set of actions occurring between two (2) or more persons relating to the conduct of business, commercial, or governmental affairs." Under the UETA (47–10–107):

> (a) A record or signature may not be denied legal effect or enforceability solely because it is in electronic form.
>
> (b) A contract may not be denied legal effect or enforceability solely because an electronic record was used in its formation.

(c) If a law requires a record to be in writing, an electronic record satisfies the law.

(d) If a law requires a signature, an electronic signature satisfies the law.

"Electronic signature" includes "an electronic sound, symbol, or process attached to or logically associated with a record and executed or adopted by a person with the intent to sign the record." *See also id.* cmt. 7 ("[T]he mere inclusion of one's name as part of an email message" qualifies as an electronic signature "so long as in each case the signer executed or adopted the symbol with the intent to sign.").

Applying the foregoing principles, we conclude that the Statute of Frauds does not bar enforcement of the settlement agreement at issue in this appeal. The parties, through their attorneys, evidenced an intent to finalize the settlement by electronic means; thus, the UETA applies. Pursuant to section 47–10–107(c), the emails counsel exchanged constitute a signed memorandum, note, or writing for purposes of the Statute of Frauds.

. . .[A]lthough Ms. Elrod did not sign the email, there is no dispute that Mr. Reed was acting as her agent when he negotiated the settlement. Had he written his signature on a printed version of the email, rather than typed his name at the end of the email, his signature would undoubtedly have been sufficient to satisfy the Statute of Frauds. The UETA, recognizing that all sorts of transactions are now routinely conducted by electronic means on a daily basis, obviates the need for a handwritten signature. Mr. Reed's typed name at the end of the email constitutes an "electronic signature." As the agent of Ms. Elrod, Mr. Reed's electronic signature on the email confirming the terms of the settlement agreement satisfies the signature requirement of the Statute of Frauds.

. . .

DISCUSSION PROBLEMS

1. Contract Renewal?

Embry worked in the sales department of the Hargadine, McKittrick Dry Goods Co. His employment contract expired on December 15, and his attempts to discuss the renewal of his contract in the days that followed with Hargadine, McKittrick president Thomas McKittrick had been unavailing.

On December 23, Embry went to McKittrick's office and insisted that his contract be extended for another year. Otherwise, he threatened, he would stop working immediately. Rather than responding directly, McKittrick asked Embry how things were going in his department, and Embry responded that the employees were very busy equipping the company's sales force with sample products. According to Embry's testimony McKittrick then said: "Go ahead, you're all right. Get your men out, and don't let that worry you." At that point, Embry returned to work. He was fired two months later. Based on this evidence, did Embry have a new one-year contract with Hargadine, McKittrick?

2. An Investment Opportunity

Rick Kaskel wanted to purchase a stake in a restaurant but lacked the necessary funds, so he proposed to share the investment with John Dennis. On February 1, 2001, Dennis sent Kaskel a document labeled "Memorandum" that included the following:

> John Dennis shall wire funds in the amount of $25,000.00 from his personal bank account to the . . . account [of Rick Kaskel] for the sole purpose of entering into an agreement with Rick Kaskel whereby John Dennis shall enjoy a percentage of the benefits that shall accrue to Rick Kaskel as a result of his position as a market partner with Texas Roadhouse—those benefits are more fully described below.
>
> . . .
>
> The benefits that shall accrue to John Dennis as a result of this investment of $25,000 and the subsequent investment of an additional $25,000, as may be required by Texas Roadhouse, shall be as follows:
>
> — A continuing interest equal to 22.5% of the annual operating bonus payable to Rick Kaskel for each store in which Rick Kaskel is involved.
>
> — 22.5% of any stock options which Rick Kaskel is granted by Texas Roadhouse.
>
> It is the stated intent to enter into a legally binding agreement that shall be constructed by an attorney(s) on behalf of John Dennis and Rick Kaskel which incorporates the above business terms not later than February 23, 2001. If such an agreement has not been signed by that time, John Dennis shall have the option to extend the time for such an agreement or demand repayment of the $25,000 investment which Rick Kaskel agrees to reimburse within (7) days of notification.

Dennis transferred to Kaskel $25,000 and then another $25,000. Kaskel deposited both sums in his Texas Roadhouse bank account. Dennis then provided Kaskel with a 14-page agreement, which Kaskel rejected as "way too complicated." Neither Kaskel nor Dennis ever signed any documents related to the Texas Roadhouse investment, and Kaskel never shared bonuses or stock options with Dennis.

Did Kaskel and Dennis have a contract?

3. Cotton from India

Raffles agreed to sell to Wichelhaus cotton that would arrive in Liverpool, England, from Bombay, India, on the ship named *Peerless*. As it happened, there were two ships named *Peerless* bound for Liverpool from Bombay, with one scheduled to depart in October and the other in December. The parties never discussed the timing of the ship's departure (or the cotton's arrival) or even the existence of more than one ship named *Peerless*. Wichelhaus knew only of the first ship, and Raffles knew only of the second.

When the second *Peerless* arrived in Liverpool, Raffles attempted to deliver the cotton to Wichelhaus, who refused to take possession of the cargo or pay the contract price. Did Raffles and Wichelhaus have a contract? If so, for which shipment?

CHAPTER 13

MISREPRESENTATION

■ ■ ■

INTRODUCTION

The misrepresentation doctrine in contract law enables parties to avoid enforcement of contracts in certain cases in which the complaining party lacked information at the time of contracting that, if known, would have caused that party to withhold assent to the agreement. Nonenforcement can be justified, in theory, by the observation that the counterpart's behavior violated customs of fair dealing, that the agreement did not reflect the counterpart's autonomous choice, or that the transaction would likely violate the principle of Pareto efficiency (i.e., that at least one party is made subjectively better off by the result and that neither is made subjectively worse off).

The difficulty in determining when the doctrine should be invoked arises from a lack of clarity as to whether the party seeking avoidance was in fact mistreated or whether that party should have taken self-protective steps to avoid entering into a contract that he would later regret. The law inevitably must balance one party's claim to protection from exploitation against the other party's claim to protection of its reliance on the other's manifestation of assent. The Restatement strikes this balance by allowing a party to avoid enforcement if three conditions are satisfied: the party's assent to the contract was induced by (a) an assertion not in accordance with the facts, that was (b) material or fraudulent, and upon which (c) he was justified in relying. Rest. (2d) Contracts §§ 159, 162, 164.

The classic case of *Vulcan Metals Co. v. Simmons Mfg. Co.* concerns the distinction between false assertions (impermissible) and a general commendation of quality (permissible). *Swinton v. Whitinsville Savings Bank* and *Weintraub v. Krobatsch* struggle with the question of whether a party's failure to disclose a material fact in the bargaining process should be treated the same as an affirmative assertion not in accordance with the facts. Put another way, should it always be a defense to a claim of misrepresentation that the defendant never actually made any affirmative statements that were false?

Restatement (Second) of Contracts § 159. Misrepresentation Defined

A misrepresentation is an assertion that is not in accord with the facts.

Comment:

a. Nature of the assertion. A misrepresentation, being a false assertion of fact, commonly takes the form of spoken or written words. Whether a statement is false depends on the meaning of the words in all the circumstances, including what may fairly be inferred from them. An assertion may also be inferred from conduct other than words. Concealment or even non-disclosure may have the effect of a misrepresentation under the rules stated in §§ 160 and 161. Whether a misrepresentation is fraudulent is determined by the rule stated in § 162(1). However, an assertion need not be fraudulent to be a misrepresentation. Thus a statement intended to be truthful may be a misrepresentation because of ignorance or carelessness, as when the word "not" is inadvertently omitted or when inaccurate language is used. But a misrepresentation that is not fraudulent has no consequences under this Chapter unless it is material. . . .

b. Half-truths. A statement may be true with respect to the facts stated, but may fail to include qualifying matter necessary to prevent the implication of an assertion that is false with respect to other facts. For example, a true statement that an event has recently occurred may carry the false implication that the situation has not changed since its occurrence. Such a half-truth may be as misleading as an assertion that is wholly false.

c. Meaning of "fact." An assertion must relate to something that is a fact at the time the assertion is made in order to be a misrepresentation. Such facts include past events as well as present circumstances but do not include future events. . . .

Restatement (Second) of Contracts § 162. When a Misrepresentation Is Fraudulent or Material

(1) A misrepresentation is fraudulent if the maker intends his assertion to induce a party to manifest his assent and the maker

(a) knows or believes that the assertion is not in accord with the facts, or

(b) does not have the confidence that he states or implies in the truth of the assertion, or

(c) knows that he does not have the basis that he states or implies for the assertion.

(2) A misrepresentation is material if it would be likely to induce a reasonable person to manifest his assent, or if the maker knows that it would be likely to induce the recipient to do so.

Comment:

c. *Meaning of "material."* Although a fraudulent misrepresentation need not be material in order to entitle the recipient to relief under the rule stated in § 164, a non-fraudulent misrepresentation will not entitle him to relief unless it is material. The materiality of a misrepresentation is determined from the viewpoint of the maker, while the justification of reliance is determined from the viewpoint of the recipient. (Contrast also the concept of a "material" failure to perform. See § 241.) The requirement of materiality may be met in either of two ways. First, a misrepresentation is material if it would be likely to induce a reasonable person to manifest his assent. Second, it is material if the maker knows that for some special reason it is likely to induce the particular recipient to manifest his assent. . . .

Illustrations:

3. A, while negotiating with B for the sale of A's race horse, tells him that the horse has run a mile in a specified time. A is honestly mistaken, and, unknown to him, the horse has never come close to that time. B is induced by A's assertion to make a contract to buy the horse. A's statement, although not fraudulent, is a material misrepresentation, and the contract is voidable by B under the rule stated in § 164.

Restatement (Second) of Contracts § 164. When a Misrepresentation Makes a Contract Voidable

(1) If a party's manifestation of assent is induced by either a fraudulent or a material misrepresentation by the other party upon which the recipient is justified in relying, the contract is voidable by the recipient.

CASES

VULCAN METALS CO. v. SIMMONS MFG. CO.

United States Court of Appeals, Second Circuit
248 F. 853 (1918)

. . .

The gist of the complaint . . . was the fraudulent procurement by the Simmons Manufacturing Company of a contract executed by the defendant Freeman on behalf of the Vulcan Metals Company, Incorporated, by which he purchased from the Simmons Company for $75,000 all the tools, dies, and equipment owned by it for the manufacture of its vacuum cleaning machines, all manufactured machines and unassembled parts, as set forth in a schedule thereto attached, and all inventions, applications, and letters patent owned by the Simmons Company in vacuum cleaners, together with certain proposed improvements to be made thereon. The complaint further alleges that the officers and agents of the Simmons Manufacturing Company made false representations as to the character of the vacuum cleaners so sold and the extent to which they had been used upon the market, to which the Vulcan Metals Company, Incorporated, acted to its prejudice, because the machines and patents were totally inefficient and unmarketable. . . . The District Judge directed a verdict for the Simmons Manufacturing Company in both actions, upon the theory that no actionable fraud had been made out, and the correctness of this ruling is the turning point in the case.

LEARNED HAND, DISTRICT JUDGE (after stating the facts as above).

The first question is of the misrepresentations touching the quality and powers of the patented machine. These were general commendations, or, in so far as they included any specific facts, were not disproved; e.g., that the cleaner would produce 18 inches of vacuum with 25 pounds water pressure. They raise, therefore, the question of law how far general 'puffing' or 'dealers' talk' can be the basis of an action for deceit.

The conceded exception in such cases has generally rested upon the distinction between 'opinion' and 'fact'; but that distinction has not escaped the criticism it deserves. An opinion is a fact, and it may be a very relevant fact; the expression of an opinion is the assertion of a belief, and any rule which condones the expression of a consciously false opinion condones a consciously false statement of fact. When the parties are so situated that the buyer may reasonably rely upon the expression of the seller's opinion, it is no excuse to give a false one. And so it makes much difference whether the parties stand 'on an equality.' For example, we should treat very differently the expressed opinion of a chemist to a layman about the properties of a composition from the same opinion between chemist and chemist, when the buyer had full opportunity to examine. The reason of the rule lies, we think, in this: There are some kinds of talk which no sensible man takes seriously, and if he does he suffers from his credulity. If we were all scrupulously honest, it would not be so; but, as it is, neither party usually believes what the seller says about his own opinions, and each knows it. Such statements, like the claims of campaign managers before election, are rather designed to allay the suspicion which would attend their absence than to be understood as having any relation to objective truth. It is quite true that they induce a compliant temper in the buyer, but it is by a much more subtle process than through the acceptance of his claims for his wares.

So far as concerns statements of value, the rule is pretty well fixed against the buyer It has been applied more generally to statements of quality and serviceability.

In the case at bar, since the buyer was allowed full opportunity to examine the cleaner and to test it out, we put the parties upon an equality. It seems to us that general statements as to what the cleaner would do, even though consciously false, were not of a kind to be taken literally by the buyer. As between manufacturer and customer, it may not be so; but this was the case of taking over a business, after ample chance to investigate. Such a buyer, who the seller rightly expects will undertake an independent and adequate inquiry into the actual merits of what he gets, has no right to treat as material in his determination statements like these. The standard of honesty permitted by the rule may not be the best; but, as Holmes, J., says in Deming v. Darling, 148 Mass. 504, 20 N.E. 107, 2 L.R.A. 743, the chance that the higgling preparatory to a bargain may be afterwards translated into assurances of quality may perhaps be a set-off to the actual wrong allowed by the rule as it stands. We therefore think that the District Court was right in disregarding all these misrepresentations.

SWINTON V. WHITINSVILLE SAVINGS BANK

Supreme Judicial Court of Massachusetts
311 Mass. 677 (1942)

QUA, J.

The declaration alleges that on or about September 12, 1938, the defendant sold the plaintiff a house in Newton to be occupied by the plaintiff and his family as a dwelling; that at the time of the sale the house "was infested with termites, an insect that is most dangerous and destructive to buildings"; that the defendant knew the house was so infested; that the plaintiff could not readily observe this condition upon inspection; that "knowing the internal destruction that these insects were creating in said house," the defendant falsely and fraudulently concealed from the plaintiff its true condition; that the plaintiff at the time of his purchase had no knowledge of the termites, exercised due care thereafter, and learned of them about August 30, 1940; and that, because of the destruction that was being done and the dangerous condition that was being created by the termites, the plaintiff was put to great expense for repairs and for the installation of termite control in order to prevent the loss and destruction of said house.

There is no allegation of any false statement or representation, or of the uttering of a half truth which may be tantamount to a falsehood. There is no intimation that the defendant by any means prevented the plaintiff from acquiring information as to the condition of the house. There is nothing to show any fiduciary relation between the parties, or that the plaintiff stood in a position of confidence toward or dependence upon the defendant. So far as appears the parties made a business deal at arm's length. The charge is concealment and nothing more; and it is concealment in the simple sense of mere failure to reveal, with nothing to show any peculiar duty to speak. The characterization of the concealment as false and fraudulent of course adds nothing in the absence of further allegations of fact. Province Securities Corp. v. Maryland Casualty Co., 269 Mass. 75, 92, 168 S.E. 252.

If this defendant is liable on this declaration every seller is liable who fails to disclose any nonapparent defect known to him in the subject of the sale which materially reduces its value and which the buyer fails to discover. Similarly it would seem that every buyer would be liable who fails to disclose any nonapparent virtue known to him in the subject of the purchase which materially enhances its value and of which the seller is ignorant. See Goodwin v. Agassiz, 283 Mass. 358. The law has not yet, we believe, reached the point of imposing upon the frailties of human nature a standard so idealistic as this. That the particular case here stated by the plaintiff possesses a certain appeal to the moral sense is scarcely to be denied. Probably the reason is to be found in the facts that the infestation of buildings by termites has not been common in Massachusetts and constitutes a concealed risk against which buyers are off their guard. But the law cannot provide special rules for termites and can hardly attempt to determine liability according to the varying probabilities of the existence and discovery of different possible defects in the subjects of trade. The rule of nonliability for bare nondisclosure has been stated and followed by this court in [numerous cases]. It is adopted in the American Law Institute's Restatement of Torts, § 551. See Williston on Contracts, Rev. Ed., §§ 1497, 1498, 1499.

The order sustaining the demurrer is affirmed, and judgment is to be entered for the defendant.

So ordered.

WEINTRAUB V. KROBATSCH

Supreme Court of New Jersey
64 N.J. 445 (1974)

JACOBS, J.

. . .Mrs. Weintraub owned and occupied a six-year-old Englishtown home which she placed in the hands of a real estate broker (The Serafin Agency, Inc.) for sale. The Krobatsches were interested in purchasing the home, examined it while it was illuminated and found it suitable. On June 30, 1971 Mrs. Weintraub, as seller, and the Krobatsches, as purchasers, entered into a contract for the sale of the property for $42,500. The contract provided that the purchasers had inspected the property and were fully satisfied with its physical condition, that no representations had been made and that no responsibility was assumed by the seller as to the present or future condition of the premises. A deposit of $4,250 was sent by the purchasers to the broker to be held in escrow pending the closing of the transaction. The purchasers requested that the seller have the house fumigated and that was done. A fire after the signing of the contract caused damage but the purchasers indicated readiness that there be adjustment at closing.

During the evening of August 25, 1971, prior to closing, the purchasers entered the house, then unoccupied, and as they turned the lights on they were, as described in their petition for certification, "astonished to see roaches literally running in all directions, up the walls, drapes, etc." On the following day their attorney wrote a letter to Mrs. Weintraub, care of her New York law firm, advising that on the previous day "it was discovered that the house is infested with vermin despite the fact that an exterminator has only recently serviced the house" and asserting that "the presence of vermin in such great quantities, particularly after the exterminator was done, rendered the house as unfit for human habitation at this time and therefore, the contract is rescinded." On September 2, 1971 an exterminator wrote to Mr. Krobatsch advising that he had examined the premises and that "cockroaches were found to have infested the entire house." He said he could eliminate them for a relatively modest charge by two treatments with a twenty-one day interval but that it would be necessary to remove the carpeting "to properly treat all the infested areas."

Mrs. Weintraub rejected the rescission by the purchasers and filed an action in the Law Division joining them and the broker as defendants. . . .At the argument on the motions it was evident that the purchasers were claiming fraudulent concealment or nondisclosure by the seller as the basis for their rescission. Thus at one point their attorney said: "Your honor, I would point out, and it is in my clients' affidavit, every time that they inspected this house prior to this time every light in the place was illuminated. Now, these insects are nocturnal by nature and that is not a point I think I have to prove through someone. I think Webster's dictionary is sufficient. By keeping the lights on it keeps them out of sight. These sellers had to know they had this problem. You could not live in a house this infested without knowing about it."

The Law Division denied the motion by the purchasers for summary judgment but granted Mrs. Weintraub's motion and directed that the purchasers pay her the sum of $4,250. . . .

Before us the purchasers contend that they were entitled to a trial on the issue of whether there was fraudulent concealment or nondisclosure entitling them to rescind; if there was, then clearly they were under no liability to either the seller or the broker and would be entitled to the return of their deposit held by the broker in escrow. See Keen v. James, 39 N.J. Eq. 527, 540 (E. & A. 1885) where Justice Dixon, speaking for the then Court of last resort, pointed out that "silence may be fraudulent" and that relief may be granted to one contractual party where the other suppresses facts which he, "under the circumstances, is bound in conscience and duty to disclose to the other party, and in respect to which he cannot, innocently, be silent." 39 N.J. Eq. at 540–541. See also 12 Williston, Contracts § 1498 (3d ed. 1970); Prosser, Torts 695–99 (4th ed. 1971).

Mrs. Weintraub asserts that she was unaware of the infestation and the Krobatsches acknowledge that, if that was so, then there was no fraudulent concealment or nondisclosure on her part and their claim must fall. But the purchasers allege that she was in fact aware of the infestation and at this stage of the proceedings we must assume that to be true. She contends, however, that even if she were fully aware she would have been under no duty to speak and that consequently no complaint by the purchasers may legally be grounded on her silence. She relies primarily on cases such as Swinton v. Whitinsville Sav. Bank, 311 Mass. 677, 42 N.E.2d 808, 141 A.L.R. 965 (1942). . . .*Swinton* is pertinent but, as Dean Prosser has noted (Prosser, Supra at 696), it is one of a line of "singularly unappetizing cases" which are surely out of tune with our times.

In *Swinton* the plaintiff purchased a house from the defendant and after he occupied it he found it to be infested with termites. The defendant had made no verbal or written representations but the plaintiff, asserting that the defendant knew of the termites and was under a duty to speak, filed a complaint for damages grounded on fraudulent concealment. The Supreme Judicial Court of Massachusetts sustained a demurrer to the complaint and entered judgment for the defendant. In the course of its opinion the court acknowledged that "the plaintiff possesses a certain appeal to the moral sense" but concluded that the law has not "reached the point of imposing upon the frailties of human nature a standard so idealistic as this." 42 N.E.2d at 808–809. That was written several decades ago and we are far from certain that it represents views held by the current members of the Massachusetts court. See Kannavos v. Annino, 356 Mass. 42 (1969). In any event we are certain that it does not represent our sense of justice or fair dealing and it has understandably been rejected in persuasive opinions elsewhere. See Obde v. Schlemeyer, 56 Wash. 2d 449 (1960); Loghry v. Capel, 257 Iowa 285 (1965); Williams v. Benson, 3 Mich. App. 9 (1966); Sorrell v. Young, 6 Wash. App. 220 (1971); Lawson v. Citizens & Southern National Bank of S.C., 259 S.C. 477 (1972); Cf. Clauser v. Taylor, 44 Cal. App. 2d 453 (1941); Simmons v. Evans, Tenn. 282, 206 S.W.2d 295 (1947); Rich v. Rankl, 6 Conn. Cir. 185, 269 A.2d 84, 88 (1969); Ford v. Broussard, 248 So. 2d 629 (La. App. 1971). See also Restatement 2d, Torts § 551 (Tent. Draft No. 12 (1966)).

. . .

If the trial judge finds such deliberate concealment or nondisclosure of the latent infestation not observable by the purchasers on their inspection, he will still be called upon to determine whether, in the light of the full presentation before him, the concealment or nondisclosure was of such significant nature as to justify rescission. Minor conditions which ordinary sellers and purchasers would reasonably disregard as of little or no materiality in the transaction would clearly not call for judicial intervention. While the described condition may not have been quite as major as in the termite cases which were concerned with structural impairments, to the purchasers here it apparently was of such magnitude and was so repulsive as to cause them to rescind immediately though they had earlier indicated readiness that there be adjustment at closing for damage resulting from a fire which occurred after the contract was signed. We are not prepared at this time to say that on their showing they acted either unreasonably or without equitable justification.

Our courts have come a long way since the days when the judicial emphasis was on formal rules and ancient precedents rather than on modern concepts of justice and fair dealing. . . .[T]he judgment entered in the Appellate Division is:

Reversed and Remanded.

DISCUSSION PROBLEMS

1. The Malfunctioning Copier

Lorraine Corporation bought a large number of copy machines from Royal Business Machines, after Royal's salesman asserted that the copiers were of "good quality" and "would last a lifetime." Not long after, the copiers began to malfunction. Lorraine filed a lawsuit against Royal seeking to rescind the contract on the grounds of misrepresentation. Who should prevail?

2. The Oil Leak

During negotiations to purchase an oil storage facility from Texaco, V.S.H. Realty asked whether there were any oil leaks on the property. Texaco never directly responded to the inquiry, but it disclosed in writing that oil had "migrated under [Texaco's] garage building across Marginal Street from the [storage facility and that] the fuel oil underground as a result of heavy rains or high tides, seeps into the boiler room of the garage building." Separately, Texaco provided a written statement that Texaco had not received "any notice, demand, or communication from any local, county, state, or federal department or agency regarding modifications or improvements to the facility or any part thereof." Ultimately, V.S.H. agreed to pay $2.8 million for the facility, and the agreement included a statement that V.S.H. had inspected the facility and accepted it "as is" without warranties by Texaco concerning its condition.

Soon after closing the transaction, V.S.H. discovered oil seeping from the ground on the storage facility property and learned that the U.S. Coast Guard was investigating the property for possible oil leaks. V.S.H. sought rescission of the contract on grounds of misrepresentation. Texaco moved to dismiss the complaint. Should the court grant Texaco's motion?

3. The End of the Blockade

On February 18, 1815, Hector Organ contracted to buy 111 hogsheads of tobacco from Laidlaw & Company in the city of New Orleans at the prevailing market price. Organ had information that the United States and Great Britain had signed the Treaty of Ghent, which ended the War of 1812. This information suggested that the British blockade of American ports, which had prevented the shipment of tobacco to Europe, would soon be lifted, but this information was not yet widely known.

When news of the peace treaty was announced, the price of tobacco increased by 50 percent almost instantly, and Laidlaw refused to deliver the contracted amount of tobacco to Organ. Organ filed suit. Which party should prevail?

CHAPTER 14

UNCONSCIONABILITY

■ ■ ■

INTRODUCTION

In the presence of mutual assent, judicial enforcement of contracts is usually consistent with the principles of both autonomy (both parties desire to be legally bound) and efficiency (the agreement, when executed, will make both parties better off than they otherwise would have been, thus increasing total social welfare). Where misrepresentation is present, enforcement of an agreement might fail to serve one or both of these core principles, justifying judicial intervention. The unconscionability doctrine can also be understood as a tool, although a less precise one than misrepresentation, for courts to intervene when a contract either fails to reflect true party autonomy or fails to improve the well-being of both parties.

The black letter law of unconscionability is a legal "standard" rather than a "rule." Courts may refuse to enforce "unconscionable agreements," but neither the Restatement nor the Uniform Commercial Code define that term. See Rest. (2d) Contracts § 208; U.C.C. § 2–302. Most courts require evidence of one or more procedural defects in the bargaining process ("procedural unconscionability") *and* substantive unfairness in the resulting agreement ("substantive unconscionability") before they will invoke the doctrine, but what facts are necessary to satisfy these dual requirements remains obscure. *Williams v. Walker-Thomas Furniture Company* is a classic example of judicial deployment of the unconscionability doctrine. But as you read the opinion, keep in mind that unconscionability claims rarely succeed, even in cases in which the contract at issue seems one-sided. The result in *Zapata v. Dairy Mart* is more typical. Is the contract at issue in *Zapata* any more troubling than the one in *Williams*? If so, why?

In unconscionability cases, plaintiffs often challenge specific terms rather than the entire agreement, which raises questions as to the appropriate remedy if the court does find unconscionability. The black letter law provides courts with little in the way of useful assistance. The Restatement states that courts may refuse to enforce the entire contract, refuse to enforce the offending term while leaving the remainder of the contract intact, or reform the offending term, but it provides no guidance as to what factors counsel in favor or against any of these options. Rest. (2d) Contracts § 208.

Restatement (Second) of Contracts § 208.
Unconscionable Contract or Term

If a contract or term thereof is unconscionable at the time the contract is made a court may refuse to enforce the contract, or may enforce the remainder of the contract without the unconscionable term, or may so limit the application of any unconscionable term as to avoid any unconscionable result.

Comment:

c. Overall imbalance. Inadequacy of consideration does not of itself invalidate a bargain, but gross disparity in the values exchanged may be an important factor in a determination that a contract is unconscionable and may be sufficient ground, without more, for denying specific performance. Such a disparity may also corroborate indications of defects in the bargaining process, or may affect the remedy to be granted when there is a violation of a more specific rule. Theoretically it is possible for a contract to be oppressive taken as a whole, even though there is no weakness in the bargaining process and no single term which is in itself unconscionable. Ordinarily, however, an unconscionable contract involves other factors as well as overall imbalance.

d. Weakness in the bargaining process. A bargain is not unconscionable merely because the parties to it are unequal in bargaining position, nor even because the inequality results in an allocation of risks to the weaker party. But gross inequality of bargaining power, together with terms unreasonably favorable to the stronger party, may confirm indications that the transaction involved elements of deception or compulsion, or may show that the weaker party had no meaningful choice, no real alternative, or did not in fact assent or appear to assent to the unfair terms. Factors which may contribute to a finding of unconscionability in the bargaining process include the following: belief by the stronger party that there is no reasonable probability that the weaker party will fully perform the contract; knowledge of the stronger party that the weaker party will be unable to receive substantial benefits from the contract; knowledge of the stronger party that the weaker party is unable reasonably to protect his interests by reason of physical or mental infirmities, ignorance, illiteracy or inability to understand the language of the agreement, or similar factors. . . .

CASES

WILLIAMS V. WALKER-THOMAS FURNITURE CO.

United States Court of Appeals, D.C. Circuit
350 F.2d 445 (1965)

J. SKELLY WRIGHT, J.

Appellee, Walker-Thomas Furniture Company, operates a retail furniture store in the District of Columbia. During the period from 1957 to 1962 each appellant in these cases purchased a number of household items from Walker-Thomas, for which payment was to be made in installments. The terms of each purchase were contained in a printed form contract which set forth the value of the purchased item and purported to lease the item to appellant for a stipulated monthly rent payment. The contract then provided, in substance, that title would remain in Walker-Thomas until the total of all the monthly payments made equaled the stated value of the item, at which time appellants could take title. In the event of a default in the payment of any monthly installment, Walker-Thomas could repossess the item.

The contract further provided that "the amount of each periodical installment payment to be made by (purchaser) to the Company under this present lease shall be inclusive of and not in addition to the amount of each installment payment to be made by (purchaser) under such prior leases, bills or accounts; and all payments now and hereafter made by (purchaser) shall be credited pro rata on all outstanding leases, bills and accounts due the Company by (purchaser) at the time each such payment is made." The effect of this rather obscure provision was to keep a balance due on every item purchased until the balance due on all items, whenever purchased, was liquidated. As a result, the debt incurred at the time of purchase of each item was secured by the right to repossess all the items previously purchased by the same purchaser, and each new item purchased automatically became subject to a security interest arising out of the previous dealings.

On May 12, 1962, appellant Thorne purchased an item described as a Daveno, three tables, and two lamps, having total stated value of $391.10. Shortly thereafter, he defaulted on his monthly payments and appellee sought to replevy all the items purchased since the first transaction in 1958. Similarly, on April 17, 1962, appellant Williams bought a stereo set of stated value of $514.95.[1] She too defaulted shortly thereafter, and appellee sought to replevy all the items purchased since December, 1957.

[1] At the time of this purchase her account showed a balance of $164 still owing from her prior purchases. [The $515 stereo thus increased her balance due to $679, which she had paid down to $400 when she defaulted.] The total of all the purchases made over the years in question came to $1,800. The total payments amounted to $1,400.

The Court of General Sessions granted judgment for appellee. The District of Columbia Court of Appeals affirmed, and we granted appellants' motion for leave to appeal to this court.

Appellants' principal contention, rejected by both the trial and the appellate courts below, is that these contracts, or at least some of them, are unconscionable and, hence, not enforceable. . . .We do not agree that the court lacked the power to refuse enforcement to contracts found to be unconscionable. In other jurisdictions, it has been held as a matter of common law that unconscionable contracts are not enforceable. While no decision of this court so holding has been found, the notion that an unconscionable bargain should not be given full enforcement is by no means novel. In Scott v. United States, 79 U.S. (12 Wall.) 443 (1870), the Supreme Court stated: "If a contract be unreasonable and unconscionable, but not void for fraud, a court of law will give to the party who sues for its breach damages, not according to its letter, but only such as he is equitably entitled to."[2] Since we have never adopted or rejected such a rule, the question here presented is actually one of first impression.

Congress has recently enacted the Uniform Commercial Code, which specifically provides that the court may refuse to enforce a contract which it finds to be unconscionable at the time it was made. 28 D.C. Code § 2–302 (Supp. IV 1965). The enactment of this section, which occurred subsequent to the contracts here in suit, does not mean that the common law of the District of Columbia was otherwise at the time of enactment, nor does it preclude the court from adopting a similar rule in the exercise of its powers to develop the common law for the District of Columbia. In fact, in view of the absence of prior authority on the point, we consider the congressional adoption of § 2–302 persuasive authority for following the rationale of the cases from which the section is explicitly derived. Comment, § 2–302, Uniform Commercial Code (1962). Accordingly, we hold that where the element of unconscionability is present at the time a contract is made, the contract should not be enforced.

Unconscionability has generally been recognized to include an absence of meaningful choice on the part of one of the parties together with contract terms which are unreasonably favorable to the other party. Whether a meaningful choice is present in a particular case can only be determined by consideration of all the circumstances surrounding the transaction. In many cases the meaningfulness of the choice is negated by a gross inequality of bargaining power. The manner in which the contract was entered is also relevant to this consideration. Did each party to the contract, considering his obvious education or lack of it, have a reasonable opportunity to understand the terms of the contract, or were the important

[2] Campbell Soup Co. v. Wentz, 3 Cir., 172 F.2d 80 (1948); Indianapolis Morris Plan Corporation v. Sparks, 132 Ind. App. 145 (1961); Henningsen v. Bloomfield Motors, Inc., 32 N.J. 358 (1960).

terms hidden in a maze of fine print and minimized by deceptive sales practices? Ordinarily, one who signs an agreement without full knowledge of its terms might be held to assume the risk that he has entered a one-sided bargain. See Restatement, Contracts § 70 (1932). But when a party of little bargaining power, and hence little real choice, signs a commercially unreasonable contract with little or no knowledge of its terms, it is hardly likely that his consent, or even an objective manifestation of his consent, was ever given to all the terms. In such a case the usual rule that the terms of the agreement are not to be questioned should be abandoned and the court should consider whether the terms of the contract are so unfair that enforcement should be withheld.

In determining reasonableness or fairness, the primary concern must be with the terms of the contract considered in light of the circumstances existing when the contract was made. The test is not simple, nor can it be mechanically applied. The terms are to be considered "in the light of the general commercial background and the commercial needs of the particular trade or case." Corbin suggests the test as being whether the terms are "so extreme as to appear unconscionable according to the mores and business practices of the time and place." 1 Corbin, Contracts § 128 (1963)[.] We think this formulation correctly states the test to be applied in those cases where no meaningful choice was exercised upon entering the contract.

Because the trial court and the appellate court did not feel that enforcement could be refused, no findings were made on the possible unconscionability of the contracts in these cases. Since the record is not sufficient for our deciding the issue as a matter of law, the cases must be remanded to the trial court for further proceedings.

So ordered.

DANAHER, J. (dissenting).

The District of Columbia Court of Appeals obviously was as unhappy about the situation here presented as any of us can possibly be. Its opinion in the *Williams* case, quoted in the majority text, concludes: "We think Congress should consider corrective legislation to protect the public from such exploitive contracts as were utilized in the case at bar."

My view is thus summed up by an able court which made no finding that there had actually been sharp practice. Rather the appellant seems to have known precisely where she stood.

There are many aspects of public policy here involved. What is a luxury to some may seem an outright necessity to others. Is public oversight to be required of the expenditures of relief funds? A washing machine, e.g., in the hands of a relief client might become a fruitful source of income. Many relief clients may well need credit, and certain business establishments will take long chances on the sale of items, expecting their pricing policies will afford a degree of protection commensurate with the risk. . . .

I mention such matters only to emphasize the desirability of a cautious approach to any such problem, particularly since the law for so long has allowed parties such great latitude in making their own contracts. I dare say there must annually be thousands upon thousands of installment credit transactions in this jurisdiction, and one can only speculate as to the effect the decision in these cases will have.

ZAPATHA V. DAIRY MART, INC.

Supreme Judicial Court of Massachusetts
381 Mass. 284 (1980)

WILKINS, J.

We are concerned here with the question whether Dairy Mart, Inc. (Dairy Mart), lawfully undertook to terminate a franchise agreement under which the Zapathas operated a Dairy Mart store on Wilbraham Road in Springfield. The Zapathas brought this action seeking to enjoin the termination of the agreement, alleging that the contract provision purporting to authorize the termination of the franchise agreement without cause was unconscionable and that Dairy Mart's conduct was an unfair and deceptive act or practice in violation of G.L. c. 93A. The judge ruled that Dairy Mart did not act in good faith, that the termination provision was unconscionable, and that Dairy Mart's termination of the agreement without cause was an unfair and deceptive act. We granted Dairy Mart's application for direct appellate review of a judgment that stated that Dairy Mart could terminate the agreement only for good cause and that the attempted termination was null and void. We reverse the judgments.

Mr. Zapatha is a high school graduate who had attended college for one year and had also taken college evening courses in business administration and business law. From 1952 to May, 1973, he was employed by a company engaged in the business of electroplating. He rose through the ranks to foreman and then to the position of operations manager, at one time being in charge of all metal finishing in the plant with 150 people working under him. In May, 1973, he was discharged and began looking for other opportunities, in particular a business of his own. Several months later he met with a representative of Dairy Mart. Dairy Mart operates a chain of franchised "convenience" stores. The Dairy Mart representative told Mr. Zapatha that working for Dairy Mart was being in business for one's self and that such a business was very stable and secure. Mr. Zapatha signed an application to be considered for a franchise. In addition, he was presented with a brochure entitled "Here's a Chance," which made certain representations concerning the status of a franchise holder.

Dairy Mart approved Mr. Zapatha's application and offered him a store in Agawam. On November 8, 1973, a representative of Dairy Mart showed him a form of franchise agreement, entitled Limited Franchise and License Agreement, asked him to read it, and explained that his wife would have to sign the agreement as well.

. . .The termination provision. . .allowed either party, after twelve months, to terminate the agreement without cause on ninety days' written notice. In the event of termination initiated by it without cause, Dairy Mart agreed to repurchase the saleable merchandise inventory at retail prices, less 20%.

The Dairy Mart representative read and explained the termination provision to Mr. Zapatha. Mr. Zapatha later testified that, while he understood every word in the provision, he had interpreted it to mean that Dairy Mart could terminate the agreement only for cause. The Dairy Mart representative advised Mr. Zapatha to take the agreement to an attorney and said "I would prefer that you did." However, he also told Mr. Zapatha that the terms of the contract were not negotiable. The Zapathas signed the agreement without consulting an attorney. When the Zapathas took charge of the Agawam store, a representative of Dairy Mart worked with them to train them in Dairy Mart's methods of operation.

In 1974, another store became available on Wilbraham Road in Springfield, and the Zapathas elected to surrender the Agawam store. They executed a new franchise agreement, on an identical printed form, relating to the new location.

In November, 1977, Dairy Mart presented a new and more detailed form of "Independent Operator's Agreement" to the Zapathas for execution. Some of the terms were less favorable to the store operator than those of the earlier form of agreement. Mr. Zapatha told representatives of Dairy Mart that he was content with the existing contract and had decided not to sign the new agreement. On January 20, 1978, Dairy Mart gave written notice to the Zapathas that their contract was being terminated effective in ninety days. The termination notice stated that Dairy Mart "remains available to enter into discussions with you with respect to entering into a new Independent Operator's Agreement; however, there is no assurance that Dairy Mart will enter into a new Agreement with you, or even if entered into, what terms such Agreement will contain." The notice also indicated that Dairy Mart was prepared to purchase the Zapathas' saleable inventory.

. . .

We consider first the plaintiffs' argument that the termination clause of the franchise agreement, authorizing Dairy Mart to terminate the agreement without cause, on ninety days' notice, was unconscionable by the standards expressed in G.L. c. 106, § 2–302. The same standards are set forth in Restatement (Second) of Contracts § 234 (Tent. Drafts Nos. 1–7, 1973). The issue is one of law for the court, and the test is to be made as of the time the contract was made. . . .

The official comment to § 2–302 states that "(t)he basic test is whether, in the light of the general commercial background and the commercial needs of the particular trade or case, the clauses involved are so one-sided as to be unconscionable under the circumstances existing at the time of the making of the contract. . . .The principle is one of prevention of oppression and unfair surprise. . .and not of disturbance of allocation of risks because of superior bargaining power." Official Comment 1 to U.C.C. § 2–302. Unconscionability is not defined in the Code, nor do the views expressed in the official comment provide a precise definition. The annotation prepared by the Massachusetts Advisory Committee on the Code states that "(t)he section appears to be intended to carry equity practice into the sales field." See 1 R. Anderson, Uniform Commercial Code § 2–302:7 (1970) to the same effect. This court has not had occasion to consider in any detail the meaning of the word "unconscionable" in § 2–302. Because there is no clear, all-purpose definition of "unconscionable," nor could there be, unconscionability must be determined on a case by case basis (see Commonwealth v. Gustafsson, 370 Mass. 181, 187, 346 N.E.2d 706 (1976)), giving particular attention to whether, at the time of the execution of the agreement, the contract provision could result in unfair surprise and was oppressive to the allegedly disadvantaged party.

. . .

We find no potential for unfair surprise to the Zapathas in the provision allowing termination without cause. We view the question of unfair surprise as focused on the circumstances under which the agreement was entered into.[13] The termination provision was neither obscurely worded, nor buried in fine print in the contract. Contrast Williams v. Walker-Thomas Furniture Co., 350 F.2d 445, 449 (D.C. Cir. 1965). The provision was specifically pointed out to Mr. Zapatha before it was signed; Mr. Zapatha testified that he thought the provision was "straightforward," and he declined the opportunity to take the agreement to a lawyer for advice. The Zapathas had ample opportunity to consider the

---

[13] As we shall note subsequently, the concept of oppression deals with the substantive unfairness of the contract term. This two-part test for unconscionability involves determining whether there was "an absence of meaningful choice on the part of one of the parties, together with contract terms which are unreasonably favorable to the other party." Williams v. Walker-Thomas Furniture Co., 350 F.2d 445, 449 (D.C. Cir. 1965). The inquiry involves a search for components of "procedural" and "substantive" unconscionability. See generally Leff, *Unconscionability and the Code—The Emperor's New Clause*, 115 Pa. L. Rev. 485 (1967).

agreement before they signed it. . . .We conclude that a person of Mr. Zapatha's business experience and education should not have been surprised by the termination provision and, if in fact he was, there was no element of unfairness in the inclusion of that provision in the agreement. See Fleischmann Distilling Corp. v. Distillers Co., 395 F. Supp. 221, 233 ("(i)t is the exceptional commercial setting where a claim of unconscionability will be allowed"). Contrast Johnson v. Mobil Oil Corp., 415 F. Supp. 264, 268–269 (illiterate service station operator incapable of reading dealer contract).

We further conclude that there was no oppression in the inclusion of a termination clause in the franchise agreement. We view the question of oppression as directed to the substantive fairness to the parties of permitting the termination provisions to operate as written. The Zapathas took over a going business on premises provided by Dairy Mart, using equipment furnished by Dairy Mart. As an investment, the Zapathas had only to purchase the inventory of goods to be sold but, as Dairy Mart concedes, on termination by it without cause Dairy Mart was obliged to repurchase all the Zapathas' saleable merchandise inventory, including items not purchased from Dairy Mart, at 80% of its retail value. There was no potential for forfeiture or loss of investment. There is no question here of a need for a reasonable time to recoup the franchisees' initial investment. See McGinnis Piano & Organ Co. v. Yamaha Int'l Corp., 480 F.2d 474, 480 (8th Cir. 1973); Gellhorn, Limitations on Contract Termination Rights Franchise Cancellations, 1967 Duke L.J. 465, 479–481.

The Zapathas were entitled to their net profits through the entire term of the agreement. They failed to sustain their burden of showing that the agreement allocated the risks and benefits connected with termination in an unreasonably disproportionate way and that the termination provision was not reasonably related to legitimate commercial needs of Dairy Mart. See Gellhorn, supra at 512. See also Central Ohio Co-op Milk Producers, Inc. v. Rowland, 29 Ohio App. 2d 236, 281 N.E.2d 42, 58 Ohio Op. 2d 421, 423 (1972); W.L. May Co. v. Philco-Ford Corp., 273 Or. 701, 708, 543 P.2d 283 (1975). To find the termination clause oppressive merely because it did not require cause for termination would be to establish an unwarranted barrier to the use of termination at will clauses in contracts in this Commonwealth, where each party received the anticipated and bargained for consideration during the full term of the agreement.

DISCUSSION PROBLEMS

1. Home Repairs

A persuasive door-to-door salesman convinced 83-year-old Pearl Maxwell to refinance her home and use the money for a variety of home repairs, including the replacement of siding and windows. Before refinancing, Maxwell owed $100,000 on her mortgage. The contract Maxwell signed was for a negative amortization mortgage loan (monthly payments were less than the interest due, so the balance owed would increase each month) at a 16 percent interest rate. The loan enabled Maxwell to pay $23,000 in cash for home repairs, but it obligated her to pay the lender $2,000 per month for five years, followed by a balloon payment of $150,000, which included over $12,000 in finance charges. Maxwell's total annual household income at the time was just over $24,000, hardly more than the total of her monthly loan payments.

Maxwell eventually stopped making the monthly payments and the lender's assignee initiated foreclosure proceedings. The assignee was unable to provide evidence that, at the time of the refinancing agreement, the original lender had provided Maxwell with various disclosure statements required by federal and state real estate law, such as statements of the percentage rate of interest, finance charges, number of payments, and total payments, that the loan included negative amortization, and that Maxwell had been given the statutorily provided number of days to rescind the agreement after entering it.

Maxwell sought rescission of the refinanced mortgage agreement, alleging that its terms were unconscionable. Should the court agree?

2. Costly Repairs

A fire caused significant damage to Wanda Gary's house. The same night, she hired Repair Masters Construction to board up the house until it could be repaired. While that work was being complete, Repair Masters' salesman persuaded Gary to sign a contract with Repair Masters for completion of all the necessary repairs, the scope (and price) of which Repair Masters would specify to Gary's insurance company. The contract included a term stating that, should Gary cancel the contract for any reason before the repair work began, she would pay Repair Masters 15 percent of the yet-to-be-determined cost of repairs.

Repair Masters later prepared an estimate for the necessary repairs, but Gary's insurance company rejected it, and so Gary notified Repair Masters that she intended to cancel the agreement. Repair Masters then billed Gary for 15 percent of its estimate, which Gary refused to pay. Repair Masters sued for breach, and Gary defended by asserting that the contract was unconscionable. Which side should prevail?

3. Employment Arbitration

After Lee Caley began working for the Gulfstream Aerospace Corporation, the company adopted a new internal dispute resolution program (DRPs). Details of the program were distributed to employees electronically, with the instruction that it would bind all employees who continued to work at the firm going forward.

The Gulfstream DRP required arbitration of employment-related legal disputes between an employee and Gulfstream with the exceptions of Employee Retirement Income Security Act (ERISA) benefits and workers' compensation claims, and it also provided that no claims covered under the agreement could be raised as class action claims in arbitration.

Caley later filed a lawsuit against Gulfstream alleging various violations of federal labor and employment statutes. Gulfstream moved for dismissal of the court action on the grounds that the DRP required Caley to arbitrate her claims. Caley defended by claiming that the DRP's arbitration requirement was unconscionable. For which party should the court rule?

CHAPTER 15

PUBLIC POLICY AND INALIENABILITY

■ ■ ■

INTRODUCTION

Courts will refuse to enforce an otherwise valid contract if the agreement contravenes "public policy." Rest. (2d) Contracts §§ 178, 179. In this way, the common law makes certain property rights "inalienable"—that is, the person or entity endowed with the right is denied the freedom to trade it for some other consideration.

But how do courts neutrally determine when "public policy" prevents alienation without imposing their personal policy preferences? This can be accomplished by analyzing the statutory pronouncements of legislatures and, in some cases, the well-established judicial pronouncements resolving disputes in common law cases.

When a legislature has either clearly prohibited a certain type of conduct altogether or prohibited payment for that conduct, invocation of the public policy doctrine is relatively uncontroversial. Contracts to commit murder are clearly unenforceable, since murder itself is illegal. Contracts for prostitution are also unenforceable, because, although sex is legal, exchanging money for it is not (in most jurisdictions). The harder cases arise when a contract's subject matter does not fall squarely into a prohibited category but the subject matter can be analogized to a course of conduct prohibited by the legislature, either out of paternalistic motives (i.e., the protection of a particular class of actors who might choose to engage in the conduct) or concern about negative externalities that arise from the conduct (i.e., negative effects of the conduct on specific third parties or society generally). In such cases, judges struggle to determine whether or not it is possible to infer legislative disapproval of the contract before them. In some circumstances, different statutes (or different common law traditions) might point in opposing directions, with the result being that the contract is consistent with one public policy and inconsistent with another.

Tunkl v. Regents of the University of California is a classic case concerning whether an individual may contract away the right to sue for negligence. In this case, which concerns admission to a hospital, the court says no, but most courts have upheld contractual waivers of negligence claims signed by customers of, for example, ski resorts. Should the validity of a negligence waiver depend on the service being purchased?

Comprehensive Technologies v. Software Artisans, Inc. and *Edwards v. Arthur Anderson, LLC* consider whether employees should be permitted to contract away their right to work for a competing employer in the future, with the courts reaching different conclusions. Is one of these decisions incorrect, or might both be legally sound?

Restatement (Second) of Contracts § 178. When a Term Is Unenforceable on Grounds of Public Policy

(1) A promise or other term of an agreement is unenforceable on grounds of public policy if legislation provides that it is unenforceable or the interest in its enforcement is clearly outweighed in the circumstances by a public policy against the enforcement of such terms.

(2) In weighing the interest in the enforcement of a term, account is taken of

(a) the parties' justified expectations,

(b) any forfeiture that would result if enforcement were denied, and

(c) any special public interest in the enforcement of the particular term.

(3) In weighing a public policy against enforcement of a term, account is taken of

(a) the strength of that policy as manifested by legislation or judicial decisions,

(b) the likelihood that a refusal to enforce the term will further that policy,

(c) the seriousness of any misconduct involved and the extent to which it was deliberate, and

(d) the directness of the connection between that misconduct and the term.

Comment:

b. Balancing of interests. Only infrequently does legislation, on grounds of public policy, provide that a term is unenforceable. When a court reaches that conclusion, it usually does so on the basis of a public policy derived either from its own perception of the need to protect some aspect of the public welfare or from legislation that is relevant to that policy although it says nothing explicitly about unenforceability. See § 179. In some cases the contravention of public policy is so grave, as when an agreement involves a serious crime or tort, that unenforceability is plain. In other cases the contravention is so trivial as that it plainly does not preclude enforcement. In doubtful cases, however, a decision as to enforceability is reached only after a careful balancing, in the light of all the circumstances, of the interest in the enforcement of the particular promise against the policy against the enforcement of such terms. . . .

Restatement (Second) of Contracts § 179. Bases of Public Policies Against Enforcement

A public policy against the enforcement of promises or other terms may be derived by the court from

(a) legislation relevant to such a policy, or

(b) the need to protect some aspect of the public welfare, as is the case for the judicial policies against, for example,

(i) restraint of trade

(ii) impairment of family relations

(iii) interference with other protected interests

Comment:

a. Development of the judicial role. Historically, the public policies against enforcement of terms were developed by judges themselves on the basis of their own perception of the need to protect some aspect of the public welfare. . . .

b. Modern role of legislation. The declaration of public policy has now become largely the province of legislators rather than judges. . . .

CASES

TUNKL V. REGENTS OF THE UNIVERSITY OF CALIFORNIA

Supreme Court of California
60 Cal.2d 92 (1963)

TOBRINER, JUSTICE.

This case concerns the validity of a release from liability for future negligence imposed as a condition for admission to a charitable research hospital. For the reasons we hereinafter specify, we have concluded that an agreement between a hospital and an entering patient affects the public interest and that, in consequence, the exculpatory provision included within it must be invalid under Civil Code section 1668.

Hugo Tunkl Brought this action to recover damages for personal injuries alleged to have resulted from the negligence of two physicians in the employ of the University of California Los Angeles Medical Center, a hospital operated and maintained by the Regents of the University of California as a nonprofit charitable institution. Mr. Tunkl died after suit was brought, and his surviving wife, as executrix, was substituted as plaintiff.

. . .

We begin with the dictate of the relevant Civil Code section 1668. The section states: 'All contracts which have for their object, directly or indirectly, to exempt anyone from responsibility for his own fraud, or willful injury to the person or property of another, or violation of law, whether willful or negligent, are against the policy of the law.'

. . .Some of the cases have applied the statute strictly, invalidating any contract for exemption from liability for negligence. . . .Other cases hold that the statute prohibits the exculpation of gross negligence only; still another case states that the section forbids exemption from active as contrasted with passive negligence.

. . .

In placing particular contracts within or without the category of those affected with a public interest, the courts have revealed a rough outline of that type of transaction in which exculpatory provisions will be held invalid. Thus the attempted but invalid exemption involves a transaction which exhibits some or all of the following characteristics. It concerns a business of a type generally thought suitable for public regulation. The party seeking exculpation is engaged in performing a service of great importance to the public, which is often a matter of practical necessity for some members of the public. The party holds himself out as willing to perform this service for any member of the public who seeks it, or at least for any member coming within certain established standards. As a result of the essential nature of the service, in the economic setting of the transaction, the party invoking exculpation possesses a decisive advantage of bargaining strength against any member of the public who seeks his services. In exercising a superior bargaining power the party confronts the public with a standardized adhesion contract of exculpation, and makes no provision whereby a purchaser may pay additional reasonable fees and obtain protection against negligence. Finally, as a result of the transaction, the person or property of the purchaser is placed under the control of the seller, subject to the risk of carelessness by the seller or his agents.

While obviously no public policy opposes private, voluntary transactions in which one party, for a consideration, agrees to shoulder a risk which the law would otherwise have placed upon the other party, the above circumstances pose a different situation. In this situation the releasing party does not really acquiesce voluntarily in the contractual shifting of the risk, nor can we be reasonably certain that he receives an adequate consideration for the transfer. Since the service is one which each member of the public, presently or potentially, may find essential to him, he faces, despite his economic inability to do so, the prospect of a compulsory assumption of the risk of another's negligence. The public policy of this state has been, in substance, to posit the risk of negligence upon the actor; in instances in which this policy has been abandoned, it has generally been to allow or require that the risk shift to another party better or equally able to bear it, not to shift the risk to the weak bargainer.

In the light of the decisions, we think that the hospital-patient contract clearly falls within the category of agreements affecting the public interest. To meet that test, the agreement need only fulfill some of the characteristics above outlined; here, the relationship fulfills all of them. Thus the contract of exculpation involves an institution suitable for, and a subject of, public regulation. That the services of the hospital to those members of the public who are in special need of the particular skill of its staff and facilities constitute a practical and crucial necessity is hardly open to question.

The hospital, likewise, holds itself out as willing to perform its services for those members of the public who qualify for its research and training facilities. While it is true that the hospital is selective as to the patients it will accept, such selectivity does not negate its public aspect or the public interest in it. The hospital is selective only in the sense that it accepts from the public at large certain types of cases which qualify for the research and training in which it specializes. But the hospital does hold itself out to the public as an institution which performs such services for those members of the public who can qualify for them.

In insisting that the patient accept the provision of waiver in the contract, the hospital certainly exercises a decisive advantage in bargaining. The would-be patient is in no position to reject the proffered agreement, to bargain with the hospital, or in lieu of agreement to find another hospital. The admission room of a hospital contains no bargaining table where, as in a private business transaction, the parties can debate the terms of their contract. As a result, we cannot but conclude that the instant agreement manifested the characteristics of the so-called adhesion contract. Finally, when the patient signed the contract, he completely placed himself in the control of the hospital; he subjected himself to the risk of its carelessness.

In brief, the patient here sought the services which the hospital offered to a selective portion of the public; the patient, as the price of admission and as a result of his inferior bargaining position, accepted a clause in a contract of adhesion waiving the hospital's negligence; the patient thereby subjected himself to control of the hospital and the possible infliction of the negligence which he had thus been compelled to waive. The hospital, under such circumstances, occupied a status different than a mere private party; its contract with the patient affected the public interest.

The judgment is reversed.

COMPREHENSIVE TECHNOLOGIES INT'L, INC. V. SOFTWARE ARTISANS, INC.

United States Court of Appeals, Fourth Circuit
3 F.3d 730 (1993)

WILLIAMS, CIRCUIT JUDGE:

Factual Background

CTI, a California corporation with its principal place of business in Chantilly, Virginia, is engaged in defense-related services. CTI was founded in 1980 by Celestino Beltran, who at the time of trial served as CTI's president, chief executive officer, and chairman of the board of directors. By 1988 Beltran was hoping to diversify CTI's operations into newly emerging technologies. . . .

With the approval of his board of directors, Beltran established a Software Products Group and designated Dean Hawkes to lead it. Hawkes was given the responsibility to design, develop, test, and market software that would enable clients to process and transmit data through EDI [electronic data interchange] technology. . . .Hawkes signed CTI's standard Confidentiality and Proprietary Information Agreement. Under the Agreement, each employee agreed not to disclose or use, directly or indirectly, during his employment and for three years thereafter any confidential, proprietary, or software-related information belonging to CTI. . . .In addition to promising confidentiality, Hawkes agreed that during the term of his employment he would not compete with CTI, solicit CTI's customers, or employ CTI's current or former employees.

The Software Products Group undertook to develop two software packages for personal computers. The first, Claims Express, is an electronic medical billing system. Claims Express transmits information that conforms to two specific insurance claims forms, the "HFCA 1500" and the "UB 82." The program has been successfully marketed. CTI's second software package, EDI Link, is not specific to the health care industry. It is designed to permit users to create generic forms, enter data on the forms electronically, test that data for errors, and store both the forms and the data on a computer. Although CTI expended substantial effort on EDI Link, at the time of trial the program had not been completed and had never been sold or marketed. Trial testimony indicated that between 35 and 85 percent of the program had been completed.

In February 1991, all of the Defendant employees left CTI. Hawkes executed a formal Termination Agreement with CTI. In that Agreement, Hawkes agreed to rescind his Employment Agreement in return for $50,000 and more than $20,000 worth of equipment. Hawkes also agreed that he would not disclose or use CTI's confidential information, and that, for a period of one year following his departure, he would not (1) compete with CTI, (2) solicit CTI's customers, or (3) hire CTI's employees.

In April 1991, the Defendants incorporated Software Artisans, Inc., located in Fairfax, Virginia. By July 1991, SA had developed and begun to market its own program called Transend. According to its User's Manual, Transend creates a "paperless office environment" by enabling its users to process business forms on a computer. (J.A. at 1592.) Transend is similar to Claims Express and EDI Link in that it is designed to prepare forms for transmission by EDI. Transend permits the user to input data, check the data for errors, and prepare the data for transmission by EDI.

. . .

In February 1991, Hawkes executed a formal Termination Agreement with CTI. In that Agreement, Hawkes agreed to rescind his Employment Agreement in return for $50,000 and more than $20,000 worth of equipment. Hawkes also agreed that he would not disclose or use CTI's confidential information, and that, for a period of one year following his departure, he would not (1) compete with CTI, (2) solicit CTI's customers, or (3) hire CTI's employees.

Covenant Not to Compete

. . .In his Termination Agreement, Hawkes agreed that, for a period of twelve months following his departure from CTI, he would not

> engage directly or indirectly in any business within the United States (financially as an investor or lender or as an employee, director, officer, partner, independent contractor, consultant or owner or in any other capacity calling for the rendition of personal services or acts of management, operation or control) which is in competition with the business of CTI. For purposes of this Agreement, the "business of CTI" shall be defined as the design, development, marketing, and sales of CLAIMS EXPRESS) and EDI LINK) type PC-based software with the same functionality and methodology.

(J.A. at 714.) Virginia has established a three-part test for assessing the reasonableness of restrictive employment covenants. Under the test, the court must ask the following questions:

(1) Is the restraint, from the standpoint of the employer, reasonable in the sense that it is no greater than is necessary to protect the employer in some legitimate business interest?

(2) From the standpoint of the employee, is the restraint reasonable in the sense that it is not unduly harsh and oppressive in curtailing his legitimate efforts to earn a livelihood?

(3) Is the restraint reasonable from the standpoint of a sound public policy?"

If a covenant not to compete meets each of these standards of reasonableness, it must be enforced. As a general rule, however, the Virginia courts do not look favorably upon covenants not to compete, and will strictly construe them against the employer. The employer bears the burden of demonstrating that the restraint is reasonable.

The district court refused to enforce the covenant not to compete because it concluded that the covenant was broader than necessary to protect CTI's legitimate business interests. First, the court held that the scope of the employment restrictions was too broad because the restrictions precluded Hawkes from working for a competitor in *any* capacity, even as a janitor. The court implied that CTI did not have a legitimate interest in preventing Hawkes from working for a competitor in a menial capacity. Second, the district court concluded that the geographic scope of the agreement was broader than necessary to protect CTI's interests. The court found that CTI had marketed Claims Express only in Virginia, Nebraska, and perhaps one other state, and therefore CTI did not have a legitimate interest in restricting Hawkes's employment throughout the United States. (J.A. at 66–67.)

We review the enforceability of the covenant not to compete *de novo. Brunswick Corp. v. Jones*, 784 F.2d 271, 274 n. 2 (7th Cir.1986).

CTI asserts that under the facts of this case the employment restrictions were reasonably necessary to protect its business interests.

Although the district court believed that the covenant was categorically overbroad because it precluded Hawkes from working for a competitor of CTI in *any* capacity, the Virginia Supreme Court has enforced similarly broad restrictions. In *Roanoke Engineering,* the Court enforced a three-year restriction on an employee's right to "own, manage, operate, control, *be employed by,* participate in, or be associated in any manner with the ownership, management, operation or control of any business similar to the type of business conducted by" the employer. *Roanoke Eng'g,* 290 S.E.2d at 882 (emphasis added). In *Blue Ridge,* the Court upheld a three-year covenant under which the employee could not "open or *be employed by* or act on behalf of any competitor of Employer which renders the same or similar services as Employer"). *Blue Ridge,* 389 S.E.2d at 468 (emphasis added). The covenant in Hawkes's agreement properly restricts him from competitive employment that would, in all likelihood, substantially interfere with CTI's business. *See Stoneman v. Wilson,* 169 Va. 239, 192 S.E. 816, 819 (1938); *cf. Grant*, 737 F.2d at 412 (covenant which restrained more than direct competition with the employer was unreasonable); *Worrie v. Boze,* 191 Va. 916, 62 S.E.2d 876, 881 (1951) (approving use of covenants to prevent injurious competition).

Moreover, as Vice President of CTI's Software Products Group, Hawkes necessarily came in contact with confidential information concerning both CTI's products and its customers. Hawkes's access to such confidential information makes the covenant not to compete more reasonable. As the Virginia Supreme Court has noted,

> [t]he fact that the employment is of such a character as to inform the employee of business methods and trade secrets which, if brought to the knowledge of a competitor, would prejudice the interests of the employer, tends to give an element of reasonableness to a contract that the employee will not engage in a similar business for a limited time after the termination of his employment, and is always regarded as a strong reason for upholding the contract.

Stoneman, 192 S.E. at 819; *Meissel,* 95 S.E.2d at 191 (possession of trade secrets and confidential information is an "important consideration" in testing the reasonableness of a restrictive covenant); *cf. Community Counselling Serv., Inc. v. Reilly*, 317 F.2d 239, 244 (4th Cir.1963) (even in absence of covenant not to compete, employee may not appropriate trade secrets and confidential information rightfully belonging to his former employer). Similarly, in *Roanoke Engineering,* an employee had access to confidential financial records, lists of customers and suppliers, and detailed knowledge of overhead factors, pricing policies, and bidding techniques. *Roanoke Eng'g,* 290 S.E.2d at 885. The Virginia Supreme Court held that this information enabled the employee to become a "formidable competitor" of his former employer, and concluded that a restriction barring the employee from working for competitors in any capacity was no greater than necessary to protect the employer's legitimate business interests. *Id.*

Hawkes poses a similar danger to CTI's business. As the individual primarily responsible for the design, development, marketing and sale of CTI's software, Hawkes became intimately familiar with every aspect of CTI's operation, and necessarily acquired information that he could use to compete with CTI in the marketplace. When an employee has access to confidential and trade secret information crucial to the success of the employer's business, the employer has a strong interest in enforcing a covenant not to compete because other legal remedies often prove inadequate. It will often be difficult, if not impossible, to prove that a competing employee has misappropriated trade secret information belonging to his former employer. On the facts of this case, we conclude that the scope of the employment restrictions is no broader than necessary to protect CTI's legitimate business interests.

. . .

Having determined that the covenant not to compete is reasonable from CTI's point of view, we must next determine whether the covenant is reasonable from Hawkes's point of view, i.e., whether the curtailment on Hawkes's ability to earn a living is unduly harsh or oppressive. Although the agreement applies throughout the United States, it restricts Hawkes from engaging in only an extremely narrow category of business. Hawkes may not render personal services to, or perform acts of management, operation, or control for, any business in competition with "the business of CTI," which the agreement defines as "the design, development, marketing and sales of CLAIMS EXPRESSTM and EDI LINKTM type PC-based software with the same functionality and methodology." (J.A. at 714.) The agreement therefore permits Hawkes to design, develop, market and sell any software of a type different from Claims Express or EDI Link, any software of the same type having a different functionality or methodology, or any software of the same type having the same functionality and methodology that is not designed to run on personal computers. Hawkes is also free to compete with any other branch of CTI's business. Because Hawkes retains broad employability under the agreement, the agreement is not unduly harsh or oppressive.

In light of the foregoing, we conclude that the covenant not to compete is no greater than necessary to protect CTI's business and is not unduly harsh or oppressive. Hawkes does not suggest, and we do not find, that the covenant is unreasonable from the standpoint of public policy. We therefore hold that the covenant is enforceable.

MURNAGHAN, CIRCUIT JUDGE, concurring in part and dissenting in part:

. . .

A restraint on an employee is unreasonable if it is greater than is necessary to protect the employer in its legitimate business interest and unreasonable from the employee's standpoint as unduly harsh in curtailing his legitimate efforts to earn his livelihood. . . .

The Supreme Court of Virginia has never approved a non-compete clause that restricts employment "within the United States." To the contrary, Virginia courts have repeatedly held that non-compete clauses should be limited to a geographical area no greater than is necessary to protect the employer's legitimate business interests. Where Virginia courts have enforced non-compete contracts, the contracts have restricted competition only within "quite narrow and well defined geographic limitations."

. . . .

Accordingly, I would hold the non-compete clause overbroad and hence invalid.

EDWARDS V. ARTHUR ANDERSEN LLP

Supreme Court of California
44 Cal.4th 937 (2008)

CHIN, J.

We granted review to address the validity of noncompetition agreements in California and the permissible scope of employment release agreements. We limited our review to the following issues: (1) To what extent does Business and Professions Code section 16600 prohibit employee noncompetition agreements; and (2) is a contract provision requiring an employee to release "any and all" claims unlawful because it encompasses nonwaivable statutory protections, such as the employee indemnity protection of Labor Code section 2802?

We conclude that section 16600 prohibits employee noncompetition agreements unless the agreement falls within a statutory exception, and that a contract provision whereby an employee releases "any and all" claims does not encompass nonwaivable statutory protections, such as the employee indemnity protection of Labor Code section 2802. We therefore affirm in part and reverse in part the Court of Appeal judgment.

FACTS

In January 1997, Raymond Edwards II (Edwards), a certified public accountant, was hired as a tax manager by the Los Angeles office of the accounting firm Arthur Andersen LLP (Andersen). Andersen's employment offer was made contingent upon Edwards's signing a noncompetition agreement, which prohibited him from working for or soliciting certain Andersen clients for limited periods following his termination. The agreement was required of all managers, and read in relevant part: "If you leave the Firm, for eighteen months after release or resignation, you agree not to perform professional services of the type you provided for any client on which you worked during the eighteen months prior to release or resignation. This does not prohibit you from accepting employment with a client. [¶] For twelve months after you leave the Firm, you agree not to solicit (to perform professional services of the type you provided) any client of the office(s) to which you were assigned during the eighteen months preceding release or resignation. [¶] You agree not to solicit away from the Firm any of its professional personnel for eighteen months after release or resignation." Edwards signed the agreement.

. . .

In July 2002, HSBC offered Edwards employment. . . . Andersen would not release Edwards from the noncompetition. . . . HSBC withdrew its offer of employment to Edwards. [Edwards filed suit against Anderson.] The court specifically decided that . . . the noncompetition agreement did not violate section 16600 because it was narrowly tailored and did not deprive Edwards of his right to pursue his profession. . . .Edwards appealed the trial court's decision. . . .[T]he Court of Appeal held: (1) the noncompetition agreement was invalid under section 16600. . . .

DISCUSSION

*A. Section **16600***

Under the common law, as is still true in many states today, contractual restraints on the practice of a profession, business, or trade, were considered valid, as long as they were reasonably imposed. This was true even in California. However, in 1872 California settled public policy in favor of open competition, and rejected the common law "rule of reasonableness," when the Legislature enacted the Civil Code. Today in California, covenants not to compete are void, subject to several exceptions discussed briefly below.

Section 16600 states: "Except as provided in this chapter, every contract by which anyone is restrained from engaging in a lawful profession, trade, or business of any kind is to that extent void." The chapter excepts noncompetition agreements in the sale or dissolution of corporations (§ 16601), partnerships (*ibid.;* § 16602), and limited liability corporations (§ 16602.5). In the years since its original enactment as Civil Code section 1673, our courts have consistently affirmed that section 16600 evinces a settled legislative policy in favor of open competition and employee mobility.

. . .

Under the statute's plain meaning, therefore, an employer cannot by contract restrain a former employee from engaging in his or her profession, trade, or business unless the agreement falls within one of the exceptions to the rule. (§ 16600.) Andersen, however, asserts that we should interpret the term "restrain" under section 16600 to mean simply to "prohibit," so that only contracts that totally prohibit an employee from engaging in his or her profession, trade, or business are illegal. It would then follow that a mere limitation on an employee's ability to practice his or her vocation would be permissible under section 16600, as long as it was reasonably based.

Andersen contends that some California courts have held that section 16600 (and its predecessor statutes, Civil Code former sections 1673, 1674, and 1675) are the statutory embodiment of prior common law, and embrace the rule of reasonableness in evaluating competitive restraints. Andersen claims that these cases show that section 16600 "prohibits only broad agreements that prevent a person from engaging entirely in his chosen business, trade or profession. Agreements that do not have this broad effect—but merely regulate some aspect of post-employment conduct, e.g., to prevent raiding [employer's personnel]—are not within the scope of [s]ection 16600."

. . .

We conclude that Andersen's noncompetition agreement was invalid. As the Court of Appeal observed, "The first challenged clause prohibited Edwards, for an 18-month period, from performing professional services of the type he had provided while at Andersen, for any client on whose account he had worked during 18 months prior to his termination. The second challenged clause prohibited Edwards, for a year after termination, from 'soliciting,' defined by the agreement as providing professional services to any client of Andersen's Los Angeles office." The agreement restricted Edwards from performing work for Andersen's Los Angeles clients and therefore restricted his ability to practice his accounting profession. The noncompetition agreement that Edwards was required to sign before commencing employment with Andersen was therefore invalid because it restrained his ability to practice his profession.

DISCUSSION PROBLEMS

1. Lobbying the MTA

Alfred Arcidi (a lobbyist), entered into a contract with the National Association of Government Employees (a union), that provided that the union would pay Arcidi $250,000 if the Massachusetts Turnpike Authority (MTA) awarded a contract to a subsidiary of the union that was bidding on an MTA project. Massachusetts law provides that "[n]o person shall make any agreement whereby any compensation or thing of value is to be paid to any person contingent upon a decision [by a Massachusetts officer or 'authority,' including the MTA]."

The MTA awarded the contract to the union subsidiary, and the union paid part of the $250,000. Arcidi then sued the union for the unpaid balance, and the union counterclaimed for the return of the partial payment. Which side should prevail?

2. A Subcontractor Spat

Pacific West Construction (Pac-West) won a public works contract to build a hospital in Idaho. It wanted to subcontract a portion of the work to

Quality Interiors (Quality), but Quality did not possess a license required by the public agency for it to work on the hospital project. To avoid the restriction, Pac-West and Quality agreed that Quality employees would perform the work under the pretense that they were actually Pac-West employees.

In the wake of a dispute over the work, Pac-West ordered the Quality workers off the jobsite and subsequently refused to make any payments on the subcontract. Quality sued Pac-West for breach of contract. Should Quality be able to recover?

3. Child Support

Ivonne Ferguson asked Joel McKiernan to provide a sperm sample at her physician's office that would be used to inseminate Ferguson through the process of *in vitro* fertilization. Ferguson agreed to release McKiernan from any claims of financial responsibility for the child if the procedure was successful, and McKiernan agreed not to seek parental rights. As a result of the procedure, Ferguson gave birth to twins, and she subsequently sued McKiernan for parental support.

Pennsylvania law provides that "in every case where children are born out of wedlock, they shall enjoy all the rights and privileges as if they had been born during the wedlock of their parents. . . ." The Uniform Parentage Act, a uniform law proposed by the American Bar Association and adopted by 19 states, but not Pennsylvania, provides that "[a] [sperm] donor is not a parent of a child conceived by means of assisted reproduction." Should Ferguson's lawsuit succeed?

CHAPTER 16

THE NATURE OF PROMISES

■ ■ ■

INTRODUCTION

The Restatement describes a contract as "a promise or set of promises for the breach of which the law gives a remedy, or the performance of which the law in some way recognizes as a duty," thus establishing the centrality of promises to the law of contract. Rest. (2d) Contracts § 1.

Just as promise is central to contract, *commitment* is central to promise. To make a promise is to commit to a particular course of action at some point in the future, even if that course of action is or becomes undesirable or costly. Speech acts that have the linguistic structure of a promise might instead indicate the speaker's present intention to take a certain action in the future (without a commitment to follow through on that intention come what may), or the speaker's opinion or prediction about what action she is likely to take in the future. The distinction between these speech acts and the making of a promise can be subtle and often depends on context. The same can be said of "jokes" or "jests."

Two of the most famous cases in American Contract Law, *Hawkins v. McGee* and *Lucy v. Zehmer* explore the nature of a promise. In both cases, the plaintiffs assert that the defendants made a promise that (along with the consideration provided by the plaintiff) established a contract, and the defendants respond that no promise was made. Which party has the better of the argument, and who—judge or jury—should decide?

Interwoven with the question of whether a speech act provides the requisite commitment to constitute a promise is whether the judgment should be made from an objective or subjective perspective. Notice that these cases reinforce the principle, established in Chapter 12 on contract formation, that contract law consistently adopts the objective perspective.

Restatement (Second) of Contracts § 1. Contract Defined

A contract is a promise or a set of promises for the breach of which the law gives a remedy, or the performance of which the law in some way recognizes as a duty.

Restatement (Second) of Contracts § 2. Promise; Promisor; Promisee; Beneficiary

(1) A promise is a manifestation of intention to act or refrain from acting in a specified way, so made as to justify a promisee in understanding that a commitment has been made.

(2) The person manifesting the intention is the promisor.

(3) The person to whom the manifestation is addressed is the promisee.

(4) Where performance will benefit a person other than the promisee, that person is a beneficiary.

Comment:

d. *Promise of event beyond human control; warranty.* Words which in terms promise that an event not within human control will occur may be interpreted to include a promise to answer for harm caused by the failure of the event to occur. An example is a warranty of an existing or past fact, such as a warranty that a horse is sound, or that a ship arrived in a foreign port some days previously. Such promises are often made when the parties are ignorant of the actual facts regarding which they bargain, and may be dealt with as if the warrantor could cause the fact to be as he asserted. It is then immaterial that the actual condition of affairs may be irrevocably fixed before the promise is made.

Words of warranty, like other conduct, must be interpreted in the light of the circumstances and the reasonable expectations of the parties. In an insurance contract, a "warranty" by the insured is usually not a promise at all; it may be merely a representation of fact, or, more commonly, the fact warranted is a condition of the insurer's duty to pay (see § 225(3)). In the sale of goods, on the other hand, a similar warranty normally also includes a promise to answer for damages (see Uniform Commercial Code § 2–715).

Illustrations:

1. A, the builder of a house, or the inventor of the material used in part of its construction, says to B, the owner of the house, "I warrant that this house will never burn down." This includes a promise to pay for harm if the house should burn down.

f. *Opinions and predictions.* A promise must be distinguished from a statement of opinion or a mere prediction of future events. The distinction is not usually difficult in the case of an informal gratuitous opinion, since there is often no manifestation of intention to act or refrain from acting or to bring about a result, no expectation of performance and no consideration. The problem is frequently presented, however, whether words of a seller of goods amount to a warranty. Under Uniform Commercial Code § 2–313(2) a statement purporting to be merely the seller's opinion does not create a warranty, but the buyer's reliance on the seller's skill and judgment may create an implied warranty that the goods are fit for a particular purpose under Uniform Commercial Code § 2–315. In any case where an expert opinion is paid for, there is likely to be an implied promise that the expert will act with reasonable care and skill.

CASES

HAWKINS V. MCGEE

Supreme Court of New Hampshire
84 N.H. 114 (1929)

BRANCH, J.

The operation in question consisted in the removal of a considerable quantity of scar tissue from the palm of the plaintiff's right hand and the grafting of skin taken from the plaintiff's chest in place thereof. The scar tissue was the result of a severe burn caused by contact with an electric wire, which the plaintiff received about nine years before the time of the transactions here involved. There was evidence to the effect that before the operation was performed the plaintiff and his father went to the defendant's office, and that the defendant, in answer to the question, "How long will the boy be in the hospital?" replied, "Three or four days, not over four; then the boy can go home and it will be just a few days when he will go back to work with a good hand." Clearly this and other testimony to the same effect would not justify a finding that the doctor contracted to complete the hospital treatment in three or four days or that the plaintiff would be able to go back to work within a few days thereafter. The above statements could only be construed as expressions of opinion or predictions as to the probable duration of the treatment and plaintiff's resulting disability, and the fact that these estimates were exceeded would impose no contractual liability upon the defendant. The only substantial basis for the plaintiff's claim is the testimony that the defendant also said before the operation was decided upon, "I will guarantee to make the hand a hundred per cent perfect hand or a hundred per cent good hand." The plaintiff was present when these words were alleged to have been spoken, and, if they are to be taken at their face value, it seems obvious that proof of their utterance would establish the giving of a warranty in accordance with his contention.

The defendant argues, however, that, even if these words were uttered by him, no reasonable man would understand that they were used with the intention of entering "into any contractual relation whatever," and that they could reasonably be understood only "as his expression in strong language that he believed and expected that as a result of the operation he would give the plaintiff a very good hand." It may be conceded, as the defendant contends, that, before the question of the making of a contract should be submitted to a jury, there is a preliminary question of law for the trial court to pass upon, i. e. "whether the words could possibly have the meaning imputed to them by the party who founds his case upon a certain interpretation," but it cannot be held that the trial court decided this question erroneously in the present case. It is unnecessary to determine at this time whether the argument of the defendant, based upon "common knowledge of the uncertainty which attends all surgical operations," and the improbability that a surgeon would ever contract to make a damaged part of the human body "one hundred per cent perfect," would, in the absence of countervailing considerations, be regarded as conclusive, for there were other factors in the present case which tended to support the contention of the plaintiff. There was evidence that the defendant repeatedly solicited from the plaintiff's father the opportunity to perform this operation, and the theory was advanced by plaintiff's counsel in cross-examination of defendant that he sought an opportunity to "experiment on skin grafting," in which he had had little previous experience. If the jury accepted this part of plaintiff's contention, there would be a reasonable basis for the further conclusion that, if defendant spoke the words attributed to him, he did so with the intention that they should be accepted at their face value, as an inducement for the granting of consent to the operation by the plaintiff and his father, and there was ample evidence that they were so accepted by them. The question of the making of the alleged contract was properly submitted to the jury.

The substance of the charge to the jury on the question of damages appears in the following quotation: "If you find the plaintiff entitled to anything, he is entitled to recover for what pain and suffering he has been made to endure and for what injury he has sustained over and above what injury he had before." To this instruction the defendant seasonably excepted. By it, the jury was permitted to consider two elements of damage: (1) Pain and suffering due to the operation; and (2) positive ill effects of the operation upon the plaintiff's hand. Authority for any specific rule of damages in cases of this kind seems to be lacking, but, when tested by general principle and by analogy, it appears that the foregoing instruction was erroneous.

"By 'damages,' as that term is used in the law of contracts, is intended compensation for a breach, measured in the terms of the contract." Davis v. New England Cotton Yarn Co., 77 N. H. 403, 404, 92 A. 732, 733. The purpose of the law is "to put the plaintiff in as good a position as he would have been in had the defendant kept his contract." 3 Williston Cont. § 1338; Hardie-Tynes Mfg. Co. v. Easton Cotton Oil Co., 150 N. C. 150, 63 S. E. 676, 134 Am. St. Rep. 899. The measure of recovery "is based upon what the defendant should have given the plaintiff, not what the plaintiff has given the defendant or otherwise expended." 3 Williston Cont. § 1341. "The only losses that can be said fairly to come within the terms of a contract are such as the parties must have had in mind when the contract was made, or such as they either knew or ought to have known would probably result from a failure to comply with its terms." Davis v. New England Cotton Yarn Co., 77 N. H. 403, 404, 92 A. 732, 733, Hurd v. Dunsmore, 63 N. H. 171.

The present case is closely analogous to one in which a machine is built for a certain purpose and warranted to do certain work. In such cases, the usual rule of damages for breach of warranty in the sale of chattels is applied, and it is held that the measure of damages is the difference between the value of the machine, if it had corresponded with the warranty, and its actual value, together with such incidental losses as the parties knew, or ought to have known, would probably result from a failure to comply with its terms.

The rule thus applied is well settled in this state. "As a general rule, the measure of the vendee's damages is the difference between the value of the goods as they would have been if the warranty as to quality had been true, and the actual value at the time of the sale, including gains prevented and losses sustained, and such other damages as could be reasonably anticipated by the parties as likely to be caused by the vendor's failure to keep his agreement, and could not by reasonable care on the part of the vendee have been avoided." Union Bank v. Blanchard, 65 N. H. 21, 23, 18 A. 90, 91; Hurd v. Dunsmore, supra; Noyes v. Blodgett, 58 N. H. 502; P. L. ch. 166, § 69, subd. 7. We therefore conclude that the true measure of the plaintiff's damage in the present case is the difference between the value to him of a perfect hand or a good hand, such as the jury found the defendant promised him, and the value of his hand in its present condition, including any incidental consequences fairly within the contemplation of the parties when they made their contract. 1 Sutherland, Damages (4th Ed.) § 92. Damages not thus limited, although naturally resulting, are not to be given.

The extent of the plaintiff's suffering does not measure this difference in value. The pain necessarily incident to a serious surgical operation was a part of the contribution which the plaintiff was willing to make to his joint undertaking with the defendant to produce a good hand. It was a legal detriment suffered by him which constituted a part of the consideration given by him for the contract. It represented a part of the price which he was willing to pay for a good hand, but it furnished no test of the value of a good hand or the difference between the value of the hand which the defendant promised and the one which resulted from the operation.

It was also erroneous and misleading to submit to the jury as a separate element of damage any change for the worse in the condition of the plaintiff's hand resulting from the operation, although this error was probably more prejudicial to the plaintiff than to the defendant. Any such ill effect of the operation would be included under the true rule of damages set forth above, but damages might properly be assessed for the defendant's failure to improve the condition of the hand, even if there were no evidence that its condition was made worse as a result of the operation.

New trial.

LUCY V. ZEHMER

Supreme Court of Appeals of Virginia
196 Va. 493 (1954)

BUCHANAN, J.

This suit was instituted by W.O. Lucy and J.C. Lucy, complainants, against A.H. Zehmer and Ida S. Zehmer, his wife, defendants, to have specific performance of a contract by which it was alleged the Zehmers had sold to W.O. Lucy a tract of land owned by A.H. Zehmer in Dinwiddie county containing 471.6 acres, more or less, known as the Ferguson farm, for $50,000. J.C. Lucy, the other complainant, is a brother of W.O. Lucy, to whom W.O. Lucy transferred a half interest in his alleged purchase.

The instrument sought to be enforced was written by A.H. Zehmer on December 20, 1952, in these words: "We hereby agree to sell to W.O. Lucy the Ferguson Farm complete for $50,000.00, title satisfactory to buyer," and signed by the defendants, A.H. Zehmer and Ida S. Zehmer.

The answer of A.H. Zehmer admitted that at the time mentioned W.O. Lucy offered him $50,000 cash for the farm, but that he, Zehmer, considered that the offer was made in jest; that so thinking, and both he and Lucy having had several drinks, he wrote out "the memorandum" quoted above and induced his wife to sign it; that he did not deliver the memorandum to Lucy, but that Lucy picked it up, read it, put it in his pocket, attempted to offer Zehmer $5 to bind the bargain, which Zehmer refused to accept, and realizing for the first time that Lucy was serious, Zehmer assured him that he had no intention of selling the farm and that the whole matter was a joke. Lucy left the premises insisting that he had purchased the farm. . . .[The lower court dismissed Lucy's complaint, holding that the complainants had failed to establish their right to specific performance.]

. . .

[At a trial on his breach of contract claim,] W.O. Lucy, a lumberman and farmer, thus testified in substance:. . .Seven or eight years ago he had offered Zehmer $20,000 for the [Ferguson] farm which Zehmer had accepted, but the agreement was verbal and Zehmer backed out. On the night of December 20, 1952,. . .[h]e entered the restaurant [owned by

Zehmer]. . . .He asked Zehmer if he had sold the Ferguson farm. Zehmer replied that he had not. Lucy said, "I bet you wouldn't take $50,000.00 for that place." Zehmer replied, "Yes, I would too; you wouldn't give fifty." Lucy said he would and told Zehmer to write up an agreement to that effect. Zehmer took a restaurant check and wrote on the back of it, "I do hereby agree to sell to W.O. Lucy the Ferguson Farm for $50,000 complete." Lucy told him he had better change it to "We" because Mrs. Zehmer would have to sign it too. Zehmer then tore up what he had written, wrote the agreement quoted above and asked Mrs. Zehmer, who was at the other end of the counter ten or twelve feet away, to sign it. Mrs. Zehmer said she would for $50,000 and signed it. . . .

The discussion leading to the signing of the agreement, said Lucy, lasted thirty or forty minutes, during which Zehmer seemed to doubt that Lucy could raise $50,000. . . .

Zehmer testified in substance as follows:

He bought this farm more than ten years ago for $11,000. He had had twenty-five offers, more or less, to buy it, including several from Lucy, who had never offered any specific sum of money. He had given them all the same answer, that he was not interested in selling it. . . .When he entered the restaurant around eight-thirty [on December 20] Lucy was there and he could see that he was "pretty high." He said to Lucy, "Boy, you got some good liquor, drinking, ain't you?" Lucy then offered him a drink. "I was already high as a Georgia pine, and didn't have any more better sense than to pour another great big slug out and gulp it down, and he took one too."

After they had talked a while Lucy asked whether he still had the Ferguson farm. He replied that he had not sold it and Lucy said, "I bet you wouldn't take $50,000.00 for it." Zehmer asked him if he would give $50,000 and Lucy said yes. Zehmer replied, "You haven't got $50,000 in cash." Lucy said he did and Zehmer replied that he did not believe it. . . .

Finally, said Zehmer, Lucy told him if he didn't believe he had $50,000, "you sign that piece of paper here and say you will take $50,000.00 for the farm. "He, Zehmer, "just grabbed the back off of a guest check there" and wrote on the back of it. . . .

After Zehmer had, as he described it, "scribbled this thing off," Lucy said, "Get your wife to sign it." Zehmer walked over to where she was and she at first refused to sign but did so after he told her that he "was just needling him [Lucy], and didn't mean a thing in the world, that I was not selling the farm." Zehmer then "took it back over there. . . .[Lucy] reached and picked it up, and when I looked back again he had it in his pocket and he dropped a five dollar bill over there, and he said, 'Here is five dollars payment on it.'. . .I said, 'Hell no, that is beer and liquor talking. I am not going to sell you the farm. I have told you that too many times before.' "

. . .

Mrs. Zehmer testified that . . . Zehmer then wrote on the back of a pad, "I agree to sell the Ferguson Place to W.O. Lucy for $50,000.00 cash." Lucy said, "All right, get your wife to sign it." Zehmer came back to where she was standing and said, "You want to put your name to this?" She said "No," but he said in an undertone, "It is nothing but a joke," and she signed it.

. . .

The evidence is convincing also that Zehmer wrote two agreements, the first one beginning "I hereby agree to sell." Zehmer first said he could not remember about that, then that "I don't think I wrote but one out." Mrs. Zehmer said that what he wrote was "I hereby agree," but that the "I" was changed to "We" after that night. The agreement that was written and signed is in the record and indicates no such change. Neither are the mistakes in spelling that Zehmer sought to point out readily apparent.

The appearance of the contract, the fact that it was under discussion for forty minutes or more before it was signed; Lucy's objection to thc first draft because it was written in the singular, and he wanted Mrs. Zehmer to sign it also; the rewriting to meet that objection and the signing by Mrs. Zehmer; the discussion of what was to be included in the sale, the provision for the examination of the title, the completeness of the instrument that was executed, the taking possession of it by Lucy with no request or suggestion by either of the defendants that he give it back, are facts which furnish persuasive evidence that the execution of the contract was a serious business transaction rather than a casual, jesting matter as defendants now contend.

. . .

If it be assumed, contrary to what we think the evidence shows, that Zehmer was jesting about selling his farm to Lucy and that the transaction was intended by him to be a joke, nevertheless the evidence shows that Lucy did not so understand it but considered it to be a serious business transaction and the contract to be binding on the Zehmers as well as on himself. . . .

Not only did Lucy actually believe, but the evidence shows he was warranted in believing, that the contract represented a serious business transaction and a good faith sale and purchase of the farm.

In the field of contracts, as generally elsewhere, "We must look to the outward expression of a person as manifesting his intention rather than to his secret and unexpressed intention. 'The law imputes to a person an intention corresponding to the reasonable meaning of his words and acts.' " First Nat'l Bank v. Roanoke Oil Co., 169 Va. 99.

. . .

The mental assent of the parties is not requisite for the formation of a contract. If the words or other acts of one of the parties have but one reasonable meaning, his undisclosed intention is immaterial except when an unreasonable meaning which he attaches to his manifestations is known to the other party. Restatement of the Law of Contracts, § 71. . . .An agreement or mutual assent is of course essential to a valid contract but the law imputes to a person an intention corresponding to the reasonable meaning of his words and acts. If his words and acts, judged by a reasonable standard, manifest an intention to agree, it is immaterial what may be the real but unexpressed state of his mind. . . .

So a person cannot set up that he was merely jesting when his conduct and words would warrant a reasonable person in believing that he intended a real agreement. . . .

Whether the writing signed by the defendants and now sought to be enforced by the complainants was the result of a serious offer by Lucy and a serious acceptance by the defendants, or was a serious offer by Lucy and an acceptance in secret jest by the defendants, in either event it constituted a binding contract of sale between the parties.

. . .

The complainants are entitled to have specific performance of the contracts sued on. . . .

Reversed and remanded.

DISCUSSION PROBLEMS

1. Until Death Do Us Part

Joseph Ellis repeatedly expressed his intention to marry Fanny Guggenheim, even telling her, "I swear to you, and God is my witness, I will never marry any other girl but you." Guggenheim, perhaps exhibiting just a bit more circumspection, responded to Ellis, "I won't swear, because we don't know what might happen; but I promise you I will never marry any other man, but will wait for you." Alas, the nuptials never occurred, and at a later date Ellis married another woman. Guggenheim sued. Did Ellis and Guggenheim have a contract?

2. Employment Benefits

When Alcon Laboratories offered Maryam Parviz-Khyavi a job, the company provided her with a letter that purported to be "a formal confirmation of our verbal offer" and indicated that Parviz-Khyavi "will be eligible for all Company benefits normally accorded employees of similar length of service and status from your first day of employment." Alcon also provided Parviz-Khyavi with a booklet titled "Short-Term Disability Income Program Policy Guideline" that described a short-term disability ("STD") insurance benefit funded by Alcon and administered by a third party. The final paragraph of the booklet provided:

> This booklet does not guarantee employment or continued employment with Alcon nor deal in any way with employment issues. . . . Alcon reserves the right to change or end the STD Program at any time. This Program also should not be interpreted as a contract or insurance policy, and it does not create any rights to continuance of the Program in favor of Employees. Accordingly, the Program may be terminated, modified, suspended, or amended in whole or in part at any time without the consent of the employees.

After working for the Alcon for two years, Parviz-Khyavi filed a claim for STD benefits. The administrator denied the claim on the grounds that her medical information did not demonstrate a disability, and that in any case, regardless of the facts concerning her health, Parviz-Khyavi did not have a contractual right to STD benefits. Parviz-Khyavi sued for breach of contract. Did Alcom promise to provide Parviz-Khyavi with disability benefits?

3. Pepsi Stuff

PepsiCo, Inc., the producer and distributor of the soft drinks Pepsi and Diet Pepsi, ran a promotion, entitled "Pepsi Stuff," in which it encouraged consumers to collect "Pepsi Points" from specially marked packages of Pepsi or Diet Pepsi and redeem these points for merchandise featuring the Pepsi logo.

A contemporaneous PepsiCo television commercial depicts a teenager preparing to leave his house for school, dressed in a shirt emblazoned with the Pepsi logo, as a subtitle on the screen states, "T-SHIRT 75 PEPSI POINTS." The teenager then exits his bedroom wearing a leather jacket, and the subtitle now reads, "LEATHER JACKET 1450 PEPSI POINTS." Walking out of the house into the sunshine, the teenager puts on a pair of sunglasses, and the new subtitle states, "SHADES 175 PEPSI POINTS." A voiceover then intones, "Introducing the new Pepsi Stuff catalog," and the picture shifts to the catalog's cover.

The scene then shifts to three boys sitting in front of a high school building, one reading the Pepsi Stuff catalog and the others drinking Pepsi. A strong wind blows and a Harrier Jet swings into view and lands next to the school building. Several students run for cover, and the velocity of the wind strips a faculty member down to his underwear. The voiceover announces, "Now the more Pepsi you drink, the more great stuff you're gonna get."

The original teenager opens the cockpit of the fighter jet with a Pepsi in hand. He exclaims, "Sure beats the bus," as the subtitle provides, "HARRIER FIGHTER 7,000,000 PEPSI POINTS." A few seconds later, the following appears in more stylized script: "Drink Pepsi—Get Stuff."

After watching the commercial, John Leonard consulted The Pepsi Stuff catalog, which described the promotion and included an order form that listed fifty-three items of Pepsi Stuff merchandise redeemable for Pepsi Points. The Harrier Fighter was not on the list, but the catalog explained that a customer who lacks sufficient points obtained from purchasing Pepsi products could purchase Pepsi Points for 10 cents each and use those for merchandise, so long as they had at least 15 Pepsi points from product purchases. Leonard submitted the order form, 15 original Pepsi points, and a check for $700,008.50. At the bottom of the Order Form, Leonard wrote in "1 Harrier Jet" in the "Item" column and "7,000,000" in the "Total Points" column. In a letter accompanying his submission, plaintiff stated that the check was to purchase additional Pepsi Points "expressly for obtaining a new Harrier jet as advertised in your Pepsi Stuff commercial."

PepsiCo refused to provide Leonard with a Harrier Jet, and Leonard sued. Did PepsiCo have an obligation to provide Leonard an airplane?

CHAPTER 17

INTERPRETATION OF CONTRACT LANGUAGE

■ ■ ■

INTRODUCTION

Given the inherent malleability of language, it is unsurprising that contracting parties often disagree about the precise substance of their contractual obligations, or "duties." Such disagreements no doubt account for the majority of contract disputes. Courts have three basic methods of ascribing substantive meaning to the language found in contracts. If the parties share the same intent as to the meaning of contractual terms, that meaning governs. If the parties intend different meanings, but one party understands the other's meaning (and the opposite is not true), the meaning that is intended by one and understood by the other governs. When parties have different intentions and neither knows the meaning intended by the other, courts will search for the most objectively reasonable meaning. See Rest. (2d) Contracts § 201. When disputes arise and parties claim conflicting intentions, courts often turn directly to the objective analysis.

The first analytic step is to determine whether the disputed term is susceptible to more than one meaning. Under the traditional "textualist" view, courts should first determine whether the term in question has a "plain meaning." If it does, that plain meaning governs, and no evidence beyond the four corners of the contract is admissible to suggest otherwise. Based on this view, extrinsic evidence—that is, evidence of meaning arising from sources other than the contract itself—is admissible to prove the meaning of the disputed term only if the court first determines that the contractual language itself is ambiguous.

The "contextualist" view, favored by the Restatement, is that words have no fixed, intrinsic meaning; they are symbols ascribed meaning by particular communities under particular circumstances. As Justice Holmes put the point, "A word is not a crystal, transparent and unchanged; it is the skin of a living thought and may vary greatly in color and content according to the circumstances and the time in which it is used." *Towne v. Eisner*, 245 U.S. 418, 425 (1918). Under this view, terms always lack a plain meaning, and the context in which the language is situated is always relevant in determining which party's interpretation should govern. Thus, contextualist courts will always consider extrinsic evidence regarding meaning. The majority of states claim to use a textualist approach, while California in particular is associated with the contextualist approach. This said, judicial opinions in almost every jurisdiction are riddled with statements that seem to support both views!

W.W.W. Associates, Inc. v. Giancontieri and *Pacific Gas & Electric Company v. G.W. Thomas Drayage & Rigging Company* illustrate the stakes in the doctrinal debate between the textualist and contextualist modes of interpretation. As you read these contrasting opinions, ask yourself whether you think the outcomes would have been different if the respective courts had adopted the alternative position on the textualist/ contextualist debate.

A second analytic step is taken by courts if and when they determine that the text in question is ambiguous as between the meanings proposed by the opposing parties. In this case, all courts must determine the relevance and relative probativeness of evidence offered to support the competing interpretations. *Frigaliment Importing Company v. B.N.S. International Sales Corporation* describes a palette of contextual tools. When reading this famous case, focus on the variety of types of evidence offered and how the court evaluates each piece of evidence separately (rather than on the case outcome).

A final complexity of contract interpretation concerns the allocation of authority between the judge and the jury. In general, the legal significance of a contract term is a matter of law for the judge to determine. If the proper meaning turns on extrinsic evidence that is reasonably subject to alternative interpretations, however, the court should defer to the trier of fact. Rest. (2d) Contracts § 212. (The "trier of fact" is the jury in a jury trial, but the judge plays that role in a "bench" trial.) Put slightly differently, if no extrinsic evidence is needed to determine the proper interpretation, or if a "reasonable" factfinder could only reach one conclusion after taking the extrinsic evidence into account, the meaning of the term at issue should be decided by the judge as a matter of law.

Restatement (Second) of Contracts
§ 201. Whose Meaning Prevails

(1) Where the parties have attached the same meaning to a promise or agreement or a term thereof, it is interpreted in accordance with that meaning.

(2) Where the parties have attached different meanings to a promise or agreement or a term thereof, it is interpreted in accordance with the meaning attached by one of them if at the time the agreement was made

(a) that party did not know of any different meaning attached by the other, and the other knew the meaning attached by the first party; or

(b) that party had no reason to know of any different meaning attached by the other, and the other had reason to know the meaning attached by the first party.

(3) Except as stated in this Section, neither party is bound by the meaning attached by the other, even though the result may be a failure of mutual assent.

Restatement (Second) of Contracts § 212. Interpretation of Integrated Agreement

(1) The interpretation of an integrated agreement is directed to the meaning of the terms of the writing or writings in the light of the circumstances, in accordance with the rules stated in this Chapter.

(2) A question of interpretation of an integrated agreement is to be determined by the trier of fact if it depends on the credibility of extrinsic evidence or on a choice among reasonable inferences to be drawn from extrinsic evidence. Otherwise a question of interpretation of an integrated agreement is to be determined as a question of law.

Comment:

a. "Objective" and "subjective" meaning. Interpretation of contracts deals with the meaning given to language and other conduct by the parties rather than with meanings established by law. But the relevant intention of a party is that manifested by him rather than any different undisclosed intention. In cases of misunderstanding, there may be a contract in accordance with the meaning of one party if the other knows or has reason to know of the misunderstanding and the first party does not. See §§ 200, 201. The meaning of one party may prevail as to one term and the meaning of the other as to another term; thus the contract as a whole may not be entirely in accordance with the understanding of either. When a party is thus held to a meaning of which he had reason to know, it is sometimes said that the "objective" meaning of his language or other conduct prevails over his "subjective" meaning. Even so, the operative meaning is found in the transaction and its context rather than in the law or in the usages of people other than the parties.

b. Plain meaning and extrinsic evidence. It is sometimes said that extrinsic evidence cannot change the plain meaning of a writing, but meaning can almost never be plain except in a context. Accordingly, the rule stated in Subsection (1) is not limited to cases where it is determined that the language used is ambiguous. Any determination of meaning or ambiguity should only be made in the light of the relevant evidence of the situation and relations of the parties, the subject matter of the transaction, preliminary negotiations and statements made therein, usages of trade, and the course of dealing between the parties. See §§ 202, 219–23. But after the transaction has been shown in all its length and breadth, the words of an integrated agreement remain the most important evidence of intention. . . .

Illustrations:

3. A agrees orally with B, a stockbroker, that in transactions between them "abracadabra" shall mean X Company. A sends a signed written order to B to buy 100 shares "abracadabra," and B buys 100 shares of X Company. The parties are bound in accordance with the oral agreement.

4. A and B are engaged in buying and selling shares of stock from each other, and agree orally to conceal the nature of their dealings by using the word "sell" to mean "buy" and using the word "buy" to mean "sell." A sends a written offer to B to "sell" certain shares, and B accepts. The parties are bound in accordancc with thc oral agreement.

d. "Question of law." Analytically, what meaning is attached to a word or other symbol by one or more people is a question of fact. But general usage as to the meaning of words in the English language is commonly a proper subject for judicial notice without the aid of evidence extrinsic to the writing. Historically, moreover, partly perhaps because of the fact that jurors were often illiterate, questions of interpretation of written documents have been treated as questions of law in the sense that they are decided by the trial judge rather than by the jury. Likewise, since an appellate court is commonly in as good a position to decide such questions as the trial judge, they have been treated as questions of law for purposes of appellate review. Such treatment has the effect of limiting the power of the trier of fact to exercise a dispensing power in the guise of a finding of fact, and thus contributes to the stability and predictability of contractual relations. In cases of standardized contracts such as insurance policies, it also provides a method of assuring that like cases will be decided alike.

e. Evaluation of extrinsic evidence. Even though an agreement is not integrated, or even though the meaning of an integrated agreement depends on extrinsic evidence, a question of interpretation is not left to the trier of fact where the evidence is so clear that no reasonable person would determine the issue in any way but one. But if the issue depends on evidence outside the writing, and the possible inferences are conflicting, the choice is for the trier of fact.

CASES

W.W.W. ASSOCIATES, INC. V. GIANCONTIERI

Court of Appeals of New York
77 N.Y.2d 157 (1990)

KAYE, J.

In this action for specific performance of a contract to sell real property, the issue is whether an unambiguous reciprocal cancellation provision should be read in light of extrinsic evidence, as a contingency clause for the sole benefit of plaintiff purchaser, subject to its unilateral waiver. Applying the principle that clear, complete writings should generally be enforced according to their terms, we reject plaintiff's reading of the contract and dismiss its complaint.

Defendants, owners of a two-acre parcel in Suffolk County, on October 16, 1986 contracted for the sale of the property to plaintiff, a real estate investor and developer. The purchase price was fixed at $750,000—$25,000 payable on contract execution, $225,000 to be paid in cash on closing (to take place "on or about December 1, 1986"), and the $500,000 balance secured by a purchase-money mortgage payable two years later.

The parties signed a printed form Contract of Sale, supplemented by several of their own paragraphs. Two provisions of the contract have particular relevance to the present dispute—a reciprocal cancellation provision (para. 31) and a merger clause (para. 19). Paragraph 31, one of the provisions the parties added to the contract form, reads: "The parties acknowledge that Sellers have been served with process instituting an action concerned with the real property which is the subject of this agreement. In the event the closing of title is delayed by reason of such litigation it is agreed that closing of title will in a like manner be adjourned until after the conclusion of such litigation provided, *in the event such litigation is not concluded, by or before 6-1-87 either party shall have the right to cancel this contract whereupon the down payment shall be returned and there shall be no further rights hereunder.*" (Emphasis supplied.) Paragraph 19 is the form merger provision, reading: "All prior understandings and agreements between *seller* and *purchaser* are merged in this contract [and it] completely expresses their full agreement. It has been entered into after full investigation, neither party relying upon any statements made by anyone else that are not set forth in this contract."

The Contract of Sale, in other paragraphs the parties added to the printed form, provided that the purchaser alone had the unconditional right to cancel the contract within 10 days of signing (para. 32), and that the purchaser alone had the option to cancel if, at closing, the seller was unable to deliver building permits for 50 senior citizen housing units (para. 29).

The contract in fact did not close on December 1, 1986, as originally contemplated. As June 1, 1987 neared, with the litigation still unresolved, plaintiff on May 13 wrote defendants that it was prepared to close and would appear for closing on May 28; plaintiff also instituted the present action for specific performance. On June 2, 1987, defendants canceled the contract and returned the down payment, which plaintiff refused. Defendants thereafter sought summary judgment dismissing the specific performance action, on the ground that the contract gave them the absolute right to cancel.

Plaintiff's claim to specific performance rests upon its recitation of how paragraph 31 originated. Those facts are set forth in the affidavit of plaintiff's vice-president, submitted in opposition to defendants' summary judgment motion.

As plaintiff explains, during contract negotiations it learned that, as a result of unrelated litigation against defendants, a lis pendens had been filed against the property. Although assured by defendants that the suit was meritless, plaintiff anticipated difficulty obtaining a construction loan (including title insurance for the loan) needed to implement its plans to build senior citizen housing units. According to the affidavit, it was therefore agreed that paragraph 31 would be added for plaintiff's sole benefit, as contract vendee. As it developed, plaintiff's fears proved groundless—the lis pendens did not impede its ability to secure construction financing. However, around March 1987, plaintiff claims it learned from the broker on the transaction that one of the defendants had told him they were doing nothing to defend the litigation, awaiting June 2, 1987 to cancel the contract and suggesting the broker might get a higher price.

Defendants made no response to these factual assertions. Rather, its summary judgment motion rested entirely on the language of the Contract of Sale, which it argued was, under the law, determinative of its right to cancel.

The trial court granted defendants' motion and dismissed the complaint, holding that the agreement unambiguously conferred the right to cancel on defendants as well as plaintiff. The Appellate Division, however, reversed and, after searching the record and adopting the facts alleged by plaintiff in its affidavit, granted summary judgment to plaintiff directing specific performance of the contract. We now reverse and dismiss the complaint.

Critical to the success of plaintiff's position is consideration of the extrinsic evidence that paragraph 31 was added to the contract solely for its benefit. The Appellate Division made clear that this evidence was at the heart of its decision: "review of the record reveals that under the circumstances of this case the language of clause 31 was intended to protect the plaintiff from having to purchase the property burdened by a notice of pendency filed as a result of the underlying action which could prevent the plaintiff from obtaining clear title and would impair its ability to obtain subsequent construction financing.". . .

We conclude, however, that the extrinsic evidence tendered by plaintiff is not material. In its reliance on extrinsic evidence to bring itself within the "party benefited" cases, plaintiff ignores a vital first step in the analysis: before looking to evidence of what was in the parties' minds, a court must give due weight to what was in their contract.

A familiar and eminently sensible proposition of law is that, when parties set down their agreement in a clear, complete document, their writing should as a rule be enforced according to its terms. Evidence outside the four corners of the document as to what was really intended but unstated or misstated is generally inadmissible to add to or vary the writing (*see, e.g., Mercury Bay Boating Club v. San Diego Yacht Club,* 76 N.Y.2d 256, 269–270, 557 N.Y.S.2d 851, 557 N.E.2d 87). That rule imparts "stability to commercial transactions by safeguarding against fraudulent claims, perjury, death of witnesses * * * infirmity of memory * * * [and] the fear that the jury will improperly evaluate the extrinsic evidence." (Fisch, New York Evidence § 42, at 22 [2d ed].) Such considerations are all the more compelling in the context of real property transactions, where commercial certainty is a paramount concern.

Whether or not a writing is ambiguous is a question of law to be resolved by the courts. In the present case, the contract, read as a whole to determine its purpose and intent, plainly manifests the intention that defendants, as well as plaintiff, should have the right to cancel after June 1, 1987 if the litigation had not concluded by that date; and it further plainly manifests the intention that all prior understandings be merged into the contract, which expresses the parties' full agreement (*see,* 3 Corbin, Contracts § 578, at 402–403). Moreover, the face of the contract reveals a "logical reason" (152 A.D.2d, at 341, 548 N.Y.S.2d 580) for the explicit provision that the cancellation right contained in paragraph 31 should run to the seller as well as the purchaser. A seller taking back a purchase-money mortgage for two thirds of the purchase price might well wish to reserve its option to sell the property for cash on an "as is" basis if third-party litigation affecting the property remained unresolved past a certain date.

Thus, we conclude there is no ambiguity as to the cancellation clause in issue, read in the context of the entire agreement, and that it confers a reciprocal right on both parties to the contract.

The question next raised is whether extrinsic evidence should be considered in order to *create* an ambiguity in the agreement. That question must be answered in the negative. It is well settled that "extrinsic and parol evidence is not admissible to create an ambiguity in a written agreement which is complete and clear and unambiguous upon its face." (*Intercontinental Planning v. Daystrom, Inc.*, 24 N.Y.2d 372, 379, 300 N.Y.S.2d 817, 248 N.E.2d 576.)

Plaintiff's rejoinder—that defendants indeed had the specified absolute right to cancel the contract, but it was subject to plaintiff's absolute prior right of waiver—suffers from a logical inconsistency that is evidence[d] in a mere statement of the argument. But there is an even greater problem. Here, sophisticated businessmen reduced their negotiations to a clear, complete writing. In the paragraphs immediately surrounding paragraph 31, they expressly bestowed certain options on the purchaser alone, but in paragraph 31 they chose otherwise, explicitly allowing both buyer and seller to cancel in the event the litigation was unresolved by June 1, 1987. By ignoring the plain language of the contract, plaintiff effectively rewrites the bargain that was struck. An analysis that begins with consideration of extrinsic evidence of what the parties meant, instead of looking first to what they said and reaching extrinsic evidence only when required to do so because of some identified ambiguity, unnecessarily denigrates the contract and unsettles the law.

. . .

Accordingly, the Appellate Division order should be reversed, with costs, defendants' motion for summary judgment granted, and the complaint dismissed.

PACIFIC GAS & ELECTRIC CO. V. G.W. THOMAS DRAYAGE & RIGGING CO.

Supreme Court of California
69 Cal. 2d 33 (1968)

TRAYNOR, C.J.

Defendant appeals from a judgment for plaintiff in an action for damages for injury to property under an indemnity clause of a contract.

In 1960 defendant entered into a contract with plaintiff to furnish the labor and equipment necessary to remove and replace the upper metal cover of plaintiff's steam turbine. Defendant agreed to perform the work "at [its] own risk and expense" and to "indemnify" plaintiff "against all loss, damage, expense and liability resulting from. . .injury to property, arising out of or in any way connected with the performance of this contract." Defendant also agreed to procure not less than $50,000 insurance to cover liability for injury to property. Plaintiff was to be an additional named insured, but the policy was to contain a cross-liability clause extending the coverage to plaintiff's property.

During the work the cover fell and injured the exposed rotor of the turbine. Plaintiff brought this action to recover $25,144.51, the amount it subsequently spent on repairs and thereafter secured judgment on the theory that the indemnity provision covered injury to all property regardless of ownership.

Defendant offered to prove by admissions of plaintiff's agents, by defendant's conduct under similar contracts entered into with plaintiff, and by other proof that in the indemnity clause the parties meant to cover injury to property of third parties only and not to plaintiff's property. Although the trial court observed that the language used was "the classic language for a third party indemnity provision" and that "one could very easily conclude that. . .its whole intendment is to indemnify third parties," it nevertheless held that the "plain language" of the agreement also required defendant to indemnify plaintiff for injuries to plaintiff's property. Having determined that the contract had a plain meaning, the court refused to admit any extrinsic evidence that would contradict its interpretation.

When the court interprets a contract on this basis, it determines the meaning of the instrument in accordance with the ". . .extrinsic evidence of the judge's own linguistic education and experience." (Corbin on Contracts (1960 ed.)) The exclusion of testimony that might contradict the linguistic background of the judge reflects a judicial belief in the possibility of perfect verbal expression. (Wigmore on Evidence (3d ed. 1940).) This belief is a remnant of a primitive faith in the inherent potency and inherent meaning of words.

The test of admissibility of extrinsic evidence to explain the meaning of a written instrument is not whether it appears to the court to be plain and unambiguous on its face, but whether the offered evidence is relevant to prove a meaning to which the language of the instrument is reasonably susceptible. (*Continental Baking Co. v. Katz* (1968) 68 Cal. 2d 512.)

A rule that would limit the determination of the meaning of a written instrument to its four-corners merely because it seems to the court to be clear and unambiguous, would either deny the relevance of the intention of the parties or presuppose a degree of verbal precision and stability our language has not attained.

Some courts have expressed the opinion that contractual obligations are created by the mere use of certain words, whether or not there was any intention to incur such obligations. Under this view, contractual obligations flow, not from the intention of the parties but from the fact that they used certain magic words. Evidence of the parties' intention therefore becomes irrelevant.

In this state, however, the intention of the parties as expressed in the contract is the source of contractual rights and duties.[5] A court must ascertain and give effect to this intention by determining what the parties meant by the words they used. Accordingly, the exclusion of relevant, extrinsic, evidence to explain the meaning of a written instrument could be justified only if it were feasible to determine the meaning the parties gave to the words from the instrument alone.

If words had absolute and constant referents, it might be possible to discover contractual intention in the words themselves and in the manner in which they were arranged. Words, however, do not have absolute and constant referents. "A word is a symbol of thought but has no arbitrary and fixed meaning like a symbol of algebra or chemistry,. . ." (*Pearson v. State Social Welfare Board* (1960) 54 Cal.2d 184, 195.) The meaning of particular words or groups of words varies with the ". . .verbal context and surrounding circumstances and purposes in view of the linguistic education and experience of their users and their hearers or readers (not excluding judges). . . .A word has no meaning apart from these factors; much less does it have an objective meaning, one true meaning." (Corbin, *The Interpretation of Words and the Parol Evidence Rule* (1965) 50 Cornell L.Q. 161, 187.) Accordingly, the meaning of a writing ". . .can only be found by interpretation in the light of all the circumstances that reveal the sense in which the writer used the words. The exclusion of parol evidence regarding such circumstances merely because the words do not appear ambiguous to the reader can easily lead to the attribution to a written instrument of a meaning that was never intended." (*Universal Sales Corp. v. California Press Mfg. Co., supra*, 20 Cal. 2d 751, 776 (concurring opinion).)

Although extrinsic evidence is not admissible to add to, detract from, or vary the terms of a written contract, these terms must first be determined before it can be decided whether or not extrinsic evidence is being offered for a prohibited purpose. The fact that the terms of an instrument appear clear to a judge does not preclude the possibility that the parties chose the language of the instrument to express different terms. That possibility is not limited to contracts whose terms have acquired a particular meaning by trade usage, but exists whenever the parties' understanding of the words used may have differed from the judge's understanding.

Accordingly, rational interpretation requires at least a preliminary consideration of all credible evidence offered to prove the intention of the parties. (Civ. Code, § 1647.) Such evidence includes testimony as to the "circumstances surrounding the making of the agreement. . .including the object, nature and subject matter of the writing. . ." so that the court can

[5] "A contract must be so interpreted as to give effect to the mutual intention of the parties as it existed at the time of contracting, so far as the same is ascertainable and lawful." (Civ. Code, § 1636;. . .*Universal Sales Corp. v. California Press Mfg. Co.* (1942) 20 Cal. 2d 751, 760. . .).

"place itself in the same situation in which the parties found themselves at the time of contracting." (*Universal Sales Corp. v. California Press Mfg. Co., supra,* 20 Cal. 2d 751, 761.) If the court decides, after considering this evidence, that the language of a contract, in the light of all the circumstances, "is fairly susceptible of either one of the two interpretations contended for. . ." (*Balfour v. Fresno C. & I. Co.* (1895) 109 Cal. 221, 225.) extrinsic evidence relevant to prove either of such meanings is admissible.

In the present case the court erroneously refused to consider extrinsic evidence offered to show that the indemnity clause in the contract was not intended to cover injuries to plaintiff's property. Although that evidence was not necessary to show that the indemnity clause was reasonably susceptible of the meaning contended for by defendant, it was nevertheless relevant and admissible on that issue. Moreover, since that clause was reasonably susceptible of that meaning, the offered evidence was also admissible to prove that the clause had that meaning and did not cover injuries to plaintiff's property.[9]

Accordingly, the judgment must be reversed [and case remanded for retrial].

. . .

The judgment is reversed.

PETERS, J., MOSK, J., BURKE, J., SULLIVAN, J., and PEEK, J., concurred.

MCCOMB, J., dissented.

---

[9] The court's exclusion of extrinsic evidence in this case would be error even under a rule that excluded such evidence when the instrument appeared to the court to be clear and unambiguous on its face. The controversy centers on the meaning of the word "indemnify" and the phrase "all loss, damage, expense and liability." The trial court's recognition of the language as typical of a third party indemnity clause and the double sense in which the word "indemnify" is used in statutes and defined in dictionaries demonstrate the existence of an ambiguity. (Compare Civ. Code, § 2772, "Indemnity is a contract by which one engages to save another from a legal consequence of the conduct of one of the parties, or of some other person," with Civ. Code, § 2527, "Insurance is a contract whereby one undertakes to indemnify another against loss, damage, or liability, arising from an unknown or contingent event." Black's Law Dictionary (4th ed. 1951) defines "indemnity" as "A collateral contract or assurance, by which one person engages to secure another against an anticipated loss or to prevent him from being damnified by the legal consequences of an act or forbearance on the part of one of the parties or of some third person." Stroud's Judicial Dictionary (2d ed. 1903) defines it as a "Contract. . .to indemnify against a liability. . . ." One of the definitions given to "indemnify" by Webster's Third New International Dict. (1961 ed.) is "to exempt from incurred liabilities.")

Plaintiff's assertion that the use of the word "all" to modify "loss, damage, expense and liability" dictates an all inclusive interpretation is not persuasive. If the word "indemnify" encompasses only third-party claims, the word "all" simply refers to all such claims. The use of the words "loss," "damage," and "expense" in addition to the word "liability" is likewise inconclusive. These words do not imply an agreement to reimburse for injury to an indemnitee's property since they are commonly inserted in third-party indemnity clauses, to enable an indemnitee who settles a claim to recover from his indemnitor without proving his liability.

FRIGALIMENT IMPORTING CO. V. B.N.S. INTERNATIONAL SALES CORP.

United States District Court, Southern District of New York
190 F.Supp. 116 (1960)

FRIENDLY, CIRCUIT JUDGE.

The issue is, what is chicken? Plaintiff says 'chicken' means a young chicken, suitable for broiling and frying. Defendant says 'chicken' means any bird of that genus that meets contract specifications on weight and quality, including what it calls 'stewing chicken' and plaintiff pejoratively terms 'fowl'. Dictionaries give both meanings, as well as some others not relevant here. To support its, plaintiff sends a number of volleys over the net; defendant essays to return them and adds a few serves of its own. Assuming that both parties were acting in good faith, the case nicely illustrates Holmes' remark 'that the making of a contract depends not on the agreement of two minds in one intention, but on the agreement of two sets of external signs—not on the parties' having meant the same thing but on their having said the same thing.' The Path of the Law, in Collected Legal Papers, p. 178. I have concluded that plaintiff has not sustained its burden of persuasion that the contract used 'chicken' in the narrower sense.

The action is for breach of the warranty that goods sold shall correspond to the description, New York Personal Property Law, McKinney's Consol. Laws, c. 41, § 95. Two contracts are in suit. In the first, dated May 2, 1957, defendant, a New York sales corporation, confirmed the sale to plaintiff, a Swiss corporation, of

> 'US Fresh Frozen Chicken, Grade A, Government Inspected, Eviscerated 2 1/2–3 lbs. and 1 1/2–2 lbs. each all chicken individually wrapped in cryovac, packed in secured fiber cartons or wooden boxes, suitable for export

75,000 lbs. 2 1/2–3 lbs.	@$33.00
25,000 lbs. 1 1/2–2 lbs.	@$36.50

per 100 lbs. FAS New York

> scheduled May 10, 1957 pursuant to instructions from Penson & Co., New York.'

The second contract, also dated May 2, 1957, was identical save that only 50,000 lbs. of the heavier 'chicken' were called for, the price of the smaller birds was $37 per 100 lbs., and shipment was scheduled for May 30. The initial shipment under the first contract was short but the balance was shipped on May 17. When the initial shipment arrived in Switzerland, plaintiff found, on May 28, that the 2 1/2–3 lbs. birds were not young chicken suitable for broiling and frying but stewing chicken or 'fowl';

indeed, many of the cartons and bags plainly so indicated. Protests ensued. Nevertheless, shipment under the second contract was made on May 29, the 2 1/2–3 lbs. birds again being stewing chicken. Defendant stopped the transportation of these at Rotterdam.

This action followed. . . .

Since the word 'chicken' standing alone is ambiguous, I turn first to see whether the contract itself offers any aid to its interpretation. Plaintiff says the 1 1/2–2 lbs. birds necessarily had to be young chicken since the older birds do not come in that size, hence the 2 1/2–3 lbs. birds must likewise be young. This is unpersuasive—a contract for 'apples' of two different sizes could be filled with different kinds of apples even though only one species came in both sizes. Defendant notes that the contract called not simply for chicken but for 'US Fresh Frozen Chicken, Grade A, Government Inspected.' It says the contract thereby incorporated by reference the Department of Agriculture's regulations, which favor its interpretation; I shall return to this after reviewing plaintiff's other contentions.

The first hinges on an exchange of cablegrams which preceded execution of the formal contracts. The negotiations leading up to the contracts were conducted in New York between defendant's secretary, Ernest R. Bauer, and a Mr. Stovicek, who was in New York for the Czechoslovak government at the World Trade Fair. A few days after meeting Bauer at the fair, Stovicek telephoned and inquired whether defendant would be interested in exporting poultry to Switzerland. Bauer then met with Stovicek, who showed him a cable from plaintiff dated April 26, 1957, announcing that they 'are buyer' of 25,000 lbs. of chicken 2 1/2–3 lbs. weight, Cryovac packed, grade A Government inspected, at a price up to 33¢ per pound, for shipment on May 10, to be confirmed by the following morning, and were interested in further offerings. After testing the market for price, Bauer accepted, and Stovicek sent a confirmation that evening. Plaintiff stresses that, although these and subsequent cables between plaintiff and defendant, which laid the basis for the additional quantities under the first and for all of the second contract, were predominantly in German, they used the English word 'chicken'; it claims this was done because it understood 'chicken' meant young chicken whereas the German word, 'Huhn,' included both 'Brathuhn' (broilers) and 'Suppenhuhn' (stewing chicken), and that defendant, whose officers were thoroughly conversant with German, should have realized this. Whatever force this argument might otherwise have is largely drained away by Bauer's testimony that he asked Stovicek what kind of chickens were wanted, received the answer 'any kind of chickens,' and then, in German, asked whether the cable meant 'Huhn' and received an affirmative response. . . .

Plaintiff's next contention is that there was a definite trade usage that 'chicken' meant 'young chicken.' Defendant showed that it was only beginning in the poultry trade in 1957, thereby bringing itself within the principle that 'when one of the parties is not a member of the trade or other circle, his acceptance of the standard must be made to appear' by proving either that he had actual knowledge of the usage or that the usage is 'so generally known in the community that his actual individual knowledge of it may be inferred.' 9 Wigmore, Evidence (3d ed. § 1940) 2464. Here there was no proof of actual knowledge of the alleged usage; indeed, continuance, so well established, so notorious, so universal and so reasonable in itself, as that the presumption is violent that the parties contracted with reference to it, and made it a part of their agreement.' Walls v. Bailey, 1872, 49 N.Y. 464, 472–473.

Plaintiff endeavored to establish such a usage by the testimony of three witnesses and certain other evidence. Strasser, resident buyer in New York for a large chain of Swiss cooperatives, testified that 'on chicken I would definitely understand a broiler.' However, the force of this testimony was considerably weakened by the fact that in his own transactions the witness, a careful businessman, protected himself by using 'broiler' when that was what he wanted and 'fowl' when he wished older birds. Indeed, there are some indications, dating back to a remark of Lord Mansfield, Edie v. East India Co., 2 Burr. 1216, 1222 (1761), that no credit should be given 'witnesses to usage, who could not adduce instances in verification.' 7 Wigmore, Evidence (3d ed. 1940), § 1954; see McDonald v. Acker, Merrall & Condit Co., 2d Dept.1920, 192 App.Div. 123, 126, 182 N.Y.S. 607.

While Wigmore thinks this goes too far, a witness' consistent failure to rely on the alleged usage deprives his opinion testimony of much of its effect. Niesielowski, an officer of one of the companies that had furnished the stewing chicken to defendant, testified that 'chicken' meant 'the male species of the poultry industry. That could be a broiler, a fryer or a roaster', but not a stewing chicken; however, he also testified that upon receiving defendant's inquiry for 'chickens', he asked whether the desire was for 'fowl or frying chickens' and, in fact, supplied fowl, although taking the precaution of asking defendant, a day or two after plaintiff's acceptance of the contracts in suit, to change its confirmation of its order from 'chickens,' as defendant had originally prepared it, to 'stewing chickens.' Dates, an employee of Urner-Barry Company, which publishes a daily market report on the poultry trade, gave it as his view that the trade meaning of it is quite plain that defendant's belief was to the contrary. In order to meet the alternative requirement, the law of New York demands a showing that 'the usage is of so long 'chicken' was 'broilers and fryers.' In addition to this opinion testimony, plaintiff relied on the fact that the Urner-Barry service, the Journal of Commerce, and Weinberg Bros. & Co. of Chicago, a large supplier of poultry, published quotations in a manner which, in one way or another, distinguish between 'chicken,' comprising broilers, fryers and certain other categories, and 'fowl,' which, Bauer acknowledged, included stewing chickens. This material would be impressive if there were nothing to the contrary. However, there was, as will now be seen.

Defendant's witness Weininger, who operates a chicken eviscerating plant in New Jersey, testified 'Chicken is everything except a goose, a duck, and a turkey. Everything is a chicken, but then you have to say, you have to specify which category you want or that you are talking about.' Its witness Fox said that in the trade 'chicken' would encompass all the various classifications. Sadina, who conducts a food inspection service, testified that he would consider any bird coming within the classes of 'chicken' in the Department of Agriculture's regulations to be a chicken. The specifications approved by the General Services Administration include fowl as well as broilers and fryers under the classification 'chickens.' Statistics of the Institute of American Poultry Industries use the phrases 'Young chickens' and 'Mature chickens,' under the general heading 'Total chickens.' and the Department of Agriculture's daily and weekly price reports avoid use of the word 'chicken' without specification.

Defendant advances several other points which it claims affirmatively support its construction. Primary among these is the regulation of the Department of Agriculture, 7 C.F.R. § 70.300–70.370, entitled, 'Grading and Inspection of Poultry and Edible Products Thereof.' and in particular 70.301 which recited:

Chickens. The following are the various classes of chickens:

(a) Broiler or fryer . . .

(b) Roaster . . .

(c) Capon . . .

(d) Stag . . .

(e) Hen or stewing chicken or fowl . . .

(f) Cock or old rooster . . .

Defendant argues, as previously noted, that the contract incorporated these regulations by reference. Plaintiff answers that the contract provision related simply to grade and Government inspection and did not incorporate the Government definition of 'chicken,' and also that the definition in the Regulations is ignored in the trade. However, the latter contention was contradicted by Weininger and Sadina; and there is force in defendant's argument that the contract made the regulations a dictionary, particularly since the reference to Government grading was already in plaintiff's initial cable to Stovicek.

Defendant makes a further argument based on the impossibility of its obtaining broilers and fryers at the 33¢ price offered by plaintiff for the 2 1/2–3 lbs. birds. There is no substantial dispute that, in late April, 1957, the price for 2 1/2–3 lbs. broilers was between 35 and 37¢ per pound, and that when defendant entered into the contracts, it was well aware of this and intended to fill them by supplying fowl in these weights. It claims that plaintiff must likewise have known the market since plaintiff had reserved shipping space on April 23, three days before plaintiff's cable to Stovicek, or, at least, that Stovicek was chargeable with such knowledge. It is scarcely an answer to say, as plaintiff does in its brief, that the 33¢ price offered by the 2 1/2–3 lbs. 'chickens' was closer to the prevailing 35¢ price for broilers than to the 30¢ at which defendant procured fowl. Plaintiff must have expected defendant to make some profit—certainly it could not have expected defendant deliberately to incur a loss.

Finally, defendant relies on conduct by the plaintiff after the first shipment had been received. On May 28 plaintiff sent two cables complaining that the larger birds in the first shipment constituted 'fowl.' Defendant answered with a cable refusing to recognize plaintiff's objection and announcing 'We have today ready for shipment 50,000 lbs. chicken 2 1/2–3 lbs. 25,000 lbs. broilers 1 1/2–2 lbs.,' these being the goods procured for shipment under the second contract, and asked immediate answer 'whether we are to ship this merchandise to you and whether you will accept the merchandise.' After several other cable exchanges, plaintiff replied on May 29 'Confirm again that merchandise is to be shipped since resold by us if not enough pursuant to contract chickens are shipped the missing quantity is to be shipped within ten days stop we resold to our customers pursuant to your contract chickens grade A you have to deliver us said merchandise we again state that we shall make you fully responsible for all resulting costs.' Defendant argues that if plaintiff was sincere in thinking it was entitled to young chickens, plaintiff would not have allowed the shipment under the second contract to go forward, since the distinction between broilers and chickens drawn in defendant's cablegram must have made it clear that the larger birds would not be broilers. However, plaintiff answers that the cables show plaintiff was insisting on delivery of young chickens and that defendant shipped old ones at its peril. Defendant's point would be highly relevant on another disputed issue—whether if liability were established, the measure of damages should be the difference in market value of broilers and stewing chicken in New York or the larger difference in Europe, but I cannot give it weight on the issue of interpretation. Defendant points out also that plaintiff proceeded to deliver some of the larger birds in Europe, describing them as 'poulets'; defendant argues that it was only when plaintiff's customers complained about this that plaintiff developed the idea that 'chicken' meant 'young chicken.' There is little force in this in view of plaintiff's immediate and consistent protests.

When all the evidence is reviewed, it is clear that defendant believed it could comply with the contracts by delivering stewing chicken in the 2 1/2–3 lbs. size. Defendant's subjective intent would not be significant if this did not coincide with an objective meaning of 'chicken.' Here it did coincide with one of the dictionary meanings, with the definition in the Department of Agriculture Regulations to which the contract made at least oblique reference, with at least some usage in the trade, with the realities of the market, and with what plaintiff's spokesman had said. Plaintiff asserts it to be equally plain that plaintiff's own subjective intent was to obtain broilers and fryers; the only evidence against this is the material as to market prices and this may not have been sufficiently brought home. In any event it is unnecessary to determine that issue. For plaintiff has the burden of showing that 'chicken' was used in the narrower rather than in the broader sense, and this it has not sustained.

This opinion constitutes the Court's findings of fact and conclusions of law. Judgment shall be entered dismissing the complaint with costs.

DISCUSSION PROBLEMS

1. Water Sports

When Debbi Krenkel checked in for a stay at the Atlantis Bahamas Resort, the resort's agent asked her to sign a one-page form labeled "Acknowledgment, Agreement and Release." The eight-paragraph document included the following language:

> I agree that any claims I may have against the Resort Parties resulting from any events occurring in The Bahamas shall be governed by and constructed in accordance with the laws of the Commonwealth of The Bahamas, and further, irrevocably agree to the Supreme Court of The Bahamas as the exclusive venue for any such proceedings whatsoever.

Krenkel asked the agent if the agreement only applied to water sports activities, he answered in the affirmative, and she signed the document. During her stay, Krenkel slipped and fell on an outdoor path on the resort grounds. If she sues the resort, is she limited by her contract with Atlantis to pursuing her claim only in the Bahamas under Bahamian law?

2. City of Angels

Disney Baseball Enterprises (Disney) purchased the "California Angels" Major League Baseball team and then entered into a stadium lease agreement with the City of Anaheim (Anaheim). One provision of the agreement required Disney to change the team name "to include the name

'Anaheim' therein." In accordance with the contractual requirement, Disney renamed the team the "Anaheim Angels." Seven years later, Disney sold the team (and assigned its stadium lease) to Angels Baseball, which changed the team's name to the "Los Angeles Angels of Anaheim." Anaheim sued, claiming that the name change constituted a breach of contract.

Evidence presented at trial demonstrated that, during the original contract negotiations, Anaheim had proposed that the team's name be "Anaheim Angels" but Disney resisted, and the parties ultimately settled on the "include the name 'Anaheim' " language. Anaheim argued that this language was intended to provide Disney with the flexibility to change the team mascot or to reverse the ordering of the city name and the mascot name (e.g., to change the official name to "Angels of Anaheim"), but that no one on either side had considered the possibility that the team name might be changed to include two different geographical identifiers. Disney did not directly contradict Anaheim's explanation, but it maintained that its goal was to maintain maximum flexibility regarding the team name in order to maximize the potential market value of the team should Disney decide to sell it, as it ultimately did. Which side should prevail?

3. The Invention of Digital Music

Prior to the invention of digital music that can be streamed or downloaded, record company Aftermath purchased exclusive rights to the works of recording artist Marshall Mathers, better known as "Eminem." The contract contained a "Records Sold" provision, which provided that Mathers would receive between 12 and 20 percent of the adjusted retail price of all "full price records sold in the United States. . . through normal retail channels." The contract separately included a "Masters Licensed" provision, which provided that "[n]otwithstanding the foregoing," Mathers would receive 50 percent of revenues earned "on masters licensed by [Aftermath] to others for their manufacture and sale of records or for any other uses."

When digital downloads emerged as a new way of distributing music, Aftermath entered into a "licensing" agreement with Apple Computer, Inc. that permitted Apple to use the master recordings of Mathers' songs to sell digital downloads to consumers through its iTunes online store. Aftermath paid Mathers royalties calculated as "Records Sold." Mathers' assignee sued, asserting it was entitled under the "Masters Licensed" term to 50 percent of the revenue Aftermath received from Apple. The parties agreed that neither side had imagined the invention of digital download technology at the time of contracting. At trial, Aftermath's expert witness testified that, according to music industry custom, the "Masters Licensed" provision concerned the use of recordings only in third-party products, such as multiple-artist compilation albums, movies, and television commercials.

Which party should prevail? Should it be a question for the judge or jury?

CHAPTER 18

CONDITIONS

■ ■ ■

INTRODUCTION

When a contract obliges a party (the obligor) to perform an act, the obligor is said to have a "duty." Failure to perform a duty constitutes a breach of the contract, which in turn gives the obligee the right to a remedy. Rest. (2d) Contracts § 235.

In many circumstances, a duty, rather than being absolute, is conditional on the occurrence of some event. If the event does not occur, then performance of the duty does not become due. Thus, a "condition" can be defined either as an event that triggers a duty or as an event that, in event of non-occurrence, discharges a duty. Rest. (2d) Contracts § 224. Put more simply, conditions usually limit obligations to perform duties.

Conditions may be "ordinary" or "promissory." An "ordinary" condition is an event beyond the control of either party. For example, home insurance contracts typically obligate the insurer to pay to rebuild the customer's home if it is destroyed by fire. The insurer's duty to pay arises only if the house burns down. Thus, a fire is a condition of to the duty to pay.

A "promissory" condition is both a duty of one party and a condition of the other party's duty. Consider, for example, a residential lease agreement that obligates a tenant to provide a security deposit and then the landlord to provide the tenant with an apartment. The tenant's obligation is a promissory condition: it is both a duty on the part of the tenant, and a condition of the landlord's duty. See Rest. (2d) Contracts § 225.

The distinction between ordinary and promissory conditions is very important because it determines the consequence of a condition's failure to occur. When an ordinary condition is not satisfied, the duty that rests on the condition does not become due, but neither party has a legal cause of action against the other. If a fire does not destroy the insured's home, the insurer's duty to pay never comes due, but neither party has grounds to sue the other. The failure of a promissory condition, in contrast, constitutes a breach of contract. Consequently, not only is the non-breaching party's conditional duty not triggered, but the non-breaching party also has a cause of action for breach. If the tenant does not provide the security deposit, the landlord not only has no duty to hand over the keys to the apartment, but she may also sue for damages caused by the tenant's breach, such as the income lost during the time period it takes to re-let the premises to another tenant.

Irving v. Town of Clinton and *Main Electric, Ltd. v. Printz Services Corporation* consider whether contractual language constitutes a condition. The former case is straightforward, and the argument that the language at issue is not a condition of the town's duty, while existent, is quite weak. The latter case is more difficult. In both cases, notice that if the events in question are conditions, they must be ordinary conditions, since it is clear that it is not the duty of either party to ensure that the events occur. As a general matter, however, such "express" conditions may be either ordinary or promissory conditions.

Contrast express conditions, which are created by the parties as a result of the language in their contract, with "constructive" conditions, which are created through the operation of law rather than by words or actions of the parties. See Rest. (2d) Contracts §§ 234, 237, 238. *Kingston v. Preston* is the seminal case establishing the important concept of constructive conditions. The language of the old English opinion is difficult to follow, but the terms of the contract at issue are actually straightforward: a business owner promises (or "covenants") to sell his business, including his inventory, to his young apprentice. The apprentice lacks the money to pay outright for the business and so promises to make monthly payments and to obtain a sufficient security (perhaps a line of credit) to cover the value of the debt if he is unable to pay. If the apprentice does not provide the security, must the owner turn over his business to the apprentice anyway? (Notice that the parties did not specify an answer to this question.) Before *Kingston*, the answer was "yes."

Restatement (Second) of Contracts § 235. Effect of Performance as Discharge and of Non-Performance as Breach

(1) Full performance of a duty under a contract discharges the duty.

(2) When performance of a duty under a contract is due any non-performance is a breach.

Restatement (Second) of Contracts § 224. Condition Defined

A condition is an event, not certain to occur, which must occur, unless its non-occurrence is excused, before performance under a contract becomes due.

Restatement (Second) of Contracts § 225. Effects of the Non-Occurrence of a Condition

(1) Performance of a duty subject to a condition cannot become due unless the condition occurs or its non-occurrence is excused.

(2) Unless it has been excused, the non-occurrence of a condition discharges the duty when the condition can no longer occur.

(3) Non-occurrence of a condition is not a breach by a party unless he is under a duty that the condition occur.

Comment:

a. *Two effects.* The unexcused non-occurrence of a condition has two possible effects on the duty subject to that condition. The first effect always follows and the second often does. The first, stated in Subsection (1), is that of preventing performance of the duty from becoming due. This follows from the definition of "condition" in § 224. Performance of the duty may still become due, however, if the condition occurs later within the time for its occurrence. The non-occurrence of the condition within that time has the additional effect, stated in Subsection (2), of discharging the duty.

Restatement (Second) of Contracts § 234. Order of Performances

(1) Where all or part of the performances to be exchanged under an exchange of promises can be rendered simultaneously, they are to that extent due simultaneously, unless the language or the circumstances indicate the contrary.

(2) Except to the extent stated in Subsection (1), where the performance of only one party under such an exchange requires a period of time, his performance is due at an earlier time than that of the other party, unless the language or the circumstances indicate the contrary.

Comment:

f. *Applicability of rule.* The rule stated in Subsection (2) usually finds its application to contracts involving services, such as construction and employment contracts. The common practice of making express provision for progress payments has diminished its importance with regard to the former, and the widespread enactment of state wage statutes giving the employee a right to the frequent periodic payment of wages has lessened its significance with regard to the latter. Nevertheless, it is a helpful rule for residual cases not otherwise provided for. It applies not only to contracts under which the performance of one party is more or less continuous, but also to contracts where performance consists of a series of acts with an interval of time between them.

Restatement (Second) of Contracts § 237. Effect on Other Party's Duties of a Failure to Render Performance

Except as stated in § 240, it is a condition of each party's remaining duties to render performances to be exchanged under an exchange of promises that there be no uncured material failure by the other party to render any such performance due at an earlier time.

Restatement (Second) of Contracts § 238. Effect on Other Party's Duties of a Failure to Offer Performance

Where all or part of the performances to be exchanged under an exchange of promises are due simultaneously, it is a condition of each party's duties to render such performance that the other party either render or, with manifested present ability to do so, offer performance of his part of the simultaneous exchange.

CASES

IRVING V. TOWN OF CLINTON

Supreme Judicial Court of Maine
711 A.2d 141 (1998)

DANA, J.

Kenneth Irving, Jr. appeals from the summary judgment entered in the Superior Court (Kennebec County, Kravchuk, C.J.) in favor of the Town of Clinton on Irving's breach of contract claim. Because we conclude that an express condition precedent to the contract did not occur, we affirm the judgment.

The underlying facts in this case are not in dispute. On June 19, 1996, Irving and a majority of the Town's selectmen signed a document entitled "Snow Plowing and Road Sanding Contract" which provided that Irving would maintain the Town's roads from October 1996 to May 1997 in return for $107,723.96. Paragraph 13 of the document states:

> 13. VOTER APPROVAL:
>
> This contract is contingent upon voter approval (Article 11, Highway Dept. Account dated June 25, 1996).

The Town held its 1996 annual town meeting on June 25, 1996, at which the residents voted on Article 11, which stated in full: "To see if the town will vote to raise and appropriate the sum of $236,503.00 for the Highway Department Account." The annual town report, which had been distributed to residents and was available at the meeting, contained a detailed breakdown of the highway department budget, including an appropriation for $107,860 for plowing. At the meeting a voter moved to amend Article 11 to reduce the snow removal line from $107,860 to $99,999. The amendment passed and the Article was approved as amended. The Town then offered Irving the snowplowing contract at the reduced amount, which he refused, opting instead to file the breach of contract lawsuit that is the subject of this appeal.

. . .

We need not address Irving's argument that the Town selectmen possess the authority to enter into contracts on behalf of the Town to carry out necessary governmental functions such as snowplowing. Even if such authority exists the contingency provided for in paragraph 13 of the parties' contract was never met. The contract was made expressly contingent on the approval of the voters at the annual town meeting. The voters did not approve the contract as written and appropriated a lesser amount of money for snow removal. An elementary rule of contract law is that the nonoccurrence of a condition discharges the parties from their duties under the contract. Restatement (Second) of Contracts § 225 (1981). Because the Town's duty to pay Irving for his snowplowing services was discharged by the failure of the Town's voters to approve the contract as written, the court properly entered a summary judgment in favor of the Town.

MAIN ELECTRIC, LTD. V. PRINTZ SERVICES CORP.

Supreme Court of Colorado (En Banc)
980 P.2d 522 (1999)

BENDER, J.

. . .

I. FACTS AND PROCEEDINGS BELOW

Respondent Printz Services Corporation was the general contractor on a casino construction project in Cripple Creek, Colorado. Petitioners C.J. Masonry and Main Electric were subcontractors on the project. The relationship between Printz and C.J. Masonry was governed by a preprinted form contract prepared by Printz, the general contractor. The form contains the following pertinent payment provisions:

> 3. SUBCONTRACT AMOUNT. In consideration of the faithful performance of the covenants and agreements herein,. . .Contractor agrees to pay, or cause to be paid, Subcontractor. . .at the times and in the manner following in Articles 4 and 5.
>
> 4. PROGRESS PAYMENTS.
>
> . . .

D. Contractor shall make payment on or before the 25th day of the next month following receipt of the Payment Request provided like payment has been made by Owner to Contractor.

. . .

5. FINAL PAYMENT. Contractor shall make final payment to Subcontractor after work is complete and accepted by Owner and Architect provided like payment shall have been made by Owner to Contractor. . . .

. . .

Before the project was complete, the owner became insolvent and lost the property in a deed of trust foreclosure. The owner failed to pay Printz, and Printz in turn failed to pay its subcontractors. C.J. Masonry and Main Electric both sought payment for breach of contract against the general contractor. Printz claimed in defense that it was obligated to pay its subcontractors only *if* it was first paid by the owner.

The trial court interpreted the payment clause "provided like payment shall have been made by Owner to Contractor" in C.J. Masonry's contract to be a promise by Printz to pay the subcontractor *when* and not *if* the general contractor was paid by the owner. In the trial court's view, the general contractor remained unconditionally obligated to pay the subcontractor provided the work was performed. The trial court ruled that Printz must pay C.J. Masonry regardless of the owner's insolvency.

. . .

The court of appeals reversed the trial court on both subcontractors' claims. *See Printz Servs. Corp.*, 949 P.2d at 79. It held that the contract between Printz and C.J. Masonry created a condition precedent rather than a promise to pay, relying substantially on language in *Orman v. Ryan*, 25 Colo. 383, 55 P. 168 (1897), in which a similarly worded clause in a construction contract was referred to as a condition precedent. *See id.* at 388, 55 P. at 170. Thus, the court of appeals ruled Printz was not obligated to pay C.J. Masonry. *See Printz Servs. Corp.*, 949 P.2d at 81–82.

. . .

III. THE PAYMENT PROVISION IN THIS CONTRACT IS NOT A PAY-IF-PAID CLAUSE

We now turn to address the interpretation of the payment clause in the contract between Printz and C.J. Masonry. Initially, we note that the interpretation of a contract is a question of law which we review de novo. *See Union Ins. Co. v. Houtz*, 883 P.2d 1057, 1061 (Colo. 1994).

We begin our analysis by reviewing basic principles of contract interpretation. The parties' intention when drafting a contract governs the interpretation of that contract. *See Centennial Enter. v. Mansfield Dev. Co.*,

193 Colo. 463, 464, 568 P.2d 50, 51 (1977). A contract term can be interpreted as either a condition precedent or a promise to perform depending on the parties' intent. *See Charles Ilfeld Co. v. Taylor*, 156 Colo. 204, 209, 397 P.2d 748, 750 (1964). In other contexts we have followed the rule that a condition precedent in a contract is not favored and will not be given effect unless established by clear and unequivocal language. *See id.; Balzano v. Bluewater Insurance Ltd.*, 801 P.2d 1, 3 (Colo. App. 1990). If there is any doubt as to the parties' intention, we interpret a clause in a contract as a promise rather than a condition. *See Ilfeld*, 156 Colo. at 209, 397 P.2d at 750. This rule of contract interpretation expresses the recognized policy of avoiding the harsh results of forfeiture against a party who has no control over the occurrence of the condition. *See Rohauer v. Little*, 736 P.2d 403, 409 (Colo. 1987); *Ilfeld*, 156 Colo. at 209, 397 P.2d at 750. As we stated in *Ilfeld:*

> The intention of the parties in making a contract controls. . . .In cases of doubt as to the intention of the parties, courts resolve the doubt in favor of an interpretation making the engagement a promise rather than a condition. And such rule of construction is founded on a policy of avoiding, if possible, forfeitures. . . .To frown upon forfeitures is part of the judicial policy of this state, too.

Ilfeld, 156 Colo. at 209, 397 P.2d at 750–751 (citations omitted).

Although we have not yet applied this reasoning to conditions precedent in payment clauses of a construction contract, we believe that our general rule of contract interpretation applies with equal force in that context. If a payment provision such as the one here creates a condition precedent, then the subcontractor will forfeit payment for work performed due to the occurrence of a condition—the owner's insolvency—over which the subcontractor has no control. *See R.N. Robinson & Son, Inc. v. Ground Improvement Techniques & Fireman's Fund Ins. Co.*, 31 F. Supp. 2d 881, 886 (D. Colo. 1998) (applying Colorado law) ("[C]onditions precedent create a risk of forfeiture, even when the party against whom the condition operates has no control over whether the condition is met.").

Typically, a subcontractor looks to the general contractor for payment and not the owner. *See Thomas J. Dyer Co. v. Bishop Int'l Eng'g Co.*, 303 F.2d 655, 660 (6th Cir. 1962). Therefore, the subcontractor need not factor in the risk of nonpayment by the owner. *See Robinson*, 31 F. Supp. 2d at 886; *Peacock Constr. Co. v. Modern Air Conditioning Inc.*, 353 So. 2d 840, 842 (Fla. 1977). If the risk of the owner's nonpayment is to be shifted from the general contractor to the subcontractor, then this shift must be clearly articulated in the agreement.

With the principle in mind that we will interpret a clause as a promise rather than a condition unless the language of the contract explicitly mandates otherwise, we analyze the relevant terms of this contract. Printz argues that the contract's terms, that the general contractor will pay its subcontractor "provided like payment shall have been made by owner to contractor," establishes a condition precedent requiring payment by the owner before payment to the subcontractor. We are not persuaded.

Although the payment clause may be read to support the argument that the parties intended the subcontractors to be paid only if the owner paid the general contractor first, this clause contains no language reflecting any intent of the parties to shift the risk of the owner's nonpayment from the general contractor to the subcontractor. There is no express acknowledgement by the subcontractor that it, rather than the general contractor, agrees to assume the risk of the owner's nonpayment. The "provided" clause does not indicate that the parties reasonably anticipated the possibility that the owner might not pay and therefore specifically addressed this contingency. The payment clause contains no specific language creating a contingency that must occur before payment must be made by the general contractor.

We conclude that the payment clause here leaves room for reasonable argument by both the general contractor and the subcontractor as to whether the parties intended to shift the risk of the owner's nonpayment from the general contractor to the subcontractor. Applying our rule interpreting a clause as a promise rather than a condition if there is any doubt of the parties' intention, we conclude that this payment clause is a pay-when-paid clause. It created a promise to pay the subcontractor that remains unconditional, although payment may be delayed because of the owner's failure to pay the general contractor. . . .

KINGSTON V. PRESTON

King's Bench
99 Eng. Rep. 434 (1781)

MANSFIELD, L.

It was an action of debt, for non-performance of covenants contained in certain articles of agreement between the plaintiff and the defendant. The declaration stated; That, by articles made the 24th of March, 1770, the plaintiff, for the considerations therein-after mentioned, covenanted, with the defendant, to serve him for one year and a quarter next ensuing, as a covenant-servant, in his trade of a silk-mercer, at £200 a year, and in consideration of the premises, the defendant covenanted, that at the end of the year and a quarter, he would give up his business of a mercer to the plaintiff, and a nephew of the defendant, or some other person to be nominated by the defendant, and give up to them his stock in trade, at a fair valuation; and that, between the young traders, deeds of partnership should be executed for 14 years, and from and immediately after the execution of the said deeds, the defendant would permit the said young traders to carry on the said business in the defendant's house.

Then the declaration stated a covenant by the plaintiff, that he would accept the business and stock in trade, at a fair valuation, with the defendant's nephew, or such other person, &c. and execute such deeds of partnership, and, further, that the plaintiff should, and would, at, and before, the sealing and delivery of the deeds, cause and procure good and sufficient security to be given to the defendant, to be approved of by the defendant, for the payment of £250 monthly, to the defendant, in lieu [half] of the monthly produce of the stock in trade, until the value of the stock should be reduced to £4000.

Then the plaintiff averred, that he had performed, and been ready to perform, his covenants, and assigned for breach on the part of the defendant, that he had refused to surrender and give up his business, at the end of the said year and a quarter.

The defendant pleaded, 1. That the plaintiff did not offer sufficient security; and, 2. That he did not give sufficient security for the payment of the £250, &c.

And the plaintiff demurred generally to both pleas.

On the part of the plaintiff, the case was argued by Mr. Buller, who contended, that the covenants were mutual and independant, and, therefore, a plea of the breach of one of the covenants to be performed by the plaintiff was no bar to an action for a breach by the defendant of one of which he had bound himself to perform, but that the defendant might have his remedy for the breach by the plaintiff, in a separate action. On the other side, Mr. Grose insisted, that the covenants were dependant in their nature, and, therefore, performance must be alleged: the security to be given for the money, was manifestly the chief object of the transaction, and it would be highly unreasonable to construe the agreement, so as to oblige the defendant to give up a beneficial business, and valuable stock in trade, and trust to the plaintiff's personal security, (who might, and, indeed, was admitted to be worth nothing,) for the performance of his part.

In delivering the judgment of the Court, Lord Mansfield expressed himself to the following effect: There are three kinds of covenants: 1. Such as are called mutual and independant, where either party may recover damages from the other, for the injury he may have received by a breach of the covenants in his favour, and where it is no excuse for the defendant, to allege a breach of the covenants on the part of the plaintiff. 2. There are covenants which are conditions and dependant, in which the performance of one depends on the prior performance of another, and, therefore, till this prior condition is performed, the other party is not liable to an action on his covenant. 3. There is also a third sort of covenants, which are mutual conditions to be performed at the same time; and, in these, if one party who is ready, and offered, to perform his part, and the other neglected, or refused, to perform his, he who was ready, and offered, has fulfilled his engagement, and may maintain an action for the default of the other; though it is not certain that either is obliged to do the first act.

His Lordship then proceeded to say, that the dependance, or independance, of covenants, was to be collected from the evident sense and meaning of the parties, and, that, however transposed they might be in the deed, their precedency must depend on the order of time in which the intent of the transaction requires their performance. That, in the case before the Court, it would be the greatest injustice if the plaintiff should prevail: the essence of the agreement was, that the defendant should not trust to the personal security of the plaintiff, but, before he delivered up his stock and business, should have good security for the payment of the money. The giving such security, therefore, must necessarily be a condition precedent.

Judgment was accordingly given for the defendant, because the part to be performed by the plaintiff was clearly a condition precedent.

DISCUSSION PROBLEMS

1. The Vineyard

In a contract for the purchase of a vineyard, buyer Merritt Hill Vineyard's obligation to close the transaction was subject to the "conditions precedent" that seller Windy Heights Vineyard obtain a title insurance policy and that Merritt Hill receive confirmation from Farmers Home Administration that the sale would not constitute a default of certain mortgages on the property. As of the date specified for closing, Windy Heights had not obtained a title insurance policy and Merritt Hills had not heard from Farmers Home Administration. Merritt Hills refused to close the transaction and sued Windy Heights for breach of contract. Which party, if either, breached the contract?

2. Not Stepping Up

The Massachusetts Municipal Wholesale Electric Company (MMWEC) entered into contracts, called "power sales agreements," with a number of small New England utilities in order to create a consortium to purchase energy. MMWEC then issued bonds and used the revenue to buy an interest in two nuclear power plants.

Each of MMWEC's power sales agreements contained an "execution and delivery" term, which provided that:

> This Agreement shall be effective upon execution and delivery of Power Sales Agreements by MMWEC and Participants whose Participant's shares total 100%.

To ensure that the consortium would have enough funds to satisfy its obligations, each power sales agreement also included a "step up" provision, which provided that, if one or more of the utilities in the consortium defaulted on its obligations, the other consortium members would be required to increase their participation *pro rata* to make up the difference.

After the power sales agreements had been signed and the bonds issued, the Vermont Supreme Court ruled that Vermont utilities, which collectively owned 15 percent of the consortium's investment, lacked authority to enter into those agreements and, thus, the power sales agreements between MMWEC and those utilities were void. In light of this ruling, the MMWEC then sought increased participation by the other consortium members under the "step up" provisions of their respective contracts. Several Massachusetts utilities sued, alleging the "step up" provisions never took effect because the condition provided by the "execution and delivery" term was never satisfied. How should the court rule?

3. Goods or Payment?

Morton contracted to purchase corn from Lamb. The contract called for Lamb to deliver the corn to Morton in the village of Shardlow within one month's time. When the month passed and no corn had been delivered, Morton brought suit. Lamb defended by arguing that Morton had not tendered payment to Lamb for the corn and so should not be permitted to recover. Who should prevail?

CHAPTER 19

SUBSTANTIAL PERFORMANCE AND MATERIAL BREACH

■ ■ ■

INTRODUCTION

Contracting parties often use conditions as a mechanism for allocating risks. When parties create an ordinary condition to allocate the risk that an uncertain event might occur, the non-occurrence of the event—in other words, the failure of the condition—typically imposes no hardship on the party who otherwise would have been entitled to performance. For example, in the case of an insurance contract that requires the insurer to rebuild the homeowner's house if it burns down, the parties' clear intent is that, in the absence of a fire, the insurer will keep the premium paid by the homeowner and the homeowner will receive nothing from the insurer. It would seem quite strange if, in the absence of fire, the homeowner were to assert that he was harmed by the fact that he received nothing from the insurer.

In some circumstances, however, the failure of a relatively minor condition—often but not always a promissory condition—may threaten to impose a significant hardship on the party expecting a subsequent performance. Imagine, for example, that the homeowner's insurance contract contains a promissory condition requiring the annual premium to be paid no later than January 1, that the homeowner's payment arrives on January 2, and that all other potential insurers charge far higher premiums than the parties' contract price. If the failure of the condition means that the insurer need not provide coverage, the cost suffered by the customer might be viewed as incommensurate with the small oversight.

The "material breach" doctrine provides that one party's breach of a promissory condition discharges the non-breaching party's subsequent duty only if the breach is *material*. If the breach is not material, the non-breaching party retains the right to sue for any damages caused by the breach but must nonetheless perform its subsequent duties as if the condition had been satisfied. See Rest. (2d) Contracts § 229. Similarly, under the doctrine of "substantial performance," incomplete but *substantial* performance of a promissory condition requires the performance of the other party, whose duty is depending on the satisfaction of the condition, although the injured party may be entitled to damages for harm caused by the breach. Rest. (2d) Contracts § 237. Both of these parallel doctrines prevent what might otherwise be seen as disproportionate forfeitures that would result if a relatively minor breach by one party were to allow the non-breaching party to suspend a much more significant or valuable performance.

The material breach and substantial performance doctrines raise two difficult questions. The more obvious of these is what exactly makes the failure of a condition significant enough to be "material" or "substantial?" Also important is whether these doctrines provide only default rules, which the parties can avoid if they wish to by drafting their contracts to require *precise* performance.

The Uniform Commercial Code (UCC) takes a different approach than the common law of contracts on the question of what quality of performance the seller of goods must provide in order to satisfy the condition of a buyer's payment. Under what is known as the "perfect tender" rule, the UCC grants the buyer thc right to reject goods that do not conform exactly to contractual requirements. The UCC dilutes the potential harshness of the perfect tender rule, however, by allowing the seller to correct any breach if time remains for performance under the contract.

Restatement (Second) of Contracts § 229. Excuse of a Condition to Avoid Forfeiture

To the extent that the non-occurrence of a condition would cause disproportionate forfeiture, a court may excuse the non-occurrence of that condition unless its occurrence was a material part of the agreed exchange.

Restatement (Second) of Contracts § 237. Effect on Other Party's Duties of a Failure to Render Performance

Except as stated in § 240, it is a condition of each party's remaining duties to render performances to be exchanged under an exchange of promises that there be no uncured material failure by the other party to render any such performance due at an earlier time.

Comment:

a. Effect of non-occurrence of condition. Under the rule stated in this Section, a material failure of performance, including defective performance as well as an absence of performance, operates as the non-occurrence of a condition. Under § 225, the non-occurrence of a condition has two possible effects on the duty subject to that condition. The first is that of preventing performance of the duty from becoming due, at least temporarily (§ 225(1)). The second is that of discharging the duty when the condition can no longer occur (§ 225(2)). A material failure of performance has, under this Section, these effects on the other party's remaining duties of performance with respect to the exchange. It prevents performance of those duties from becoming due, at least temporarily, and it discharges those duties if it has not been cured during the time in which performance can occur. The occurrence of conditions of the type dealt with in this Section is required out of a sense of fairness rather than as a result of the agreement of the parties. Such conditions are therefore sometimes referred to as "constructive conditions of exchange.". . .

b. First material failure of performance. In many disputes over failure of performance, both parties fail to finish performance, and the question is whether one of them is justified in so doing by the other party's failure. This Section states the fundamental rule under which that question is to be answered. . . . The rule is based on the principle that where performances are to be exchanged under an exchange of promises, each party is entitled to the assurance that he will not be called upon to perform his remaining duties of performance with respect to the expected exchange if there has already been an uncured material failure of performance by the other party. The central problem is in determining which party is chargeable with the first uncured material failure of performance.

d. Substantial performance. In an important category of disputes over failure of performance, one party asserts the right to payment on the ground that he has completed his performance, while the other party refuses to pay on the ground that there is an uncured material failure of performance.) A typical example is that of the building contractor who claims from the owner payment of the unpaid balance under a construction contract. In such cases it is common to state the issue, not in terms of whether there has been an uncured material failure by the contractor, but in terms of whether there has been substantial performance by him. This manner of stating the issue does not change its substance, however, and the rule stated in this Section also applies to such cases. If there has been substantial although not full performance, the building contractor has a claim for the unpaid balance and the owner has a claim only for damages. If there has not been substantial performance, the building contractor has no claim for the unpaid balance, although he may have a claim in restitution (§ 374). The considerations in determining whether performance is substantial are those listed in § 241 for determining whether a failure is material. . . .If, however, the parties have made an event a condition of their agreement, there is no mitigating standard of materiality or substantiality applicable to the non-occurrence of that event. If, therefore, the agreement makes full performance a condition, substantial performance is not sufficient and if relief is to be had under the contract, it must be through excuse of the non-occurrence of the condition to avoid forfeiture.

Illustrations:

11. A contracts to build a house for B, for which B promises to pay \$50,000 in monthly progress payments equal to 85% of the value of the work with the balance to be paid on completion. When A completes construction, B refuses to pay the \$7,500 balance claiming that there are defects that amount to an uncured material breach. If the breach is material, A's performance is not substantial and he has no claim under the contract against B, although he may have a claim in restitution (§ 374). If the breach is not material, A's performance is said to be substantial, he has a claim under the contract against B for \$7,500, and B has a claim against A for damages because of the defects.

CASES

JACOB & YOUNGS V. KENT

Court of Appeals of New York
230 N.Y. 239 (1921)

CARDOZO, J.

The plaintiff built a country residence for the defendant at a cost of upwards of \$77,000, and now sues to recover a balance of \$3,483.46, remaining unpaid. The work of construction ceased in June, 1914, and the defendant then began to occupy the dwelling. There was no complaint of defective performance until March, 1915. One of the specifications for the plumbing work provides that "all wrought iron pipe must be well galvanized, lap welded pipe of the grade known as 'standard pipe' of Reading manufacture." The defendant learned in March, 1915, that some of the pipe, instead of being made in Reading, was the product of other factories. The plaintiff was accordingly directed by the architect to do the work anew. The plumbing was then encased within the walls except in a few places where it had to be exposed. Obedience to the order meant more than the substitution of other pipe. It meant the demolition at great expense of substantial parts of the completed structure. The plaintiff left the work untouched, and asked for a certificate that the final payment was due. Refusal of the certificate was followed by this suit.

The evidence sustains a finding that the omission of the prescribed brand of pipe was neither fraudulent nor willful. It was the result of the oversight and inattention of the plaintiff's subcontractor. Reading pipe is distinguished from Cohoes pipe and other brands only by the name of the manufacturer stamped upon it at intervals of between six and seven feet.

Even the defendant's architect, though he inspected the pipe upon arrival, failed to notice the discrepancy. The plaintiff tried to show that the brands installed, though made by other manufacturers, were the same in quality, in appearance, in market value and in cost as the brand stated in the contract—that they were, indeed, the same thing, though manufactured in another place. The evidence was excluded, and a verdict directed for the defendant. The Appellate Division reversed, and granted a new trial.

We think the evidence, if admitted, would have supplied some basis for the inference that the defect was insignificant in its relation to the project. The courts never say that one who makes a contract fills the measure of his duty by less than full performance. They do say, however, that an omission, both trivial and innocent, will sometimes be atoned for by allowance of the resulting damage, and will not always be the breach of a condition to be followed by a forfeiture. The distinction is akin to that between dependent and independent promises, or between promises and conditions. Some promises are so plainly independent that they can never by fair construction be conditions of one another. Others are so plainly dependent that they must always be conditions. Others, though dependent and thus conditions when there is departure in point of substance, will be viewed as independent and collateral when the departure is insignificant. Considerations partly of justice and partly of presumable intention are to tell us whether this or that promise shall be placed in one class or in another. The simple and the uniform will call for different remedies from the multifarious and the intricate. The margin of departure within the range of normal expectation upon a sale of common chattels will vary from the margin to be expected upon a contract for the construction of a mansion or a "skyscraper." There will be harshness sometimes and oppression in the implication of a condition when the thing upon which labor has been expended is incapable of surrender because united to the land, and equity and reason in the implication of a like condition when the subject-matter, if defective, is in shape to be returned. From the conclusion that promises may not be treated as dependent to the extent of their uttermost minutiae without a sacrifice of justice, the progress is a short one to the conclusion that they may not be so treated without a perversion of intention. Intention not otherwise revealed may be presumed to hold in contemplation the reasonable and probable. If something else is in view, it must not be left to implication. There will be no assumption of a purpose to visit venial faults with oppressive retribution.

Those who think more of symmetry and logic in the development of legal rules than of practical adaptation to the attainment of a just result will be troubled by a classification where the lines of division are so wavering and blurred. Something, doubtless, may be said on the score of consistency and certainty in favor of a stricter standard. The courts have balanced such considerations against those of equity and fairness, and found the latter to be the weightier. The decisions in this state commit us to the liberal view, which is making its way, nowadays, in jurisdictions slow to welcome it. Where the line is to be drawn between the important and the trivial cannot be settled by a formula. "In the nature of the case precise boundaries are impossible." Williston on Contracts. The same omission may take on one aspect or another according to its setting. Substitution of equivalents may not have the same significance in fields of art on the one side and in those of mere utility on the other. Nowhere will change be tolerated, however, if it is so dominant or pervasive as in any real or substantial measure to frustrate the purpose of the contract. There is no general license to install whatever, in the builder's judgment, may be regarded as "just as good." The question is one of degree. . . .We must weigh the purpose to be served, the desire to be gratified, the excuse for deviation from the letter, the cruelty of enforced adherence. Then only can we tell whether literal fulfilment is to be implied by law as a condition. This is not to say that the parties are not free by apt and certain words to effectuate a purpose that performance of every term shall be a condition of recovery. That question is not here. This is merely to say that the law will be slow to impute the purpose, in the silence of the parties, where the significance of the default is grievously out of proportion to the oppression of the forfeiture. The willful transgressor must accept the penalty of his transgression. For him there is no occasion to mitigate the rigor of implied conditions. The transgressor whose default is unintentional and trivial may hope for mercy if he will offer atonement for his wrong.

In the circumstances of this case, we think the measure of the allowance is not the cost of replacement, which would be great, but the difference in value, which would be either nominal or nothing. It is true that in most cases the cost of replacement is the measure. The owner is entitled to the money which will permit him to complete, unless the cost of completion is grossly and unfairly out of proportion to the good to be attained. When that is true, the measure is the difference in value. Specifications call, let us say, for a foundation built of granite quarried in Vermont. On the completion of the building, the owner learns that through the blunder of a subcontractor part of the foundation has been built of granite of the same quality quarried in New Hampshire. The measure of allowance is not the cost of reconstruction.

. . .

The order should be affirmed, and judgment absolute directed in favor of the plaintiff upon the stipulation, with costs in all courts.

MCLAUGHLIN, J. (dissenting).

I dissent. The plaintiff did not perform its contract. Its failure to do so was either intentional or due to gross neglect which, under the uncontradicted facts, amounted to the same thing, nor did it make any proof of the cost of compliance, where compliance was possible.

Under its contract it obligated itself to use in the plumbing only pipe (between 2,000 and 2,500 feet) made by the Reading Manufacturing Company. The first pipe delivered was about 1,000 feet and the plaintiff's superintendent then called the attention of the foreman of the subcontractor, who was doing the plumbing, to the fact that the specifications annexed to the contract required all pipe used in the plumbing to be of the Reading Manufacturing Company. They then examined it for the purpose of ascertaining whether this delivery was of that manufacture and found it was. Thereafter, as pipe was required in the progress of the work, the foreman of the subcontractor would leave word at its shop that he wanted a specified number of feet of pipe, without in any way indicating of what manufacture. Pipe would thereafter be delivered and installed in the building, without any examination whatever. Indeed, no examination, so far as appears, was made by the plaintiff, the subcontractor, defendant's architect, or any one else, of any of the pipe except the first delivery, until after the building had been completed. Plaintiff's architect then refused to give the certificate of completion, upon which the final payment depended, because all of the pipe used in the plumbing was not of the kind called for by the contract. After such refusal, the subcontractor removed the covering or insulation from about 900 feet of pipe which was exposed in the basement, cellar and attic, and all but 70 feet was found to have been manufactured, not by the Reading Company, but by other manufacturers, some by the Cohoes Rolling Mill Company, some by the National Steel Works, some by the South Chester Tubing Company, and some which bore no manufacturer's mark at all. The balance of the pipe had been so installed in the building that an inspection of it could not be had without demolishing, in part at least, the building itself.

I am of the opinion the trial court was right in directing a verdict for the defendant. The plaintiff agreed that all the pipe used should be of the Reading Manufacturing Company. Only about two-fifths of it, so far as appears, was of that kind. The question of substantial performance of a contract of the character of the one under consideration depends in no small degree upon the good faith of the contractor. If the plaintiff had intended to, and had complied with the terms of the contract except as to minor omissions, due to inadvertence, then he might be allowed to recover the contract price, less the amount necessary to fully compensate the defendant for damages caused by such omissions. But that is not this case. It installed between 2,000 and 2,500 feet of pipe, of which only 1,000 feet at most complied with the contract. No explanation was given why pipe called for by the contract was not used, nor was any effort made to show what it would cost to remove the pipe of other manufacturers and install that of the Reading Manufacturing Company. The defendant had a right to contract for what he wanted. He had a right before making payment to get what the contract called for. It is no answer to this suggestion to say that the pipe put in was just as good as that made by the Reading Manufacturing Company, or that the difference in value between such pipe and the pipe made by the Reading Manufacturing Company would be either "nominal or nothing." Defendant contracted for pipe made by the Reading Manufacturing Company. What his reason was for requiring this kind of pipe is of no importance. He wanted that and was entitled to it. It may have been a mere whim on his part, but even so, he had a right to this kind of pipe, regardless of whether some other kind, according to the opinion of the contractor or experts, would have been "just as good, better, or done just as well." He agreed to pay only upon condition that the pipe installed were made by that company and he ought not to be compelled to pay unless that condition be performed. The rule, therefore, of substantial performance, with damages for unsubstantial omissions, has no application.

HISCOCK, Ch. J., HOGAN and CRANE, JJ., concur with CARDOZO, J.; POUND and ANDREWS, JJ., concur with MCLAUGHLIN, J.

MAXTON BUILDERS, INC. V. LO GALBO

Court of Appeals of New York
68 N.Y.2d 373 (1986)

WATCHLER, C.J.

. . .

In 1983 the defendants contracted to purchase a newly constructed house from the plaintiff for $210,000. At the contract signing on August 3, the defendants gave the plaintiff a check for $21,000 as a down payment to be held in escrow. A handwritten rider, included in the contract at the defendants' request, provided: "If real estate taxes are in excess of $3,500 based on a full assessment of house sold for $210,000.00, buyer shall have the right to cancel this contract upon written notice to the seller within three days of date and escrow funds to be returned."

The following day defendant Cynthia Lo Galbo and plaintiff's president, Scott Seeman, went to the county tax assessor's office to obtain an estimate of the taxes on the new house. The assessment was in excess of $3,500.

The defendants' attorney then called the plaintiff's counsel and informed him that the defendants had decided to exercise their option to cancel. He also sent a certified letter to the defendants' attorney informing him in writing of the defendants' decision to cancel. The letter was mailed on Friday August 5 and was received by plaintiff's attorney on August 9.

Several days later plaintiff's attorney also received a bank notice that defendants had stopped payment on their check.

On September 20, 1983, the plaintiff commenced this action against the defendants to recover the amount of the down payment claiming that the defendants breached the contract when they stopped payment on the check. . . .

On this appeal the defendants again urge that their refusal to perform did not constitute a breach because they had reserved and adequately exercised a right to terminate. Although the plaintiff did not receive written notice of termination within three days, as the contract required, the defendants contend that this is not fatal when, as here, the contract does not provide that time is of the essence. The defendants argue that under these circumstances all that is required is reasonable notice and that this requirement was met here when the defendants mailed the notice and gave the plaintiff's attorney actual oral notice within the three-day period. It is settled, however, that when a contract requires that written notice be given within a specified time, the notice is ineffective unless the writing is actually received within the time prescribed (*see, Peabody v. Satterlee*, 166 N.Y. 174, 59 N.E. 818; *Kantrowitz v. Dairymen's League Co-op. Assn.*, 272 App. Div. 470, 71 N.Y.S.2d 821, *aff'd* 297 N.Y. 991, 80 N.E.2d 366; *cf. Sy Jack Realty Co. v. Pergament Syosset Corp.*, 27 N.Y.2d 449, 318 N.Y.S.2d 720, 267 N.E.2d 462). In short, the defendants bargained for and obtained a limited right to cancel which they failed to exercise within the time agreed upon. The cancellation was, therefore, ineffective and the defendants' refusal to perform constituted a breach (*Morgan & Brother Manhattan Stor. Co. v. Balin*, 39 N.Y.2d 848, 386 N.Y.S.2d 100, 351 N.E.2d 748).

. . .

SAHADI V. CONTINENTAL ILLINOIS NAT'L BANK & TRUST CO. OF CHICAGO

United States Court of Appeals, Seventh Circuit
706 F.2d 193 (1983)

HARLINGTON WOOD, JR., J.

This is an appeal from the district court's order granting partial summary judgment in favor of the defendant-appellee Continental Illinois Bank (the Bank) in an action alleging that the Bank breached its agreement with the plaintiff-appellant's business, Great Lakes and European Lines, Inc. (GLE), by calling a $7 million loan when GLE tendered interest payments less than one day after they were due. . . .

I.

Viewing the facts in the light most favorable to the plaintiffs, as we must, there emerges a story of financial brinkmanship and opaque dealing in which neither side emerges wholly blameless. GLE, an international shipping line, began its relationship with the Bank in 1976 with a $3 million loan, personally guaranteed by the Sahadis. The Bank increased its loan commitment to $11 million in 1977, a commitment upon which GLE relied in expanding its business, but which was repudiated by the Bank, to the detriment of GLE, when personal and institutional friction developed between the parties. The parties quickly reached a stalemate, with GLE threatening to sue the Bank for breach of its loan commitment and the Bank threatening to call the loans already extended. Meanwhile, GLE successfully interested another lender which conditioned its backing on GLE's settlement of its differences with the Bank.

Negotiations ensued in which, the evidence indicated, the Bank primarily sought to obtain release from the Sahadis and GLE of their claims stemming from the Bank's purported breach of its loan commitment, and to obtain further collateral from the Sahadis to secure their guarantee of the outstanding loan. The Bank also sought to have GLE's outstanding interest payments, which had been withheld during the several months of the dispute, brought up to date.

The negotiations resulted in two agreements executed on October 25, 1977. One agreement [stated:]

> 1. [The Bank] hereby agrees to forbear from demanding payment of the Liabilities during the period ending December 31, 1977, except for payment of current interest thereon as more fully set forth in clause (i) of paragraph 3 below.

The agreement went on to state:

> 3. Notwithstanding the foregoing, [the Bank] may demand payment in full of the Liabilities prior to December 31, 1977 if. . .(i) [GLE] shall fail to make payment of interest accrued on the Liabilities through September 30, 1977 on or before November 15, 1977.

This latter paragraph, as initially drafted, provided for October 7, 1977 as the deadline for the payment of accrued interest. This date was changed to November 15, 1977 at Sahadi's request with no objection by the Bank; moreover, there was no evidence that the precise date on which accrued interest was to be paid was ever a point of contention in the negotiations.

. . .

Sahadi was reminded by a subordinate on November 14 of the November 15 interest payment date, but Sahadi responded that the payment should be delayed so that GLE monies in Chicago would be available to satisfy other immediate liabilities. As Sahadi noted in his affidavit, "There was no great significance attached to the payment of interest in this covenant; it did not occur to us that the bank would treat the interest payment date any differently than it had treated previous payment dates." On the morning of November 16, a GLE representative was queried by the Bank as to whether the interest payments had been made; when the GLE representative responded negatively but indicated that the payment would be made by the end of the week, the Bank representative responded that the matter could be discussed later that day. At that later meeting, the Bank presented the surprised GLE representative with notification that the loan was called. The GLE representative immediately offered to tender payment for the due interest from the company's account with the Bank, but the Bank refused. The calling of the loan destroyed GLE and subjected the Sahadis to liability on the personal guarantee.

The Sahadis, indirectly as assignees of GLE, thereafter filed this action against the Bank, seeking release from their personal guarantee agreement and damages for the destruction of GLE. Chiefly, they contended that GLE's brief delay in tender of the November 15 interest payment did not amount to a "material" breach of the October 25 agreements justifying the Bank's cessation of forbearance. . . .

. . .

II.

. . .

It is black letter law in Illinois and elsewhere that only a "material" breach of a contract provision by one party will justify non-performance by the other party. *See Janssen Bros. v. Northbrook Trust and Savings Bank*, 12 Ill. App. 3d 840, 299 N.E.2d 431, 434 (2d Dist. 1973); *Herbert Shaffer Associates, Inc. v. First Bank of Oak Park*, 30 Ill. App. 3d 647, 332 N.E.2d 703, 710 (1st Dist. 1975); *Anderson v. Long Grove Country Club Estates*, 111 Ill. App. 2d 127, 249 N.E.2d 343, 349 (2d Dist. 1969); *Wright v. Douglas Furniture Corp.*, 98 Ill. App. 2d 137, 240 N.E.2d 259, 262 (1st Dist. 1968); *See also C.G. Caster Co. v. Regan*, 88 Ill. App. 3d 280, 43 Ill. Dec. 422, 426, 410 N.E.2d 422–426 (1st Dist. 1980); *John Kubinski & Sons, Inc. v. Dockside Development Corp.*, 33 Ill. App. 3d 1015, 339 N.E.2d 529, 534 (1st Dist. 1975); 5 *Williston on Contracts* §§ 675, 805 (3d ed. 1961); Restatement (Second) of Contracts § 229 (1979). Moreover, the determination of "materiality" is a complicated question of fact, involving an inquiry into such matters as whether the breach worked to defeat the bargained-for objective of the parties or caused disproportionate prejudice to the non-breaching party, whether custom and usage considers such a breach to be material, and whether the allowance of reciprocal non-performance by the non-breaching party will result in his accrual of an unreasonable or unfair advantage. *Wright*, 240 N.E.2d at 262; *Anderson*, 249 N.E.2d at 349; *C.G. Caster Co.*, 43 Ill. Dec. at 426, 410 N.E.2d at 426; *National Importing & Trading Co. v. E.A. Bear Co.*, 324 Ill. 346, 155 N.E. 343, 346 (1927); *Cantrell v. Kruck*, 25 Ill. App. 3d 1060, 324 N.E.2d 260, 263 (2d Dist. 1975); *Janssen Bros.*, 299 N.E.2d at 433. All of these issues must be resolved with reference to the intent of the parties as evidenced in large part by the full circumstances of the transaction, thus making these issues especially unsuited to resolution by summary judgment. *Conrad v. Delta Airlines, Inc.*, 494 F.2d 914, 918 (7th Cir. 1974); *Janssen Bros.*, 299 N.E.2d at 433.

The need for a complete factual inquiry into the underlying circumstances and commercial custom is especially acute where, as here, the purportedly breaching party claims that time was not of the essence of the contract. Even where the contract contains a provision, not present here, explicitly stipulating that "time is of the essence," the Illinois courts will inquire into the situation of the parties and the underlying circumstances to determine whether a delay in performance resulted in a "material" breach. *Janssen Bros.*, 299 N.E.2d at 434; *John Kubinski & Sons, Inc.*, 339 N.E.2d at 531, 534; *Cantrell*, 324 N.E.2d at 263. *See also* 3A *Corbin on Contracts* § 715 (1960); 6 *Williston on Contracts* § 846 (1961); Restatement (Second) of Contracts § 229 (1979). The record in the case at bar discloses evidence that would permit a trier of fact to find that payment of the interest due precisely on November 15 was *not* "of the essence" of the agreement from the Bank's point of view. For example, Sahadi himself was allowed unilaterally to choose the payment date, and there was no contention in negotiations over the fixing of that date; the prejudice to the Bank's rights stemming from a payment delay of several hours was *de minimis* in view of the Bank's retention of the enhanced collateralization, its retention of the complete release of legal claims stemming from the reneged-upon loan commitment, and the Bank's clear knowledge that GLE had on hand in the Bank, and tendered, funds sufficient to satisfy the interest requirement; the Bank had previously accepted late payments in its course of dealings with GLE; and there was evidence that calling a loan for such a brief delay was without precedent in the banking community. Significantly, even the Bank conceded at oral argument on appeal, "The important thing. . .is not the date of the fifteenth in that sense; it's the fact of the promise." Whether or not these facts would be sufficient to prove non-materiality in light of all the other evidence adduced at trial, they at least raise a genuine issue as to whether the "promise" was in any important way defeated by the hours of delay in tender of payment. Indeed, it would be difficult to posit a set of alleged facts making summary resolution of the issue of "materiality" in favor of the defendant less appropriate.

The Bank. . .argues, the contract before us presents a uniquely attractive case for the rigid and summary application of time requirements because it contains a specific provision allowing the cessation of the Bank's forbearance if interest was not paid on or before November 15, 1977. However, this argument merely assumes what it seeks to prove: that the payment of interest on precisely the named date was an essential part of that specific provision, and that whether the precise day of payment was essential can be determined without the benefit of a full inquiry at trial.

The Illinois courts have rightly spurned such conclusory logic. In *Janssen Bros. v. Northbrook Trust & Savings Bank*, 12 Ill. App. 3d 840, 299 N.E.2d 431 (2d Dist. 1973), for example, a real estate contract specifically provided that time was of the essence and that if certain payments were not made by the named date, certain deeds would be automatically recorded and the purchase price refunded. 299 N.E.2d at 432. Notwithstanding this explicit recitation of the consequences of late payment, the court refused to undertake a wooden reading of the provision, let alone to do so through a summary procedure. Noting that even where the parties clearly intended to regard a specific payment date as crucial, "equity will refuse to enforce such a provision when to do so would be unconscionable or would give one party an unfair advantage over the other," *id.* at 434, the court also underscored that "summary procedure is not. . .suited to situations in which substantial questions are present relating to the formation and terms of a settlement agreement or its construction, and evidence or testimony is required to satisfactorily resolve the issue," *id.* at 433. *Accord Elliott v. Snyder*, 246 S.C. 186, 143 S.E.2d 374, 375, 376 (1965). . . .

The Bank contends alternatively that no room for a "materiality" analysis and its concomitant factual inquiry exists here because the payment of the interest on or before November 15 was an "express condition" of the Bank's forbearance, and thus its terms were required to be exactly fulfilled. This second argument, like the Bank's first, suffers from its conclusory assumption of what it seeks to prove—that the payment of the interest on the precise named date rather than payment of the interest in a reasonably prompt manner was of threshold importance to the completion of the contract. In short, asking whether a provision is a "condition" is similar to stating the "materiality" question: both seek to determine whether its performance was a *sine qua non* of the contract's fulfillment. And that determination may not be made through a mechanical process.

In general, contractual terms are presumed to represent independent promises rather than conditions. 3A *Corbin on Contracts* § 635 (1960); 5 *Williston on Contracts* §§ 665, 666 (1961). Determining whether this presumption may be upset entails a full inquiry into the "intention of the parties and the good sense of the case" including such factors as whether the protected party can achieve its principal goal without literal performance of the contractual provision. *Foreman State Trust and*

Savings Bank v. Tauber, 348 Ill. 280, 180 N.E. 827, 831, 832 (1932); *Palmer v. Meriden Britannia Co.*, 188 Ill. 508, 59 N.E. 247, 252 (1900). So reluctant are courts to elevate a term to the status of a condition that the factual inquiry will often be undertaken in spite of the existence of explicit language, not present here, creating liability only "on condition" of the occurrence of a required, prior act. *Rooks Creek Evangelical Lutheran Church v. First Lutheran Church*, 290 Ill. 133, 129 N.E. 793, 795 (1919); 5 *Williston on Contracts* § 665 (1961) ("Especially words literally appropriate for conditions have not been given their natural meaning where the consequence would lead to injustice and a violation of the probable intent of the parties."). The Bank points to a confirmatory telex message from Sahadi stating that the Bank's forbearance was to be "on condition" that interest was paid by the named date, but such evidence is but one tile in the evidentiary mosaic; the law requires that the Sahadis be given the opportunity to present evidence that the parties only considered the payment of the interest, not its payment by an exact hour, to be the relevant "condition," if, indeed, that term as used in the telex is to be given its formal legal meaning. The Sahadis have been denied this opportunity by the district court's summary disposition.

Moreover, even if the payment of interest by the named date could be summarily construed as a necessary "condition," the district court would *still* be required to conduct a full-ranging factual inquiry into whether that condition had been "materially" breached or whether the technical breach was without "pecuniary importance." 5 *Williston on Contracts* § 805 at 839–40 (1961). Restatement (Second) of Contracts § 229 (1979) ("To the extent that the non-occurrence of a condition would cause disproportionate forfeiture, a court may excuse the non-occurrence of that condition unless its occurrence was a material part of the agreed exchange."); *see also* Restatement (Second) of Contracts § 229, Illustrations 3 and 4 (demonstrating that day-late payments are not "material" breaches). At either level of the "promise/condition" analysis, then, summary judgment would not be appropriate in this case.

. . .

REVERSED AND REMANDED.

DISCUSSION PROBLEMS

1. Failure to Close

Real estate developer Ocean Atlantic Woodland Corp. contracted to purchase a parcel of Illinois farmland from Elda Arnhold and John Argoudelis. A series of disputes and attempts at renegotiation caused years of delays in finalizing the transaction and, eventually, litigation between the parties. Ultimately, the parties settled that lawsuit by agreeing to some substantive revisions to the contract, as well as the following provision concerning the time for closing the sale:

> "If Ocean Atlantic, for any reason whatsoever, fails to close on the property within 90 days from the execution of [the] settlement document, it shall forfeit any and all rights it may have to purchase the property."

Soon after this settlement agreement was signed, Ocean Atlantic provided notice that it intended to close on January 24, 2001, one day before the end of the 90-day period. Ocean Atlantic's lender demanded additional documents at the last minute, however, resulting in the company failing to close on January 24 or 25. When Ocean Atlantic tendered payment on January 26—one day late—the sellers refused accept the payment and tender the property. Ocean Atlantic sued. Was the sellers' duty discharged, or is Ocean Atlantic entitled to enforce the agreement?

2. The Cramped Living Room

Eugene Plante built a new house for the Jacobs family according to a "stock" floor plan with minor individualized modifications. Failing to precisely follow the floorplan that he had provided, Plante placed the wall between the living room and kitchen such that the living room was one foot narrower than set out in the plan and the kitchen one foot wider. The Jacobses then refused to make the last in a series of progress payments, which was approximately one-fifth of the contract price, and Plante sued. At trial, Plante provided expert testimony, which the Jacobses did not dispute, that the misplacement of the wall would not affect the market value of the house if and when the Jacobses were to sell. Were the Jacobses legally justified in withholding the final payment?

3. Insurance Coverage

When George Murphy terminated the lease for his dental office and moved out, the owner of the property sued him for damage caused to the premises. Two years after that lawsuit was instituted, Murphy sought coverage from his insurance carrier, Chubb. Chubb denied coverage, and when Murphy sued Chubb, the insurer filed a motion to dismiss on the ground Murphy failed to satisfy the insurance contract's notice provision, which stated that, "[i]n the event of an occurrence, written notice. . .shall be given by or for the insured to the company. . .as soon as practicable." Should the court grant Chubb's motion to dismiss?

CHAPTER 20

UNANTICIPATED CIRCUMSTANCES

■ ■ ■

INTRODUCTION

Contracts often serve to allocate risks between parties for events or circumstances that might or might not occur in the future. But what happens when the future transpires in ways that the parties did not anticipate, and this increases the costs of performing contractual duties or decreases the value provided by the contract?

Unexpected events occur every day, often disappointing the expectations of a contracting party. If an oil refinery contracts to purchase oil for delivery in six months from a drilling company for a price of $100 per barrel, an unexpected increase in gasoline consumption that increases the spot market price for oil could make the drilling company unhappy with the terms of the contract. An unexpected decrease in driving that reduces demand for gasoline could mean that the refinery finds itself obligated to purchase more oil than it can profitably use, making the refinery unhappy. But such common events do not release either party from their contractual obligations. By agreeing to future obligations, sellers implicitly accept the risk that the price of inputs or the demand for its goods and services might increase, and buyers implicitly accept the risk that its need or desire for those goods and services might decline in the intervening time.

The doctrines of "impracticability" (sometimes also referred to as "impossibility") and "frustration of purpose" can be invoked to excuse the performance of contractual duties, however, in a relatively circumscribed subset of situations in which a supervening event causes disappointment. In these situations, both doctrines can be understood as imposing on contracts a constructive condition of performance that the unanticipated event in question does not occur. If the event does occur, the buyer is excused from tendering payment, or the seller is excused from providing goods and services.

What situations justify excusing express duties? In the language of the Restatement, the non-occurrence of the event in question must be a "basic assumption" of the contract. Additionally, the occurrence of the event must not be the fault of the adversely affected party. Importantly, the excuse doctrines may be invoked only when the contract does not explicitly or implicitly allocate the risk of the unanticipated development to one of the parties. See Rest. (2d) Contracts §§ 261, 263. This means that these doctrines should be understood as creating default conditions that the parties are free to contract around. For example, even if a contractor might otherwise be excused from meeting a deadline if he or she suffers an illness on the ground that good health was a "basic assumption" of the contract, a contract term specifying that illness is not an excuse for delay will be enforced.

When a supervening event renders performance difficult for sellers of goods or services, they may attempt to invoke the doctrine of impracticability. *Taylor v. Caldwell* typifies a classic claim involving the physical destruction of the contract's subject matter. Should the owner of a theater be excused from its contractual duties to renters when the building burns down? Notice that what is at stake in the case is not whether the owner must provide the theater space to its renters—the fire made this obviously impossible—but whether the owner must compensate a renting theater troupe for the losses it suffers as a result.

While unanticipated events can, theoretically, give rise to a claim of "impracticability" for buyers, supervening events usually do not render contractual performance itself unusually difficult for buyers. More often, the problem for buyers is that the unanticipated event reduces the value of executing a contract. For this reason, the proper claim for buyers is usually "frustration of purpose": specifically, that their duty to perform should be discharged because the purpose for which they entered into an agreement no longer exists.

Krell v. Henry provides an excellent example of such a claim. A person who contracts to rent an apartment from which to view the coronation parade of the King of England is still just as able to pay the rental fee when the King's illness causes the event to be canceled; the problem is that he would obtain no value from doing so. Should the renter be excused from performing his contractual duty? *NIPSCO v. Carbon Coal* considers the extent to which unanticipated events should be evaluated differently if the parties have included what is known as a "*force majeure*" clause in their contract.

When the doctrines of impracticability or frustration of purpose are successfully invoked, the harmed party is usually entitled to rescission of the contract, excusing both parties from the performance of further duties and entitling them to restitution of benefits previously conferred (if any). Depending on the nature of the obstacle posed by the unanticipated event, however, the complaining party might be entitled only to temporarily suspend the performance of a duty.

Restatement (Second) of Contracts § 261. Discharge by Supervening Impracticability

Where, after a contract is made, a party's performance is made impracticable without his fault by the occurrence of an event the non-occurrence of which was a basic assumption on which the contract was made, his duty to render that performance is discharged, unless the language or the circumstances indicate the contrary.

Comment:

b. Basic assumption. In order for a supervening event to discharge a duty under this Section, the non-occurrence of that event must have been a "basic assumption" on which both parties made the contract (see Introductory Note to this Chapter). This is the criterion used by Uniform Commercial Code § 2–615(a). Its application is simple enough in the cases of the death of a person or destruction of a specific thing necessary for performance. The continued existence of the person or thing (the non-occurrence of the death or destruction) is ordinarily a basic assumption on which the contract was made, so that death or destruction effects a discharge. Its application is also simple enough in the cases of market shifts or the financial inability of one of the parties. The continuation of existing market conditions and of the financial situation of the parties are ordinarily not such assumptions, so that mere market shifts or financial inability do not usually effect discharge under the rule stated in this Section. In borderline cases this criterion is sufficiently flexible to take account of factors that bear on a just allocation of risk. The fact that the event was foreseeable, or even foreseen, does not necessarily compel a conclusion that its non-occurrence was not a basic assumption.

Illustrations:

1. On June 1, A agrees to sell and B to buy goods to be delivered in October at a designated port. The port is subsequently closed by quarantine regulations during the entire month of October, no commercially reasonable substitute performance is available (see Uniform Commercial Code § 2–614(1)), and A fails to deliver the goods. A's duty to deliver the goods is discharged, and A is not liable to B for breach of contract.

2. A contracts to produce a movie for B. As B knows, A's only source of funds is a $100,000 deposit in C bank. C bank fails, and A does not produce the movie. A's duty to produce the movie is not discharged, and A is liable to B for breach of contract.

Restatement (Second) of Contracts § 263. Destruction, Deterioration or Failure to Come Into Existence of Thing Necessary for Performance

If the existence of a specific thing is necessary for the performance of a duty, its failure to come into existence, destruction, or such deterioration as makes performance impracticable is an event the non-occurrence of which was a basic assumption on which the contract was made.

Restatement (Second) of Contracts § 265. Discharge by Supervening Frustration

Where, after a contract is made, a party's principal purpose is substantially frustrated without his fault by the occurrence of an event the non-occurrence of which was a basic assumption on which the contract was made, his remaining duties to render performance are discharged, unless the language or the circumstances indicate the contrary.

Comment:

a. *Rationale*. This Section deals with the problem that arises when a change in circumstances makes one party's performance virtually worthless to the other, frustrating his purpose in making the contract. . . . The rule stated in this Section sets out the requirements for the discharge of that party's duty. First, the purpose that is frustrated must have been a principal purpose of that party in making the contract. It is not enough that he had in mind some specific object without which he would not have made the contract. The object must be so completely the basis of the contract that, as both parties understand, without it the transaction would make little sense. Second, the frustration must be substantial. It is not enough that the transaction has become less profitable for the affected party or even that he will sustain a loss. The frustration must be so severe that it is not fairly to be regarded as within the risks that he assumed under the contract. Third, the non-occurrence of the frustrating event must have been a basic assumption on which the contract was made. This involves essentially the same sorts of determinations that are involved under the general rule on impracticability. The foreseeability of the event is here, as it is there, a factor in that determination, but the mere fact that the event was foreseeable does not compel the conclusion that its non-occurrence was not such a basic assumption.

CASES

TAYLOR V. CALDWELL

Court of Queen's Bench
122 Eng. Rep. 309 (1863)

BLACKBURN, J.

In this case the plaintiffs and the defendants, on the 27th May 1861, entered into a contract by which the defendants agreed to let the plaintiffs have the use of The Surrey Gardens and Music Hall on four days then to come, viz., the 17th June, 15th July, 5th August and 19th August, for the purpose of giving a series of four grand concerts, and day and night fêtes at the Gardens and Hall on those days respectively; and the plaintiffs agreed to take the Gardens and Hall on those days, and pay 100£. for each day.

The parties inaccurately call this a "letting," and the money to be paid a "rent"; but the whole agreement is such as to shew that the defendants were to retain the possession of the Hall and Gardens so that there was to be no demise of them, and that the contract was merely to give the plaintiffs the use of them on those days. Nothing however, in our opinion, depends on this. The agreement then proceeds to set out various stipulations between the parties as to what each was to supply for these concerts and the entertainments, and as to the manner in which they should be carried on. The effect of the whole is to shew that the existence of the Music Hall in the Surrey Gardens in a state fit for a concert was essential for the fulfilment of the contract,—such entertainments as the parties contemplated in their agreement could not be given without it.

After the making of the agreement, and before the first day on which a concert was to be given, the hall was destroyed by fire. This destruction, we must take it on the evidence, was without fault of either party, and was so complete that in consequence the concerts could not be given as intended. And the question we have to decide is whether, under these circumstances, the loss which the plaintiffs have sustained is to fall upon the defendants. The parties when framing their agreement evidently had not present to their minds the possibility of such a disaster, and have made no express stipulation with reference to it, so that the answer to the question must depend on the general rules of law applicable to such a contract.

There seems no doubt that where there is a positive contract to do a thing, not in itself unlawful, the contractor must perform it or pay damages for not doing it, although in consequence of unforeseen accident, the performance of his contract has become unexpectedly burdensome, or even impossible. . . .But this rule is only applicable when the contract is positive and absolute, and not subject to any condition either expressed or implied;

and there are authorities which, as we think, establish the principle that where, from the nature of the contract, it appears that the parties must from the beginning have known that it could not be fulfilled unless when the time for the fulfilment of the contract arrived some particular specified thing continued to exist, so that, when entering into the contract they must have contemplated such continuing existence as the foundation of what was to be done; there, in the absence of any expressed or implied warranty that the thing shall exist, the contract is not to be construed as a positive contract, but as subject to an implied condition that the parties shall be excused in case, before breach, performance becomes impossible from the perishing of the thing without default of the contractor.

There seems little doubt that this implication tends to further the great object of making the legal construction such as to fulfil the intention of those who enter into the contract. For in the course of affairs men in making such contracts in general would, if it were brought to their minds, say that there should be such a condition.

. . .

There is a class of contracts in which a person binds himself to do something which requires to be performed by him in person, and such promises, e.g. promises to marry, or promises to serve for a certain time, are never in practice qualified by an express exception of the death of the party; and therefore in such cases, the contract is in terms broken if the promisor dies before fulfillment. Yet it was very early determined that, if the performance is personal, the executors are not liable; *Hyde v. The Dean of Windsor* (Cro. Eliz. 552, 553). See 2 Wms. Exers. 1560, 5th ed., where a very apt illustration is given. "Thus," says the learned author: "if an author undertakes to compose a work, and dies before completing it, his executors are discharged from this contract: for the undertaking is merely personal in its nature, and, by the intervention of the contractor's death, has become impossible to be performed."

. . .

It seems that, in these cases, the only ground on which the parties or their executors, can be excused from the consequences of the breach of the contract is that from the nature of the contract there is an implied condition of the continued existence of the life of the contractor, and, perhaps, in the case of the painter of his eyesight. . . .

These are instances where the implied condition is of the life of a human being, but there are others in which the same implication is made as to the continued existence of a thing. . . .

It may, we think, be safely asserted to be now English law, that in all contracts of loan of chattels or bailments if the performance of the promise of the borrower or bailee to return the things lent or bailed, becomes impossible because it has perished, this impossibility (if not arising from the fault of the borrower or bailee from some risk which he has taken upon himself) excuses the borrower or bailee from the performance of his promise to redeliver the chattel.

. . .

In none of these cases is the promise in words other than positive, nor is there any express stipulation that the destruction of the person or thing shall excuse the performance; but that excuse is by law implied, because from the nature of the contract it is apparent that the parties contracted on the basis of the continued existence of the particular person or chattel. In the present case, looking at the whole contract, we find that the parties contracted on the basis of the continued existence of the Music Hall at the time when the concerts were to be given, that being essential to their performance.

We think, therefore, that, the Music Hall having ceased to exist, without fault of either party, both parties are excused, the plaintiffs from taking the gardens and paying the money, the defendants from performing their promise to give the use of the Hall and Gardens and other things. Consequently the rule must be absolute to enter the verdict for the defendants.

Rule absolute.

KRELL V. HENRY

G.B. Court of Appeal
All E.R. Rep. 20 (1903)

VAUGHAN WILLIAMS, L.J.

The real question in this case is the extent of the application in English law of the principle of the Roman law which has been adopted and acted on in many English decisions, and notably in *Taylor v. Caldwell.* That case at least makes it clear that "where, from the nature of the contract, it appears that the parties must from the beginning have known that it could not be fulfilled unless, when the time for the fulfilment of the contract arrived, some particular specified thing continued to exist, so that when entering into the contract they must have contemplated such continuing existence as the foundation of what was to be done; there, in the absence of any express or implied warranty that the thing shall exist, the contract is not to be construed as a positive contract, but as subject to an implied condition that the parties shall be excused in case, before breach, performance becomes impossible from the perishing of the thing without default of the contractor."

. . .[T]he English law applies the principle not only to cases where the performance of the contract becomes impossible by the cessation of existence of the thing which is the subject-matter of the contract, but also to cases where the event which renders the contract incapable of performance is the cessation or nonexistence of an express condition or state of things, going to the root of the contract, and essential to its performance. It is said, on the one side, that the specified thing, state of things, or condition the continued existence of which is necessary for the fulfilment of the contract, so that the parties entering into the contract must have contemplated the continued existence of that thing, condition, or state of things as the foundation of what was to be done under the contract, is limited to things which are either the subject-matter of the contract, or a condition or state of things, present or anticipated, which are expressly mentioned in the contract. But, on the other side, it is said that the condition or state of things need not be expressly specified, but that it is sufficient if such condition or state of thing, clearly appears by extrinsic evidence to have been assumed by the parties to be the foundation or basis of the contract and the event which causes the impossibility is of such a character that it cannot reasonably be supposed to have been in the contemplation of the contracting parties when the contract was made. In such a case the contracting parties will not be held bound by general words which, though large enough to include, were not used with reference to a possibility of a particular event rendering performance of the contract impossible.

I do not think that the principle of the civil law as introduced into the English law is limited to cases in which the event causing the impossibility of performance is the destruction or non-existence of some thing which is the subject-matter of the contract or of some condition or state of things expressly specified as a condition of it. I think that you first have to ascertain, not necessarily from the terms of the contract, but if necessary from necessary inferences, drawn from surrounding circumstances recognised by both contracting parties, what is the substance of the contract, and then to ask the question whether that substantial contract needs for its foundation the assumption of the existence of a particular state of things. If it does, this will limit the operation of the general words, and in such case if the contract becomes impossible of performance by reason of the non-existence of the state of things assumed by both contracting parties, as the foundation of the contract, there will be no breach of the contract thus limited.

What are the facts of the present case? The contract is contained in two letters of 20 June 1902, which passed between the defendant and the plaintiff's agent, Mr. Cecil Bisgood. These letters do not mention the coronation, but speak merely of the taking of Mr. Krell's chambers, or, rather, of the use of them, in the daytime of 26 and 27 June 1902, for the sum of 75 pounds, 25 pounds then paid, balance 50 pounds to be paid on the 24th. But the affidavits, which by agreement between the parties are to be taken as stating the facts of the case, show that the plaintiff exhibited on his premises, third floor, 56A, Pall Mall, an announcement to the effect that windows to view the royal coronation processions were to be let, and that the defendant was induced by that announcement to apply to the housekeeper on the premises, who said that the owner was willing to let the suite of rooms for the purpose of seeing the royal procession for both days, but not nights, of 26 and 27 June. In my judgment, the use of the rooms was let and taken for the purpose of seeing the royal processions. It was not a demise of the rooms or even an agreement to let and take the rooms. It was a licence to use rooms for a particular purpose and none other. And in my judgment the taking place of those processions on the days proclaimed along the proclaimed route, which passed 56A, Pall Mall, was regarded by both contracting parties as the foundation of the contract. I think that it cannot reasonably be supposed to have been in the contemplation of the contracting parties, when the contract was made, that the coronation would not be held on the proclaimed days, or the processions not take place on those days along the proclaimed route; and I think that the words imposing on the defendant the obligation to accept and pay for the use of the rooms for the named days, although general and unconditional, were not used with reference to the possibility of the particular contingency which afterwards occurred.

It was suggested in the course of the argument that if the occurrence, on the proclaimed days, of the coronation and the processions in this case were the foundation of the contract, and if the general words are thereby limited or qualified, so that in the event of the non-occurrence of the coronation and processions along the proclaimed route they would discharge both parties from further performance of the contract, it would follow that if a cabman was engaged to take someone to Epsom on Derby-day at a suitable enhanced price for such a journey, both parties to the contract would be discharged in the contingency of the race at Epsom for some reason becoming impossible, but I do not think this follows, for I do not think that in the cab case the happening of the race would be the foundation of the contract. No doubt the purpose of the engager was to go to see the Derby, and that the price was proportionately high; but the cab had no special qualifications for the purpose which led to the selection of the cab for this particular occasion. Any other cab would have done as well. Moreover, I think that, under the cab contract, the hirer, even if the race went off, could have said: "Drive me to Epsom, I will pay you the agreed sum, you have nothing to do with the purpose for which I hired the cab"—and that if the cabman refused he would have been guilty of a breach of contract, there being nothing to qualify his promise to drive the hirer to Epsom on a particular day, whereas, in the case of the coronation, there is not merely the purpose of the hirer to see the coronation processions, but it is the coronation processions and the relative position of the rooms which is the basis of the contract as much for the lessor as the hirer; and I think that if the King, before the coronation day and after the contract, had died, the hirer could not have insisted on having the rooms on the days named. It could not in the cab case be reasonably said that seeing the Derby race was the foundation of the contract, as viewing the processions was of the licence in this case, whereas, in the present case, where the rooms were offered and taken, by reason of their peculiar suitability from the position of the rooms for a view of the coronation processions, surely the view of the coronation processions was the foundation of the contract, which is a very different thing from the purpose of the man who engaged the cab—viz, to see the race—being held to be the foundation of the contract.

Each case must be judged by its own circumstances. In each case one must ask oneself, first: What, having regard to all the circumstances, was the foundation of the contract?; secondly: Was the performance of the contract prevented?; and thirdly: Was the event which prevented the performance of the contract of such a character that it cannot reasonably be said to have been in the contemplation of the parties at the date of the contract? If all these questions arc answered in the affirmative (as I think they should be in this case) I think both parties are discharged from further performance of the contract. I think that the coronation processions were the foundation of this contract, and that the non-happening of them prevented the performance of the contract; and, secondly, I think that the non-happening of the processions, to use the words of Sir James Hannen in *Baily v. De Crespigny* (LR 4 QB at p 185) was an event "of such a character that it cannot reasonably be supposed to have been in the contemplation of the contracting parties when the contract was made, and that they are not to be held bound by general words which, though large enough to include, were not used with reference to the possibility of the particular contingency which afterwards happened."

The test seems to be, whether the event which causes the impossibility was or might have been anticipated and guarded against. It seems difficult to say, in a case where both parties anticipate the happening of an event, which anticipation in the foundation of the contract, that either party must be taken to have anticipated, and ought to have guarded against, the event which prevented the performance of the contract. . . .

NORTHERN INDIANA PUBLIC SERVICE CO. V. CARBON COUNTY COAL CO.

United States Court of Appeals, Seventh Circuit
799 F.2d 265 (1986)

POSNER, J.

These appeals bring before us various facets of a dispute between Northern Indiana Public Service Company (NIPSCO), an electric utility in Indiana, and Carbon County Coal Company, a partnership that until recently owned and operated a coal mine in Wyoming. In 1978 NIPSCO and Carbon County signed a contract whereby Carbon County agreed to sell and NIPSCO to buy approximately 1.5 million tons of coal every year for 20 years, at a price of $24 a ton subject to various provisions for escalation which by 1985 had driven the price up to $44 a ton.

NIPSCO's rates are regulated by the Indiana Public Service Commission. In 1983 NIPSCO requested permission to raise its rates to reflect increased fuel charges. Some customers of NIPSCO opposed the increase on the ground that NIPSCO could reduce its overall costs by buying more electrical power from neighboring utilities for resale to its customers and producing less of its own power. Although the Commission granted the requested increase, it directed NIPSCO, in orders issued in December 1983 and February 1984 (the "economy purchase orders"), to make a good faith effort to find, and wherever possible buy from, utilities that would sell electricity to it at prices lower than its costs of internal generation. The Commission added ominously that "the adverse effects of entering into long-term coal supply contracts which do not allow for renegotiation and are not requirement contracts, is a burden which must rest squarely on the shoulders of NIPSCO management." Actually the contract with Carbon County did provide for renegotiation of the contract price—but one-way renegotiation in favor of Carbon County; the price fixed in the contract (as adjusted from time to time in accordance with the escalator provisions) was a floor. And the contract was indeed not a requirements contract: it specified the exact amount of coal that NIPSCO must take over the 20 years during which the contract was to remain in effect. NIPSCO was eager to have an assured supply of low-sulphur coal and was therefore willing to guarantee both price and quantity.

Unfortunately for NIPSCO, however, as things turned out it was indeed able to buy electricity at prices below the costs of generating electricity from coal bought under the contract with Carbon County; and because of the "economy purchase orders," of which it had not sought judicial review, NIPSCO could not expect to be allowed by the Public Service Commission to recover in its electrical rates the costs of buying coal from Carbon County. NIPSCO therefore decided to stop accepting coal deliveries from Carbon County, at least for the time being; and on April 24, 1985, it brought this diversity suit against Carbon County in a federal district court in Indiana, seeking a declaration that it was excused from its obligations under the contract either permanently or at least until the economy purchase orders ceased preventing it from passing on the costs of the contract to its ratepayers. In support of this position it argued that. . .NIPSCO's performance was excused or suspended—either under the contract's *force majeure* clause or under the doctrines of frustration or impossibility—by reason of the economy purchase orders.

[A jury found in favor of Carbon County on its claim for breach of contract and awarded damages of $181 million. NIPSCO appealed.] . . .

The contract permits NIPSCO to stop taking delivery of coal "for any cause beyond [its] reasonable control. . .including but not limited to. . .orders or acts of civil. . .authority. . .which wholly or partly prevent. . .the utilizing. . .of the coal." This is what is known as a *force majeure* clause. See, e.g., *Northern Illinois Gas Co. v. Energy Coop., Inc.*, 122 Ill. App. 3d 940, 949–52, 461 N.E.2d 1049, 1057–58, 78 Ill. Dec. 215 (1984). NIPSCO argues that the Indiana Public Service Commission's "economy purchase orders" prevented it, in whole or part, from using the coal that it had agreed to buy, and it complains that the district judge instructed the jury incorrectly on the meaning and application of the clause. The complaint about the instructions is immaterial. The judge should not have put the issue of *force majeure* to the jury. It is evident that the clause was not triggered by the orders.

All that those orders do is tell NIPSCO it will not be allowed to pass on fuel costs to its ratepayers in the form of higher rates if it can buy electricity cheaper than it can generate electricity internally using Carbon County's coal. Such an order does not "prevent," whether wholly or in part, NIPSCO from using the coal; it just prevents NIPSCO from shifting the burden of its improvidence or bad luck in having incorrectly forecasted its fuel needs to the backs of the hapless ratepayers. The purpose of public utility regulation is to provide a substitute for competition in markets (such as the market for electricity) that are naturally monopolistic. Suppose the market for electricity were fully competitive, and unregulated. Then if NIPSCO signed a long-term fixed-price fixed-quantity contract to buy coal, and during the life of the contract competing electrical companies were able to produce and sell electricity at prices below the cost to NIPSCO of producing electricity from that coal, NIPSCO would have to swallow the excess cost of the coal. It could not raise its electricity prices in order to pass on the excess cost to its consumers, because if it did they would buy electricity at lower prices from NIPSCO's competitors. By signing the kind of contract it did, NIPSCO gambled that fuel costs would rise rather than fall over the life of the contract; for if they rose then the contract price would give it an advantage over its (hypothetical) competitors who would have to buy fuel at the current market price. If such a gamble fails, the result is not *force majeure.*

This is all the clearer when we consider that the contract price was actually fixed just on the downside; it put a floor under the price NIPSCO had to pay, but the escalator provisions allowed the actual contract prices to rise above the floor, and they did. This underscores the gamble NIPSCO took in signing the contract. It committed itself to paying a price at or above a fixed minimum and to taking a fixed quantity at that price. It was willing to make this commitment to secure an assured supply of low-sulphur coal, but the risk it took was that the market price of coal or substitute fuels would fall. A *force majeure* clause is not intended to buffer a party against the normal risks of a contract. The normal risk of a fixed-price contract is that the market price will change. If it rises, the buyer gains at the expense of the seller (except insofar as escalator provisions give the seller some protection); if it falls, as here, the seller gains at the expense of the buyer. The whole purpose of a fixed-price contract is to allocate risk in this way. A *force majeure* clause interpreted to excuse the buyer from the consequences of the risk he expressly assumed would nullify a central term of the contract.

. . .

If the Commission had ordered NIPSCO to close a plant because of a safety or pollution hazard, we would have a true case of *force majeure*. As a regulated firm NIPSCO is subject to more extensive controls than unregulated firms and it therefore wanted and got a broadly worded *force majeure* clause that would protect it fully (hence the reference to partial effects) against government actions that impeded its using the coal. But as the only thing the Commission did was prevent NIPSCO from using its monopoly position to make consumers bear the risk that NIPSCO assumed when it signed a long-term fixed-price fuel contract, NIPSCO cannot complain of *force majeure*; the risk that has come to pass was one that NIPSCO voluntarily assumed when it signed the contract.

The district judge refused to submit NIPSCO's defenses of impracticability and frustration to the jury, ruling that Indiana law does not allow a buyer to claim impracticability and does not recognize the defense of frustration. Some background (on which see Farnsworth, Contracts §§ 9.5–9.7 (1982)) may help make these rulings intelligible. In the early common law a contractual undertaking unconditional in terms was not excused merely because something had happened (such as an invasion, the passage of a law, or a natural disaster) that prevented the undertaking. See *Paradine v. Jane*, Aleyn 26, 82 Eng. Rep. 897 (K.B. 1647). Excuses had to be written into the contract; this is the origin of *force majeure* clauses. Later it came to be recognized that negotiating parties cannot anticipate all the contingencies that may arise in the performance of the contract; a legitimate judicial function in contract cases is to interpolate terms to govern remote contingencies—terms the parties would have agreed on explicitly if they had had the time and foresight to make advance provision for every possible contingency in performance. Later still, it was recognized that physical impossibility was irrelevant, or at least inconclusive; a promisor might want his promise to be unconditional, not because he thought he had superhuman powers but because he could insure against the risk of nonperformance better than the promisee, or obtain a substitute performance more easily than the promisee. See *Field Container Corp. v. ICC*, 712 F.2d 250, 257 (7th Cir. 1983); Holmes, The

Common Law 300 (1881). Thus the proper question in an "impossibility" case is not whether the promisor could not have performed his undertaking but whether his nonperformance should be excused because the parties, if they had thought about the matter, would have wanted to assign the risk of the contingency that made performance impossible or uneconomical to the promisor or to the promisee; if to the latter, the promisor is excused.

. . .

Since impossibility and related doctrines are devices for shifting risk in accordance with the parties' presumed intentions, which are to minimize the costs of contract performance, one of which is the disutility created by risk, they have no place when the contract explicitly assigns a particular risk to one party or the other. As we have already noted, a fixed-price contract is an explicit assignment of the risk of market price increases to the seller and the risk of market price decreases to the buyer, and the assignment of the latter risk to the buyer is even clearer where, as in this case, the contract places a floor under price but allows for escalation. If, as is also the case here, the buyer forecasts the market incorrectly and therefore finds himself locked into a disadvantageous contract, he has only himself to blame and so cannot shift the risk back to the seller by invoking impossibility or related doctrines.

[Judgment affirmed.]

. . . .

DISCUSSION PROBLEMS

1. Nuclear Waste Disposal

In 1966, Florida Light & Power Company (FL&P) hired Westinghouse Electric Corporation to build a nuclear power plant. The contract gave FL&P the option to require Westinghouse to "remove the [spent] fuel [after processing] and dispose of it as Westinghouse sees fit." At the time, the industry expected that private entities would soon begin to purchase and reprocess spent nuclear fuel, and the U.S. Government had issued a formal assurance that it would reprocess spent fuel from nuclear reactors in the absence of private buyers.

In 1971, FL&P provided notice that it was exercising its option to require Westinghouse to dispose of the spent fuel. By this time, however, environmental concerns had not only eliminated any private market for spent nuclear fuel, the government had, unexpectedly, discontinued its commitment to provide that option. Instead, spent fuel had to be held in long-term storage at a significant cost. Westinghouse estimated that rather than earning $18 to $20 million selling the spent fuel, as it has anticipated at the time it contracted with FL&P, it would have to spend more than $80 million to store it.

Westinghouse refused to take responsibility for the spent fuel. When FL&P sued for breach of contract, Westinghouse claimed impracticability. How should the court rule on FL&P's breach of contract claim?

2. The Empty Lot

Prior to World War II, Harold Murphy leased a lot in Los Angeles from Caroline Lloyd for the purpose of selling new cars. When the United States entered the war, in order to help facilitate a massive shift in industrial production to military purposes, the government restricted sales of cars to a small percentage of the population. This restriction substantially impacted Murphy's business, and Murphy stopped paying rent on the lot. Lloyd sued for breach of contract. Should Lloyd prevail, or is Murphy excused?

3. The World Football League

In 1974, the Birmingham Americans franchise of the new World Football League signed Dallas Cowboys offensive tackle Larry Rayfield Wright to a three-year contract set to begin in 1977. The team paid Wright an immediate signing bonus, but most of the compensation was scheduled to be paid as salary annually between 1977 and 1979, when Wright would actually play for Birmingham. Plagued by low attendance, the World Football League went bankrupt and ceased to exist in 1975. Was Wright still due his contracted salary?

CHAPTER 21

MONEY DAMAGES OR INJUNCTIONS

■ ■ ■

INTRODUCTION

According to Oliver Wendell Holmes, "[t]he duty to keep a contract at common law means a prediction that you must pay damages if you do not keep it—and nothing else." The Path of the Law, 10 Harv. L. Rev. 457, 462 (1897). One implication of Holmes's description is that a party that breaches a contract should be required to provide compensation but should not be morally condemned. One of contract law's most clearly articulated bright-line rules would seem to support this view: "punitive" damages—which by definition are intended to punish the defendant rather than to compensate the plaintiff—are not recoverable in actions for breach of contract. See Rest. (2d) Contracts § 355.

A second implication of Holmes's claim is that a party that suffers a breach of contract may only turn to the courts for monetary compensation. This is not correct, but it is the case that a monetary award is the standard remedy for breach of contract, and that injunctive relief, in the form of a court order requiring the breaching party to "specifically perform" its duties, is exceptional. According to the Restatement, courts will not order specific performance or other injunctive relief "if damages would be adequate to protect the expectation interest of the injured party." Rest. (2d) Contracts § 359.

If specific performance—a court order requiring a breaching party to perform his contractual duties—is available but only when a monetary remedy is not "adequate," much rides on one obvious question: when is monetary compensation considered to be adequate and when is it not? *Van Wagner Advertising Corporation v. S & M Enterprises* concerns the breach of a contract to lease a particular billboard location, which is physically different from any other location that the plaintiff might have leased. *Laclede Gas Company v. Amoco Oil Company* concerns the breach of a contract to provide propane fuel, which is presumably indistinguishable from any other propane fuel the plaintiff might have contracted to purchase. Yet the court in *Van Wagner* limits the plaintiff to money damages, while the court in *Laclede* grants specific performance. Do you agree that monetary compensation is adequate in the first case but not the second, or do you think that one or both courts reached the wrong conclusion?

Restatement (Second) of Contracts § 355. Punitive Damages

Punitive damages are not recoverable for a breach of contract unless the conduct constituting the breach is also a tort for which punitive damages are recoverable.

Restatement (Second) of Contracts § 359. Effect of Adequacy of Damages

(1) Specific performance or an injunction will not be ordered if damages would be adequate to protect the expectation interest of the injured party.

(2) The adequacy of the damage remedy for failure to render one part of the performance due does not preclude specific performance or injunction as to the contract as a whole.

(3) Specific performance or an injunction will not be refused merely because there is a remedy for breach other than damages, but such a remedy may be considered in exercising discretion under the rule stated in § 357.

Comment:

a. *Bases for requirement.* The underlying objective in choosing the form of relief to be granted is to select a remedy that will adequately protect the legally recognized interest of the injured party. If, as is usually the case, that interest is the expectation interest, the remedy may take the form either of damages or of specific performance or an injunction. . . .

During the development of the jurisdiction of courts of equity, it came to be recognized that equitable relief would not be granted if the award of damages at law was adequate to protect the interests of the injured party. There is, however, a tendency to liberalize the granting of equitable relief by enlarging the classes of cases in which damages are not regarded as an adequate remedy. This tendency has been encouraged by the adoption of the Uniform Commercial Code, which "seeks to further a more liberal attitude than some courts have shown in connection with the specific performance of contracts of sale." Comment 1 to Uniform Commercial Code § 2–716. In accordance with this tendency, if the adequacy of the damage remedy is uncertain, the combined effect of such other factors as uncertainty of terms, insecurity as to the agreed exchange and difficulty of enforcement should be considered. Adequacy is to some extent relative, and the modern approach is to compare remedies to determine which is more effective in serving the ends of justice. Such a comparison will often lead to the granting of equitable relief. Doubts should be resolved in favor of the granting of specific performance or injunction.

Because the availability of equitable relief was historically viewed as a matter of jurisdiction, the parties cannot vary by agreement the requirement of inadequacy of damages, although a court may take appropriate notice of facts recited in their contract. . . .

CASES

VAN WAGNER ADVERTISING CORP. V. S & M ENTERPRISES

Court of Appeals of New York
67 N.Y.2d 186 (1986)

KAYE, JUDGE.

. . .

By agreement dated December 16, 1981, Barbara Michaels leased to plaintiff, Van Wagner Advertising, for an initial period of three years plus option periods totaling seven additional years space on the eastern exterior wall of a building on East 36th Street in Manhattan. Van Wagner was in the business of erecting and leasing billboards, and the parties anticipated that Van Wagner would erect a sign on the leased space, which faced an exit ramp of the Midtown Tunnel and was therefore visible to vehicles entering Manhattan from that tunnel.

In early 1982 Van Wagner erected an illuminated sign and leased it to Asch Advertising, Inc. for a three-year period commencing March 1, 1982. However, by agreement dated January 22, 1982, Michaels sold the building to defendant S & M Enterprises. Michaels informed Van Wagner of the sale in early August 1982, and on August 19, 1982 S & M sent Van Wagner a letter purporting to cancel the lease [which constituted a breach of contract].

. . .

Given defendant's unexcused failure to perform its contract, we next turn to a consideration of remedy for the breach: Van Wagner seeks specific performance of the contract, S & M urges that money damages are adequate but that the amount of the award was improper.

Whether or not to award specific performance is a decision that rests in the sound discretion of the trial court, and here that discretion was not abused. Considering first the nature of the transaction, specific performance has been imposed as the remedy for breach of contracts for the sale of real property (*Judnick Realty Corp. v. 32 W. 32nd St. Corp.*, 61 N.Y.2d 819, 823, 473 N.Y.S.2d 954, 462 N.E.2d 131; *Da Silva v. Musso*, 53

N.Y.2d 543, 545, 444 N.Y.S.2d 50, 428 N.E.2d 382; *S.E.S. Importers v. Pappalardo*, 53 N.Y.2d 455, 442 N.Y.S.2d 453, 425 N.E.2d 841), but the contract here is to lease rather than sell an interest in real property. While specific performance is available, in appropriate circumstances, for breach of a commercial or residential lease, specific performance of real property leases is not in this State awarded as a matter of course (*see, Gardens Nursery School v. Columbia Univ.*, 94 Misc. 2d 376, 378, 404 N.Y.S.2d 833).

Van Wagner argues that specific performance must be granted in light of the trial court's finding that the "demised space is unique as to location for the particular advertising purpose intended." The word "uniqueness" is not, however, a magic door to specific performance. A distinction must be drawn between physical difference and economic interchangeability. The trial court found that the leased property is physically unique, but so is every parcel of real property and so are many consumer goods. Putting aside contracts for the sale of real property, where specific performance has traditionally been the remedy for breach, uniqueness in the sense of physical difference does not itself dictate the propriety of equitable relief.

By the same token, at some level all property may be interchangeable with money. Economic theory is concerned with the degree to which consumers are willing to substitute the use of one good for another (*see*, Kronman, *Specific Performance*, 45 U. Chi. L. Rev. 351, 359), the underlying assumption being that "every good has substitutes, even if only very poor ones," and that "all goods are ultimately commensurable" (*id.*). Such a view, however, could strip all meaning from uniqueness, for if all goods are ultimately exchangeable for a price, then all goods may be valued. Even a rare manuscript has an economic substitute in that there is a price for which any purchaser would likely agree to give up a right to buy it, but a court would in all probability order specific performance of such a contract on the ground that the subject matter of the contract is unique.

The point at which breach of a contract will be redressable by specific performance thus must lie not in any inherent physical uniqueness of the property but instead in the uncertainty of valuing it: "What matters, in measuring money damages, is the volume, refinement, and reliability of the available information about substitutes for the subject matter of the breached contract. When the relevant information is thin and unreliable, there is a substantial risk that an award of money damages will either exceed or fall short of the promisee's actual loss. Of course this risk can always be reduced—but only at great cost when reliable information is difficult to obtain. Conversely, when there is a great deal of consumer behavior generating abundant and highly dependable information about substitutes, the risk of error in measuring the promisee's loss may be reduced at much smaller cost. In asserting that the subject matter of a particular contract is unique and has no established market value, a court is really saying that it cannot obtain, at reasonable cost, enough information about substitutes to permit it to calculate an award of money damages without imposing an unacceptably high risk of undercompensation on the injured promisee. Conceived in this way, the uniqueness test seems economically sound." (45 U. Chi. L. Rev., at 362.) This principle is reflected in the case law (*see, e.g., Erie R.R. Co. v. City of Buffalo*, 180 N.Y. 192, 200, 73 N.E. 26; *St. Regis Paper Co. v. Santa Clara Lbr. Co.*, 173 N.Y. 149, 160, 65 N.E. 967; *Dailey v. City of New York*, 170 App. Div. 267, 276–277, 156 N.Y.S. 124, *affd.* 218 N.Y. 665, 113 N.E. 1053), and is essentially the position of the Restatement (Second) of Contracts, which lists "the difficulty of proving damages with reasonable certainty" as the first factor affecting adequacy of damages (Restatement [Second] of Contracts § 360[a]).

Thus, the fact that the subject of the contract may be "unique as to location for the particular advertising purpose intended" by the parties does not entitle a plaintiff to the remedy of specific performance.

. . .Van Wagner asserts that while lost revenues on the Asch contract may be adequate compensation, that contract expired February 28, 1985, its lease with S & M continues until 1992, and the value of the demised space cannot reasonably be fixed for the balance of the term.

. . .[I]t is hardly novel in the law for damages to be projected into the future. Particularly where the value of commercial billboard space can be readily determined by comparisons with similar uses—Van Wagner itself has more than 400 leases—the value of this property between 1985 and 1992 cannot be regarded as speculative.

LACLEDE GAS CO. V. AMOCO OIL CO.

United States Court of Appeals, Eighth Circuit
522 F.2d 33 (1975)

ROSS, J.

The Laclede Gas Company (Laclede), a Missouri corporation, brought this diversity action alleging breach of contract against the Amoco Oil Company (Amoco), a Delaware corporation. It sought relief in the form of a mandatory injunction prohibiting the continuing breach or, in the alternative, damages. . . .

On September 21, 1970, Midwest Missouri Gas Company (now Laclede), and American Oil Company (now Amoco), the predecessors of the parties to this litigation, entered into a written agreement which was designed to provide central propane gas distribution systems to various residential developments in Jefferson County, Missouri, until such time as natural gas mains were extended into these areas. The agreement contemplated that as individual developments were planned the owners or developers would apply to Laclede for central propane gas systems. If

Laclede determined that such a system was appropriate in any given development, it could request Amoco to supply the propane to that specific development. This request was made in the form of a supplemental form letter, as provided in the September 21 agreement; and if Amoco decided to supply the propane, it bound itself to do so by signing this supplemental form.

Once this supplemental form was signed the agreement placed certain duties on both Laclede and Amoco. Basically, Amoco was to "(i)nstall, own, maintain and operate. . .storage and vaporization facilities and any other facilities necessary to provide (it) with the capability of delivering to (Laclede) commercial propane gas suitable. . .for delivery by (Laclede) to its customers' facilities." Amoco's facilities were to be "adequate to provide a continuous supply of commercial propane gas at such times and in such volumes commensurate with (Laclede's) requirements for meeting the demands reasonably to be anticipated in each Development while this Agreement is in force." Amoco was deemed to be "the supplier," while Laclede was "the distributing utility."

For its part Laclede agreed to "(i)nstall, own, maintain and operate all distribution facilities" from a "point of delivery" which was defined to be "the outlet of (Amoco) header piping." Laclede also promised to pay Amoco "the Wood River Area Posted Price for propane plus four cents per gallon for all amounts of commercial propane gas delivered" to it under the agreement. Since it was contemplated that the individual propane systems would eventually be converted to natural gas. . .the agreement provided that Laclede should give Amoco 30 days written notice of [impending conversions], after which the agreement would no longer be binding for the converted development.

. . .

For a time the parties operated satisfactorily under this agreement, and some 17 residential subdivisions were brought within it by supplemental letters. However, for various reasons, including conversion to natural gas, the number of developments under the agreement had shrunk to eight by the time of trial. These were all mobile home parks.

During the winter of 1972–73 Amoco experienced a shortage of propane and voluntarily placed all of its customers, including Laclede, on an 80% Allocation basis, meaning that Laclede would receive only up to 80% of its previous requirements. Laclede objected to this and pushed Amoco to give it 100% of what the developments needed. Some conflict arose over this before the temporary shortage was alleviated.

Then, on April 3, 1973, Amoco notified Laclede that its Wood River Area Posted Price of propane had been increased by three cents per gallon. Laclede objected to this increase also and demanded a full explanation. None was forthcoming. Instead Amoco merely sent a letter dated May 14,

1973, informing Laclede that it was "terminating" the September 21, 1970, agreement effective May 31, 1973.

Generally the determination of whether or not to order specific performance of a contract lies within the sound discretion of the trial court. However, this discretion is, in fact, quite limited; and it is said that when certain equitable rules have been met and the contract is fair and plain "specific performance goes as a matter of right." Miller v. Coffeen, 365 Mo. 204 (1955). . . .

With this in mind we have carefully reviewed the very complete record on appeal and conclude that the trial court should grant the injunctive relief prayed. We are satisfied that this case falls within that category in which specific performance should be ordered as a matter of right. Miller v. Coffeen, supra, 280 S.W.2d at 102.

. . .

It is axiomatic that specific performance will not be ordered when the party claiming breach of contract has an adequate remedy at law. Jamison Coal & Coke Co. v. Goltra, 132 F.2d 889, 894 (8th Cir.), *cert. denied*, 323 U.S. 769 (1944). This is especially true when the contract involves personal property as distinguished from real estate.

However, in Missouri, as elsewhere, specific performance may be ordered even though personalty is involved in the "proper circumstances." Mo. Rev. Stat. § 400.2–716(1); Restatement of Contracts, supra, § 361. . . .

One of the leading Missouri cases allowing specific performance of a contract relating to personalty because the remedy at law was inadequate is *Boeving v. Vandover*, 240 Mo. App. 117 (1949). In that case the plaintiff sought specific performance of a contract in which the defendant had promised to sell him an automobile. At that time (near the end of and shortly after World War II) new cars were hard to come by, and the court held that specific performance was a proper remedy since a new car "could not be obtained elsewhere except at considerable expense, trouble or loss, which cannot be estimated in advance."

We are satisfied that Laclede has brought itself within this practical approach taken by the Missouri courts. As Amoco points out, Laclede has propane immediately available to it under other contracts with other suppliers. And the evidence indicates that at the present time propane is readily available on the open market. However, this analysis ignores the fact that the contract involved in this lawsuit is for a long-term supply of propane to these subdivisions. The other two contracts under which Laclede obtains the gas will remain in force only until March 31, 1977, and April 1, 1981, respectively; and there is no assurance that Laclede will be able to receive any propane under them after that time. Also it is unclear as to whether or not Laclede can use the propane obtained under these contracts to supply the Jefferson County subdivisions, since they were originally entered into to provide Laclede with propane with which to "shave" its natural gas supply during peak demand periods.[4] Additionally, there was uncontradicted expert testimony that Laclede probably could not find another supplier of propane willing to enter into a long-term contract such as the Amoco agreement, given the uncertain future of worldwide energy supplies. And, even if Laclede could obtain supplies of propane for the affected developments through its present contracts or newly negotiated ones, it would still face considerable expense and trouble which cannot be estimated in advance in making arrangements for its distribution to the subdivisions.

Specific performance is the proper remedy in this situation, and it should be granted by the district court.

DISCUSSION PROBLEMS

1. The Gulfstream II

Eugene Klein contracted to purchase a Gulfstream II corporate jet (G-II) from PepsiCo for $4.6 million. When PepsiCo refused to deliver the plane, Klein sued for breach of contract and sought specific performance of the agreement. At trial, the court found that of the 21 other G-IIs available on the market at the time Klein was shopping for a jet, only 3 were roughly comparable to the PepsiCo plane, and that considerable expense would have been required for Klein to locate a replacement. Klein testified that he did not purchase a replacement plane because prices rose sharply following the breach. Is Klein entitled to specific performance of the contract, or should he be limited to money damages for PepsiCo's breach?

2. The Special-Edition Corvette

To celebrate the Corvette being chosen as the official pace car of the Indianapolis 500 automobile race, Chevrolet announced that it would produce 6,000 special-edition, commemorative models of the car. Charlie's Chevrolet dealership learned it would be allotted one of these special-edition Corvettes, and it contracted to sell that car to collector Joseph Sedmak at the "manufacturer's suggested retail price," which had not yet been set. At Sedmak's request, Charlie's ordered the car equipped with a special engine, a four-speed standard transmission, and an AM-FM radio with a cassette tape deck. The car eventually arrived at Charlie's, as ordered, with a manufacturer's suggested retail price of $15,000. But

[4] During periods of cold weather, when demand is high, Laclede does not receive enough natural gas to meet all this demand. It, therefore, adds propane to the natural gas it places in its distribution system. This practice is called "peak shaving."

because of higher-than-expected demand for the commemorate models, Charlie's refused to deliver its Corvette to Sedmak and instead notified him that the dealership would be auctioning the car to the highest bidder.

Sedmak sued Charlie's for breach of contract and requested specific performance. Charlie's contended that monetary damages would be an adequate remedy. Which party should prevail on this issue?

3. Equipment Purchased for Resale

Ace Equipment Company contracted to purchase a used, 6,000 KVA General Electric Transformer—a very large piece of industrial equipment—from Aqua Chem for $1,800. Ace then contracted to resell the transformer to Frank Lunney for $7,500. When Aqua Chem refused to deliver the transformer, Ace sued for breach of contract and requested an order of specific performance so that it could fulfill its obligation to Lunney. Is this a proper case for specific performance, or are money damages adequate?

CHAPTER 22

CALCULATING EXPECTATION DAMAGES

■ ■ ■

INTRODUCTION

When courts award monetary damages for breach of contract, the proper measure of damages is the non-breaching party's "expectation" interest. So-called "expectation damages" are the amount of money necessary to make the non-breaching party as well off as it would have been had the breaching party performed its contractual obligations. See Rest. (2d) Contracts § 347.

It might seem as though money would rarely be a *perfect* substitute for an expected performance, but it is a sufficient substitute in many commercial transactions. The most obvious example is when a buyer whose sole contractual obligation is to pay money for goods or services breaches an agreement. If the seller is awarded the contract price minus the costs it saves by not having to fulfill the buyer's order, the seller will end up in the same position as if the buyer had not breached and should be indifferent to the outcome. Non-breaching buyers also typically can be made whole by an award of damages, because a monetary award equal to the cost of purchasing the goods or services at issue from an alternative seller can enable the buyer to "cover" and end up with the same goods or services it expected to receive. For example, assume that a restaurant chain contracts to buy 100,000 eggs from an egg supplier for $10,000, and an alternate supplier would charge $12,000 for that order. If the supplier breaches, an award of $2000 plus any additional amount needed to pay for any higher costs of collecting the eggs from the substitute supplier (known as an "incidental" costs) would enable the restaurant to end up with exactly the product it expected to receive under the original contract.

When the available market substitutes are not identical to the promised performance—in attributes, quality, timing, or in some other material characteristic—calculating the non-breaching party's expectation damages becomes more complicated. *Egerer v. CSR West, LLC* illustrates how the law attempts to deal with such circumstances. Although *Egerer* is decided under the Uniform Commercial Code (because the contract is for the sale of goods), the reasoning is applicable to non-UCC cases as well.

An important caveat to the principle of expectation damages is that contract law treats non-breaching parties as if they took reasonable steps to minimize the extent of the damages suffered as a result of the breach. The "as if" qualification is important. The non-breaching party is not required to *actually* mitigate her damages, but courts will calculate her damages—and thus limit her award—on the assumption that she did. See Rest. (2d) Contracts § 350. *Parker v. Twentieth Century-Fox Film Corporation* explores the question of what actions are expected of the non-breaching party in the context of whether an actress's damage award should be limited when she was offered (and declined) a different acting contract as a substitute for the one that the production company breached. *In re WorldCom, Inc.* considers the important question of how to treat what is known as the "lost volume seller" problem, which arises when the non-breaching seller enters into a substitute transaction that replaces its income lost as the direct result of the breach but suffers a net reduction in its total number of sales as a result.

Restatement (Second) of Contracts § 347. Measure of Damages in General

Subject to the limitations stated in §§ 350–53, the injured party has a right to damages based on his expectation interest as measured by

(a) the loss in the value to him of the other party's performance caused by its failure or deficiency, plus

(b) any other loss, including incidental or consequential loss, caused by the breach, less

(c) any cost or other loss that he has avoided by not having to perform.

Comment:

b. Loss in value. The first element that must be estimated in attempting to fix a sum that will fairly represent the expectation interest is the loss in the value to the injured party of the other party's performance that is caused by the failure of, or deficiency in, that performance. If no performance is rendered, the loss in value caused by the breach is equal to the value that the performance would have had to the injured party. . . .

c. Other loss. Subject to the limitations stated in §§ 350–53, the injured party is entitled to recover for all loss actually suffered. Items of loss other than loss in value of the other party's performance are often characterized as incidental or consequential. Incidental losses include costs incurred in a reasonable effort, whether successful or not, to avoid loss, as where a party pays brokerage fees in arranging or attempting to arrange a substitute transaction. Consequential losses include such items as injury to person or property resulting from defective performance. The terms used to describe the type of loss are not, however, controlling, and the general principle is that all losses, however described, are recoverable.

d. Cost or other loss avoided. Sometimes the breach itself results in a saving of some cost that the injured party would have incurred if he had had to perform. See Illustration 5. Furthermore, the injured party is expected to take reasonable steps to avoid further loss. See § 350. Where he does this by discontinuing his own performance, he avoids incurring additional costs of performance. . . .This cost avoided is subtracted from the loss in value caused by the breach in calculating his damages. If the injured party avoids further loss by making substitute arrangements for the use of his resources that are no longer needed to perform the contract, the net profit from such arrangements is also subtracted. . . .The value to him of any salvageable materials that he has acquired for performance is also subtracted. . . .Loss avoided is subtracted only if the saving results from the injured party not having to perform rather than from some unrelated event. . . .If no cost or other loss has been avoided, however, the injured party's damages include the full amount of the loss in value with no subtraction, subject to the limitations stated in §§ 350–53. . . .

f. Lost volume. Whether a subsequent transaction is a substitute for the broken contract sometimes raises difficult questions of fact. If the injured party could and would have entered into the subsequent contract, even if the contract had not been broken, and could have had the benefit of both, he can be said to have "lost volume" and the subsequent transaction is not a substitute for the broken contract. The injured party's damages are then based on the net profit that he has lost as a result of the broken contract. Since entrepreneurs try to operate at optimum capacity, however, it is possible that an additional transaction would not have been profitable and that the injured party would not have chosen to expand his business by undertaking it had there been no breach. It is sometimes assumed that he would have done so, but the question is one of fact to be resolved according to the circumstances of each case. See also Uniform Commercial Code § 2–708(2).

Restatement (Second) of Contracts § 350. Avoidability as a Limitation on Damages

(1) Except as stated in Subsection (2), damages are not recoverable for loss that the injured party could have avoided without undue risk, burden or humiliation.

(2) The injured party is not precluded from recovery by the rule stated in Subsection (1) to the extent that he has made reasonable but unsuccessful efforts to avoid loss.

CASES

EGERER V. CSR WEST, LLC

Court of Appeals of Washington
67 P.3d 1128 (2003)

BECKER, C.J.

Appellant CSR West breached a contract to supply fill for land development. Issues on appeal include the calculation of damages based on "hypothetical cover"; the allowance of prejudgment interest; and the denial of the plaintiff's requests to include sales tax and consequential damages in the award of damages. We affirm in all respects.

MEASURE OF DAMAGES

According to unchallenged findings of fact entered after a bench trial, Robert Egerer owned a 10 acre parcel of land in Skagit County that he planned to develop into commercial property. The property required a considerable amount of fill to make it suitable for development.

Egerer first purchased fill material in 1995, when he contracted at the rate of $1.10 per cubic yard to have Wilder Construction haul to his property some material being excavated from the shoulders of Interstate 5 as a part of a highway improvement project. In its suitability to serve as structural fill, the shoulder material resembled a gravel known as "pit run," but it was cheaper than pit run because it contained asphalt grindings.

Beyond what Wilder Construction could supply, Egerer needed roughly 17,000 cubic yards of fill material. In May 1997, Egerer learned that CSR West had contracted with the Washington State Department of Transportation to excavate material from the shoulder areas of Interstate 5 near Lake Samish. He met with John Grisham, CSR's sales manager, and they reached an agreement to have CSR transport "all" the shoulder excavations from the project to Egerer's site at the rate of $.50 per cubic yard.

CSR brought fill material to Egerer's property on only two nights: July 9 and 10, 1997. Shortly thereafter, the Department of Transportation issued a change order that allowed CSR to use the excavated shoulder material in the reconstruction of the shoulder area. It was more profitable for CSR to supply the material for the State's use than to fulfill its contract with Egerer. CSR excavated a total of 16,750 cubic yards of material during its work on the shoulder project in 1997, and supplied virtually all of it to the Department of Transportation.

Egerer did not purchase replacement fill at the time of the breach in July 1997. Asked about this at trial, he explained that it would have been too expensive, and he also did not think there was time to find replacement fill and get it onto his property before the end of the summer. Egerer said that his window of opportunity to place fill on the property was June through September, before the weather became too wet. In January and February 1998, he obtained price quotes for pit run ranging from $8.25 per cubic yard to $9.00 per cubic yard. These prices exceeded Egerer's budget, and he did not contract for replacement fill at that time either.

In the summer of 1999, Egerer learned of an unexpected landslide at a gravel pit not far from his property. The company agreed to sell Egerer the unwanted slide material at a cost of $6.39 per cubic yard, including the cost of hauling and spreading.

Egerer filed suit in November 2000, alleging that CSR breached its contract by failing to deliver all the excavated shoulder material in the summer of 1997. After a bench trial, the court found breach. The court then turned to the Uniform Commercial Code to determine the measure of damages. CSR raises several legal issues with respect to the award of damages.

The findings, which are unchallenged, are deemed verities on appeal. We review conclusions of law de novo to see if they are supported by the trial court's findings of fact. *Bingham v. Lechner*, 111 Wash. App. 118, 127, 45 P.3d 562 (2002).

Where a seller fails to make delivery of goods sold to a buyer, the buyer has two alternative remedies under the Uniform Commercial Code. One is the remedy of "cover": the buyer may purchase substitute goods and recover as damages the difference between the cost of this cover and the contract price, provided the buyer covers in good faith and without unreasonable delay. RCW 62A.2–712. The other, a complete alternative, is damages for non-delivery, also known as "hypothetical cover": the buyer may recover as damages from the seller "the difference between the market price at the time when the buyer learned of the breach and the contract price." RCW 62A.2–713. This measure applies only when and to the extent that the buyer does not cover. Uniform Commercial Code Comment 5, RCWA 62A.2–713. "The general baseline adopted in this section uses as a yardstick the market in which the buyer would have obtained cover had he sought that relief." U.C.C. Comment 1, RCWA 62A.2–713. "The market or current price to be used in comparison with the contract price under this section is the price for goods of the same kind and in the same branch of trade." U.C.C. Comment 2, RCWA 62A.2–713.

The court determined that Egerer was limited to damages for non-delivery under section 2–713: "Mr. Egerer is limited to damages reflecting the difference between CSR contract price and the price he could have obtained replacement material for at the time of the breach in 1997. *See* RCW 62A.2–713(1) and Comment 3." The court found that Egerer could have obtained replacement material at the time of the breach for a cost of \$8.25 per cubic yard—a price quoted to Egerer in early 1998. The court calculated his damages for the non-delivery of fill to be \$129,812.50, which was the difference between the market price of \$8.25 per cubic yard and the contract price of \$.50 per cubic yard.

CSR accepts the trial court's decision to apply the remedy furnished by section 2–713, but contends the court erred by calculating damages based on a market price of \$8.25 per cubic yard for pit run. CSR argues that \$8.25 was not "the price for goods of the same kind" (as U.C.C. Comment 2 calls for) because pit run is a product superior to shoulder excavations containing asphalt grindings. CSR further argues that \$8.25 was not "the market price at the time when the buyer learned of the breach" (as section 2–713 calls for) because the breach was in July 1997 and the \$8.25 price was as of six months later—in January, 1998. CSR takes the position that the trial court should instead have used the \$1.10 per cubic yard price reflected in Egerer's 1995 contract with Wilder Construction, because that was the only evidence in the record of a price for shoulder excavations. Use of the much higher price for pit run resulted in a windfall for Egerer, according to CSR.

The trial court expressly relied on Comment 3 to U.C.C. 2 713 in determining that \$8.25 per cubic yard was the price for which Egerer could have obtained replacement material at the time of the breach. That comment states in part, "When the current market price under this section is difficult to prove the section on determination and proof of market price is available to permit a showing of a comparable market price or, where no market price is available, evidence of spot sale prices is proper." U.C.C. Comment 3, RCWA 62A.2–713. The section on determination and proof of market price provides,

> If evidence of a price prevailing at the times or places described in this Article is not readily available the price prevailing within any reasonable time before or after the time described or at any other place which in commercial judgment or under usage of trade would serve as a reasonable substitute for the one described may be used, making any proper allowance for the cost of transporting the goods to or from such other place.

RCW 62A.2–723(2).

A court is granted a "reasonable leeway" in measuring market price under section 2–723. *Sprague v. Sumitomo Forestry Co., Ltd.*, 104 Wash. 2d 751, 760, 709 P.2d 1200 (1985). Contrary to CSR's argument, a trial court may use a market price for goods different in quality from those for which the buyer contracted. That possibility is encompassed in the reference to "price. . .which in commercial judgment or under usage of trade would serve as a reasonable substitute for the one described." And section 2–723 expressly permits looking to a price "prevailing within any reasonable time before or after the time described."

We conclude the trial court did not misapply the law in concluding that the January 1998 price for pit run was the relevant market price. The court found the 1998 quotes for replacement material and hauling "were reasonable and customary," and noted that CSR "did not offer evidence that suitable replacement material was available at a lower price at the time of breach." There was testimony that shoulder excavation material, though cheap when available, is rarely available. John Grisham, CSR's sales manager, acknowledged that it would have been difficult for Egerer to locate an alternative supplier of shoulder excavations in 1997 because "quantities like that are few and far between." Grisham said he was unaware of any other pit in the area that would have had similar material available at a price anywhere near $.50 per cubic yard in the summer of 1997. Egerer's eventual purchase in 1999 was possible only because of the landslide that unexpectedly deposited unwanted fill material in a local gravel pit. If Egerer had covered at the time of the breach, higher-priced pit run would have been a reasonable substitute for the shoulder excavations.

Egerer, in his cross-appeal, argues that the relevant market price was much higher. He contends the trial court should have based its calculation of damages on figures showing that the Washington Department of Transportation was paying CSR between $33.33 and $46.80 per cubic yard for gravel pit material at that time. But the record does not indicate that Egerer made any argument below based on figures in CSR's contract with the State, and we will not consider it for the first time on appeal.

PARKER V. TWENTIETH CENTURY-FOX FILM CORP.

Supreme Court of California
3 Cal.3d 176 (1970)

BURKE, J.

Defendant Twentieth Century-Fox Film Corporation appeals from a summary judgment granting to plaintiff [Shirley MacLaine Parker] the recovery of agreed compensation under a written contract for her services as an actress in a motion picture. As will appear, we have concluded that the trial court correctly ruled in plaintiff's favor and that the judgment should be affirmed.

Plaintiff is well known as an actress, and in the contract between plaintiff and defendant is sometimes referred to as the "Artist." Under the contract, dated August 6, 1965, plaintiff was to play the female lead in defendant's contemplated production of a motion picture entitled "Bloomer Girl." The contract provided that defendant would pay plaintiff a minimum "guaranteed compensation" of $53,571.42 per week for 14 weeks commencing May 23, 1966, for a total of $750,000. Prior to May 1966 defendant decided not to produce the picture and by a letter dated April 4, 1966, it notified plaintiff of that decision and that it would not "comply with our obligations to you under" the written contract.

By the same letter and with the professed purpose "to avoid any damage to you," defendant instead offered to employ plaintiff as the leading actress in another film tentatively entitled "Big Country, Big Man" (hereinafter, "Big Country"). The compensation offered was identical, as were 31 of the 34 numbered provisions or articles of the original contract. Unlike "Bloomer Girl," however, which was to have been a musical production, "Big Country" was a dramatic "western type" movie. "Bloomer Girl" was to have been filmed in California; "Big Country" was to be produced in Australia. Also, certain terms in the proffered contract varied from those of the original.[2] Plaintiff was given one week within which to accept; she did not and the offer lapsed. Plaintiff then commenced this action seeking recovery of the agreed guaranteed compensation.

The complaint sets forth two causes of action. The first is for money due under the contract; the second, based upon the same allegations as the first, is for damages resulting from defendant's breach of contract. Defendant in its answer admits the existence and validity of the contract, that plaintiff complied with all the conditions, covenants and promises and stood ready to complete the performance, and that defendant breached and "anticipatorily repudiated" the contract. It denies, however, that any money is due to plaintiff either under the contract or as a result of its breach, and pleads as an affirmative defense to both causes of action plaintiff's allegedly deliberate failure to mitigate damages, asserting that she unreasonably refused to accept its offer of the leading role in "Big Country."

Plaintiff moved for summary judgment, the motion was granted, and summary judgment for $750,000 plus interest was entered in plaintiff's favor. This appeal by defendant followed.

The familiar rules are that the matter to be determined by the trial court on a motion for summary judgment is whether facts have been presented which give rise to a triable factual issue. The court may not pass upon the issue itself. Summary judgment is proper only if the affidavits or declarations in support of the moving party would be sufficient to sustain a judgment in his favor and his opponent does not by affidavit show facts

---

[2] Article 29 of the original contract specified that plaintiff approved the director already chosen for "Bloomer Girl" and that in case he failed to act as director plaintiff was to have approval rights of any substitute director. Article 31 provided that plaintiff was to have the right of approval of the "Bloomer Girl" dance director, and Article 32 gave her the right of approval of the screenplay. Defendant's letter of April 4 to plaintiff, which contained both defendant's notice of breach of the "Bloomer Girl" contract and offer of the lead in "Big Country," eliminated or impaired each of those rights.

sufficient to present a triable issue of fact. The affidavits of the moving party are strictly construed, and doubts as to the propriety of summary judgment should be resolved against granting the motion. Such summary procedure is drastic and should be used with caution so that it does not become a substitute for the open trial method of determining facts. . . .

As stated, defendant's sole defense to this action which resulted from its deliberate breach of contract is that in rejecting defendant's substitute offer of employment plaintiff unreasonably refused to mitigate damages.

The general rule is that the measure of recovery by a wrongfully discharged employee is the amount of salary agreed upon for the period of service, less the amount which the employer affirmatively proves the employee has earned or with reasonable effort might have earned from other employment. (W.F. Boardman Co. v. Petch (1921) 186 Cal. 476, 484; De Angeles v. Roos Bros., Inc. (1966) 244 Cal. App. 2d 434, 441–442; de la Falaise v. Gaumont-British Picture Corp. (1940) 39 Cal. App. 2d 461, 469, and cases cited; see also Wise v. Southern Pac. Co. (1970) 1 Cal. 3d 600, 607–608.) However, before projected earnings from other employment opportunities not sought or accepted by the discharged employee can be applied in mitigation, the employer must show that the other employment was comparable, or substantially similar, to that of which the employee has been deprived; the employee's rejection of or failure to seek other available employment of a different or inferior kind may not be resorted to in order to mitigate damages. (Gonzales v. Internat. Assn. of Machinists (1963) 213 Cal. App. 2d 817, 822–824; Harris v. Nat. Union etc. Cooks, Stewards (1953) 116 Cal. App. 2d 759, 761; Crillo v. Curtola (1949) 91 Cal. App. 2d 263, 275; de la Falaise v. Galumont-British Picture Corp., supra, 39 Cal. App. 2d 461, 469; Schiller v. Keuffel & Esser Co. (1963) 21 Wis. 2d 545; 28 A.L.R. 736, 749; 22 Am. Jur. 2d, Damages, §§ 71–72, p. 106.)

In the present case defendant has raised no issue of *reasonableness of efforts* by plaintiffs to obtain other employment; the sole issue is whether plaintiff's refusal of defendant's substitute offer of "Big Country" may be used in mitigation. Nor, if the "Big Country" offer was of employment different or inferior when compared with the original "Bloomer Girl" employment, is there an issue as to whether or not plaintiff acted reasonably in refusing the substitute offer. Despite defendant's arguments to the contrary, no case cited or which our research has discovered holds or suggests that reasonableness is an element of a wrongfully discharged employee's option to reject, or fail to seek, different or inferior employment lest the possible earnings therefrom be charged against him in mitigation of damages.[5]

---

[5] Instead, in each case the reasonableness referred to was that of the *efforts* of the employee to obtain other employment that was not different or inferior; his right to reject the latter was declared as an unqualified rule of law. . . .

Applying the foregoing rules to the record in the present case, with all intendments in favor of the party opposing the summary judgment motion—here, defendant—it is clear that the trial court correctly ruled that plaintiff's failure to accept defendant's tendered substitute employment could not be applied in mitigation of damages because the offer of the "Big Country" lead was of employment both different and inferior, and that no factual dispute was presented on that issue. The mere circumstance that "Bloomer Girl" was to be a musical revue calling upon plaintiff's talents as a dancer as well as an actress, and was to be produced in the City of Los Angeles, whereas "Big Country" was a straight dramatic role in a "Western Type" story taking place in an opal mine in Australia, demonstrates the difference in kind between the two employments; the female lead as a dramatic actress in a western style motion picture can by no stretch of imagination be considered the equivalent of or substantially similar to the lead in a song-and-dance production.

Additionally, the substitute "Big Country" offer proposed to eliminate or impair the director and screenplay approvals accorded to plaintiff under the original "Bloomer Girl" contract (see fn. 2, ante), and thus constituted an offer of inferior employment. No expertise or judicial notice is required in order to hold that the deprivation or infringement of an employee's rights held under an original employment contract converts the available "other employment" relied upon by the employer to mitigate damages, into inferior employment which the employee need not seek or accept.

. . .

In view of the determination that defendant failed to present any facts showing the existence of a factual issue with respect to its sole defense—plaintiff's rejection of its substitute employment offer in mitigation of damages—we need not consider plaintiff's further contention that for various reasons, including the provisions of the original contract set forth in footnote 1, ante, plaintiff was excused from attempting to mitigate damages.

The judgment is affirmed.

MCCOMB, J., PETERS, J., TOBRINER, J., KAUS, J., and ROTH, J., concurred.

SULLIVAN, Acting C.J.

The basic question in this case is whether or not plaintiff acted reasonably in rejecting defendant's offer of alternate employment. The answer depends upon whether that offer (starring in "Big Country, Big Man") was an offer of work that was substantially similar to her former employment (starring in "Bloomer Girl") or of work that was of a different or inferior kind. To my mind this is a factual issue, which the trial court should not have determined on a motion for summary judgment. The majority have not only repeated this error but have compounded it by applying the rules governing mitigation of damages in the employer-employee context in a misleading fashion. Accordingly, I respectfully dissent.

. . .

Although the majority appear to hold that there was a difference "in kind" between the employment offered plaintiff in "Bloomer Girl" and that offered in "Big Country," an examination of the opinion makes crystal clear that the majority merely point out differences between the *two films* (an obvious circumstance) and then apodictically asserts that these constitute a difference in the *kind of employment.* The entire rationale of the majority boils down to this; that the "*mere circumstances*" that "Bloomer Girl" was to be a musical revue while "Big Country" was a straight drama "demonstrates the difference in kind" since a female lead in a western is not "the equivalent of or substantially similar to" a lead in a musical. This is merely attempting to prove the proposition by repeating it. It shows that the vehicles for the display of the star's talents are different but it does not prove that her employment as a star in such vehicles is of necessity different *in kind* and either inferior or superior.

I believe that the approach taken by the majority (a superficial listing of differences with no attempt to assess their significance) may subvert a valuable legal doctrine. The inquiry in cases such as this should not be whether differences between the two jobs exist (there will always be differences) but whether the differences which are present are substantial enough to constitute differences in the *kind* of employment or, alternatively, whether they render the substitute work employment of an *inferior kind.*

. . .

I believe that the judgment should be reversed so that the issue of whether or not the offer of the lead role in "Big Country, Big Man" was of employment comparable to that of the lead role in "Bloomer Girl" may be determined at trial.

IN RE WORLDCOM, INC.

United States Bankruptcy Court, Southern District of New York
361 B.R. 675 (2007)

GONZALEZ, B.J.

On or about July 10, 1995, [Michael] Jordan and the Debtors entered into an endorsement agreement (the "Agreement"). At that time, Jordan was considered to be one of the most popular athletes in the world. The Agreement granted MCI a ten-year license to use Jordan's name, likeness, "other attributes," and personal services to advertise and promote MCI's telecommunications products and services beginning in September 1995 and ending in August 2005. The Agreement did not prevent Jordan from endorsing most other products or services, although he could not endorse the same products or services that MCI produced. In addition to a $5 million signing bonus, the Agreement provided an annual base compensation of $2 million for Jordan. The Agreement provided that Jordan would be treated as an independent contractor and that MCI would not withhold any amount from Jordan's compensation for tax purposes. The Agreement provided that Jordan was to make himself available for four days, not to exceed four hours per day, during each contract year to produce television commercials and print advertising and for promotional appearances. The parties agreed that the advertising and promotional materials would be submitted to Jordan for his approval, which could not be unreasonably withheld, fourteen days prior to their release to the general public. From 1995 to 2000, Jordan appeared in several television commercials and a large number of print ads for MCI.

On July 1, 2002, MCI commenced a case under chapter 11 of title 11 of the United States Code (the "Bankruptcy Code") in the Bankruptcy Court for the Southern District of New York. . . .On July 18, 2003, the Debtors rejected the Agreement. . . .As of the rejection in July 2003, two years remained under the Agreement.

. . .MCI argues that Jordan had an obligation to mitigate his damages and failed to do so. . . .MCI argues that it is under no obligation to pay Jordan for contract years 2004 and 2005. . . .Jordan argues that the objection should be overruled and dismissed for three independent reasons (1) Jordan was a "lost volume seller" and thus mitigation does not apply, (2) there is no evidence that Jordan could have entered into a "substantially similar" endorsement agreement, and (3) Jordan acted reasonably when he decided not to pursue other endorsements after MCI's rejection of the Agreement.

. . .

C. MITIGATION

The doctrine of avoidable consequences, which has also been referred to as the duty to mitigate damages, "bars recovery for losses suffered by a non-breaching party that could have been avoided by reasonable effort and without risk of substantial loss or injury." *Edward M. Crough, Inc. v. Dep't of Gen. Servs. of D.C.*, 572 A.2d 457, 466 (D.C. 1990). The burden of proving that the damages could have been avoided or mitigated rests with the party that committed the breach. *See Obelisk Corp. v. Riggs Nat'l Bank of Washington, D.C.*, 668 A.2d 847, 856 (D.C. 1995); *see also Norris v. Green*, 656 A.2d 282, 287 (D.C. 1995) ("The failure to mitigate damages is an affirmative defense and the [breaching party] has the burden of showing the absence of reasonable efforts to mitigate"). The efforts to avoid or mitigate the damages do not have to be successful, as long as they are reasonable. *See Edward M. Crough*, 572 A.2d at 467.

. . .

1. Whether Jordan Was a "Lost Volume Seller"

Jordan argues that MCI's mitigation defense does not apply here because Jordan is akin to a "lost volume seller." Jordan points to testimony demonstrating that he could have entered into additional endorsement contracts even if MCI had not rejected the Agreement. Thus, he argues, any additional endorsement contracts would not have been substitutes for the Agreement and would not have mitigated the damages for which MCI is liable.

"A lost volume seller is one who has the capacity to perform the contract that was breached in addition to other potential contracts due to unlimited resources or production capacity." *Precision Pine & Timber, Inc. v. United States*, 72 Fed. Cl. 460, 490 (Fed. Cl. 2006). A lost volume seller does not minimize its damages by entering into another contract because it would have had the benefit of both contracts even if the first were not breached. *See Jetz Service Co. v. Salina Props.*, 19 Kan. App. 2d 144, 865 P.2d 1051, 1055–56 (1993). The lost volume seller has two expectations, the profit from the breached contract and the profit from one or more other contracts that it could have performed at the same time as the breached contract. *See Snyder v. Herbert Greenbaum & Assocs.*, 38 Md. App. 144, 380 A.2d 618, 624 (1977). "The philosophical heart of the lost volume theory is that the seller would have generated a second sale irrespective of the buyer's breach" and that "[i]t follows that the lost volume seller cannot possibly mitigate damages." D. Matthews, *Should the Doctrine of Lost Volume Seller Be Retained? A Response to Professor Breen*, 51 U. Miami L. Rev. 1195, 1214 (July 1997); *see also Snyder*, 380 A.2d at 625 (under this theory, "the original sale and the second sale are independent events").

The lost volume seller theory is recognized in the Restatement (2d) of Contracts, §§ 347, 350 (1981) (the "Restatement (2d)").

The lost volume seller theory applies to contracts for services as well as goods. *See* Restatement (2d), § 347, ill. 16; *see also Jetz Service*, 865 P.2d at 1055–56 (applying theory to seller of services); *Gianetti v. Norwalk Hosp.*, 64 Conn. App. 218, 779 A.2d 847, 853 (2001) (applying theory to provider of medical services), *aff'd in part, rev'd in part*, 266 Conn. 544, 833 A.2d 891 (2003).

This case offers a twist on the typical lost volume seller situation. In what the Court regards as the typical situation, the non-breaching seller has a near-inexhaustible supply of inventory. *See, e.g., Katz Commc'ns, Inc. v. Evening News Ass'n*, 705 F.2d 20, 26 (2d Cir. 1983). In the typical situation, when a buyer breaches an agreement to buy a good or service from the seller, the item is returned to inventory and the lost volume seller continues in its efforts to sell its goods or services. However, the transactions that occur following the breach are not necessarily the result of the breach but fundamentally the result of the seller continuing efforts to market its goods and services. It is this continuous effort coupled with a virtually limitless supply that warrants the lost volume exception to mitigation. As stated above, the transactions that may occur after the breach would in the context of the lost volume seller have occurred independent of the breach. Here, Jordan lacked a nearly limitless supply and had no intention of continuing to market his services as a product endorser.

. . .

To claim lost volume seller status, Jordan must establish that he would have had the benefit of both the original and subsequent contracts if MCI had not rejected the Agreement. *See Ullman-Briggs*, 754 F. Supp. at 1008. Although there is no definitive set of elements that the non-breaching party must show, many cases seem to follow the language from the Restatement (2d), Section 347, that the non-breaching party must show that it "could and would have entered into" a subsequent agreement. *See, e.g., Donald Rubin, Inc. v. Schwartz*, 191 A.D.2d 171, 172, 594 N.Y.S.2d 193, 194–95 (1st Dep't 1993); *Precision Pine,* 72 Fed. Cl. at 496–97; *Gianetti*, 833 A.2d at 897; *Jetz Service*, 865 P.2d at 1056; *see also Green Tree Financial*, 2002 WL 31163072, at *9 ("[t]o recover lost profits under this theory, a non-breaching party must prove three things: (1) that the seller of services had the capability to perform both contracts simultaneously; (2) that the second contract would have been profitable; and (3) that the seller of service would have entered into the second contract if the first contract had not been terminated").

In his arguments, Jordan focuses primarily on his *capacity* to enter subsequent agreements, arguing that the loss of MCI's sixteen-hour annual time commitment hardly affected his ability to perform additional endorsement services. On this prong alone, Jordan likely would be considered a lost volume seller of endorsement services because he had sufficient time to do multiple endorsements. Although he does not have the "infinite capacity" that some cases discuss, a services provider does not need unlimited capacity but must have the requisite capacity and intent to perform under multiple contracts at the same time. *See Gianetti*, 266 Conn. at 561–62, 833 A.2d 891 (plastic surgeon could be considered a lost volume seller if it were determined that he had the capacity and intent to simultaneously work out of three or four hospitals profitably).

Contrary to Jordan's analysis, courts do not focus solely on the seller's capacity. The seller claiming lost volume status must also demonstrate that it *would* have entered into subsequent transactions. *See Diasonics*,

826 F.2d at 684; *Green Tree Financial*, 2002 WL 31163072, at *9; *Gianetti*, 779 A.2d at 853 ("for sellers of personal services to come within the purview of the Restatement's lost volume seller theory. . ., they must establish," in addition to capacity, that additional sales would have been profitable and that they would made the additional sale regardless of the buyer's breach). Jordan has not shown he could and *would have* entered into a subsequent agreement. Rather, the evidence shows that Jordan did not have the "subjective intent" to take on additional endorsements. *See Ullman-Briggs*, 754 F. Supp. at 1008. The testimony from Jordan's representatives establishes that although Jordan's popularity enabled him to obtain additional product endorsements in 2003, Jordan desired to scale back his level of endorsements. Jordan's financial and business advisor, Curtis Polk ("Polk"), testified that at the time the Agreement was rejected, Jordan's desire was "not to expand his spokesperson or pitchman efforts with new relationships." *See* Debtors' Mot. Summ. J., App. 5, at 32. Polk testified that had Jordan wanted to do additional endorsements after the 2003 rejection, he could have obtained additional deals. *See id.* at 64–65. Jordan's agent, David Falk ("Falk"), testified that "there might have been twenty more companies that in theory might have wanted to sign him" but that Jordan and his representatives wanted to avoid diluting his image. *See* Debtors' Mot. Summ J., App. 6, at 24. Jordan's Memorandum for Summary Judgment stated that at the time the Agreement was rejected, Jordan had implemented a strategy of not accepting new endorsements because of a belief that new deals would jeopardize his ability to achieve his primary goal of National Basketball Association ("NBA") franchise ownership.

. . .

One of the classic examples of the lost volume seller is found in *Neri v. Retail Marine Corp.*, 30 N.Y.2d 393, 399–400, 334 N.Y.S.2d 165, 169–70, 285 N.E.2d 311 (N.Y. 1972)[:]

> [I]f a private party agrees to sell his automobile to a buyer for $2,000, a breach by the buyer would cause the seller no loss (except incidental damages, i.e., expense of a new sale) if the seller was able to sell the automobile to another buyer for $2,000. But the situation is different with dealers having an unlimited supply or standard-priced goods. Thus, if an automobile dealer agrees to sell a car to a buyer at the standard price of $2,000, a breach by the buyer injures the dealer, even though he is able to sell the automobile to another for $2,000. If the dealer has an inexhaustible supply of cars, the resale to replace the breaching buyer costs the dealer a sale, because, had the breaching buyer performed, the dealer would have made two sales instead of one. The buyer's breach, in such a case, depletes the dealer's sales to

the extent of one, and the measure of damages should be the dealer's profit on one sale.

This example would surely have a different result if the car dealership was winding down its business and had agreed to sell one of its last cars to a buyer. If that buyer subsequently breached the contract and did not purchase the car, the dealership could hardly be expected to recover lost profits damages if the dealer put the car back onto a deserted car lot, made no attempts to sell it, and kept the dealership shuttered to new customers. Those modifications are analogous to Jordan's situation, with his stated desire to withdraw his services from the endorsement marketplace, and the lost volume seller theory accordingly does not apply to his circumstances.

Jordan states that it is a "red herring" to speculate under the lost volume analysis on what he *would* have done because that ignores the central point of the lost volume principle: if Jordan had. . .accepted a substantially similar endorsement opportunity—exactly what [MCI] argues he was required to do to mitigate damages—the damages for which [MCI] is liable would not have been reduced by one penny because the lost volume principle would allow Jordan to retain the benefits of both the [MCI] Agreement and the hypothetical additional endorsement. *See* Michael Jordan's Reply Brief, at 14–15.

Jordan overlooks an important point about the lost volume seller theory—that the "original sale and the second sale are independent events," *Snyder*, 380 A.2d at 625, because the lost volume seller's intent to enter into new contracts is the same before and after a purchaser's breach. The lost volume seller's desire to sell more units of goods or services is virtually unaffected by the loss of a single sale or agreement.

Next, even if Jordan had mitigated damages by entering one subsequent endorsement agreement, this, without more, does not mean that Jordan was a lost volume seller. The lost volume seller has the intent and capacity to sell multiple units despite the breach of a contract for one transaction.

Finally, if Jordan had entered into a subsequent agreement or agreements, and if he had showed both the capacity and the intent to make subsequent sales, that might have had the effect of helping him to establish his status as a lost volume seller, which generally would relieve him of the duty to mitigate. This would not be a novel situation but it ignores the fact that he did not do so. *See, e.g., Storage Tech. Corp. v. Trust Co. of N.J.*, 842 F.2d 54, 57 (3d Cir. 1988) ("The lost volume seller theory is a response to a breaching buyer's right to have a non-breaching seller mitigate damages. In other words, a seller can avoid the effect of its failure to mitigate by proving that it was a lost volume seller."); *Chicago Title Ins. Corp. v. Magnuson*, No. 2:03-CV-368, 2005 WL 2373430, at *23 (S.D. Ohio Sept. 26, 2005) (when there is no evidence in the record that plaintiff "turned away or would have turned away business during the relevant period" and the "only evidence on the issue supports that the [plaintiff] could and would have completed such transactions," the consequent instructions to the jury that the plaintiff was a lost volume seller and therefore had no duty to mitigate its damages were not erroneous).

Because the evidence establishes, among other things, that Jordan would not have entered into subsequent agreements, Jordan has not established that he is a lost volume seller. This theory thus does not relieve Jordan from the duty to mitigate damages.

. . .

The Court finds that Jordan failed to mitigate damages but a further evidentiary hearing is necessary to determine what Jordan could have received had he made reasonable efforts to mitigate, a determination that consequently will affect the Claim.

DISCUSSION PROBLEMS

1. Challenger Fallout

NASA contracted to launch a series of commercial satellites owned by Hughes Communications Galaxy into space from NASA's space shuttles. Following the explosion that destroyed the space shuttle "Challenger" in January 1986, President Reagan decided that NASA shuttles would no longer be used for commercial satellite launches. At that time, NASA was still contractually obligated to launch five of Hughes's HS-393 satellites over a period of several years. Without access to the space shuttles, Hughes turned to expendable launch vehicles (ELVs)—essentially, large rockets—to launch its satellites. Launching satellites using ELVs was more expensive than Hughes's contracted price with NASA. In addition, the HS-393 satellites were not well suited for ELV launches, so after launching three HS-393 satellites on ELVs, Hughes developed and launched HS-601 satellites, which were better suited to the ELV technology and, in addition, more powerful satellites.

(i) At a trial on the issue of damages, Hughes calculated the difference in the cost of launching an HS-393 satellite using ELVs and the cost it would have paid under the NASA contract and requested five times that amount (for the five launches it had left on its contract with NASA at the time of breach). NASA contended that, because Hughes only launched three HS-393s, it was only entitled to three times the cost differential.

(ii) The NASA contract with Hughes included a "reflight" clause, which would provide Hughes with a free relaunch on a later space shuttle if a satellite was not deployed or if its deployment deviated from the proper orbit. Reflight was not available in Hughes's contracts with the ELV providers, so Hughes purchased "launch insurance," which would have reimbursed the company for the cost of an unsuccessful launch. Hughes sought reimbursement for the cost of the launch insurance, and NASA objected on the ground that such insurance was not included in its contract with Hughes.

(iii) As a result of NASA's breach of contract and the subsequent increase in costs of launching satellites, Hughes increased the price it charged its customers for satellite space. NASA sought to have these revenues subtracted from the damages it owed to Hughes as "losses avoided." Hughes argued that it would be improper to consider price concessions obtained by Hughes subsequent to the breach as part of the damage calculation.

How should the court rule on these three issues concerning the calculation of damages?

2. The Red Lion Inn

The Red Lion Inn fired its employee, Patricia Fair, two weeks before she was scheduled to return from a medical leave of absence. When Fair threatened a lawsuit for breach of contract, Red Lion offered to reinstate her in her job as a room service server. When Red Lion refused to agree to a series of additional conditions, Fair declined reinstatement and proceeded with her suit.

In her trial testimony, Fair provided three reasons that she declined the reinstatement offer: she feared retaliatory termination in the future, she was concerned about the physical demands of the job because she had become pregnant while on the medical leave, and she was uncertain about whether her reinstated medical benefits would cover her during the period of time between her firing and her reinstatement. Red Lion claimed Fair's refusal to accept reinstatement constituted a failure to mitigate her damages and moved to limit Fair's recovery to wages lost prior to that point in time. How should the judge rule on Red Lion's motion?

3. The Call Center

Sprint Spectrum contracted with Penncro Associates to staff a call center with employees who would seek to collect unpaid charges owed to Sprint by cell phone customers. The contract obligated Penncro to provide 500 employees to service the Sprint contract, but difficulties with hiring and retention made it continually difficult for Penncro to sustain this level of staffing.

After Sprint breached the contract, Penncro was able to sign a similar agreement with another consumer telecom company, AT&T, based on its experience having worked for Sprint, as well as another contract with

American Water. Penncro serviced these two accounts from the same facility that it had used for the Sprint call center, using the same employees who had serviced the Sprint account. Penncro sued Sprint for damages, seeking the $25 million in profits it had expected to earn from the remaining period of the Sprint contract ($53 million due under the contract minus $28 million that Penncro saved by not having to service the Sprint account). Sprint argued that $6.5 million in profits that Penncro earned from the AT&T and American Water contracts Sprint should be subtracted. How should the court rule?

CHAPTER 23

LIMITATIONS ON DAMAGES

■ ■ ■

INTRODUCTION

When a non-breaching party can respond to a breach by entering into a substitute transaction, the expectation damages principle is generally workable, although complications determining the precise valuation often arise when the substitute transaction differs from the original transaction in material ways. When a contract is breached and there is no substitute transaction that is available to and suitable for the non-breaching party, the principle underlying expectation damages, that the non-breaching party must be made whole, suggests that the breaching party should be liable for the difference between the contract price and the full value of the expected performance to the non-breaching party. Applying this principle, however, can lead to liability that is both substantial and unpredictable, which could reduce the *ex ante* value of contract law to both buyers and sellers of goods and services.

As an example, imagine that a band breaches a contract to perform at a wedding just hours ahead of the nuptials, leaving no time for the bride and groom to find a replacement. To some couples, the inconvenience would seem minor, and a minimal amount of damages would make them indifferent to the result. To others, the breach would be devastating, and a very large sum, perhaps many times the contract price, would be required to make them truly indifferent to celebrating such a significant occasion without live music. The unpredictability of the couple's expectation damages would make it difficult for the band to price its services (knowing that circumstances beyond its control might force it to breach) and to determine what steps to prevent a breach would be cost effective to take (imagine, for example, that the band suffers a flat tire on its way to the ceremony).

The limitations on expectation damages provided by the "foreseeability" and "certainty" doctrines attempt to respond to these problems by placing limits on liability. In *Hadley v. Baxendale,* one of the most famous cases in Anglo-American contract law, the court considers the problem that the damages suffered by a delay in fixing a mill's broken crankshaft depend on whether the mill has a spare on site or not. It deals with the problem by limiting expectation damages to those that are reasonably foreseeable by the breaching party at the time of contracting. See Rest. (2d) Contracts § 351.

Kenford Company, Inc. v. County of Erie and *Florafax International, Inc. v. GTE Market Resources, Inc.* consider what evidence is necessary to prove lost profits suffered as a result of a breach to the standard of "reasonable certainty." Rest. (2d) Contracts § 352. Should the non-breaching party be able to recover for its projected lost profits in one case but not in the other?

Restatement (Second) of Contracts § 351. Unforeseeability and Related Limitations on Damages

(1) Damages are not recoverable for loss that the party in breach did not have reason to foresee as a probable result of the breach when the contract was made.

(2) Loss may be foreseeable as a probable result of a breach because it follows from the breach

(a) in the ordinary course of events, or

(b) as a result of special circumstances, beyond the ordinary course of events, that the party in breach had reason to know.

(3) A court may limit damages for foreseeable loss by excluding recovery for loss of profits, by allowing recovery only for loss incurred in reliance, or otherwise if it concludes that in the circumstances justice so requires in order to avoid disproportionate compensation.

Comment:

a. Requirement of foreseeability. A contracting party is generally expected to take account of those risks that are foreseeable at the time he makes the contract. He is not, however, liable in the event of breach for loss that he did not at the time of contracting have reason to foresee as a probable result of such a breach. The mere circumstance that some loss was foreseeable, or even that some loss of the same general kind was foreseeable, will not suffice if the loss that actually occurred was not foreseeable. It is enough, however, that the loss was foreseeable as a probable, as distinguished from a necessary, result of his breach. Furthermore, the party in breach need not have made a "tacit agreement" to be liable for the loss. Nor must he have had the loss in mind when making the contract, for the test is an objective one based on what he had reason to foresee. There is no requirement of foreseeability with respect to the injured party. In spite of these qualifications, the requirement of foreseeability is a more severe limitation of liability than is the requirement of substantial or "proximate" cause in the case of an action in tort or for breach of warranty. . . .Uniform Commercial Code § 2–715(2)(b). Although the recovery that is precluded by the limitation of foreseeability is usually based on the expectation interest and takes the form of lost profits. . .the limitation may also preclude recovery based on the reliance interest[.]

Restatement (Second) of Contracts § 352. Uncertainty as a Limitation on Damages.

Damages are not recoverable for loss beyond an amount that the evidence permits to be established with reasonable certainty.

CASES

HADLEY V. BAXENDALE

Court of Exchequer
156 Eng. Rep. 1220 (1854)

At the trial before Crompton, J., at the last Gloucester Assizes, it appeared that the plaintiffs carried on an extensive business as millers at Gloucester; and that, on the 11th of May, their mill was stopped by a breakage of the crank shaft by which the mill was worked. The steam-engine was manufactured by Messrs. Joyce & Co., the engineers, at Greenwich, and it became necessary to send the shaft as a pattern for a new one to Greenwich. The fracture was discovered on the 12th, and on the 13th the plaintiffs sent one of their servants to the office of the defendants, who are the well-known carriers trading under the name of Pickford & Co., for the purpose of having the shaft carried to Greenwich. . . .[I]n answer to the inquiry when the shaft would be taken, the answer was, that if it was sent up by twelve o'clock any day, it would be delivered at Greenwich on the following day. . . .The delivery of the shaft at Greenwich was delayed by some neglect; and the consequence was, that the plaintiffs did not receive the new shaft for several days after they would otherwise have done, and the working of their mill was thereby delayed, and they thereby lost the profits they would otherwise have received.

On the part of the defendants, it was objected that these damages were too remote, and that the defendants were not liable with respect to them. The learned Judge left the case generally to the jury, who found a verdict with 25£ damages beyond the amount paid into Court.

ALDERSON, B.

We think that there ought to be a new trial in this case; but, in so doing, we deem it to be expedient and necessary to state explicitly the rule which the Judge, at the next trial, ought, in our opinion, to direct the jury to be governed by when they estimate the damages.

It is, indeed, of the last importance that we should do this; for, if the jury are left without any definite rule to guide them, it will, in such cases as these, manifestly lead to the greatest injustice. . . .

"There are certain established rules," this Court says, in *Alder v. Keighley* (15 M. & W. 117), "according to which the jury ought to find." And the Court, in that case, adds: "and here there is a clear rule, that the amount which would have been received if the contract had been kept, is the measure of damages if the contract is broken."

Now we think the proper rule in such a case as the present is this: Where two parties have made a contract which one of them has broken, the damages which the other party ought to receive in respect of such breach of contract should be such as may fairly and reasonably be considered either arising naturally, i.e., according to the usual course of things, from such breach of contract itself, or such as may reasonably be supposed to have been in the contemplation of both parties, at the time they made the contract, as the probable result of the breach of it. Now, if the special circumstances under which the contract was actually made were communicated by the plaintiffs to the defendants, and thus known to both parties, the damages resulting from the breach of such a contract, which they would reasonably contemplate, would be the amount of injury which would ordinarily follow from a breach of contract under these special circumstances so known and communicated. But, on the other hand, if these special circumstances were wholly unknown to the party breaking the contract, he, at the most, could only be supposed to have had in his contemplation the amount of injury which would arise generally, and in the great multitude of cases not affected by any special circumstances, from such a breach of contract. For, had the special circumstances been known, the parties might have specially provided for the breach of contract by special terms as to the damages in that case; and of this advantage it would be very unjust to deprive them.

Now the above principles are those by which we think the jury ought to be guided in estimating the damages arising out of any breach of contract. . . .Now, in the present case, if we are to apply the principles above laid down, we find that the only circumstances here communicated by the plaintiffs to the defendants at the time the contract was made, were, that the article to be carried was the broken shaft of a mill, and that the plaintiffs were the millers of that mill. But how do these circumstances shew reasonably that the profits of the mill must be stopped by an unreasonable delay in the delivery of the broken shaft by the carrier to the third person? Suppose the plaintiffs had another shaft in their possession put up or putting up at the time, and that they only wished to send back the broken shaft to the engineer who made it; it is clear that this would be quite consistent with the above circumstances, and yet the unreasonable delay in the delivery would have no effect upon the intermediate profits of the mill. Or, again, suppose that, at the time of the delivery to the carrier, the machinery of the mill had been in other respects defective, then, also, the same results would follow. Here it is true that the shaft was actually sent back to serve as a model for a new one, and that the want of a new one was the only cause of the stoppage of the mill, and that the loss of profits really arose from not sending down the new shaft in proper time, and that this arose from the delay in delivering the broken one to serve as a model. But it is obvious that, in the great multitude of cases of millers sending off broken shafts to third persons by a carrier under ordinary circumstances, such consequences would not, in all probability, have occurred; and these special circumstances were here never communicated by the plaintiffs to the defendants.

It follows, therefore, that the loss of profits here cannot reasonably be considered such a consequence of the breach of contract as could have been fairly and reasonably contemplated by both the parties when they made this contract. For such loss would neither have flowed naturally from the breach of this contract in the great multitude of such cases occurring under ordinary circumstances, nor were the special circumstances, which, perhaps, would have made it a reasonable and natural consequence of such breach of contract, communicated to or known by the defendants. The Judge ought, therefore, to have told the jury, that, upon the facts then before them, they ought not to take the loss of profits into consideration at all in estimating the damages. There must therefore be a new trial in this case.

Rule absolute.

KENFORD CO. V. COUNTY OF ERIE

Court of Appeals of New York
67 N.Y.2d 257 (1986)

PER CURIAM.

The issue in this appeal is whether a plaintiff, in an action for breach of contract, may recover loss of prospective profits for its contemplated 20-year operation of a domed stadium which was to be constructed by defendant County of Erie (County).

On August 8, 1969, pursuant to a duly adopted resolution of its legislature, the County of Erie entered into a contract with Kenford Company, Inc. (Kenford) and Dome Stadium, Inc. (DSI) for the construction and operation of a domed stadium facility near the City of Buffalo. The contract provided that construction of the facility by the County would commence within 12 months of the contract date and that a mutually acceptable 40-year lease between the County and DSI for the operation of said facility would be negotiated by the parties and agreed upon within three months of the receipt by the County of preliminary plans, drawings and cost estimates. It was further provided that in the event a mutually acceptable lease could not be agreed upon within the three-month period, a separate management contract between the County and DSI, as appended to the basic agreement, would be executed by the parties, providing for the operation of the stadium facility by DSI for a period of 20 years from the completion of the stadium and its availability for use [with DSI compensation set as a percentage of revenues.]

Although strenuous and extensive negotiations followed, the parties never agreed upon the terms of a lease, nor did construction of a domed facility begin within the one-year period or at any time thereafter. A breach of the contract thus occurred and this action was commenced in June 1971 by Kenford and DSI.

[A trial on the issue of damages resulted in] a multimillion dollar jury verdict in plaintiffs' favor. An appeal to the Appellate Division resulted in a modification of the judgment. . . . On appeal to this court, we are concerned only with that portion of the verdict which awarded DSI money damages for loss of prospective profits during the 20-year period of the proposed management contract, as appended to the basic contract. That portion of the verdict was set aside by the Appellate Division and the cause of action dismissed. The court concluded that the use of expert opinion to present statistical projections of future business operations involved the use of too many variables to provide a rational basis upon which lost profits could be calculated and, therefore, such projections were insufficient as a matter of law to support an award of lost profits. We agree with this ultimate conclusion, but upon different grounds.

Loss of future profits as damages for breach of contract have been permitted in New York under long-established and precise rules of law. First, it must be demonstrated with certainty that such damages have been caused by the breach and, second, the alleged loss must be capable of proof with reasonable certainty. In other words, the damages may not be merely speculative, possible or imaginary, but must be reasonably certain and directly traceable to the breach, not remote or the result of other intervening causes (*Wakeman v. Wheeler & Wilson Mfg. Co.*, 101 NY 205). In addition, there must be a showing that the particular damages were fairly within the contemplation of the parties to the contract at the time it was made (*Witherbee v. Meyer*, 155 NY 446). If it is a new business seeking to recover for loss of future profits, a stricter standard is imposed for the obvious reason that there does not exist a reasonable basis of experience upon which to estimate lost profits with the requisite degree of reasonable certainty (*Cramer v. Grand Rapids Show Case Co.*, 223 NY 63; 25 CJS, Damages, § 42[b]).

These rules must be applied to the proof presented by DSI in this case. We note the procedure for computing damages selected by DSI was in accord with contemporary economic theory and was presented through the testimony of recognized experts. Such a procedure has been accepted in this State and many other jurisdictions (*see, De Long v. County of Erie*, 60 NY2d 296). DSI's economic analysis employed historical data, obtained from the operation of other domed stadiums and related facilities throughout the country, which was then applied to the results of a comprehensive study of the marketing prospects for the proposed facility in the Buffalo area. The quantity of proof is massive and, unquestionably, represents business and industry's most advanced and sophisticated method for predicting the probable results of contemplated projects. Indeed, it is difficult to conclude what additional relevant proof could have been submitted by DSI in support of its attempt to establish, with reasonable certainty, loss of prospective profits. Nevertheless, DSI's proof is insufficient to meet the required standard.

. . .[Despite the massive quantity of expert proof submitted by DSI, the ultimate conclusions are still projections, and as employed in the present day commercial world, subject to adjustment and modification. We of course recognize that any projection cannot be absolute, nor is there any such requirement, but it is axiomatic that the degree of certainty is dependent upon known or unknown factors which form the basis of the ultimate conclusion. Here, the foundations upon which the economic model was created undermine the certainty of the projections. DSI assumed that the facility was completed, available for use and successfully operated by it for 20 years, providing professional sporting events and other forms of entertainment, as well as hosting meetings, conventions and related commercial gatherings. At the time of the breach, there was only one other facility in this country to use as a basis of comparison, the Astrodome in Houston. Quite simply, the multitude of assumptions required to establish projections of profitability over the life of this contract require speculation and conjecture, making it beyond the capability of even the most sophisticated procedures to satisfy the legal requirements of proof with reasonable certainty.

The economic facts of life, the whim of the general public and the fickle nature of popular support for professional athletic endeavors must be given great weight in attempting to ascertain damages 20 years in the future. New York has long recognized the inherent uncertainties of predicting profits in the entertainment field in general (*see, Broadway Photoplay Co. v. World Film Corp.*, 225 NY 104) and, in this case, we are dealing, in large part, with a new facility furnishing entertainment for the public. It is our view that the record in this case demonstrates the efficacy of the principles set forth by this court in *Cramer v. Grand Rapids Show Case Co.* (223 NY 63), principles to which we continue to adhere. In so doing, we specifically reject the "rational basis" test enunciated in *Perma Research & Dev. Co. v. Singer Co.* (542 F2d 111, *cert denied* 429 US 987) and adopted by the Appellate Division.

Accordingly, that portion of the order of the Appellate Division being appealed from should be affirmed.

FLORAFAX INTERNATIONAL, INC. V. GTE MARKET RESOURCES, INC.

Supreme Court of Oklahoma
1997 Ok. 7 (1997)

LAVENDER, J.

Florafax is generally a flowers-by-wire company acting as a clearinghouse to allow the placement and receipt of orders between florists throughout the United States and internationally. Basically the system works as follows: retail florists become members of the Florafax network (apparently, thousands of retail florists join Florafax's wire service). Florafax maintains a list of the members and circulates a directory to them. The members are then able to send and receive orders among each other throughout the system. In other words, a consumer orders flowers at a retail florist at a certain location (e.g. Oklahoma City) to be delivered to someone in another location (e.g. Los Angeles). Florafax assists the transactions by collecting money from the florist taking the order from the customer and guarantying payment to the florist delivering the flowers. It processes the credit card activity on the transactions and charges a fee or fees for this service. Florafax also maintains a computer network whereby member florists can send and receive orders by computer—if they have such technology—without using the telephone. It also has a division that advertises floral products by the use of brochures, and other sales and promotional materials, allowing consumers to place a telephone order for floral products directly without going through a florist in their hometowns.

Evidence at trial showed at the time the agreements giving rise to this dispute were entered that Florafax was one of the largest floral wire services of its kind in the nation, and, in fact, certain evidence placed it third world-wide behind Florists' Transworld Delivery Association (FTD) and a company known as Teleflora. Evidence also showed Florafax had been headquartered in Tulsa, Oklahoma since, at least, 1979.

In addition to the above activities, Florafax solicits agreements with third party clients such as supermarket chains, American Express and other entities that advertise the sale of floral products by various methods (e.g. television, radio, newspapers, billing circulars, mass mailings to consumers) which allow a consumer to order floral arrangements via the use of a 1-800 telephone call, with Florafax agreeing to handle the actual inbound and outbound communication aspects of the transactions. In other words, when a consumer responds to an advertisement, it is not the advertiser that answers the telephone call to take the order, or that makes a telephone call or computer communication to a retail florist for fulfillment, but it is Florafax who handles these activities. Such orders would, of course, be fulfilled, if possible, by retail florist members taken from the Florafax directory maintained by it and, again, Florafax would handle the mechanics of processing the transactions, e.g. credit card processing. The advertiser would pay Florafax a certain fee or fees for its services.

One client that signed up for an arrangement like that described immediately above was Bellerose Floral, Inc., d/b/a Flora Plenty, a leading marketer of floral products advertising sales through use of the telephone number 1-800-FLOWERS. Florafax and Bellerose entered a contract in early October 1989 whereby Florafax and/or its designee would accept direct consumer orders (i.e. inbound calls and orders) placed via the 1-800-FLOWERS number and, of course, it also agreed to handle the outbound placement of orders either by telephone or computer transmission. The Florafax/Bellerose contract provided Florafax would be paid certain fee(s) per order. As we read the contract its initial term was for one year, to be automatically renewed from month to month thereafter, but that either party, with or without cause, could terminate the agreement upon sixty (60) days written notice.

GTE, on the other hand, was a company providing telecommunication and/or telemarketing services for other businesses. It provided for other businesses a call answering center where telemarketing sales representatives (TSRs) physically answered telephones when orders from promotional activities came in from consumers and took care of transmitting the orders by telephone or computer for fulfillment. For certain management and business-related reasons Florafax subcontracted out much of the telecommunication and telemarketing services of its business.

In mid-October 1989, about two weeks after Florafax signed its agreement with Bellerose, the Florafax/GTE contract was entered. In essence, it provided GTE would via a call answering center (apparently located in the Dallas, Texas area) handle much, if not all, of the activities connected with taking incoming orders and placing outgoing calls or computer transmissions directed to it by Florafax associated with the purchase and fulfillment of floral orders throughout the United States and internationally. The agreement required Florafax to pay GTE certain fees for this service depending on the type of order.

The Florafax/GTE contract generally ran for a term of three years from the effective date the parties anticipated Florafax would begin directing calls to GTE for floral orders—a date anticipated to be in early December

1989. It also contained certain provisions that in essence might result in termination after a two year period based upon application of a price/fee renegotiation clause. In answer to one of the questions submitted via a special verdict form, the jury determined the Florafax/GTE contract could be terminated after two years based on this clause.

. . .

[The evidence produced at trial indicated that GTE breached its agreement with Florafax and, as a consequence, Bellarose terminated its contract with Florafax.] The jury. . ., in addition to other damages, awarded Florafax $750,000.00 in lost profits that would have been earned under the Florafax/Bellerose contract over a two year period of time.

. . .

Generally speaking, this Court has long espoused the view that loss of future or anticipated profit—i.e. loss of expected monetary gain—is recoverable in a breach of contract action: 1) if the loss is within the contemplation of the parties at the time the contract was made, 2) if the loss flows directly or proximately from the breach—i.e. if the loss can be said to have been caused by the breach—and 3) if the loss is capable of reasonably accurate measurement or estimate. *Groendyke Transport, Inc. v. Merchant*, 380 P.2d 682 *Second Syllabus* (Okla. 1962).

. . .

. . .When a breach of a contractual obligation with resulting damages has been established, although the amount of damages may not be based on mere speculation, conjecture and surmise alone, the mere uncertainty as to the exact amount of damages will not preclude the right of recovery. *Larrance Tank Corporation v. Burrough*, 476 P.2d 346, 350 (Okla. 1970). It is sufficient if the evidence shows the extent of damage by just and reasonable inference. *Id.* We believe sufficient evidence was presented so that Florafax carried its burden to prove the fact, cause and amount of its lost profit damages with the requisite degree of reasonable certainty.

The fact of lost profit damage beyond merely a sixty (60) day period is shown by the testimony of Bellerose's President. Although not absolute, his testimony was, in essence, he considered the relationship with Florafax a long-term one had things worked out and that the most important issues to him in making the decision to terminate were issues concerning performance. This testimony showed the relationship in all probability would have continued long after it was terminated had GTE adequately performed. Although it is true—given the existence of the sixty (60) day notice provision—Bellerose might have terminated the Florafax/Bellerose contract at some point in time even had GTE performed, the state of this record does not require a conclusion Bellerose would have exercised its right of termination for some other reason.

We are also of the view the fact of damage is partially shown by the projections for profits of both the damage experts presented by the parties. Although they differed in their ultimate conclusions as to the extent or amount of lost profits, both presented estimates that Florafax could have made profits from the Florafax/Bellerose relationship had it survived.

. . .

As to the exact extent or amount of damages, the record contains sufficient evidence to take the matter out of the realm of mere speculation, conjecture or surmise. A track record existed which showed the calls coming to GTE from Bellerose during the five to seven months Bellerose business was actually being routed to GTE. There was also evidence that although the business relationship between Florafax and Bellerose was relatively new, Bellerose had been in business for a number of years, and it had experienced 100,000–200,000 orders annually. Such evidence clearly was appropriate to consider on the issue of the extent of lost profits. Although this case is not exactly like our cases dealing with the destruction of an established business by a breach of contract, it is sufficiently close to be analogized to the established business situation, where we have allowed the recovery of lost profits. *See e.g. Firestone Tire & Rubber Co. v. Sheets, supra,* 62 P.2d at 93; *See also Hardesty v. Andro Corporation-Webster Division,* 555 P.2d 1030, 1034–1035 (Okla. 1976), *disapproved on other grounds; Old Albany Estates, Ltd. v. Highland Carpet Mills, Inc.*, 604 P.2d 849 (Okla. 1979); and *City of Collinsville v. Brickey,* 115 Okla. 264, 242 P. 249, 249–250 *Fifth Syllabus* (1925) (tort case where nuisance resulted in destruction of established business).

Evidence also existed which showed that Bellerose, after terminating its relationship with Florafax, experienced a substantial increase in its sales volume in 1991. In other words, there was not only evidence tending to show a certain volume of orders prior to the breach, but evidence tending to show that level of sales would have in all probability increased substantially during part of the term of the Florafax/GTE contract had Bellerose continued its relationship with Florafax. This post-breach evidence is proper to be considered at arriving at a reasonable estimate of the loss caused by a breach of contract [*Ft. Smith & Western Railroad Co. v. Williams, supra,* 121 P. at 278] because all facts which would reasonably tend to make certain the amount of injury inflicted are admissible. *Cloe v. Rogers,* 31 Okla. 255, 121 P. 201, 208 (1912). Although the jury apparently did not totally credit the testimony or documentation presented by either Florafax's or GTE's experts as to their projections of profits lost, the $750,000.00 awarded for the two year period was within the range of the estimates of the two experts. Accordingly, not only was the fact and causation of lost profit damages adequately shown to a reasonable certainty, but the amount of lost profit damages awarded was sufficiently shown through competent evidence contained in this record to take the matter out of the realm of mere speculation, conjecture and surmise.

DISCUSSION PROBLEMS

1. A Last-Minute Change of Plans

Maine Rubber International hired Environmental Management Group (EMG) to test a potential new factory site for contaminants, telling EMG that it was considering purchasing the property in question but providing no specific information about the company's relocation plans.

For a fee of $1,900, EMG determined that the property was clean, and Maine Rubber made extensive preparations for a phased move of its factory operations to the new location. Just before the move was about to take place, government regulators discovered significant environmental hazards on the new site that EMG had failed to identify. Because the toxins on the property could not be remediated before the closing date, Maine Rubber canceled the purchase and completed an expedited, and much more expensive, move to another site. It then sued EMG for breach of contract.

Maine Rubber sought $200,000 in damages as compensation for the costs of preparing for the phased move and $500,000 for lost profits during the period in which its operations needed to be shuttered because of the unanticipated, last-minute need to move to a different location. Assuming that EMG breached the contract with Maine Rubber, how should the court rule on Maine Rubber's claim for damages?

2. A Modern Drama

Professor Philip Freund contracted with Washington Square Press to publish Freund's manuscript on modern drama, first in a hardcover edition and then later in paperback. The contract called for the press to pay Freund an advance of $2,000 and royalties of 10 percent of retail sales proceeds. Washington Square paid the advance, but soon after it stopped publishing in hardcover, and it never published Freund's book. Freund sued and presented expert testimony at trial that it would have cost Washington Square $10,000 to publish the book. He presented no evidence of any costs he incurred in producing the book or any evidence concerning how many copies the book might have sold. What damages, if any, should the court award?

3. Restaurant Service and Hotel Occupancy

In 1989, Apted-Hulling, the owner of the Cheshire Lodge in suburban St. Louis, leased its adjoining restaurant, the Cheshire Inn, to L&S

Properties Limited for a term of 25 years. The lease agreement required that the Inn provide room service and breakfast service to guests staying at the Lodge. By all accounts, the relationship worked well for a decade before Lodge guests began to complain that room service was slow or even nonexistent and that breakfast was often unavailable. From 1999 to 2004, the room vacancy rate at the Lodge increased significantly.

In 2004, Apted-Hulling sued L&S for breach of contract. The Lodge's business manager, Margaret Piot, testified without challenge that the Lodge rented 6,263 fewer single-occupancy rooms in 2003 and 6,543 fewer in 2004 than in 1991. She also testified that, using a conservative estimate of revenue per guest and the Lodge's profit margin of 40 percent, the reduction in occupancy resulted in a $244,000 decline in profit for those two years compared to 1991 levels. Finally, Piot also testified that the Lodge had received numerous complaints about the restaurant's service, and that the reduction in occupancy was due entirely to the actions of L&S. On cross examination, Piot testified that the Lodge had no direct competitors for business travelers within three miles of its location but, when the L&S attorney listed several hotels nearby, Piot conceded that at least two were competitors. She also testified that she did not know if the number of corporate headquarters had increased or decreased in St. Louis during the period of time in question, or whether the demolition of a nearby sports venue could have affected the Lodge's occupancy rates.

The trial judge, sitting as the trier of fact, awarded the plaintiff $244,000 in damages for lost profits, and L&S appealed. Assuming L&S breached the contract by providing sub-par quality food service, how should the appellate court rule on the issue of damages?

CHAPTER 24

STIPULATED DAMAGES

■ ■ ■

INTRODUCTION

When a contracting party breaches its duties, the non-breaching party is generally entitled to recover its expectation damages, limited by the mitigation principle, subject to the foreseeability and certainty doctrines. If the non-breaching party cannot prove its full expectation damages to the level of reasonable certainty, it will still be entitled to recover any reliance damages suffered (the amount of money or other resources expended to satisfy its contractual obligations), which will be less than expectation damages if the contract would have been profitable to that party. If money damages would be "inadequate" and performance remains possible and desirable to the non-breaching party, it should be able to obtain a grant of specific performance.

But are these rules concerning remedies for breach immutable, or are they only default rules that apply if the parties have not agreed on their own set of remedies for breach? Often, a contract states the amount of damages one or both parties should be entitled to in the case of breach. Such party-specified remedies for breach are called "stipulated damages." Do stipulated damages terms displace the general rules of remedies covered in the previous three chapters?

With few exceptions, parties may use a contract to specify their own duties, and a thoroughly drafted agreement generally reduces the court's job to interpretation and gap-filling. But contract law does not treat stipulated damages terms as flexibly as it treats most other terms. Stipulated damages are enforceable as "liquidated damages," but only if they constitute a *reasonable* approximation of either anticipated or actual damages. If stipulated damages exceed reasonable estimates of damages a party would be likely to suffer in the event of breach, those terms are classified as "penalty clauses" and are unenforceable. Rest. (2d) Contracts § 356. *TAL Financial Corporation v. CSC Consulting, Inc.* and *NPS, LLC v. Minihane* grapple with this distinction, with the court enforcing the stipulated damages term in one contract but not in the other. Notice that the two cases were decided by the same court within a two-year period of time. Are they distinguishable?

Restatement (Second) of Contracts § 356. Liquidated Damages and Penalties

(1) Damages for breach by either party may be liquidated in the agreement but only at an amount that is reasonable in the light of the anticipated or actual loss caused by the breach and the difficulties of proof of loss. A term fixing unreasonably large liquidated damages is unenforceable on grounds of public policy as a penalty.

(2) A term in a bond providing for an amount of money as a penalty for non-occurrence of the condition of the bond is unenforceable on grounds of public policy to the extent that the amount exceeds the loss caused by such non-occurrence.

CASES

TAL FINANCIAL CORP. v. CSC CONSULTING, INC.

Supreme Judicial Court of Massachusetts
446 Mass. 422 (2006)

GREANEY, J.

. . .TAL is a boutique finance company, located in Framingham, that specializes in extending credit to small companies through equipment leasing. TAL's president and sole shareholder is Howard D. Siegel. CSC is a company with headquarters in Waltham that provides information technology consulting services for businesses. In the summer of 1997, Onward was a start-up company, located in Natick, engaged in the business of website development.

On July 28, 1997, TAL and Onward entered into an agreement for the lease of computer hardware, telephone equipment, software, and office furniture needed by Onward to start its business. The agreement consisted of a master lease and the first of what would be a series of three schedules incorporating the terms of the master lease. The first schedule (schedule one) identified computer hardware, telephone equipment, and software licensed to Onward, and provided for monthly payments from Onward to TAL of $1,692.55, including taxes, for thirty-six months. On September 3, 1997, Onward and TAL executed a second schedule (schedule two) which identified additional computer hardware, used furniture, and software licensed to Onward. Schedule two provided for monthly payments of $2,587.55, including taxes, for thirty-six months. On January 28, 1998, Onward and TAL executed a third and final schedule (schedule three) to the master lease, also identifying computer hardware, used furniture, and software licensed to Onward. Schedule three provided for monthly payments of $716.07, including taxes, for thirty-six months.

The master lease provided that each schedule would begin as of the first day of the month following Onward's acceptance of the leased equipment and end as of the last day of the calendar month in which the schedule was executed. Thus, schedule one began on August 1, 1997, and was to end July 31, 2000; schedule two began on October 1, 1997, and was to end September 30, 2000; and schedule three began on February 1, 1998, and was to end on January 31, 2001. The schedules provided for TAL to receive a total of $179,862.12 over thirty-six months. At the time each schedule was executed, Onward paid TAL in advance the first, thirty-fifth, and thirty-sixth payments due.

TAL paid a total of $140,433.62 for all of the items listed in the schedules, including $76,590.15 for computer hardware and telephone equipment, $33,305.40 for used furniture, and $30,538.07 for software. . . .

. . .Section 20 of the master lease provides that, in the event of a default by Onward, then TAL "at its sole option" may elect one or more of several alternatives, including (1) declaring a default and demanding payment of the entire amount of rent remaining to be paid over the balance of the lease, and (2) recovering "as liquidated damages for loss of a bargain and not as a penalty (X) an amount equal to the present value of all moneys to be paid by [Onward] during the remaining Initial Term or any renewal period then in effect. . .discounted at the rate of six percent (6.0%). . .plus (Y) eighteen percent (18%) of the Acquisition Cost to [TAL] of such Equipment and/or any Other Equipment." Section 20 additionally provides that Onward's failure to return any of the leased items would entitle TAL to recover "as liquidated damages for breach of this Lease, and not as a penalty, an amount equal to the sum of the amounts specified in items (X) and (Y) [set forth] above.". . .

On or about March 31, 1998, CSC acquired the stock of Onward, which merged into CSC. . . .CSC continued to make monthly payments set forth in the schedules. On or about August, 1999, Onward's employees moved from Natick to CSC's Waltham offices. Either before or during the move, CSC discarded most of the equipment and furniture covered by the master lease. CSC also misplaced the lease documents.

The case proceeded to trial on TAL's claim that. . .CSC's failure to return any of the leased items constituted a default entitling TAL to liquidated damages in the amount of eighteen per cent of its acquisition costs. In sum, TAL claimed damages in the amount of $112,156 (the remaining rental payments it claimed were due on a sixty-month lease, plus late charges, plus liquidated damages). [CSC questioned] whether the liquidated damages provision in the master lease calling for eighteen per cent of TAL's acquisition costs was enforceable as a reasonable estimate of actual damages under principles set forth in *Kelly v. Marx*, 428 Mass. 877, 880, 705 N.E.2d 1114 (1999), or void as an unconscionable penalty.

. . .

The judge determined that the liquidated damages provision calling for the present value of all future rent, plus eighteen per cent of the acquisition costs of all the items listed in the schedules, was an unreasonable estimate of any actual damage that could have been anticipated at the time the schedules were executed and, therefore, unenforceable. The judge's reasoning incorporated her findings that (a) the majority of items to be leased were not yet identified at the time the parties agreed to the provision in the master lease; (b) the lease did not provide for the reduction of the liquidated payment if the lease extended beyond the original thirty-six month term; and (c) it could have been anticipated that the leased items had little or no residual value after three years and, thus, the eighteen per cent figure was "grossly disproportionate" to a reasonable estimate of actual damages at the time of contract formation. We agree with the judge's conclusion and much of her reasoning. Before elaborating, however, we consider a matter intrinsically related to our resolution of the liquidated damages issue, but one not raised by the parties, or mentioned by the judge, at trial: which party bears the burden of proof when a clause in a contract providing for payment of liquidated damages is challenged as unenforceable.

. . .

Under freedom of contract principles, generally, parties are held to the express terms of their contract, and the burden of proof is on the party seeking to invalidate an express term. The burden of proof regarding the enforceability of a liquidated damages clause, therefore, should rest squarely on the party seeking to set it aside. See *Town Planning & Eng'g Assocs., Inc. v. Amesbury Specialty Co.*, 369 Mass. 737, 744, 342 N.E.2d 706 (1976); *Hastings Assocs., Inc. v. Local 369 Bldg. Fund, Inc.*, 42 Mass. App. Ct. 162, 173, 675 N.E.2d 403 (1997). Any reasonable doubt as to whether a provision constitutes a penalty or a legitimate liquidated damages clause should be resolved in favor of the aggrieved party. We thus join the majority of courts in other States that have considered the question.

. . .

It has long been the rule in Massachusetts that a contract provision that clearly and reasonably establishes liquidated damages should be enforced, so long as it is not so disproportionate to anticipated damages as to constitute a penalty. See *Kaplan v. Gray*, 215 Mass. 269, 270–273, 102 N.E. 421 (1913). There is no bright line separating an agreement to pay a reasonable measure of damages from an unenforceable penalty clause. In *Kelly v. Marx, supra,* we provided guidance as to how a judge should analyze the enforceability of a liquidated damages clause in a purchase and sale agreement. We squarely rejected the "second look" approach, where actual damages resulting from the breach are measured to determine whether enforcement of the agreement for liquidated damages would serve unfairly to punish one party rather than compensate the other "who suffered no loss from the [first party's] breach." *Id.* at 879, 705 N.E.2d 1114. Generally, a liquidated damages provision will be enforced when, at the time the agreement was made, potential damages were difficult to determine and the clause was a reasonable forecast of damages expected to occur in the event of a breach. Conversely, "[l]iquidated damages will not be enforced if the sum is 'grossly disproportionate to a reasonable estimate of actual damages' made at the time of contract formation." *Id.* at 880, 705 N.E.2d 1114, quoting *Lynch v. Andrew*, 20 Mass. App. Ct. 623, 628, 481 N.E.2d 1383 (1985). This approach, we concluded, will most accurately reflect the expectations of the parties when they contracted for liquidated damages. See *Kelly v. Marx, supra* at 880–881, 705 N.E.2d 1114.

. . .We conclude that CSC carried its burden of establishing that this provision called for damages that were "grossly disproportionate" to a reasonable estimate of anticipated damages at the time the schedules were executed. A reasonable estimate of such damages, occurring after a lease term of thirty-six months (a term guaranteed under the lease), would have been a negligible amount. Failing to provide any recognition for the type, or timing, of the default, while by no means determinative, tends to indicate that the provision's intended purpose was not to estimate the different types of damages that might arise from a future default, but to penalize for any failure, however immaterial. Although we cautioned in *Kelly v. Marx, supra* at 879, 705 N.E.2d 1114, against use of the "second look approach," the disparity between the stipulated sum (eighteen per cent of acquisition costs, or $25,278) and actual damages (here, none) cannot be ignored in this case, because that disparity was known at the time of the agreement. The set figure of eighteen per cent of acquisition costs bears no rational relation to the parties' expectation of the true value of the leased items[13] and, moreover, does not take into account TAL's independent ability to collect all future monthly payments still due under the lease. . . .

[13] CSC submitted evidence, through the testimony of an expert appraiser, that software that is licensed, typically, has no resale value, and that computer hardware, after three years, would have little or no resale value. The expert conceded, on cross-examination, that the software might have "some value" if the particular software at issue were transferable. We reject TAL's claim that the judge's findings with respect to the anticipated value of the leased items were not supported by the expert's testimony.

NPS, LLC v. MINIHANE

Supreme Judicial Court of Massachusetts
451 Mass. 417 (2008)

COWIN, J.

In this case we decide whether an acceleration clause in a ten-year license agreement for luxury seats for New England Patriots professional football games at Gillette Stadium is enforceable. The agreement requires the purchaser of the license to pay, upon default, the amounts due for all years remaining on the license. The plaintiff contends that the clause is a lawful liquidated damages provision; the defendant, who defaulted in the first year of the agreement, argues that it is an unlawful penalty. A judge in the Superior Court agreed with the defendant and refused to enforce the provision. Because we conclude the provision is enforceable, we modify the judgment accordingly.

. . .The plaintiff, NPS, LLC (NPS), is the developer of Gillette Stadium (stadium), the home field of the New England Patriots professional football team (Patriots). In 2002, while the stadium was still under construction, NPS entered into an agreement with the defendant, Paul Minihane, for the purchase of a ten-year license for two luxury seats in the Club Level III section. The agreement called for the defendant to pay $3,750 per seat annually for each of the ten seasons from 2002 to 2011. The agreement included a liquidated damages provision, set forth in the margin,[2] which provides that in the event of a default, including failure to pay any amount due under the license agreement, the payments would be accelerated so that the defendant would be required to pay the balance for all the years remaining on the contract. Upon executing the agreement, the defendant paid a $7,500 security deposit; he later made a payment of $2,000 toward the license fee for the 2002 season. Although he or his guests attended all but one of the 2002 preseason and regular season Patriots games at the stadium using the tickets for the Club Seats, he made no further payments.

After giving notice to the defendant, NPS accelerated the payments and filed a complaint in the Superior Court seeking the full amount due

---

[2] "15. *Default.* The following shall constitute an 'Event of Default' under this Agreement: (i) Licensee fails to pay when due any amounts to be paid by Licensee pursuant to the Agreement. . . .In the event of any such Event of Default, Owner may, at its option: (a) withhold distribution of tickets to Licensee for games and/or other Stadium Events until such time as such default is cured; and/or (b) terminate the rights of Licensee under the Agreement after giving Licensee not less than twenty (20) days prior written notice of such default or breach. . . .In the event that Licensee shall not have cured the default or breach specified in said notice by the date specified in said notice, Owner may terminate the right of Licensee to the use and possession of the Club Seats and all other rights and privileges of Licensee under the Agreement and declare the entire unpaid balance of the License Fee (which for the purposes hereof shall include the total aggregate unpaid balance of the annual License Fees for the remainder of the Term) immediately due and payable, whereupon Owner shall have no further obligation of any kind to Licensee. Owner shall have no duty to mitigate any damages incurred by it as a result of a default by Licensee hereunder. . . ."

under the contract. After a bench trial, the judge ruled that the liquidated damages provision was unenforceable because the amount due was "grossly disproportionate to a reasonable estimate of actual damages made at the time of contract formation." After taking further evidence on the issue of actual damages, the judge issued a memorandum of decision and order in which he awarded damages to NPS in the amount of $6,000. This appeal followed, and we transferred the case to this court on our own motion.

. . .

It is well settled that "a contract provision that clearly and reasonably establishes liquidated damages should be enforced, so long as it is not so disproportionate to anticipated damages as to constitute a penalty." *TAL Fin. Corp. v. CSC Consulting, Inc., supra* at 431, 844 N.E.2d 1085. A liquidated damages provision will usually be enforced, provided two criteria are satisfied: first, that at the time of contracting the actual damages flowing from a breach were difficult to ascertain; and second, that the sum agreed on as liquidated damages represents a "reasonable forecast of damages expected to occur in the event of a breach." *Cummings Props., LLC v. National Communications Corp., supra* at 494, 869 N.E.2d 617. Where damages are easily ascertainable, and the amount provided for is grossly disproportionate to actual damages or unconscionably excessive, the court will award the aggrieved party no more than its actual damages. *A–Z Servicenter, Inc. v. Segall,* 334 Mass. 672, 675, 138 N.E.2d 266 (1956). Since there is "no bright line separating an agreement to pay a reasonable measure of damages from an unenforceable penalty clause," *TAL Fin. Corp. v. CSC Consulting, Inc., supra,* the reasonableness of the measure of anticipated damages depends on the circumstances of each case. *A–Z Servicenter, Inc. v. Segall, supra.* In assessing reasonableness, we look to the circumstances at the time of contract formation; we do not take a "second look" at the actual damages after the contract has been breached. *Kelly v. Marx,* 428 Mass. 877, 878, 705 N.E.2d 1114 (1999).

In this case, the trial judge found that, at the time the parties entered into the license agreement, the harm resulting from a possible breach was difficult to ascertain. That finding was supported by the evidence, which indicated that the damages sustained by NPS would vary depending on the demand for tickets at the time of breach. Although the Patriots had won their first Super Bowl championship in 2002, shortly before the parties entered into their agreement, the demand for luxury stadium seats was then and remains variable and depends, according to the evidence, on the current performance of the team, as well as other factors, such as the popularity of the players and the relative popularity of other sports, that are unpredictable at the time of contract. Therefore, to predict at the time of contract how long it would take NPS to resell the defendant's seat license would be extremely difficult, if not impossible.

The judge went on to find, however, that the sum provided for in the agreement—acceleration of all payments for the remaining term of the contract—was "grossly disproportionate to a reasonable estimate of actual damages made at the time of contract formation." That finding was not supported by the evidence. It is the defendant's burden to show that the amount of liquidated damages is "unreasonably and grossly disproportionate to the real damages from a breach" or "unconscionably excessive." See *TAL Fin. Corp. v. CSC Consulting, Inc., supra* at 423, 844 N.E.2d 1085; *A–Z Servicenter, Inc. v. Segall, supra* at 675, 138 N.E.2d 266. Having presented little evidence beyond his assertion that the contract as a whole was unconscionable, the defendant in this case has not sustained that burden.

The liquidated damages provision here is similar to one we upheld in *Cummings Props., LLC v. National Communications Corp., supra* (*Cummings*). In that case, a tenant who defaulted on a commercial lease was required by the terms of the agreement to pay the entire amount of rent remaining under the lease. *Id.* at 491–492, 869 N.E.2d 617. . . .In upholding the liquidated damages provision in *Cummings*, we noted that "to the extent that the liquidated damages amount represented the agreed rental value of the property over the remaining life of the lease, decreasing in amount as the lease term came closer to expiration, it appears to be a reasonable anticipation of damages that might accrue from the nonpayment of rent." *Id.* at 496–497, 869 N.E.2d 617. The same is true here. This, like *Cummings*, is a case where the damages were difficult to estimate at the outset, and the defendant is required to pay no more than the total amount he would have paid had he performed his obligations under the agreement. The sum provided for therefore bears a reasonable relationship to the anticipated actual damages resulting from a breach. It anticipates a worst-case scenario, that is, NPS's inability to resell the seat for the remaining term of the license.[7] However, the defendant has not shown that this outcome is sufficiently unlikely that it renders the amount grossly disproportionate to a reasonable estimate of actual damages.

The defendant stood to receive a substantial benefit from this agreement: guaranteed luxury seating for all Patriots home games, as well as a hedge against future price increases over ten years. He was not deprived of an opportunity to learn and consider the terms of the agreement. Those terms may be harsh, especially when, as here, the breach occurred early in the life of the agreement. But the defendant has not shown that in the circumstances they are "unreasonably and grossly

---

[7] We note in passing that there was evidence at trial that NPS in fact had not been able to resell the defendant's seat, some four years after the defendant committed a breach of the agreement. Although *Kelly v. Marx*, 428 Mass. 877, 878, 705 N.E.2d 1114 (1999), prevents our consideration of this fact, it suggests that it was not unduly pessimistic to think that NPS might have difficulty reselling the defendant's seat in the event of breach.

disproportionate to the real damages from a breach." *A–Z Servicenter, Inc. v. Segall*, 334 Mass. 672, 675, 138 N.E.2d 266 (1956).

On appeal, the parties have not raised the issue whether, if the liquidated damages provision is enforced, mitigation should be considered. . . .[W]e consider the issue, which appears to be one of first impression in Massachusetts.

We will follow the rule in many other jurisdictions[9] and hold that, in the case of an enforceable liquidated damages provision, mitigation is irrelevant and should not be considered in assessing damages. When parties agree in advance to a sum certain that represents a reasonable estimate of potential damages, they exchange the opportunity to determine actual damages after a breach, including possible mitigation, for the "peace of mind and certainty of result" afforded by a liquidated damages clause. *Kelly v. Marx*, 428 Mass. 877, 881, 705 N.E.2d 1114 (1999), quoting *Kelly v. Marx*, 44 Mass. App. Ct. 825, 833, 694 N.E.2d 869 (1998) (Spina, J., dissenting). In such circumstances, to consider whether a plaintiff has mitigated its damages not only is illogical, but also defeats the purpose of liquidated damages provisions. See *Barrie School v. Patch*, 401 Md. 497, 513–514, 933 A.2d 382 (2007) (sum that stipulates damages in advance "replaces any determination of actual loss," so that if liquidated damages provision is enforceable, court need not consider mitigation). Since the liquidated damages provision at issue here is enforceable, the question is irrelevant.

Conclusion. The ruling of the Superior Court that the liquidated damages provision of the license agreement is unenforceable is set aside, and the judgment is modified to award NPS the total amount of unpaid license fees due under the agreement, $65,500, plus interest. . . .

So ordered.

DISCUSSION PROBLEM

1. Resale

Donald Leeber contracted to purchase a condominium from the Deltona Corporation for $150,200. As specified in the contract, he made a 15-percent down payment ($22,530) at the time of signing. According to the

[9] See, e.g., *Federal Realty Ltd. Partnership v. Choices Women's Med. Ctr., Inc.*, 289 A.D.2d 439, 442, 735 N.Y.S.2d 159 (N.Y. 2001); *Lake Ridge Academy v. Carney*, 66 Ohio St. 3d 376, 385, 613 N.E.2d 183 (1993); *Cady v. IMC Mtge. Co.*, 862 A.2d 202, 219 (R.I. 2004) (applying Florida law). See also 24 S. Williston, Contracts § 65.31, at 364 (4th ed. 2002) ("Since the effect of a stipulated damages provision is to substitute a predetermined amount for actual damages. . ., the existence of an enforceable liquidated damages provision has the effect of making the mitigation of damages irrelevant").

contract, Deltona would be entitled to retain the deposit as liquidated damages if Leeber were to fail to close on the purchase. When Leeber failed to close, Deltona provided him with notice that it was retaining the deposit, per the contract. Only four days later, it sold the unit to another buyer for $167,500 (including a $25,125 deposit). Deltona incurred costs of $5,704 as a result of the breach, in the form of administrative costs and a commission it paid to a real estate agent for reselling the condominium. Leeber sued for the return of his deposit, arguing that the stipulated damages term was unenforceable. Should he prevail?

2. The Fiber-Optic Cable

The City of Coffeeville, Kansas, hired Hutton Contracting Company to construct a power and fiber-optic cable line, for approximately $1,132,000. Hutton was to complete the project within 45 days, with specified extensions in the case of inclement weather. The contract also included the following stipulated damages clause:

> The time of the Completion of Construction of the Project is of the essence of the Contract. Should [Hutton] neglect, refuse or fail to complete the construction within the time herein agreed upon, after giving effect to extensions of time, if any, herein provided, then, in that event and in view of the difficulty of estimating with exactness damages caused by such delay, the [City] shall have the right to deduct from and retain out of such monies which may be then due, or which may become due and payable to [Hutton], the sum of **FIVE HUNDRED DOLLARS ($500.00)** per day for each and every day that such construction is delayed on its completion beyond the specified time, as liquidated damages and not as a penalty.

Hutton was nearly six months late in completing the project, and the city withheld $85,500 from the final payment. Hutton sued. At trial, the city presented evidence, which Hutton did not challenge, that it had suffered $76,000 in increased engineering and inspection costs as a result of the delay. Is Hutton entitled to any additional payment?

3. Late Notice

John Carney enrolled his son, Michael, in the fourth-grade class of the Lake Ridge Academy private school for the following school year. The contract obligated Carney to pay $6,240 for the academic year for tuition, books, and supplies. It provided that Carney could cancel the enrollment in writing prior to August 1, but that he would be obligated to pay the full charge if enrollment were canceled after that date. On August 7, Carney notified Lake Ridge that Michael would not be enrolling that fall. Lake Ridge sued for the tuition. At trial, the Lake Ridge headmaster testified that "we feel that August 1st is as far as we want to go prior to the start of the school year in order for us to be able to collect our revenue for expenses that are ongoing regarding the operations of the school." He claimed that any savings that the school enjoyed as a result of Michael not enrolling were "minuscule." Should Lake Ridge be permitted to recover the full tuition charge?

INDEX

References are to Pages